and
.oating
Physically
Abused
Children
and
Their
Families

Interpersonal Violence:
The Practice Series

Jon R. Conte, Series Editor

Assessing and Treating Physically Abused Children and Their Families

A Cognitive-Behavioral Approach

David J. Kolko
University of Pittsburgh School of Medicine
Western Psychiatric Institute and Clinic

Cynthia Cupit Swenson
Medical University of South Carolina

Interpersonal Violence:
The Practice Series

SAGE Publications
International Educational and Professional Publisher
Thousand Oaks ▪ London ▪ New Delhi

Copyright © 2002 by Sage Publications, Inc.

For information:

> Sage Publications, Inc.
> 2455 Teller Road
> Thousand Oaks, California 91320
> E-mail: order@sagepub.com

> Sage Publications Ltd.
> 6 Bonhill Street
> London EC2A 4PU
> United Kingdom

> Sage Publications India Pvt. Ltd.
> M-32 Market
> Greater Kailash I
> New Delhi 110 048
> India

Printed in the United States of America

Library of Congress Cataloging-in-Publication Data

Kolko, David J.
    Assessing and treating physically abused children and their families : a cognitive-behavioral approach / by David J. Kolko and Cynthia Cupit Swenson.
      p. cm. — (Interpersonal violence, the practice series)
    Includes bibliographical references and index.
    ISBN 978-0-7619-2148-6 (c) ISBN 978-0-7619-2149-3 (p)
    1. Abused children.   2. Cognitive therapy.   I. Swenson, Cynthia Cupit. II. Title. III. Interpersonal violence.
    RJ507.A29 K65 2002
    618.92'858223^dc21   2001006683

This book is printed on acid-free paper.

07 08 09 10 11 8 7 6 5 4 3

Acquiring Editor:	Margaret H. Seawell
Editorial Assistant:	Alicia Carter
Production Editor:	Diana E. Axelsen
Copy Editor:	Stacey Shimizu
Typesetter/Designer:	Doreen Barnes
Indexer:	Rachel Rice
Cover Designer:	Sandra Ng

Contents

Foreword

In recent years, expanding research in the field of child maltreatment has taken us toward a broader understanding of the problems that abused children may encounter and the potential solutions for those problems. Given that the individual problems and family circumstances associated with child physical maltreatment are so varied and complex, the solutions also must be comprehensive.

In this book, Drs. Kolko and Swenson integrate a large body of research literature with real-world information from clinical practice. To their credit, the authors have carefully described and illustrated an array of procedures that nicely lend themselves to efficient application. The pleasing result is a careful description and thoughtful illustration of ways that practitioners can apply a comprehensive, empirically based model for intervening in cases involving child physical abuse.

Historically, the field of child maltreatment has emphasized individually focused interventions for abusive or at-risk parents or, in some cases, abused or maltreated children. These interventions often vary considerably in the extent to which they are based on empirical evidence of their efficacy. Surprisingly, the field has held to individually focused interventions for the most part, even though the occurrence of physical abuse relates to certain factors within the child, parent, family, and community domains. Kolko and Swenson present one of the few integrated models that appreciate the empirically based, individually focused interventions, while at the same time taking us a step further through the incorporation of family-systems interventions.

Throughout the volume, Kolko and Swenson cite evidence for the efficacy of various techniques designed to address an array of child, adult, and family concerns. Readers are provided with extensive knowledge of general physical abuse information and an understanding of why and how the techniques may be useful. These empirically validated techniques are illustrated through concrete examples, transcripts, and case description to maximize clinical intervention and equip the reader to put research into practice. Beyond description of the precise application of these techniques is the strong implication that professional systems (i.e., the court and child protection) and the family's greater ecology are important partners in the treatment process.

This book is especially important given the recent focus by health care programs on both clinician accountability and the measurement of client outcomes. Because child physical abuse is not a diagnosis but can lead to a variety of mental health problems, an efficient assessment that articulates both specific strengths and weaknesses is essential to the effective resolution of problem behaviors and reduction of further risk. The model illustrated in this book provides a guide for assessing factors that contribute to abuse risk, as well as various clinical disorders resulting from experiences of child physical abuse. The development of a comprehensive treatment plan in accord with this model is nicely demonstrated.

This practice manual is a welcome addition to this expanding field, and will be a well-used and often-cited resource for beginning and experienced therapists.

David A. Wolfe, PhD
The University of Western Ontario

Acknowledgments

This book is the culmination of several rewarding years of professional training, clinical service, and applied research, but it would not have been possible without the influence and inspiration of many individuals. First, I am grateful to my wife, Judith, for her encouragement of my clinical research work with abuse victims and offenders. My parents, Dvorah and Myron, have been unwavering models of the supportive and constructive approaches to behavior change described in this book. For their support of my professional interests in this field, I wish to acknowledge the early and current mentoring of Alan Kazdin, PhD, and David Brent, MD, respectively. My colleagues Lucy Berliner, Mark Chaffin, Judith Cohen, Esther Deblinger, and Tony Mannarino have provided for more than a decade sound advice and exceptional professional examples in treating and evaluating child abuse victims and their families using cognitive-behavioral treatment procedures. In particular, David Wolfe's original work on the treatment of child physical abuse was both pioneering and insightful. Other colleagues—notably, Sharon Hicks, Diane Holder, and James Alexander—provided advice and assistance in developing or administering our family treatment procedures. I also am grateful to the former National Center on Child Abuse and Neglect for the funds that supported my initial outcome study with physically abused children and their offending caregivers (90-CA-1459) and a subsequent services research study (90-CA-1547), and to the Office of Children, Youth, and Families of Allegheny County

(Pittsburgh) for collaborating in these studies. This outcome study, subsequently referred to as Project IMPACT (Interventions to Maximize Parent-Child Togetherness), incorporated many of the techniques and materials described in this book. Finally, I wish to acknowledge the collegiality and ongoing academic encouragement of my many friends and associates at the University of Pittsburgh and Children's Hospital of Pittsburgh.

David Kolko

I would like to thank a number of people who have offered either personal or professional support and guidance. Foremost, I would like to thank my husband, Marshall. His sacrifices and belief in me and my work made my part of this endeavor possible. Much love and appreciation go to Theresa, Kevin, and Ricky for constant strength, and to Sarah, Elizabeth, and Holly for teaching me what is important to children. I would also like to thank my grandmothers, Elsie and Aline, who are my heart; Paporan; and my parents—Bobbie Lewis Cupit, Joseph Cupit, Mary Margaret Marshall McClure and Ralph Swenson—for being a guiding force even at times when they did not realize it.

I thank my very wise mentors, Wally Kennedy and Scott Henggeler, for professional guidance and support of my ideas. To Cathy Joyner, for help in trying out the techniques and helping me stay on the path, and to Kevin Taylor for his help in demonstrating the breathing techniques. I would like to thank the Camp Stern group and Renae, Eve, Sonja, Julie, Elissa, Wahini, and Jay Basco for days, months, and years of love and support. Thanks to Art, Claudia, Elizabeth, Kelly, Mary, and Todd for teaching me to go the distance. To Toby, for being primarily responsible for keeping my sanity intact for the last year. Finally, I owe a great debt of gratitude for the support of my many friends and adopted family in Union Heights, especially Ida Taylor who daily helps me keep my understanding in the right place.

Cindy Swenson

This book is dedicated to my wife, Judith, and my children, Rachel and Aaron, who bring love and fulfillment to my life. Their support and affection defy even the thought of mistreatment of any kind. (DJK)

This book is dedicated to Marshall, a truly great person with whom I have had the fortune of spending a large portion of my life.

This book is also dedicated to the memory of my children who gave me an understanding of the urgency with which we must cherish and protect all children for they are so precious and time is so short. (CCS)

1

Introduction and Overview

Child physical abuse (CPA), including physical maltreatment, is a problem that has a significant impact on children, adults, families, an extensive professional service sector, and the larger society. In this chapter, we describe the prevalence and incidence of CPA based on recent statistics and detail some of the specific factors that document why treating physically abused children and their families is so important. These factors include high prevalence rates, the salient social impact of physical abuse, and the significant costs associated with this problem.

❏ Significance of the Problem

PREVALENCE

Assessment of the prevalence of CPA has been approached using a variety of methods, each yielding different information. These methods include a compilation of Child Protective Services (CPS) data and national prevalence studies. Annually, the U.S. Department of Health and Human Services aggregates data from CPS in each of the states to determine the prevalence of a variety of types of child maltreatment.

The most recent report (U.S. Department of Health and Human Services, 1999), based on 45 states, indicates that in 1996, reports of suspected abuse were made to CPS agencies on nearly 3 million children. Considering the general population of children younger than 18 years of age in the United States, approximately 42 children per 1,000 children were reported to CPS for abuse and neglect. Of these reported children, 24.6% were investigated for physical abuse. These rates are lower than those reported for neglect (55.9%) but higher than other forms of abuse (12.5% sexual, 6.1% psychological, 12.2% other). The majority of children allegedly physically abused were male and above the age of 8 years. One problem inherent in the Department of Health and Human Services report is that it includes only reported cases and may underestimate the actual number of children abused.

National prevalence studies based on violence surveys capture a sample of the general population and may detect abuse that was never reported to an official agency. Several major studies have shown varied prevalence rates. Finkelhor and Dziuba-Leatherman (1994) conducted a study funded by the Boy Scouts of America. A nationally representative sample of 2,000 youths, ages 10 to 16 years, and their caregivers were interviewed via telephone. Twenty-two percent of youths reported experiencing a completed nonfamily assault and 7.5% reported a family assault in their lifetime. Interestingly, 7.5% of youths reported experiencing violence to their genitals at some point in their lifetime.

In 1985, the Second National Family Violence Survey was conducted through the Family Violence Research Program at the University of Rhode Island (Gelles & Straus, 1987). This study included a national probability sample of 6,002 households and was conducted over the telephone. According to study results, approximately 700,000 children were subjected to very severe violent behavior. An estimated 6.9 million children were assaulted (i.e., kicking, biting, punching, choking, beating, and using weapons) by parents at a rate of 110 incidents per 1,000 children during a one-year period (Straus & Gelles, 1990).

The Third National Incidence Study of Child Abuse and Neglect (NIS-3; Sedlak & Broadhurst, 1996) was a congressionally mandated study preceded by two studies published in 1981 and 1988. This study included children investigated by CPS and those not reported to CPS but seen by community professionals. According to study results, 1,553,800 children in the United States were abused or neglected in 1993. The estimated number of physically abused children was 381,700. These data were based on a very stringent definition of abuse or neglect, in that demonstrable harm must have occurred. When a less stringent criterion was included (i.e., when children who were not yet harmed by maltreatment but were considered by a non-CPS sentinel to be endangered, or when maltreatment was substantiated or indicated by CPS), the estimated number of maltreated children was 2,815,600 and the number of children physically abused was 614,000.

Altogether, CPA affects hundreds of thousands of children annually with physical trauma ranging from the mild (e.g., bruising) to the very severe (e.g., broken bones or skull fractures). However, the impact extends well beyond the physical and emotional injury to the individual child and family, and includes consequences for society in general.

SOCIAL IMPACT

The immediate and long-term impact of child maltreatment carries significant social and financial costs. The social costs are incurred by the victim and family in the form of pain, emotional trauma, serious injury or risk of death, and sometimes prolonged involvement with the legal and child protective systems. However, those costs also affect the majority of individuals in society. For example, child maltreatment strongly correlates with committing juvenile and adult crime (Luntz & Widom, 1994; McCord, 1983; Pollock et al., 1990; Widom, 1989). These crimes may be against property or persons, and many individuals may suffer emotional and financial consequences. However, such crimes may take the form of parents abusing their own children. Research on the intergenerational transmission of child abuse indicates that roughly one third of abuse victims go on to commit physical abuse against their own children (Kaufman & Zigler, 1987). In such cases, the social cost of abuse spirals upward and without apparent limits.

COSTS

The immediate dollar costs associated with child maltreatment are vast, including mental health treatment, court and legal services, law enforcement investigation, outpatient and emergency medical services, and time lost on the job or at school. In addition, for children who are unsafe in their family home or who are having extreme psychiatric difficulties, the costs associated with out-of-home placements are staggering, especially when considering they may be required on a long-term basis. Over 10 years ago, Daro (1988) estimated that reported cases of child maltreatment in the United States cost, at a minimum, $460 million annually in administration and foster care placements. However, these data do not include repeated psychiatric hospitalizations or residential placements, the types of costly services with which physical abuse has been associated (Barber, Rosenblatt, Harris, & Attkisson, 1992). In general, federal trends for dollars spent on out-of-home placements show a sharp rise in expenditures for foster care and adoption maintenance payments and administration (from $610 million to $3.67 billion) from 1986 to 1996. The dollars spent on services to families and child protection (from $198 million to $277 million) increased to a much lesser degree in that same time span (Courtney, 1999).

Interestingly, the dollars spent on foster care cover only a minority of the children. In 1997, only 16.1% of child victims reported to the states were placed in foster care (U.S. Department of Health and Human Services, 1999). These figures indicate that a majority of dollars is spent on a small number of children and that the services do not necessarily address mental health difficulties or preservation or reunification with the family. Rather, they address providing a safe and stable residence and the administration of those programs.

When a broader range of costs to society is considered, the figures become quite substantial. Miller, Cohen, and Wiersema (1996) report that crime victimizations cost $105 billion annually in property and productivity losses, and medical expenses. When the values of pain, emotional trauma, disability, and death risk are added, they estimate that the annual cost of victimization rises to roughly $450 billion annually. Of course, these figures include those costs associated with adult victims of crime. Considering losses due to violence against children only, the costs were estimated to exceed $164 billion annually.

As shown above, several estimates have sought to determine the financial costs of child maltreatment. Current estimates are far from accurate but do point out that billions of dollars could be saved annually if we determined ways to stop child maltreatment, lower the risk of reabuse for children, and make it possible for children to grow up safely with their own families.

❏ The Challenge Before Us

As explained throughout this chapter, CPA, like other forms of maltreatment, is a serious problem that exacts costs for all involved and even those who are not directly involved in a specific incident. In fact, many people who feel the effects of maltreatment will not be people who abuse their children or even know the names or faces of children included in the abuse statistics above. The ripples from abuse are so pervasive that they touch each of us.

The challenge before us is not only to develop effective ways of preventing abuse, but also to apply effective treatments to all of those who experience abuse, bringing about positive clinical outcomes and safety within the family. To date, our success in doing such has been modest.

❏ Purpose and Overview of the Book

This book is an effort to rise to the challenge before us. We describe a model, Comprehensive Individual and Family Cognitive-Behavioral Therapy (CIF-CBT) to guide efforts to integrate assessment and treatment of families where physical abuse has occurred. The intent of the book is to present a model that clinicians can use to provide comprehensive, evidence-based practice. The treatment proposed in this model is designed to target those multiple factors necessary to help the child victim adjust from the abuse experiences; the parent manage social emotional difficulties, which may result in prevention of further abuse; and the family make changes that support a safe environment. The clinical techniques proposed within the model have empirical support from the research world and utility from the practice world.

In Chapter 2, we show that the child victim may experience varied consequences. Furthermore, we demonstrate that physical abuse is contributed to by multiple factors from the child, parent, family, and community. As shown in Chapter 3, although abuse is attributable to multiple factors, the major clinical and research approaches have been to attack a portion of the problem. That is, typically, either parents have been provided some type of limited treatment or children have been treated to the exclusion of the family. We will show that individual approaches have little hope of bringing about desired clinical outcomes.

Chapter 4 provides a comprehensive model for assessing the multiple etiological factors. Chapter 5 details the CIF-CBT model. Before discussing specific treatment techniques, Chapter 6 discusses factors that may facilitate the treatment process and provides tips for orientation to treatment. Chapters 7 through 10 present child treatment strategies that address the many potential consequences of abuse. Chapters 11 through 13 present treatment strategies to be considered with the maltreating adult. Chapter 14 discusses abuse-focused procedures for bridging child/adult and family treatment. Chapter 15 expounds on family approaches. Chapter 16 shows how other systems are key to involvement in treating abusive families. In the final chapters, case examples are provided to show how the individual and family techniques are integrated.

References

Barber, C. C., Rosenblatt, A., Harris, L., & Attkisson, C. C. (1992). Use of mental health services among severely emotionally disturbed children and adolescents in San Francisco. *Journal of Child and Family Studies, 1*(2), 183–207.

Courtney, M. E. (1999). The economics. *Child Abuse & Neglect, 23,* 975–986.

Daro, D. (1988). *Confronting child abuse: Research for effective program design.* New York: Free Press.

Finkelhor, D., & Dziuba-Leatherman, J. (1994). Children as victims of violence: A national survey. *Pediatrics, 94,* 413–420.

Gelles, R. J., & Straus, M. A. (1987). Is violence toward children increasing? A comparison of 1975 and 1985 National Survey rates. *Journal of Interpersonal Violence, 2,* 212–222.

Kaufman, J., & Zigler, E. (1987). Do abused children become abusive parents? *American Journal of Orthopsychiatry, 57,* 186–192.

Luntz, B. K., & Widom, C. S. (1994). Antisocial personality disorder in abused and neglected children grown up. *American Journal of Psychiatry, 151*(5), 670–674.

McCord, J. (1983). A forty year perspective on effects of child abuse and neglect. *Child Abuse & Neglect, 7,* 265–270.

Miller, T. R., Cohen, M. A., & Wiersema, B. (1996). *Victim costs and consequences: A new Look.* Washington, DC: National Institute on Justice.

Pollock, V. E., Briere, J., Schneider, L., Knop, J., Mednick, S. A., & Goodwin, D. W. (1990). Childhood antecedents of antisocial behavior: Parental alcoholism and physical abusiveness. *American Journal of Psychiatry, 147*(10), 1290–1293.

Sedlak, A. J., & Broadhurst, D. D. (1996). *Executive summary of the Third National Incidence Study of Child Abuse and Neglect.* Washington, DC: U.S. Department of Health and Human Services.

Straus, M. A., & Gelles, R. J. (Eds.). (1990). *Physical violence in American families: Risk factors and adaptations to violence in 8,145 families.* New Brunswick, NJ: Transaction.

U.S. Department of Health and Human Services, Administration on Children, Youth and Families. (1999). *Child Maltreatment 1997: Reports from the states to the National Child Abuse and Neglect Data System.* Washington, DC: Government Printing Office.

Widom, C. S. (1989). Child abuse, neglect, and adult behavior: Research design and findings on criminality, violence, and child abuse. *American Journal of Orthopsychiatry, 59,* 355–367.

2

Characteristics and Correlates of Child Physical Abuse

In this chapter we examine the multiple characteristics and correlates of child physical abuse (CPA). We use the term *correlates* because at present the state of the research is such that we cannot say with certainty that these factors either cause or are caused by physical abuse. Rather, current research simply shows a relationship between physical abuse and multiple correlates.

We begin with child correlates and show that children may exhibit varied symptomatology related to the abuse experience. Next, we review parent correlates with abuse and show that multiple and varied parent characteristics may relate to CPA. Third, we review the multiple family factors that correlate with CPA. Finally, we discuss community characteristics that seem to relate to physical abuse. The overall purpose of the chapter is to make the reader aware of the many factors that may need to be addressed when working with physically abused children and their families. As such, we begin to build the case for a comprehensive treatment model.

❏ **Child Characteristics and Correlates**

SUMMARY OF EMPIRICAL FINDINGS

In this section we examine child factors that relate to CPA. Much of our knowledge regarding what we believe to be the impact of CPA has been gained from research that broadly examined the various forms of child maltreatment (e.g., neglect, sexual abuse, and physical abuse). Unfortunately, many studies in the literature contain serious methodological shortcomings, such as lack of control groups, failure to assess theoretically relevant moderator variables (such as level of family stress), inattention to sampling issues, inconsistent definitions of maltreatment, failure to differentiate subtypes of maltreatment, poor operationalization of constructs, and use of unvalidated measurement instruments (see Azar & Wolfe, 1998; Kolko, 2002). However, findings from the better designed studies have identified, across the developmental continuum, five domains of impaired functioning in physically abused children including aggression and behavioral difficulties, poor social competence, trauma-related emotional symptoms, developmental deficits in relationship skills, and cognitive/neuropsychological deficits. Here, we discuss the empirical support for the relationship between physical abuse and social-emotional difficulties in each of these domains. Several important long-term sequelae of physical abuse have also been identified and are described herein. These characteristics are summarized in Box 2.1. Other sources provide additional study details and research findings for the interested reader (see Kaplan, Pelcovitz, & Labruna, 1999; Kolko, 2002).

Box 2.1   Child Victim Characteristics and Correlates

Aggression/behavioral dysfunction
- Most consistent finding
- Persists into latency/adolescence
- Towards adults and peers

Poor social competence/interpersonal problems
- General social skills deficits
- Problems in peer interactions

> ### Box 2.1 *continued*
>
> - Poor social problem solving
> - Peer rejection
>
> Trauma-related emotional symptoms
> - Anxiety and hypervigilance
> - Depression, suicidality, and low self-esteem
> - PTSD (less than 50% of cases)
> - Subclinical PTSD
>
> Developmental deficits in relationship skills
> - Anxious attachment
> - Limited positive affect, enthusiasm
> - Low frustration tolerance
> - Less secure readiness to learn
> - Less outer directedness
> - Difficulty managing conflict with attachment figures
>
> Cognitive/neuropsychological impairment
> - Receptive/expressive language
> - Reading ability and comprehension/abstraction
> - Use of motoric expression in absence of language skills
> - Limited solving of interpersonal conflicts through language
> - Low performance in math and reading skills
>
> Long-term effects
> - Interpersonal aggression, violent crime
> - Suicide and self-injurious behavior
> - Relationship problems
> - PTSD
> - Depression
> - Substance abuse

Aggression/Behavioral Dysfunction

One of the most consistent findings in the literature is that physically abused children tend to exhibit externalizing and aggressive behavior problems (Conaway & Hansen, 1989; Kolko, 2002; National

Academy of Sciences, 1993). In studies using retrospective and cross-sectional designs, parents and teachers of abused children consistently rate them as more oppositional and aggressive than do parents and teachers of nonabused agemates (Cummings, Hennessy, Rabideau, & Cicchetti, 1994; Dodge, Pettit, & Bates, 1997; Hoffman-Plotkin & Twentyman, 1984; Jaffe, Wolfe, Wilson, & Zak, 1986; Manly, Cicchetti, & Barnett, 1994; Reid, Kavanagh, & Baldwin, 1987; Reidy, 1977; Wolfe & Mosk, 1983). Similar findings have been shown on self-ratings (Pelcovitz et al., 1994; Wolfe, Werkele, Reitzel-Jaffe, & Lefebvre, 1998).

Observational studies have shown that physically abused children are more aggressive than are nonabused counterparts toward peers (George & Main, 1979; Haskett & Kistner, 1991; Hoffman-Plotkin & Twentyman, 1984), siblings (Burgess & Conger, 1978), and adults (George & Main, 1979; Hoffman-Plotkin & Twentyman, 1984; Reidy, 1977) in both home and social/academic settings. Externalizing behavior problems documented include increased rule violations, oppositional behavior (Trickett & Kuczynski, 1986) delinquency (Walker, Downey, & Bergman, 1989), property offenses and arrests (Gelles & Straus, 1990), substance use and cigarette smoking (Gelles & Straus, 1990; Hotaling, Straus, & Lincoln, 1990; Kaplan et al., 1998). Longitudinal data also indicate that physically abused infants display continuity in negative behaviors and negative affect through the toddler, preschool, and early school years (Egeland, 1991; Egeland, Sroufe, & Erickson, 1983).

Poor Social Competence/Interpersonal Problems

Extensive evidence shows that physically abused children are less socially competent than their nonabused peers. For example, physically abused preschoolers have been rated as initiating fewer positive interactions with peers and adults (Howes & Espinosa, 1985), avoiding peers more often (George & Main, 1979), and engaging in fewer prosocial behaviors (Hoffman-Plotkin & Twentyman, 1984) and less parallel or group play (Alessandri, 1991) than comparison children. Longitudinal evidence suggests that such problems tend to persist, at least through early childhood (Egeland, 1991; Egeland et al., 1983). Older children have been observed to have fewer positive social interactions, both with peers and adults (Burgess & Conger, 1978; Kaufman & Cicchetti, 1989). Similarly, parents perceive physically abused children to be less socially involved, socially skilled, and socially mature than nonabused counterparts (Hoffman-Plotkin & Twentyman, 1984; Kravic, 1987; Mash, Johnston, & Kovitz, 1983; Perry, Doran, & Wells,

1983; Wolfe & Mosk, 1983). In fact, classroom teachers and children report greater peer rejection among abused children (Rosgosch, Cicchetti, & Abre, 1995). In addition, abused children have performed more poorly than comparison children on indices of sensitivity to social cues, identification of others' emotional displays, empathy, generation of solutions to hypothetical problems, and social role flexibility, which did not appear to be due to between-group differences in intelligence or socioeconomic status (Barahal, Waterman, & Martin, 1981; Frodi & Smetana, 1984; Haskett, 1990; Main & George, 1985; Straker & Jacobson, 1981).

Trauma-Related Emotional Symptoms

Symptoms whose principal manifestation is emotional distress include fear, anxiety, low self-esteem, and sadness/depression. Because CPA is a potentially traumatic event, researchers have assessed posttraumatic symptoms among physically abused children and found rates ranging from 0% to 50% (Deblinger, McLeer, Atkins, Ralphe, & Foa, 1989; Famularo, Fenton & Kinscherff, 1993; Kiser, Heston, Millsap, & Pruitt, 1991; Pelcovitz, et al., 1994). For some children, posttraumatic stress disorder (PTSD) symptoms are enduring. Famularo and colleagues (Famularo, Fenton, Kinscherff, Ayoub, & Barnum, 1994) found a PTSD prevalence rate of 36% among CPA victims. A subset of 33% of those with PTSD retained that diagnosis at a two-year follow-up (Famularo, Fenton, Augustyn, & Zuckerman, 1996). Although the majority of CPA victims across extant studies actually were not diagnosed with PTSD, many reported numerous PTSD symptoms. Finally, several investigations (e.g., Flisher et al., 1997; Kazdin, Moser, Colbus, & Bell, 1985; Kinard, 1980, 1982) have indicated that CPA is associated with psychiatric diagnoses such as depression, agoraphobia, overanxious disorder, and generalized anxiety disorder. CPA has also been found to contribute to lifetime disorders such as dysthymia and conduct disorder when added to other risk factors (Kaplan et al., 1998).

In part, the child's attributions regarding the abusive event may contribute to emotional difficulties. In the sexual abuse literature, abuse-related self-blame has been shown to relate to greater levels of depression and lower self-esteem in adolescents and adults (Frazier, 1991; Morrow, 1991; Wyatt & Newcomb, 1990). Furthermore, in sexually abused school-aged children, perceiving oneself as feeling different from peers, self-blame for negative events, lower perceived credibility, and reduced interpersonal trust have been found to relate to greater anxiety and depression, and to reduced self-esteem (Mannarino,

Cohen, & Berman, 1994). Among physically abused children, abuse-specific attributions (e.g., self-blame and guilt) have been associated with abuse-specific symptoms. Furthermore, negative self-oriented attributions (e.g., *"When other children don't play with me, they are mad at me"*) have been associated with internalizing symptoms, whereas negative other-oriented attributions (e.g., *"People say bad things behind my back"*) have been associated with externalizing behavior problems (Brown & Kolko, 1999).

Developmental Deficits in Relationship Skills

A significant body of research suggests that maltreatment of infants and toddlers is associated with insecure attachment and developmental problems (e.g., Carlson, Cicchetti, Barnett, & Braunwald, 1989; Crittenden & Ainsworth, 1989). Furthermore, there is evidence showing that among maltreated children, secure attachments may become insecure as the child develops (Cicchetti & Barnett, 1992). Anxiously attached children are expected to develop poor relationship skills and demonstrate aggressive or hostile behavior in established relationships because of an internalized approach-avoidance conflict with adults who are important to them. Some empirical data support this prediction. For example, nonsecure attachment status in infancy is associated with poorer social competence and increased aggression during the school years (Lamb & Nash, 1989; Mueller & Silverman, 1989), less secure readiness to learn in school (e.g., less curiosity and less variability seeking), and less outer directedness (e.g., less seeking of approval, less verbal attention seeking; Aber & Allen, 1987).

An emerging body of literature is focusing on attachment beyond infancy, throughout the life course. Attachment is hypothesized to undergo transformations as children renegotiate the balance between being connected with others and being independent (Cicchetti, Cummings, Greenberg, & Marvin, 1990). Studies are showing that attachment patterns and their impact may persist beyond infancy. For example, among adolescents, attachment is positively related to psychosocial adjustment (Noom, Dekovic, & Meeus, 1999). In late adolescence and early adulthood, insecure attachment has been found to relate to difficulty managing conflict with attachment figures and low confidence in one's ability to regulate negative mood (Creasey, Kershaw, & Boston, 1999). Among maltreated children, negative attachment patterns have shown some persistence. Child maltreatment in infancy is associated with an insecure or disorganized attachment through at least the toddler years. Among adolescents with a history of child sexual abuse, attachment style has been shown to mediate the effects of abuse on coping and psychological distress. That is, the quality of attachment may determine the level of psychological distress experienced by a sexual abuse victim (Shapiro & Levendosky, 1999).

In summary, attachment patterns established in early relationships between a child and parent can persist and affect the child's later functioning. For maltreated children, the risk of later interpersonal distress and poor adjustment may be increased because of the relationship between early maltreatment and disorganized or insecure attachment.

Cognitive/Neuropsychological Impairment

Early research on the sequelae of child physical abuse documented intellectual deficits associated with brain damage and other central nervous system impairment (Kempe, Silverman, Steele, Droegemueller, & Silver, 1962; Martin & Rodeheoffer, 1976). Later studies, however, failed to find differences between physically abused and control children in overall intellectual functioning (Alessandri, 1991; Lynch & Roberts, 1982). However, other studies suggest that physically abused children of varying ages display deficits in specific cognitive skills rather than global cognitive functioning. These skills include receptive language skills (McFayden & Kitson, 1996; Vondra, Barnett, and Cicchetti, 1989), reading ability and expressive language skills (Burke, Crenshaw, Green, Schlosser, & Strocchia-Rivera, 1989), initiation of tasks (Aber & Allen, 1987; Allen & Tarnowski, 1989), comprehension and abstraction abilities (Tarter, Hegedus, Winsten, & Alterman, 1984), communication (Perry et al., 1983), comprehension of social roles (Barahal et al., 1981), and auditory attention and verbal fluency (Tarter et al, 1984, 1985). Such cognitive deficits most likely affect the overall social functioning of physically abused children. Burke et al. (1989), for example, suggested that physical aggression observed in physically abused children might be due, in part, to their reliance on motoric forms of expression in the absence of adequate language skills.

Academically, physically abused children have performed lower on math and reading tests. Furthermore, they show increased school discipline referrals and suspensions and are 2.5 times more likely to repeat a grade (Eckenrode, Laird, & Doris, 1993).

More recent work in the area of cognitive neuroscience has focused on the effects of trauma on brain development and emotion processing. De Bellis and colleagues (De Bellis, Baum, et al., 1999;

De Bellis, Keshavan, et al., 1999) compared maltreated children who had PTSD to overanxious, nonmaltreated children and healthy children on several biological measures. Study results indicated that maltreatment was associated with alterations of biological stress systems. In the first study (De Bellis, Baum, et al., 1999), maltreated children with PTSD excreted greater concentrations of baseline urinary norepinephrine and dopamine than overanxious nonmaltreated children and healthy children. They also had greater concentrations of urinary free cortisol than healthy controls and greater concentrations of urinary epinephrine than overanxious nonmaltreated children. In animal models, activation of these systems produces behavior consistent with anxiety and hypervigilance. In De Bellis's second study (De Bellis, Keshavan, et al., 1999), children with PTSD had smaller intracranial and cerebral volumes than control participants. Investigators concluded that the stress of maltreatment is associated with adverse brain development.

With regard to emotion processing, Pollak, Cicchetti, Klorman, and Brumaghim (1997) compared maltreated to nonmaltreated children on cognitive event-related potentials, an index of central nervous system functioning believed to reflect neurological processing of discrete stimuli. Results indicated that maltreated children processed emotional information differently than those who were nonmaltreated. Maltreated children used different cognitive resources when attending to cues for negative versus positive affect.

Long-Term Sequelae of Physical Abuse

The long-term effects of physical abuse can be divided into those that persist throughout the course of a child's development and may be a barrier to accomplishing certain developmental tasks (Cicchetti & Carlson, 1989) and those effects that are demonstrable in adulthood. With regard to effects across development, Egeland and his colleagues (Egeland, 1991; Egeland et al., 1983; Pianta, Egeland, & Erickson, 1989) have provided evidence that physical abuse at an early developmental stage influences adaptation at later stages. These researchers followed 267 at-risk families from the time of their eldest child's birth. Those children who were identified as physical abuse victims during infancy exhibited poorer functioning on developmental tasks than children from the same cohort who were not physically abused. Deficits have been noted in attachment security during infancy, emotional functioning and individuation skills in toddlerhood, peer relatedness and school readiness in the preschool period, and intellectual, academic, and social competence in the elementary school years (Egeland, 1991).

Longitudinal and retrospective data indicate that physical abuse is a risk factor for mental health problems in adulthood. Longitudinal data comparing adults who were physically abused as children with nonabused controls suggest that differences in adaptational outcomes persist beyond childhood. McCord (1983), for example, followed 253 males from early childhood over a 30-year period and found that men who had been physically abused, rejected, or neglected were more likely to have been juvenile delinquents and had higher rates of criminal conviction, mental illness, and substance abuse problems in adulthood than men who came from nonabusive homes. Furthermore, in a longitudinal study of 699 young adults, Widom and colleagues (Luntz & Widom, 1994; Perez & Widom, 1994) found that, in comparison with nonabused peers, individuals maltreated as children had higher rates of criminal offenses and antisocial personality disorder, and both lower IQ and reading ability. Retrospective data from clinical samples (e.g., Surrey, Swett, Michaels, & Levin, 1990) and community samples (e.g., Duncan, Saunders, Kilpatrick, Hanson, & Resnick, 1996; Pollock et al., 1990) also indicate that CPA victims are likely to have higher rates of substance abuse and psychiatric, interpersonal, vocational, and antisocial behavior problems than adults without histories of CPA. In a review of the long-term consequences of CPA, Malinosky-Rummell and Hansen (1993) found that physical abuse in childhood was associated with dating violence, marital violence, substance abuse, and suicidal attempts in adulthood.

SECTION SUMMARY

In this section, we have summarized evidence showing that physically abused children are at risk of several significant and potentially long-term social and emotional difficulties. The behavioral, psychiatric, interpersonal, and legal problems that are potentially experienced indicate that long-term management may be necessary (Swenson & Kolko, 2000). However, it must be noted that no symptom picture characterizes all physically abused children. In fact, some children who experience physical abuse will not show mental health problems. Preliminary data indicate that fear of injury and death during physical abuse relates to internalizing symptoms (e.g., fear or depression) and PTSD (Brown, Swenson, & Kirk, 1996). At present, the state of the research with physical abuse is too premature to definitively identify robust factors that predict mental health problems.

❏ Maltreating Adult Characteristics and Correlates

SUMMARY OF EMPIRICAL FINDINGS

This section describes some of the characteristics that, based on descriptive reports and descriptive comparison studies, have been associated with a range of physically abusive adults. A summary of these maltreating adult characteristics is shown in Box 2.2. Much of this literature has been examined in considerable detail elsewhere (see Emery & Laumann-Billings, 1998; Milner & Dopke, 1997). It is important to point out that these characteristics represent only a subset of the many possible characteristics that could be examined to describe a maltreating individual. Furthermore, these characteristics are fairly static and are best conceptualized and understood along with other family and contextual factors that may influence caregiver behavior. What follows is a brief overview of the most commonly reported maltreating adult characteristics.

Box 2.2   Maltreating Adult Characteristics and Correlates

History of childhood abuse
    Intergenerational transmission in about 30% of cases
Cognitive problems
- Attributional biases—negative perception of child
- Belief in need for physical punishment
- Limited empathy
- Unrealistic/high developmental expectations
- External locus of control
- Reduced self-esteem

Affective expression/regulation problems
- Negative affect/irritability, anger, hostility/explosiveness
- Personal distress/symptoms
- Health problems

Behavioral problems
- Poor impulse control
- Excessive physical punishment

Box 2.2 *continued*

- Inconsistent child management practices—monitoring, discipline
- Limited use of positive consequences or problem solving
- Social isolation

Psychiatric disorders
- Depression
- Substance abuse
- PTSD
- Personality disorder

Biological factors
- Heightened physiological reactivity
- Neuropsychological dysfunction

History of Childhood Abuse

An early childhood history of exposure to or the experience of physically abusive behavior is not uncommon among abusive parents. An early review estimated that about 30% of abused children appear to become abusive parents (Kaufman & Zigler, 1987), with some empirical studies finding a relationship between early physical punishment and later physical violence or abusive behavior (Coohey & Braun, 1997; Merrill, Hervig, & Milner, 1996). Still, although such a history may be of significance in certain cases, most abused children do not grow up to be abusers. Furthermore, the specific mechanism by which early exposure to harsh punishment in childhood influences the expression of abusive behavior has not been examined thoroughly, and some findings are mixed about the strength of this relationship (see Cappell & Heiner, 1990; Straus & Smith, 1990). It bears mentioning that few controlled studies have examined this particular background characteristic in recent years.

Cognitive Problems

Several cognitive factors have been described among abusive parents in empirical studies. One of these factors reflects parental attributional biases. Abusive parents may exhibit a negative cognitive-attributional style or perceive their children in a more negative light than nonabusive parents (Azar & Siegel, 1990; Whipple & Webster-Stratton, 1991), which may exacerbate reports of the severity of their children's behavior problems. Studies with high-risk parents suggest the presence of cognitive rigidity, more critical evaluations, and attributions of child noncompliance that implicate the child's negative intentions (Caselles & Milner, 2000; Dopke & Milner, 2000; Nayak & Milner, 1998). Parents occasionally report possible distortions or exaggerations in their beliefs about their children's motives (e.g., malicious intent, "He spilled his milk just to make me late for work") or responsibility for certain events, the parent's welfare, or other personal circumstances (see Azar, 1991, 1997). Abusers may also take responsibility for success but attribute responsibility for failure to their children (Bradley & Peters, 1991; Bugental, Mantyla, & Lewis, 1989). In this context, negative child perceptions may cause parents to be less accepting of and less empathic towards their children (see Mash & Johnston, 1990), as well as more reactive to them (Bradley & Peters, 1991).

Related cognitive factors involve having high expectations of their children's behavior (Azar, Robinson, Hekimian, & Twentyman, 1984), which again may reinforce parental perceptions of a child's deviance or inappropriateness. Having unrealistic expectations may precipitate frustration and, ultimately, child-directed aggression. It has also been reported that abusive parents believe in the appropriateness of harsh physical discipline, which may result in their use of harsh parenting (Simons, Whitbeck, Conger, & Chyi-in, 1991) and their greater acceptance of physical punishment than comparison parents (Kelly, Grace, & Elliot, 1990). Low self-esteem has been found to be more common in abusive than nonabusive parents and to be related to later child maltreatment.

Affective Expression/Regulation Problems

Various emotional reactions or personality characteristics have been reported among abusive parents. Harsh parenting has been associated with negative affective states, such as irritability, sadness, and anxiety (Simons et al., 1991), as well as explosiveness, hostility, anger, and the use of threats (Caspi & Elder, 1988; Patterson, DeBaryshe, & Ramsey, 1989). The latter are more commonly targeted in assessment and intervention studies, suggesting the need to examine more carefully parental internalizing symptoms. At the same time, abusive parents have shown patterns of coping characterized by heightened emotion-focused coping, reflecting their reactivity to stressful circumstances (Cantos, Neale, & O'Leary, 1997).

Abusive parents have also been found to report higher numbers of stressful life events and to perceive their lives as more stressful than comparison parents. Some laboratory data support the view that some abusive parents show more adverse reactions to various stressful stimuli (see Milner, 1998). This more general level of distress may be real or simply perceived, but, regardless of the source, may have implications for parental tolerance and reactivity. Of course, there is limited evidence as to the ways in which these emotional states influence parental aggression or to whether they reflect consequences rather than causes of abusive activity. Furthermore, whether these affective problems reflect specific symptoms, personality traits, or more general psychiatric disorders cannot be determined at this time.

Behavioral Problems

Several patterns of behavior have been used to characterize the abusive parent. The parent may exhibit impulse control problems that may result in several inappropriate or dangerous actions. Such actions may include frequent negative or critical comments, physical coercion or threats, power assertion, or direct aggressive management practices (Caselles & Milner, 2000; Dolz, Cerezo, & Milner, 1997; Trickett & Kuczynski, 1986; Whipple & Webster-Stratton, 1991). At the same time, evidence suggests that abusers show deficits in various positive behaviors, such as attention, positive affect and social behavior, and physical affection (Kavanagh, Youngblade, Reid, & Fagot, 1988), poor problem solving (Azar et al., 1984; Hansen, Pallotta, Tishelman, Conaway, & MacMillan, 1988), and prosocial control techniques (Alessandri, 1992), with most evidence based on behavioral observations. In some instances, parents may have deficits in or rely infrequently upon basic parent management procedures, such as monitoring or consequating their children's behavior. Not surprisingly, a given parent may fluctuate between these two extremes, in effect creating the appearance of inconsistency in their child-rearing practices (Susman, Trickett, Iannotti, Hollenbeck, & Zahn-Waxler, 1985).

Reports have also acknowledged the isolation and loneliness of physically abusive parents (see Milner & Dopke, 1997). Abusive parents show a propensity toward limited contact with or alienation from friends and general dissatisfaction with their social supports (Crittenden, 1985; Egeland, Breitenbucher, & Rosenberg, 1980). Compounding the problem, abusive families tend not to use available community resources (Corse, Schmid, & Trickett, 1990). Isolated parents who experience limited social support may be more susceptible to the effects of stress and family problems. Furthermore, they remain less receptive to the positive influences of those within their social network.

These findings suggest that limitations in parents' repertoires of coping skills may be found in several domains (e.g., self-control or discipline) related to their adaptive functioning and ability to fulfill various roles. At the same time, it is important to mention that abusive parents may also experience multiple personal and family stressors (e.g., low parental social support, depression, and marital discord) likely to affect adversely their coping efforts and ability to be psychologically available to their families (Pianta et al., 1989; Whipple & Webster-Stratton, 1991).

Psychiatric Disorders

Some of the aforementioned problems may manifest themselves as psychiatric disturbances, with the most notable ones being depression (Whipple & Webster-Stratton, 1991), substance abuse, and PTSD (Famularo, Kinscherff, & Fenton, 1992a, 1992b; Kelleher, Chaffin, Hollenberg, & Fischer, 1994; Murphy et al., 1991; Whipple & Webster-Stratton, 1991). Even though evidence suggests the presence of individual disorders, each of these difficulties may also exist as individual symptoms or problems that may still restrict parental functioning. Specifically, these forms of dysfunction, especially parental substance abuse, may decrease parental involvement in family activities and increase intolerance for unwanted behaviors, not to mention increasing the potential for out-of-home placement of the child (Famularo et al., 1992b; Kelley, 1992; Murphy et al., 1991). Still, few comparison studies of abusive and other psychiatrically controlled samples have been conducted to determine either the specificity of these findings to CPA, per se, or whether these parents do indeed suffer from psychiatric disorders at a higher rate than other samples. Furthermore, some studies have failed to find differences between abusive and nonabusive parents on measures of depression or self-worth (Kinard, 1996).

Biological Factors

Few biological variables have been examined in relation to CPA in recent years. Existing evidence suggests that abusive parents have increased psychophysiological reactivity, described in some studies as hyperarousal to stressful child-related and non–child-related stimuli (e.g., Casanova, Domanic, McCanne, & Milner, 1991; McCanne & Milner, 1991). What is not clear is whether hyperarousal appears in adults prior to any exposure to child stressors and whether it is associated with cognitive, affective, or behavioral reactions to abusive behavior. Some unpublished work cited by Milner and Dopke (1997) suggests that physically abusive parents perform less poorly on tests of neuropsychological functioning that evaluate conceptual ability, conceptual flexibility, and problem-solving ability, as well as attention, distractibility, and verbal fluency. Thus, while plausible, these features are at best tentative until more scientific evidence has been presented.

❏ Family-System Characteristics and Correlates

SUMMARY OF EMPIRICAL FINDINGS

This section describes some of the characteristics that have been associated with families in which physical abuse occurs. Box 2.3 lists some of the more common family-system correlates and characteristics.

Box 2.3 | Family-System Characteristics and Correlates

Volatile home environment
- Family and/or partner conflict
- Coercion and family violence

Limited psychosocial resources
- Social supports (isolation)
- Finances (poverty, unemployment)

General family stressors
- Family disruptions/separations
- Chaos and instability

Volatile Home Environment

In terms of family processes or functions, observational studies have documented heightened aggressive or coercive behavior and violent family behavior. Family interactions may be characterized by critical, hostile, or verbally abusive behaviors (Claussen & Crittenden, 1991). Partner hostility also may be common in such families (Fantuzzo et al., 1991; Salzinger, Feldman, Hammer, & Rosario, 1991).

Limited Psychosocial Resources

Evidence also suggests low levels of general family cohesion and support among various family members (see Kolko, 1992). Physical abuse potential has been associated with low levels of family cohesion and expressiveness (Mollerstrom, Patchner, & Milner, 1992). Indeed, limited positive interactions actually may be more characteristic of abusive families than excessive negativity (Caliso & Milner, 1992). Limited social networks and interactions have been found in some studies (Coohey, 2000), but not others (Howes, Cicchetti, Toth, & Rogosch, 2000; Kinard, 1996). The study by Howes et al. (2000) found no group differences between physically and sexually abusive families on several measures of family climate and structure.

General Family Stressors

Family stressors, such as disruptions, moves, and other forms of instability, also are common among abusive families (Emery & Laumann-Billings, 1998). Abusive families have experienced numerous child and parent stressors (Holden, Willis, & Foltz, 1989) and social disadvantages (Pianta et al., 1989). Exposure to family violence is a related stressor common in such families (Appel & Holden, 1998; Coohey & Braun, 1997). The social insularity of these families is related potentially to the child's limited social competence, and to the family's lack of connectiveness to prosocial (normative) sources of influence, support, and assistance. Limited financial resources (e.g., limited income, unemployment, inadequate housing, large family size, or single parenthood) are common stressors. Indeed, poverty alone is a salient correlate and predictor of abuse status (Gillham et al., 1998; Whipple & Webster-Stratton, 1991).

SECTION SUMMARY

There is evidence to suggest that abusive parents experience psychological distress, report problematic parenting practices, and reside in conflictual, unsupportive, and/or stressful family environments (Milner, 1998; National Academy of Sciences, 1993). All told, these characteristics reflect numerous domains rather than a few specific problem areas. Perhaps what can be said about abusive adults and their families is that they are characterized by no single attribute or set of characteristics, but, instead, by a variety of possible clinical features. Indeed, numerous psychological or contextual factors, such as childhood abuse, parental aggressivity, and depression, high IQ, poverty, poor parenting practices, limited social support/competence, and stress, among other factors, may influence the likelihood of CPA (Cappell & Heiner, 1990; Mash & Johnston, 1990; Simons et al., 1991; Webster-Stratton, 1985, 1990; Whipple & Webster-Stratton, 1991; Widom, 1989). Parents may show such features as parental worries, dissatisfaction with their children and the parenting role, limited emotional expressiveness, social isolation, and lack of encouragement for the development and autonomy of their children (Trickett, Aber, Carlson, & Cicchetti, 1991). Accordingly, assessment must be directed toward both individual parental functioning and family functioning, and toward both processes and structures, in order to identify worthy targets for intervention.

Despite such information, however, recent descriptive evidence is meager at best. Moreover, the role of the characteristics influencing abusive family interactions has also not been well documented, highlighting the need to critically evaluate the literature and to conduct longitudinal studies.

❏ Community Characteristics and Correlates

SUMMARY OF EMPIRICAL FINDINGS

This section describes characteristics of communities that have been associated with the occurrence of physical abuse. To date, studies are limited, but several factors do appear associated with abuse. Box 2.4 lists common community characteristics and correlates.

Box 2.4	Community Characteristics and Correlates

Limited finances and economic disadvantage
Instability, isolation, and poor organization
Neighborhood burden

Limited Finances and Economic Disadvantage

Studies encompassing many regions in the United States have found some consistent community predictors of child maltreatment. The circumstances of abusive families are influenced by level of disadvantage in their social and community resources. Thus, communities with economic disadvantages tend to have higher maltreatment rates (Coulton, Korbin, Su, & Chow, 1995; Drake & Pandey, 1996; Zuravin, 1989). As noted by Emery and Laumann-Billings (1998), the disadvantages may also include limits in other resources, such as the absence of available social services.

Instability, Isolation, and Poor Organization

In addition to having limited resources, communities with high rates of maltreatment tend to be unstable, isolated, and poorly organized (Coulton et al., 1995). In some neighborhoods, the instability is due to the high mobility of residents. When residential turnover in a neighborhood is high, the likelihood of bringing organization to the neighborhood and having internal controls is reduced (Bursik & Grasmich, 1993). In addition, as residents move away from their homes, these structures may be left vacant, a factor related to maltreatment (Zuravin, 1989). These problems, coupled with the presence of high rates of crime and antisocial activities, may serve as additional stressors to a given family.

Neighborhood Burden

In more recent work, Coulton, Korbin, and Su (1999) examined the relationship of child abuse potential to neighborhood structural variables (i.e., impoverishment, childcare burden, and instability) and process variables (i.e., resident's perception of resources and control). This study differed from others addressing community factors in that, instead of using aggregate rates of maltreatment, the investigators used an individual measure of abuse potential. Impoverishment and childcare burden significantly affected abuse potential. Interestingly, the variation in potential for child abuse was greater within a given neighborhood than between neighborhoods.

SECTION SUMMARY

Although infrequently addressed in treatment programs, empirical findings show that neighborhood factors relate to the occurrence of

CPA. Heightened risk for maltreatment is found in those neighborhoods characterized by economic disadvantage, instability, and isolation. Furthermore, greater neighborhood burden relates to the potential to abuse a child. Though research points to the importance of neighborhood-wide intervention to reduce the factors that relate to child maltreatment, at present, additional research is needed to understand factors that might mediate the relationship between the above-noted factors and child maltreatment. Furthermore, we have a limited understanding of what protective factors might reduce the risk of maltreatment and how to intervene with these neighborhood risk factors to help neighborhoods create protective families.

❏ What Causes Child Physical Abuse?

At present, there is no known single factor or set of factors that cause child abuse. As shown in this chapter, CPA relates to multiple factors within the child, parent, and family. Furthermore, it is unclear at this time whether the factors that correlate with CPA are a cause or result of it. Certainly, the set of factors that determines whether a particular child in a particular family will be abused varies on a case-by-case basis. Given that there are no well-defined and empirically validated causal models giving support to the strength of some factors over others, when trying to determine etiology, the most conservative approach is to look at multiple factors that may increase risk for abuse. As such, the assessment and treatment model we present will consider child, parent, and family factors, as well as other community systems.

References

Aber, J. L., & Allen, J. P. (1987). Effects of maltreatment on young children's socioemotional development: An attachment theory perspective. *Developmental Psychology, 23*, 406–414.

Alessandri, S. M. (1991). Play and social behavior in maltreated preschoolers. *Development and Psychopathology, 3*, 191–205.

Alessandri, S. M. (1992). Mother-child interactional correlates of maltreated and non-maltreated children's play behavior. *Development and Psychopathology, 4*, 257–270.

Allen, D. M., & Tarnowski, K. J. (1989). Depressive characteristics of physically abused children. *Journal of Abnormal Child Psychology, 17*, 1–11.

Appel, A. E., & Holden, G. W. (1998). The occurrence of spouse and physical child abuse: A review and appraisal. *Journal of Family Psychology, 12*, 578–599.

Azar, S. T. (1991). Models of child abuse: A metatheoretical analysis. *Criminal Justice and Behavior, 18*, 30–46.

Azar, S. T. (1997). A cognitive behavioral approach to understanding and treating parents who physically abuse their children. In D. Wolfe, R. J. McMahon, & R. D. Peters (Eds.), *Child abuse: New directions in prevention and treatment across the lifespan* (Vol. 4, pp. 79–101). Thousand Oaks, CA: Sage.

Azar, S. T., Robinson, D. R., Hekimian, E., & Twentyman, C. T. (1984). Unrealistic expectations and problem-solving ability in maltreating and comparison mothers. *Journal of Consulting and Clinical Psychology, 52,* 687–691.

Azar, S. T., & Siegel, B. R. (1990). Behavioral treatment of child abuse: A developmental perspective. *Behavior Modification, 14,* 279–300.

Azar, S. T., & Wolfe, D. A. (1998). Child physical abuse and neglect. In E. J. Mash & R. A. Barkley (Eds.), *Treatment of childhood disorders* (2nd ed., pp. 501–544). New York: Guilford.

Barahal, R. M., Waterman, J., & Martin, H. P. (1981). The social cognitive development of abused children. *Journal of Consulting and Clinical Psychology, 49,* 508–516.

Bradley, E. J., & Peters, R. D. (1991). Physically abusive and nonabusive mothers' perceptions of parenting and child behavior. *American Journal of Orthopsychiatry, 61,* 455–460.

Brown, E. J., & Kolko, D. J. (1999). Child victims' attributions about being physically abused: An examination of factors associated with symptom severity. *Journal of Abnormal Child Psychology, 27,* 311–322.

Brown, E. J., Swenson, C. C., & Kirk, L. C. (1996, June). *The impact of physical abuse on children.* Paper presented at the Annual Colloquium of the American Professional Society on the Abuse of Children, Chicago, IL.

Bugental, D. B., Mantyla, S. M., & Lewis, J. (1989). Parental attributions as moderators of affective communication to children at risk for physical abuse. In D. Cicchetti & V. Carlson (Eds.), *Child maltreatment: Theory and research on the causes and consequences of child abuse and neglect* (pp. 254–279). New York. Cambridge University Press.

Burgess, R. L., & Conger, R. D. (1978). Family interaction in abusive, neglectful, and normal families. *Child Development, 49,* 1163–1173.

Burke, A. E., Crenshaw, D. A., Green, J., Schlosser, M. A., & Strocchia-Rivera, L. (1989). Influence of verbal ability on the expression of aggression in physically abused children. *Journal of the American Academy of Child Psychiatry, 28,* 215–218.

Bursik, R. J., & Grasmich, H. G. (1993). *Neighborhood and crime.* New York: Lexington Books.

Caliso, J. A., & Milner, J. S. (1992). Childhood history of abuse and child abuse screening. *Child Abuse & Neglect, 16,* 647–659.

Cantos, A. L., Neale, J. M., & O'Leary, K. D. (1997). Assessment of coping strategies of child abusing mothers. *Child Abuse & Neglect, 21,* 631–636.

Cappell, C., & Heiner, R. B. (1990). The intergenerational transmission of family aggression. *Journal of Family Violence, 5,* 135–151.

Carlson, V., Cicchetti, D., Barnett, D., & Braunwald, K. G. (1989). Finding order in disorganization: Lessons from research on maltreated infants' attachments to their caregivers. In D. Cicchetti & V. Carlson (Eds.), *Child maltreatment: Theory and research on the causes and consequences of child abuse and neglect* (pp. 494–528). New York: Cambridge University Press.

Casanova, G. M., Domanic, J., McCanne, T. R., & Milner, J. S. (1991). Physiological responses to non-child-related stressors in mothers at risk for child abuse. *Child Abuse & Neglect, 16,* 31–44.

Caselles, C. E., & Milner, J., S. (2000). Evaluation of child transgressions, disciplinary choices, and expected child compliance in a no-cry and a crying infant condition in physically abusive and comparison mothers. *Child Abuse & Neglect, 24,* 477–491.

Caspi, A., & Elder, G. H. (1988). Emergent family patterns: The intergenerational construction of problem behaviour and relationships. In R. A. Hinde & J. Stevenson-Hinde (Eds.), *Relationships with families: Mutual influences* (pp. 218–240). Oxford: Clarendon.

Cicchetti, D., & Barnett, D. (1992). Attachment organization in maltreated preschoolers. *Development and Psychopathology, 3,* 397–411.

Cicchetti, D., & Carlson, V. (1989). *Child maltreatment: Theory and research on the causes and consequences of child abuse and neglect.* New York: Cambridge University Press.

Cicchetti, D., Cummings, E. M., Greenberg, M. T., & Marvin, R. S. (1990). An organizational perspective on attachment beyond infancy: Implications for theory, measurement, and research. In M. T. Greenberg, D. Cicchetti, & E. M. Cummings (Eds.), *Attachment in the preschool years: Theory, research, and intervention* (pp. 3–49). Chicago: University of Chicago Press.

Claussen, A. H., & Crittenden, P. M. (1991). Physical and psychological maltreatment: Relations among types of maltreatment. *Child Abuse & Neglect, 15,* 5–8.

Conaway, L. P., & Hansen, D. J. (1989). Social behavior of physically abused and neglected children: A critical review. *Clinical Psychology Review, 9,* 627–652.

Coohey, C. (2000). The role of friends, in-laws, and other kin in father-penetrated child physical abuse. *Child Welfare, 79,* 373–402.

Coohey, C., & Braun, N. (1997). Toward an integrated framework for understanding child physical abuse. *Child Abuse & Neglect, 21,* 1081–1094.

Corse, S. J., Schmid, K., & Trickett, P. K. (1990). Social network characteristics of mothers in abusing and nonabusing families and their relationships to parenting beliefs. *Journal of Community Psychology, 18,* 44–59.

Coulton, C. J., Korbin, J. E., & Su, M. (1999). Neighborhoods and child maltreatment: A multi-level study. *Child Abuse & Neglect, 23,* 1019–1040.

Coulton, C. J., Korbin, J. E., Su, M., & Chow, J. (1995). Community level factors and child maltreatment rates. *Child Development, 66,* 1262–1276.

Creasey, G., Kershaw, K., & Boston, A. (1999). Conflict management with friends and romantic partners: The role of attachment and negative mood regulation expectancies. *Journal of Youth and Adolescence, 28,* 523–543.

Crittenden, P. M. (1985). Social networks, quality of childrearing, and child development. *Child Development, 56,* 1299–1313.

Crittenden, P. M., & Ainsworth, M. S. (1989). Child maltreatment and attachment theory. In D. Cicchetti & V. Carlson (Eds.), *Child maltreatment: Theory and research on the causes and consequences of child abuse and neglect* (pp. 432–463). New York: Cambridge University Press.

Cummings, E. M., Hennessy, K. D., Rabideau, G. J., & Cicchetti, D. (1994). Responses of physically abused boys to interadult anger involving their mothers. *Development and Psychopathology, 6,* 31–41.

De Bellis, M. D., Baum, A. S., Birmaher, B., Keshavan, M. S., Eccard, C. H., Boring, A. M., Jenkins, F. J., & Ryan, N. D. (1999a). Developmental traumatology, part I: Biological stress systems. *Biological Psychiatry, 45,* 1259–1270.

De Bellis, M. D., Keshavan, M. S., Clark, D. B., Casey, B. J., Giedd, J. N., Boring, A. M., Frustaci, K., and Ryan, N. D. (1999b). Developmental traumatology, part II: Brain development. *Biological Psychiatry, 45,* 1271–1284.

Deblinger, E., McLeer, S. V., Atkins, M. S., Ralphe, D., & Foa, E. (1989). Post-traumatic stress in sexually abused, physically abused, and nonabused children. *Child Abuse & Neglect, 13,* 403–408.

Dodge, K. A., Pettit, G. S., & Bates, J. E. (1997). How the experience of early physical abuse leads children to become chronically aggressive. *Developmental perspectives on trauma: Theory, research and intervention* (Vol. 8, pp. 263–288). Rochester, NY: University of Rochester Press.

Dolz, L., Cerezo, M. A., & Milner, J. S. (1997). Mother-child interactional patterns in high- and low-risk mothers. *Child Abuse & Neglect, 21,* 1149–1158.

Dopke, C. A., & Milner, J. S. (2000). Impact of child compliance on stress appraisals, attributions, and disciplinary choices in mothers at high and low risk for child physical abuse. *Child Abuse & Neglect, 24,* 493–504.

Drake, B., & Pandey, S. (1996). Understanding the relationship between neighborhood poverty and specific types of child maltreatment. *Child Abuse & Neglect, 20,* 1003–1018.

Duncan, R. D., Saunders, B. E., Kilpatrick, D. G., Hanson, R. F., & Resnick, H. S. (1996). Childhood physical assault as a risk factor for PTSD, depression, and substance abuse: Findings from a national survey. *American Journal of Orthopsychiatry, 66,* 437–448.

Eckenrode, J., Laird, M., & Doris, J. (1993). School performance and disciplinary problems among abused and neglected children. *Developmental Psychology, 29*(1), 53–62.

Egeland, B. (1991). A longitudinal study of high-risk families: Issues and findings. In R. H. Starr, Jr., & D. A. Wolfe (Eds.), *The effects of child abuse and neglect.* New York: Guilford.

Egeland, B., Sroufe, L. A., & Erickson, M. (1983). The developmental consequence of different patterns of attachment. *Child Abuse & Neglect, 7,* 459–469.

Egeland, B. R., Breitenbucher, M., & Rosenburg, D. (1980). Prospective study of the significance of life stress in the etiology of child abuse. *Journal of Consulting and Clinical Psychology, 48,* 195–205.

Emery, R. E., & Laumann-Billings, L. (1998). An overview of the nature, causes and consequences of abusive family relationships. *American Psychologist, 53,* 121–135.

Famularo, R., Fenton, T., Augustyn, M., & Zuckerman, B. (1996). Persistence of pediatric post traumatic stress disorder after two years. *Child Abuse & Neglect, 20,* 1245–1248.

Famularo, R., Fenton, T., & Kinscherff, R. (1993). Child maltreatment and the development of posttraumatic stress disorder. *American Journal of the Diseases of Children, 147,* 755–760.

Famularo, R., Fenton, T., Kinscherff, R., Ayoub, C., & Barnum, R. (1994). Maternal and child posttraumatic stress disorder in cases of child maltreatment. *Child Abuse & Neglect, 13,* 507–514.

Famularo, R., Kinscherff, R., & Fenton, T. (1992a). Parental substance abuse and the nature of child maltreatment. *Child Abuse & Neglect, 16,* 475–483.

Famularo, R., Kinscherff, R., & Fenton, T. (1992b). Psychiatric diagnoses of abusive mothers. *Journal of Nervous and Mental Disease, 180,* 658–661.

Fantuzzo, J. W., DePaola, L. M., Lambert, L., Martino, T., Anderson, G., & Sutton, S. (1991). Effects of interparental violence on the psychological adjustment and competencies of young children. *Journal of Consulting and Clinical Psychology, 59,* 258–265.

Flisher, A. J., Kramer, R. A., Hoven, C. W., Greenwald, S. M. A., Bird, H. R., Canino, G., Connell, R., & Moore, R. E. (1997). Psychosocial characteristics of physically abused children and adolescents. *Journal of the American Academy of Child and Adolescent Psychiatry, 36*(1), 123–131.

Frazier, P. A. (1991). Self-blame as a mediator of post-rape depressive symptoms. *Journal of Social and Clinical Psychology, 10,* 47–57.

Frodi, A., & Smetana, J. (1984). Abused, neglected, and nonmaltreated preschoolers' ability to discriminate emotions in others: The effects of IQ. *Child Abuse & Neglect, 8,* 459–465.

Gelles, R. J., & Straus, M. A. (1990). The medical and psychological costs of family violence. In M. A. Straus & R. J. Gelles (Eds.), *Physical violence in American families: Risk factors and adaptations to violence in 8,145 families* (pp. 431–470). New Brunswick, NJ: Transaction.

Gillham, B., Tanner, G., Cheyne, B., Freeman, I., Rooney, M., & Lambie, A. (1998). Unemployment rates, single parent density, and indices of child poverty: Their relationship in different categories of child abuse and neglect. *Child Abuse & Neglect, 22*, 79–90.

George, C., & Main, M. (1979). Social interactions of young abused children: Approach, avoidance, and aggression. *Child Development, 50*, 306–318.

Hansen, D. J., Pallotta, G. M., Tishelman, A. C., Conaway, L. P., & MacMillan, V. M. (1988). Parental problem-solving skills and child behavior problems: A comparison of physically abusive, neglectful, clinic, and community families. *Journal of Family Violence, 4*, 353–368.

Haskett, M. E. (1990). Social problem-solving skills of young physically abused children. *Child Psychiatry and Human Development, 21*(2), 109–119.

Haskett, M. E., & Kistner, J. A. (1991). Social interactions and peer perceptions of young physically abused children. *Child Development, 62*, 979–990.

Hoffman-Plotkin, D., & Twentyman, C. T. (1984). A multimodal assessment of behavioral and cognitive deficits in abused and neglected preschoolers. *Child Development, 55*, 794–802.

Holden, E. W., Willis, D. J., & Foltz, L. (1989). Child abuse potential and parenting stress: Relationships in maltreating parents. *Psychological Assessment: A Journal of Consulting and Clinical Psychology, 1*, 64–67.

Hotaling, G. T., Straus, M. A., & Lincoln, A. J. (1990). Intrafamily violence and crime and violence outside the family. In M. A. Straus & R. J. Gelles (Eds.), *Physical violence in American families: Risk factors and adaptations to violence in 8,145 families* (pp. 431–470). New Brunswick, NJ: Transaction.

Howes, C., & Espinosa, M. P. (1985). The consequences of child abuse for the formation of relationships with peers. *Child Abuse & Neglect, 9*, 397–404.

Howes, P. W., Cicchetti, D., Toth, S., & Rogosch, F. A. (2000). Affective, organizational, and relational characteristics of maltreating families: A system's perspective. *Journal of Family Psychology, 14*, 95–110.

Jaffe, P. G., Wolfe, D. A., Wilson, S. K., & Zak, L. (1986). Similarities in behavioral and social maladjustment among child victims and witnesses to family violence. *American Journal of Orthopsychiatry, 56*, 142–146.

Kaplan, S. J., Pelcovitz, D., & Labruna, V. (1999). Child and adolescent abuse and neglect research: A review of the past 10 years. Part I: Physical and emotional abuse and neglect. *Journal of the American Academy of Child and Adolescent Psychiatry, 38*, 1214–1222.

Kaplan, S. J., Pelcovitz, D., Salzinger, S., Weiner, M., Mandel, F. S., Lesser, M. L., & Labruna, V. E. (1998). Adolescent physical abuse: Risk for adolescent psychiatric disorders. *American Journal of Psychiatry, 155*(7), 954–959.

Kaufman, J., & Cicchetti, D. (1989). Effects of maltreatment on school-age children's socioemotional development: Assessments in day-camp setting. *Developmental Psychology, 25*, 516–524.

Kaufman, J., & Zigler, E. (1987). Do abused children become abusive parents? *American Journal of Orthopsychiatry, 57*, 186–192.

Kavanagh, K. A., Youngblade, L., Reid, J. B., & Fagot, B. I. (1988). Interactions between children and abusive versus control parents. *Journal of Clinical Child Psychology, 17*, 137–142.

Kazdin, A. E., Moser, J., Colbus, D., & Bell, R. (1985). Depressive symptoms among physically abused and psychiatrically disturbed children. *Journal of Abnormal Psychology, 94*(3), 298–307.

Kelleher, K., Chaffin, M., Hollenberg, J., & Fischer, E. (1994). Alcohol and drug disorders among physically abusive and neglectful parents in a community-based sample. *American Journal of Public Health, 84*, 1586–1590.

Kelley, S. J. (1992). Parenting stress and child maltreatment in drug-exposed children. *Child Abuse & Neglect, 16,* 317–328.

Kelly, M. L., Grace, N., & Elliot, S. N. (1990). Acceptability of positive and punitive discipline methods: Comparisons among abusive, potentially abusive, and nonabusive parents. *Child Abuse & Neglect, 14,* 219–226.

Kempe, C. H., Silverman, F. N., Steele, B. F., Droegemueller, W., & Silver, H. K. (1962). The battered child syndrome. *Journal of the American Medical Association, 191,* 17–24

Kinard, E. M. (1980). Emotional development in physically abused children. *American Journal of Orthopsychiatry, 50,* 686–695.

Kinard, E. M. (1982). Experiencing child abuse: Effects on emotional adjustment. *American Journal of Orthopsychiatry, 52,* 82–91.

Kinard, E. M. (1996). Social support, self-worth, and depression in offending and nonoffending mothers of maltreated children. *Child Maltreatment, 1,* 272–283.

Kiser, L. J., Heston, J., Millsap, P. A., & Pruitt, D. B. (1991). Physical and sexual abuse in childhood: Relationship with post-traumatic stress disorder. *Journal of the American Academy of Child and Adolescent Child Psychiatry, 30,* 776–783.

Kolko, D. J. (1992). Characteristics of child victims of physical violence: Research findings and clinical implications. *Journal of Interpersonal Violence, 7,* 244–276.

Kolko, D. J. (2002). Child physical abuse. In: J. E. B. Myers, L. Berliner, J. Briere, C. T. Hendrix, C. Jenny, & T. Reid (Eds.), *The APSAC handbook of child maltreatment* (2nd ed., pp. 21–54). Thousand Oaks, CA: Sage Publications.

Kravic, J. N. (1987). Behavior problems and social competence of clinic-referred abused children. *Journal of Family Violence, 2*(2), 111–120.

Lamb, M. E. & Nash, A. (1989). Infant-mother attachment, sociability, and peer competence. In T. J. Berndt & G. W. Ladd (Eds.), *Peer relationships in child development* (pp. 219–245). New York: John Wiley.

Luntz, B. K., & Widom, C. S. (1994). Antisocial personality disorder in abused and neglected children grown up. *American Journal of Psychiatry, 151*(5), 670–674.

Lynch, M. A., & Roberts, J. (1982). *Consequences of child abuse.* London: Academic Press.

Main, M., & George, C. (1985). Responses of abused and disadvantaged toddlers to distress in agemates: A study in the daycare setting. *Developmental Psychology, 21,* 407–412.

Malinosky-Rummell, R., & Hansen, D. J. (1993). Long-term consequences of childhood physical abuse. *Psychological Bulletin, 114,* 68–79.

Manly, J. T., Cicchetti, D., & Barnett, D. (1994). The impact of subtype, frequency, chronicity, and severity of child maltreatment on social competence and behavior problems. *Development and Psychopathology, 6*(1), 121–143.

Mannarino, A. P., Cohen, J. A., & Berman, S. R. (1994). The Children's Attributions and Perceptions Scale: A new measure of sexual abuse-related factors. *Journal of Clinical Child Psychology, 23,* 204–211.

Martin, H. P., & Rodeheoffer, M. A. (1976). The psychological impact of abuse on children. *Journal of Pediatric Psychology, 1,* 12–15.

Mash, E. J., & Johnston, C. (1990). Determinants of parenting stress: Illustrations from families of hyperactive children and families of physically abused children. *Journal of Clinical Psychology, 19,* 313–328.

Mash, E. J., Johnston, C., & Kovitz, K. (1983). A comparison of the mother-child interactions of physically abused and non-abused children during play and task situations. *Journal of Clinical Child Psychology, 12,* 337–346.

McCanne, T. R., & Milner, J. S. (1991). Physiological reactivity of physically abusive and at-risk subjects to child-related stimuli. In J. S. Milner (Ed.), *Neuropsychology of aggression* (pp. 147–166). Norwell, MA: Kluwer.

McCord, J. (1983). A forty-year perspective on effects of child abuse and neglect. *Child Abuse & Neglect, 7,* 265–270.

McFayden, R. G., & Kitson, W. J. H. (1996). Language comprehension and expression among adolescents who have experienced childhood physical abuse. *Journal of Child Psychology and Psychiatry and Allied Disciplines, 37*(5), 551–562.

Merrill, L. L., Hervig, L. K., & Milner, J. S. (1996). Childhood parenting experiences, intimate partner conflict resolution, and adult risk for child physical abuse. *Child Abuse & Neglect, 20,* 1049–1065.

Milner, J. S. (1998). Individual and family characteristics associated with intrafamilial child physical and sexual abuse. In P. K. Trickett & C. J. Schellenbach (Eds.), *Violence against children in the family and community* (pp. 141–170). Washington, DC: American Psychological Association.

Milner, J. S., & Dopke, C. (1997). Child physical abuse: review of offender characteristics. In D. A. Wolfe & R. J. McMahon (Eds.), *Child Abuse: New directions in prevention and treatment across the lifespan* (pp. 27–54). Thousand Oaks, CA: Sage.

Mollerstrom, W. W., Patchner, M. M., & Milner, J. S. (1992). Family functioning and child abuse potential. *Journal of Clinical Psychology, 48,* 445–454.

Morrow, K. B. (1991). Attributions of female adolescent incest victims regarding their molestation. *Child Abuse & Neglect, 15,* 477–483.

Mueller, E., & Silverman, N. (1989). Peer relations in maltreated children. In D. Cicchetti & V. Carlson (Eds.), *Child maltreatment: Theory and research on the causes and consequences of child abuse and neglect* (pp. 529–578). New York: Cambridge University Press.

Murphy, J. M., Jellineck, M., Quin, D., Smith, G., Poitrast, F. G., & Goshko, M. (1991). Substance abuse and serious child mistreatment: Prevalence, risk, and outcome in a court sample. *Child Abuse & Neglect, 15,* 197–212.

National Academy of Sciences. (1993). *Understanding child abuse and neglect.* Washington, DC: National Academy Press.

Nayak, M. B., & Milner, J. S. (1998). Neuropsychological functioning: Comparison of mothers at high- and low-risk for child abuse. *Child Abuse & Neglect, 22,* 687–703.

Noom, M. J., Dekovic, J., & Meeus, W. H. J. (1999). Autonomy, attachment and psychosocial adjustment during adolescence: A double-edged sword? *Journal of Adolescence, 22,* 771–783.

Patterson, G. R., DeBaryshe, B. D., & Ramsey, E. (1989). A developmental perspective on antisocial behavior. *American Psychologist, 44,* 329–335.

Pelcovitz, D., Kaplan, S., Goldenberg, B., Mandel, F., Lehane, J., & Guarrera, J. (1994). Post-traumatic stress disorder in physically abused adolescents. *Journal of American Academic Child and Adolescent Psychiatry, 33*(3), 305–312.

Perez, C. M., & Widom, C. S. (1994). Childhood victimization and long-term intellectual and academic outcomes. *Child Abuse & Neglect, 18,* 617–632.

Perry, M. A., Doran, L. D., & Wells, E. A. (1983). Developmental and behavioral characteristics of the physically abused child. *Journal of Clinical Child Psychology, 12,* 320–324.

Pianta, R., Egeland, B., & Erickson, M. F. (1989). The antecedents of maltreatment: Results of the mother-child interaction research project. In D. Cicchetti & V. Carlson (Eds.), *Child maltreatment: Theory and research on the causes and consequences of child abuse and neglect* (pp. 203–253). New York: Cambridge University Press.

Pollak, S. D., Cicchetti, D., Klorman, R., & Brumaghim, J. T. (1997). Cognitive brain event-related potentials and emotion processing in maltreated children. *Child Development, 68,* 773–787.

Pollock, V. E., Briere, J., Schneider, L., Knop, J., Mednick, S. A., & Goodwin, D. W. (1990). Childhood antecedents of antisocial behavior: Parental alcoholism and physical abusiveness. *American Journal of Psychiatry, 147*(10), 1290–1293.

Reid, J. B., Kavanagh, K., & Baldwin, D. V. (1987). Abusive parents' perceptions of child problem behaviors: An example of parental bias. *Journal of Abnormal Child Psychology, 15,* 457–466.

Reidy, T. J. (1977). The aggressive characteristics of abused and neglected children. *Journal of Clinical Psychology, 33*(4), 1140–1145.

Rosgosch, F., Cicchetti, D., & Abre, J. L. (1995). The role of child maltreatment in early deviations in cognitive and affective processing abilities and later peer relationships problems. *Development and Psychopathology, 7*(4), 591–609.

Salzinger, S., Feldman, R. S., Hammer, M., & Rosario, M. (1991). Risk for physical child abuse and the personal consequences for its victims. *Criminal Justice and Behavior, 18,* 64–81.

Shapiro, D. L., & Levendosky, A. A. (1999). Adolescent survivors of childhood sexual abuse: The mediating role of attachment style and coping in psychological and interpersonal functioning. *Child Abuse & Neglect, 23,* 1175–1191.

Simons, R. L., Whitbeck, L. B., Conger, R. D., & Chyi-in, W. (1991). Intergenerational transmission of harsh parenting. *Developmental Psychology, 27,* 159–171.

Straker, G., & Jacobson, R. S. (1981). Aggression, emotional maladjustment, and empathy in the abused child. *Developmental Psychology, 17,* 762–765.

Straus, M. A., & Smith, C. (1990). Family patterns and child abuse. In M. A. Straus & R. J. Gelles (Eds.), *Physical violence in American families. Risk factors and adaptations to violence in 8,145 families* (pp. 258–259). New Brunswick, NJ: Transaction.

Surrey, S., Swett, C., Michaels, A., & Levin, S. (1990). Reported history of physical and sexual abuse and severity of symptomatology in women psychiatric outpatients. *American Journal of Orthopsychiatry, 60,* 412–417.

Susman, E. J., Trickett, P. K., Iannotti, R. J., Hollenbeck, B. E., & Zahn-Waxler, C. (1985). Child-rearing patterns in depressed, abusive, and normal mothers. *American Journal of Orthopsychiatry, 55,* 237–251.

Swenson, C. C., & Kolko, D. J. (2000). Long-term management of the developmental consequences of child physical abuse. In R. M. Reece (Ed.), *The treatment of child abuse* (pp. 135–154). Baltimore, MD: Johns Hopkins University Press.

Tarter, R. E., Hegedus, A. M., Winsten, N. E., & Alterman, A. I. (1984). Neuropsychological, personality, and familial characteristics of physically abused children. *Journal of the American Academy of Child Psychiatry, 23,* 668–674.

Tarter, R. E., Hegedus, A. M., Winsten, N. E., & Alterman, A. I. (1985). Intellectual profiles and violent behavior in juvenile delinquents. *The Journal of Psychology, 119,* 125–128.

Trickett, P. K., Aber, J. L., Carlson, V., & Cicchetti, D. (1991). Relationship of socioeconomic status to the etiology and developmental sequelae of physical child abuse. *Developmental Psychology, 27,* 148–158.

Trickett, P. K., & Kuczynski, L. (1986). Children's misbehaviors and parental discipline strategies in abusive and nonabusive families. *Developmental Psychology, 22,* 115–123.

Vondra, J. A., Barnett, D., & Cicchetti, D. (1989). Perceived and actual competence among maltreated and comparison school children. *Development and Psychopathology, 1,* 237–255.

Walker, E., Downey, G., & Bergman, A. (1989). The effects of parental psychopathology and maltreatment on child behavior: A test of the diathesis-stress model. *Child Development, 60,* 15–24.

Webster-Stratton, C. (1985). Comparison of abusive and nonabusive families with conduct-disordered children. *American Journal of Orthopsychiatry, 55,* 59–68.

Webster-Stratton, C. (1990). Stress: A potential disruptor of parent perceptions and family interactions. *Journal of Clinical Child Psychology, 19,* 302–312.

Whipple, E. E., & Webster-Stratton, C. (1991). The role of parental stress in physically abusive families. *Child Abuse & Neglect, 15,* 279–291.

Widom, C. S. (1989, April). The cycle of violence. *Science, 244,* 160–165.

Wolfe, D. A., & Mosk, M. D. (1983). Behavioral comparisons of children from abusive and distressed families. *Journal of Consulting and Clinical Psychology, 51,* 702–708.

Wolfe, D. A., Werkele, C., Reitzel-Jaffe, D., & Lefebvre, L. (1998). Factors associated with abusive relationships among maltreated and nonmaltreated youth. *Development and Psychopathology, 10,* 61–85.

Wyatt, G. E., & Newcomb, M. (1990). Internal and external mediators of women's sexual abuse in childhood. *Journal of Consulting and Clinical Psychology, 48,* 758–767.

Zuravin, S. (1989). The ecology of child abuse and neglect: Review of the literature and presentation of data. *Violence and Victims, 4,* 101–120.

3

Treatment Outcome Studies
Clinical and Research Implications

❏ What Have We Learned?

OVERVIEW OF STUDY FINDINGS

Considerable progress has been made over the past two decades in applying and evaluating treatments for children, parents, and their families involved with child physical abuse (CPA). These intervention studies are described in some detail in several reviews, but are summarized briefly in this chapter to provide some understanding of the nature and outcomes of this work (see Azar & Wolfe, 1998; Corcoran, 2000; Kolko, 1998a, 1998b; Oates & Bross, 1995; Stevenson, 1999; Wolfe, 1994). Most treatment approaches reported for this population have been based on the application of cognitive-behavioral treatment (CBT) procedures applied individually or to a lesser extent, at the family level, in conjunction with specific educational, clinical, or support services (Graziano & Mills, 1992; Wolfe & Wekerle, 1993). Although generally applied in traditional clinic settings, such interventions have been extended to more naturalistic "ecological" settings and directed towards child, parent, family, and social system variables (Belsky, 1993).

It is important to indicate that these studies describe interventions that vary in several parameters of treatment, such as the age ranges of the clients (children vs. adolescents), type of treatment approach used (CBT vs. psychoeducation), diversity of the treatment content and procedures, setting for the treatment (clinic vs. home), format of treatment (group vs. individual therapy), and length or duration of treatment. Within the child maltreatment area, the impact of these parameters is generally unknown. Much of this work has emphasized parent-focused applications, followed by family-based and child-focused interventions. A summary of the findings of this research is found in Box 3.1.

Box 3.1 | Literature Review: Summary of Findings From Recent Outcome Studies

Target/Outcome	Amount of Change		
Common Outcomes Following Parental Family Intervention			
Parenting skill acquisition	+	+	+
Parenting practices	+	+	
Other negative parental behaviors	+	+	
Severity of child behavior problems	+	+	
Positive parent-child interactions	+	+	
Family support-conflict	+	+	
Abuse indicators	+		
Common Outcomes Following Child Intervention			
Social initiations/interactions	+	+	+
Severity of behavioral/emotional problems	+	+	
Parental behavior	+		
Number of Studies Targeting Different Groups			
Offenders (adults)	+	+	+
Family treatments	+	+	
School-aged children	+		

Individual and Group Parent Treatment

Parent training in positive/nonviolent child management practices, anger control skills, or stress management techniques is one of the most common and effective treatment approaches (see National

Academy of Sciences, 1993; Wolfe & Wekerle, 1993). Behaviorally oriented parent training has successfully taught psychological forms of discipline and discouraged the use of excessive, harsh, or physical forms of punishment. Related studies have reported improved parental knowledge of alternative disciplinary practices and normal child development (Golub, Espinosa, Damon, & Card, 1987), and reductions in negative or coercive parenting behaviors (Sandler, Van Dercar, & Milhoan, 1978). To improve generalization from the clinic to the home, parent training has extended clinic-based training (e.g., in child management and self-control) to the home with reports of the maintenance of these improvements at a one-year follow-up (Wolfe, Sandler, & Kaufman, 1981).

An extension of this approach found that individualized parent-child sessions contributed to key clinical outcomes beyond the effects of a parent information group alone (Wolfe, Edwards, Manion, & Koverola, 1988). This study found that the combination condition showed greater improvements on some measures (e.g., fewer and less intense child behavior problems, fewer parental adjustment problems, and lowered risk of maltreatment), but not in other outcomes (e.g., quality of child-rearing environment and children's adaptive abilities). Moreover, these gains were maintained at follow-up and associated with reduced risk for reabuse.

Other cognitive-behavioral applications for parents conducted in a group format have reported positive outcomes in terms of anger control, positive communication, and problem-solving skills (Acton & During, 1992; Nurius, Lovell, & Edgar, 1988; Whiteman, Fanshel, & Grundy, 1987), although these studies suffer from certain methodological limitations, such as a lack of comparison groups. In terms of more recent studies, programs that combine these elements report improvements in both parent targets (e.g., child abuse potential and parental depression) and child targets (e.g., behavior problems) after treatment and at short-term follow-up (Wolfe et al., 1988).

A related protocol for offending parents was based on social learning principles designed to address their cognitive, affective, and behavioral-social repertoires, incorporating instruction in both intrapersonal and interpersonal skills (Kolko, 1996a, 1996b). Accordingly, this parent protocol emphasized parental views on violence and physical punishment, attributional style and expectations, self-control (e.g., anger control and cognitive coping), and contingency management (e.g., attention, reinforcement, and time-out). Several technical materials were adapted for this protocol (e.g., Fleischman, Horne, & Arthur, 1983; Walker, Bonner, and Kaufman, 1988).

Individual and Group Child Treatment

In contrast to the many child-directed interventions examined in studies with child sexual abuse (CSA) victims, few interventions have been conducted for physically abused children on an outpatient or inpatient basis. Indeed, only one study of school-aged children (Kolko, 1996c) included specialized individual child therapy, which emphasized training in various CBT procedures and skills based on several protocol materials (e.g., Feindler & Ecton, 1986; Jaffe, Wilson, & Wolfe, 1986, 1988; Wilson, Cameron, Jaffe, & Wolfe, 1986, 1989). Treatment for children covered their views of family stressors and violence, and their coping and self-control skills training (e.g., safety/support planning and relaxation), followed by training in interpersonal effectiveness skills to enhance social competence (e.g., using social supports, social skills, and assertion).

Other studies of individualized interventions with preschoolers have evaluated specific behavioral and social learning procedures directed toward improving their peer relations and social adjustment by arranging play-buddy sessions in which withdrawn, maltreated children were exposed to social initiation techniques demonstrated by trained peer confederates (Fantuzzo, Stovall, Schachtel, Goins, & Hall, 1987). Experimental evidence has shown that this intervention, called resilient peer treatment or RPT, is more effective than adult initiations in improving children's social adjustment and peer initiations (Davis & Fantuzzo, 1989; Fantuzzo, Jurecic, Stovall, Hightower, & Goins, 1988). In particular, RPT has been effective with withdrawn children but not with aggressive children, who actually exhibited higher levels of deviant behavior following intervention (Davis & Fantuzzo, 1989; Fantuzzo et al., 1987, 1988). Maintenance effects two-months following RPT also have been documented (Fantuzzo et al., 1996). These systematic research studies suggest some important differences among intervention procedures and have documented short-term follow-up gains, but would benefit from further evaluations of long-term follow-up and their impact on recidivism.

To our knowledge, no controlled group therapy studies have been reported with CPA victims, although controlled outcome studies have been reported for CSA victims (e.g., Berliner & Saunders, 1996) or children exposed to domestic violence (Jaffe et al., 1988; Wagar & Rodway, 1995). One recent application described a multiple-module cognitive-behavioral group conducted over a 16-week period with six physically abused children, four of whom completed the group (Swenson & Brown, 1999). The program emphasized content in three primary domains: trauma-specific work, anger management, and social skills training. Outcome assessment based on child reports revealed improvements (e.g., in anger reactions and posttraumatic symptoms) for some, but not all, group participants, with parent reports indicating some increase in emotional and behavioral problems at posttreatment. Certainly, further evaluation of the feasibility and efficacy of this type of structured group program is warranted. Other group applications for this population are currently under investigation (Silovsky, Valle, & Chaffin, 1999). There are potential advantages to group work, especially the ability to draw upon shared group experiences and problems, although it is not always easy to find suitable group members at a given time. Certainly, therapists should keep in mind that grouping children who have antisocial behavior problems or severe aggression may lead to increased behavioral problems (Arnold & Hughes, 1999).

Day and Residential Treatment

Day and residential treatment programs have provided maltreated children and their families access to an array of therapeutic activities. One intensive day-treatment program for young children incorporated a diverse developmental stimulation curriculum involving play, speech, and physical therapy; family therapy; support group counseling; parent education; and crisis line over an average nine-month period. Compared to a control group, the program was associated with several child improvements in cognitive performance, peer and maternal acceptance, and developmental achievement based on parent and teacher ratings (Culp, Little, Letts, & Lawrence, 1991). These improvements notwithstanding, most children still remained below the "normal" range in most of these areas.

Another program, KEEPSAFE (Kempe Early Education Project Serving Abused Families) consisting of a therapeutic preschool and home visitation also found improved intellectual functioning and receptive language at discharge one year later (Oates, Gray, Schweitzer, Kempe, & Harmon, 1995). Several of these children were able to enter regular classrooms. Yet, because of the absence of a controlled design, it is not possible to conclude that the program is responsible for these improvements.

Parent-Child and Family Treatment

Although family therapy (FT) techniques have been incorporated in some of the aforementioned studies, few studies have formally evaluated family treatment protocols per se. Kolko (1996a, 1996b) evaluated one protocol designed to enhance family functioning and relationships by promoting various objectives with all family members (e.g., cooperation and motivation, understanding of coercive behavior, and instruction in communication and problem-solving skills). The three phases of FT entailed engagement (e.g., assessment, reframing, and a no-force contract), skill building (e.g., problem-solving and communication skills training), and application/termination (e.g., establishing problem-solving family routines) based on the functional FT model. Sessions were conducted in the clinic and in the home. In this study, family treatment was compared with CBT and routine community services.

The study by Wolfe et al. (1988), noted earlier, examined the incremental benefit of providing individualized parent-child sessions beyond the effects of participation in an information group alone with parents who were referred for treatment because of frequent abusive or punitive behaviors. The parent-child sessions consisted of teaching parents to give clear demands to children, reward compliance, and implement time-out, among other procedures. The combination condition was found to be associated with several benefits (e.g., fewer and less intense child behavior problems, fewer parental adjustment problems, and a lowered risk of maltreatment). Both conditions led to a higher quality of child-rearing environment and improved children's adaptive abilities.

In another outcome study with school-aged children and their offending parents (Kolko, 1996a, 1996b), cases that were assigned to CBT or FT were found to show greater improvements in child-to-parent violence and child externalizing behavior, parental distress and abuse risk, and family conflict and cohesion, than those cases who received routine community service (RCS). All three conditions did report several improvements across time (e.g., in parental anger, parental practices, and children's fears). Based on official records, recidivism rates reflecting the percentage of children from the CBT, FT, and RCS groups who were involved in another incident of child maltreatment during follow-up differed, but not significantly (10%, 12%, and 30%, respectively). In terms of the adults who participated in treatment, one adult each in CBT (5%) and FT (6%), and three in RCS (30%) had been reported as having maltreated a participating child during follow-up. No differences between CBT and FT were observed on consumer satisfaction or maltreatment risk ratings at termination; unfortunately, such information could not be assessed in RCS. These evaluation findings highlight some of the benefits associated with the application of individual and family treatments involving child victims of physical abuse.

Treatment course data obtained from this study were also reported to describe rates of behavioral indicators of abusive activity (Kolko, 2002). During treatment, the overall levels of parental anger and physical discipline/force based on weekly reports from children and their offending parents decreased more rapidly in CBT than FT families, though each group showed a reduction on these items from the early to late treatment sessions. Between 20% and 23% of all children and their parents independently reported high levels of physical discipline/force during the early and late phases of treatment, although few incidents seemed to result in injuries, and an even higher percentage of cases reported heightened parental anger and family problems. Early treatment reports from both informants predicted late period reports, but only parent reports were related to validity measures. Thus, it may be important to monitor clinical indicators of problem behaviors on a regular basis to gauge family response to treatment.

One specific program having both behavioral and systemic components, Parent-Child Interaction Training or PCIT (Eisenstadt, Eyberg, McNeil, Newcomb, & Funderburk, 1993), has been advocated for clinical application to the treatment of CPA with children no older than seven years of age (Urquiza & Bodiford-McNeil, 1996). To support this development, Urquiza and Bodiford-McNeil (1996) contend that parent-child interactions in abusive families are often conflictual and problematic, that PA children show poor behavioral controls and heightened behavioral dysfunction, and that social learning factors influence parental use of coercive discipline. PCIT may address these issues by providing parents with opportunities to establish more positive relationships with their children and to learn appropriate parenting techniques through ongoing coaching efforts during observed interactions. Although outcome evidence for abusive families must await the completion of two ongoing PCIT studies, numerous benefits to PCIT have been found with behavior problem children. This model nicely describes various stages in the treatment process that lend themselves to training and evaluation (e.g., assessment, training in behavioral play skills, discipline training, and booster sessions).

Family-Based, In-Home Services

Several interventions have been directed at various contextual risk factors associated with abuse and have reported positive benefits (e.g., in problem behaviors and communication skills), but few of these reports permit adequate experimental evaluation of their outcomes (Amundson, 1989; Whittaker, Kinney, Tracy, & Booth, 1990). In fact, initial program evaluation reports failed to find improvements in child placement rates for family preservation versus routine services (Nelson, 1990). In one early study (Nicol et al., 1988), behaviorally oriented family casework (e.g., modeling or reinforcement) was more effective than individual child play therapy in reducing family coercion, but not in increasing positive interactions. However, the study is limited by a large attrition rate (44%), and the absence of both treatment integrity and follow-up data.

Turning to more CBT-derived intervention programs, Multisystemic Therapy or MST (Brunk, Henggeler, & Whelan, 1987; Henggeler & Borduin, 1990) and Project 12-Ways (Lutzker, Frame, & Rice, 1982) are widely recognized ecological models that address the multiple child, parent, family, and social system correlates of abuse. In an earlier clinical trial of MST, Brunk et al. (1987) randomly assigned families who had been investigated for abuse and neglect to home-based MST or office-based group parent training (see Wolfe et al., 1981). MST and parent training were effective in reducing parents' psychiatric symptoms and stress, and in improving individualized family problems. However, maltreating parents who received MST controlled their children's behavior more effectively, and their children exhibited less passive noncompliance than those whose parents received parent training. Parent training was superior to MST in decreasing parents' reports of problems with their social system. Unfortunately, no follow-up data were reported for either condition.

The PEACE Project (Project Empowering Adults, Children, and Their Ecology), *Betta Fuh Fambly* ("For the Family"), a 5-year, National Institute for Mental Health–funded study currently in progress, is comparing MST to parent training (Swenson, 2000). This project targets physically abused adolescents and their families, and measures specific change across multiple systems (i.e., individual child, parent, family, and social network systems). Importantly, the PEACE Project brings together the scientific strength of a university-based study and the day-to-day issues of practice in the real world through the use of random assignment, monitoring of treatment adherence and treatment integrity, minimal exclusion criteria for participants, following families over 16 months, and the conduct of the treatment via a community-based outpatient clinic, the Charleston/Dorchester Mental Health Center.

The Project 12-Ways (Lutzker, Van Hasselt, Bigelow, Greene, & Kessler, 1998) program has documented multiple gains in various targeted areas (e.g., interactions, child management training, social support, assertion training, job training, and home safety/finances training) following individualized skills training in the home.

Program evaluations of Project 12-Ways also demonstrate important benefits in terms of reduced recidivism relative to comparison families (1 vs. 5 families; Lutzker & Rice, 1984). These short-term improvements have been replicated in a more extensive evaluation (Lutzker & Rice, 1987), but this difference was not maintained at long-term follow-up (Wesch & Lutzker, 1991). Other reports from this innovative program illustrate the diversity in treatment needs and outcomes across families (see Lutzker & Campbell, 1994), highlighting the need for individualized programming and outcome assessment measures (Greene, Norman, Searle, Daniels, & Lubeck, 1995). Extensions of this ecobehavioral program for families with very young children at risk for abuse or neglect may yield more substantial program benefits (Bigelow, Kessler, & Lutzker, 1995; Taub, Kessler, & Lutzker, 1995).

❏ What Do We Need to Learn in Research to Make Treatment More Effective?

OVERVIEW OF STUDY LIMITATIONS AND DIRECTIONS

This brief literature review highlights some of the developments that have been achieved in addressing the diverse consequences of an abusive experience and in documenting the impact of intervention based on experimentally rigorous methodologies. Other studies reported in the general child psychotherapy literature provide some insights regarding the types of characteristics associated with clinical improvement (e.g., structured treatments, behaviorally oriented treatment models, and use of manuals; see Weisz, Donenberg, Han, & Weiss, 1995). Collectively, the outcomes from these studies suggest that individual and family treatments have been associated with modest improvements in certain parental practices, child behaviors, and appropriate family functions. When follow-up data have been collected, studies have documented the maintenance of various improvements. There are also indications in a few studies that recidivism rates following treatment are fairly low. Concomitantly, improvements in the methodologies (e.g., independent abuse assessment, multiple outcome measures and sources, adequate comparison groups, and use of treatment manuals and assessment of treatment integrity) of these outcome studies, especially the more recent ones, are being reported more frequently, which may strengthen the conclusions derived from these studies.

These clinical and methodological advances notwithstanding, there are still numerous limitations in the scope, significance, and sophistication of the treatment outcome literature in this area. For example, few studies of psychotherapeutic treatments have been conducted with child victims (whereas several applications have been directed toward preschoolers) have evaluated program maintenance at follow-up, or have examined the social validity or significance of intervention procedures and targets. Thus, additional studies are needed to document the efficacy of alternative modalities and formats (e.g., individual or group) that are designed to minimize the effects of abuse with child victims or to minimize a child's risk for reabuse (see Kolko, 2002; Mannarino & Cohen, 1990; Oates & Bross, 1995; Wolfe, 1994). The impact of these efforts may be enhanced to the extent that multiple forms of child and parental functioning are addressed (e.g., psychiatric disorders and functional impairments).

Based on this collective work, several areas of further program development and evaluation seem warranted. There is a need to accumulate additional evidence regarding the efficacy of new treatments and the real-world effectiveness of existing ones. Many of the interventions reported in the abuse field have some modest level of efficacy, but are in need of replication. Further investigation of the utility of existing treatments could include comparisons to a minimal-care condition or an alternative treatment. Ultimately, replication may be the most rigorous form of experimental validation. Additionally, investigators must include measures that capture the magnitude or clinical significance of change following experimental interventions (see Jacobson & Revenstorf, 1988). In many instances, interventions may achieve statistical significance, but with questionable clinical significance. Better documentation of the impact of treatment on primary measures of child and parent functioning is a high priority for this field.

As intervention programs gain empirical support, tests of the impact of specific procedures become an important next step. Most interventions in the abuse field consist of multiple therapeutic techniques, many of which have not been evaluated independently. By examining the constituents of such packages in next-generation studies, we may be able to determine the active ingredients in these programs. Potential ingredients worth evaluating include discussion of and psychoeducation about the victim's experience and its impact, exposure and discussion of the experience, teaching psychological and coping skills, and working with parents and families to provide support, among other procedures. An understanding of effective parameters of treatment in the child abuse field has received limited empirical attention. It may be the case that specific procedures work best under particular conditions, suggesting the need to evaluate treatment moderators and mediators. Recent work by Cohen and Mannarino (1998) indicates that certain variables may influence treatment outcome in conducting CBT with young sexually abused children.

Perhaps some of the more important developments in the application of treatment reflect the articulation of clinical guidelines used to enhance service participation and overall impact. Noteworthy recommendations have been made for enhancing treatment adherence, promoting generalization, and increasing the validity of treatment targets (Lundquist & Hansen, 1998), assessing and targeting abusive parents' educational and therapeutic needs (Tymchuk, 1998; Webster-Stratton, 1998), and establishing effective community partnerships to maximize the helpfulness of the service delivery system (Fantuzzo, Weiss, & Coolahan, 1998). Aspects of these and other clinical recommendations are addressed in a clinical approach to treatment that is outlined in the next chapter.

Finally, more attention ought to be paid to the ways in which treatments and interventions are applied in existing clinical practice or service delivery systems. Other studies are needed to determine if the efficacy of laboratory-based research treatments exceeds that found in routine clinical practice. Furthermore, most of the existing studies in this area have been conducted in specialized research treatment settings. Therefore, treatment applications are needed in community clinic and other real-world settings in order to understand their limitations and any need for modifications. The ultimate test of an intervention's utility may reflect its successful application under the real-world or naturalistic conditions of existing clinical practice.

❏ What Would Make Clinical Practice More Effective?

SOME LESSONS LEARNED FROM STUDIES OF CHILD/FAMILY PSYCHOTHERAPY

An extensive literature has documented the efficacy of child and adolescent psychotherapy (see Weisz & Jensen, 1999; Weisz, Weiss, & Donenberg, 1992). Rigorous reviews of these studies have described the effects of therapy across a range of important treatment parameters. Some of these findings bear implications for improving the treatment of CPA.

One implication of these findings is that therapy with children and adolescents, when applied in research settings, was found to be beneficial overall, although there was wide diversity in clinicians, patients, and methods. Much more modest effects were found in studies that were conducted in everyday clinical settings. Thus, fewer effects of psychotherapy were found in routine clinic settings.

Some of this work has identified the conditions under which treatments conducted in clinics are most effective. Weisz, Donenberg, Han, and Kauneckis (1995) explored possible reasons for these differences by examining various study characteristics. Several factors were not associated with the differential efficacy of research and clinic treatment studies (e.g., age and rigor of studies, severity of clinical problems, or training of therapists). However, they did find greater efficacy among studies that draw upon structured (vs. unstructured) interventions and the use of treatment manuals or clinical guidelines. Attention to these variables may enhance the impact of child psychotherapy.

In terms of other factors associated with the greater efficacy of research treatments, Weisz, Weiss, Han, Granger, and Morton (1995) found that behavioral interventions were more effective than non–behavioral treatments and their effects were well maintained. These effects were generally greater for adolescents than for children, and for females than males, even when controlling for problem type (e.g., externalizing behavior). Paraprofessionals had greater overall effects than professionals or students, recruited cases showed greater improvement than clinic cases, and individual treatment was more effective than group treatment. Other analyses revealed that the effects of treatment were greater when there was a match between the target problem and the outcome measure that was used, highlighting the need to try to focus specifically on changing problems that were directly being targeted by the treatment. Treatment effects generally reflected the specific and intended outcomes of treatment, rather than generalized positive effects. In contrast, no difference was found between the effectiveness of treatment on the types of problems that were targeted (overcontrolled vs. undercontrolled).

These general findings provide some indication of those characteristics of treatment that may contribute to positive outcomes. In particular, the reader can appreciate the potential benefits to treatments that incorporate structure and a behavioral focus, and the use of treatments specifically designed to target a given problem. Incorporating these treatment parameters might be expected to enhance the efficacy of treatment outcome with physically abused children and their families. Many of these treatment parameters are addressed in the chapters devoted to specific treatment procedures in the later sections of this book.

It is also important to recognize that, because there is no profile of the physically abused child, treatment targets must be assessed on a case-by-case basis, and the potential range of clinical problems worth addressing may be quite extensive. Thus, the relevance and impact of treatment is likely to be maximized if a comprehensive assessment is conducted that examines different aspects of functioning in several important domains. Relevant dimensions of clinical outcome that may bear examination have been described by Hoagwood, Jensen, Petti, and Burns (1996) in their interactional model of outcomes of mental health care. The model posts five domains that reflect primary outcomes important for the evaluation of treatments administered in diverse settings. Three domains relevant to understanding client problems are as follows: (1) severity of symptoms and diagnoses (e.g., fewer posttraumatic stress disorder [PTSD] symptoms or less serious depressive or aggressive behavior); (2) child functional status or level of impairment (e.g., role efficacy or enhanced social and problem-solving skill); and (3) child or family functioning in its environmental context, such as at home, at school, and in other community settings (e.g., appropriate parenting practices and family support, involvement with deviant peers, or school behavior problems).

One can appreciate the relevance of each domain to assessing the outcome of treatment in cases of child abuse. For example, most evaluations of outcome include children's symptoms, such as PTSD, depression, aggression, and anxiety, and parental or family functioning. However, few studies have evaluated the children's level of impairment, school and peer behavior, consumer satisfaction, and service system involvement. Given the possibility of extended system contact, multiple interventions, and a history of multiple traumas and family adversities, an outcome assessment with both depth and breath seems warranted.

An implication of this model is the need to understand and possibly target the effects of treatment in different settings and contexts. Targeting the child's ecology directly may enhance the impact of treatment in various community settings, such as the child's home, school, and neighborhood. Indeed, favorable outcomes have been reported by studies that have conducted treatment in the natural environment (see Burns, Farmer, Angold, Costello, & Behar, 1996; Coie, Underwood, & Lochman, 1991; Conduct Problems Prevention Research Group, 1992; Cunningham, Bremner, & Boyle, 1995; Henggeler, Schoenwald, & Pickrel, 1995; Kolko, 1996b, 1996c). There may be several benefits to targeting ecological factors in the community (e.g., enhancing family involvement, reducing obstacles to attendance, and targeting of contextual problems).

In general, there is emerging evidence to support specific treatment approaches in this area (Cohen, Berliner, & Mannarino, 2000) and the articulation of clinical guidelines for treating abuse-specific sequelae and more general psychological dysfunction or skills deficiencies. The development of multicomponent interventions that target several problems seems reasonable when various child and family problems require attention and when it is complemented by the use of highly specific interventions targeting discrete clinical problems. Such interventions could also help in addressing common therapeutic obstacles to treatment participation and progress (e.g., limited motivation, attrition, or poor skills acquisition or generalization; see Corcoran, 2000).

❏ Summary

In sum, there is modest, but increasing, evidence for the efficacy of specific interventions for physically abusive parents or families and, to a lesser extent, for children who have been physically abused. Improvements have been documented following treatment and, in some cases, at follow-up in individual skill or behavior problem areas and in family processes related to coercive behavior. For all of these positive outcomes, however, studies have been limited in treatment conceptualization, analytic technique, and study design, among other areas, such that more work needs to be done to document the impact, generality, and replicability of treatment.

On the practical side, it is clear that innovative clinical models and methods are needed to guide the selection of particular treatment techniques for children, parents, and families. Such interventions must begin to address at least two service aims, namely, promoting prosocial repertoires and minimizing the psychological sequelae of abusive behavior. Furthermore, interventions should be sufficiently comprehensive in scope as to be able to target the various sequelae and risk factors associated with CPA, many of which are described in subsequent chapters. Thus, interventions that integrate clinical and psychoeducational work with both the victim and the offender are called for in order to enhance the social-psychological development of both participants (Graziano & Mills, 1992). After all, only through continued advances in technique and methodology will the benefits of treatment for abused children and their families be maximized.

References

Acton, R. G., & During, S. M. (1992). Preliminary results of aggression management training for aggressive parents. *Journal of Interpersonal Violence, 7*, 410–417.

Amundson, M. J. (1989). Family crisis care: A home-based intervention program for child abuse. *Issues in Mental Health Nursing, 10*, 285–296.

Arnold, M. E., & Hughes, J. N. (1999). First do no harm: Adverse effects of grouping deviant youth for skills training. *Journal of School Psychology, 37*, 99–115.

Azar, S. T., & Wolfe, D. A. (1998). Child physical abuse and neglect. In E. J. Mash & R. A. Barkley (Eds.), *Treatment of childhood disorders* (2nd ed., pp. 501–544). New York: Guilford.

Belsky, J. (1993). Etiology of child maltreatment: A developmental-ecological analysis. *Psychological Bulletin, 114*, 413–434.

Berliner, L., & Saunders, B. (1996). Treating fear and anxiety in sexually abused children: Results of a controlled two-year follow-up study. *Child Maltreatment, 1*, 294–309.

Bigelow, K. M., Kessler, M. L., & Lutzker, J. R. (1995). Improving the parent-child relationship in abusive and neglectful families. In M. L. Kessler (Chair), *Treating physical abuse and neglect: Four approaches*. Symposium conducted at the 3rd Annual APSAC Colloquium, Tucson, AZ.

Brunk, M., Henggeler, S. W., & Whelan, J. P. (1987). Comparison of multisystemic therapy and parent training in the brief treatment of child abuse and neglect. *Journal of Consulting and Clinical Psychology, 55*, 171–178.

Burns, B. J., Farmer, E. M., Angold, A., Costello, E. J., & Behar, L. (1996). A randomized trial of case management for youths with serious emotional disturbance. *Journal of Clinical Child Psychology, 25*, 476–486.

Cohen, J. A., Berliner, L., & Mannarino, A. (2000). Treating traumatized children. *Trauma, Violence and Abuse, 1*, 29–46.

Cohen, J. A., & Mannarino, A. P. (1998). Factors that mediate treatment outcome of sexually abused preschool children: Six- and twelve-month follow-up. *Journal of the American Academy of Child and Adolescent Psychiatry, 37*, 44–51.

Coie, J. D., Underwood, M., & Lochman, J. E. (1991). Programmatic intervention with aggressive children in the school setting. In D. J. Pepler & K. H. Rubin (Eds.), *The development and treatment of childhood aggression* (pp. 389–407). Hillsdale, NJ: Lawrence Erlbaum.

Conduct Problems Prevention Research Group. (1992). A developmental and clinical model for the prevention of conduct disorder. *Development and Psychopathology, 4*, 509–527.

Corcoran, J. (2000). Family interventions with child physical abuse and neglect: A critical review. *Children and Youth Services Review, 22*, 563–591.

Culp, R. E., Little, V., Letts, D., & Lawrence, H. (1991). Maltreated children's self-concept: Effects of a comprehensive treatment program. *American Journal of Orthopsychiatry, 61*, 114–121.

Cunningham, C. E., Bremner, R., & Boyle, M. (1995). Large group community-based parenting programs for families of preschoolers at risk for disruptive behavior disorders: Utilization, cost effectiveness, and outcome. *Journal of Child Psychology and Psychiatry, 36*, 1141–1159.

Davis, S., & Fantuzzo, J. W. (1989). The effects of adult and peer social initiations on social behavior of withdrawn and aggressive maltreated preschool children. *Journal of Family Violence, 4*, 227–248.

Eisenstadt, T. H., Eyberg, S., McNeil, C. B., Newcomb, K., & Funderburk, B. (1993). Parent-child interaction therapy with behavior problem children: Relative effectiveness of two stages and overall treatment outcome. *Journal of Clinical Child Psychology, 22*, 42–51.

Fantuzzo, J. W., Jurecic, L., Stovall, A., Hightower, A. D., & Goins, C. (1988). Effects of adult and peer social initiations on the social behavior of withdrawn, maltreated preschool children. *Journal of Consulting and Clinical Psychology, 56*, 34–39.

Fantuzzo, J. W., Stovall, A., Schachtel, D., Goins, C., & Hall, R. (1987). The effects of peer social initiations on the social behavior of withdrawn maltreated preschool children. *Journal of Behavior Therapy and Experimental Psychiatry, 18,* 357–363.

Fantuzzo, J., Sutton-Smith, B., Atkins, M., Meyers, R., Stevenson, H., Coolahan, K., Weiss, A., & Manz, P. (1996). Community-based resilient peer treatment of withdrawn maltreated preschool children. *Journal of Consulting and Clinical Psychology, 64,* 1377–1386.

Fantuzzo, J., Weiss, A. D., & Coolahan, K. C. (1998). Community-based partnership-directed research: Actualizing community strengths to treatment child victims of physical abuse and neglect. In J. R. Lutzker (Ed.), *Handbook of child abuse research and treatment: Issues in clinical child psychology* (pp. 213–237). New York, NY: Plenum.

Feindler, E. L., & Ecton, R. B. (1986). *Adolescent anger control: Cognitive behavioral techniques.* New York: Pergamon.

Fleischman, M. J., Horne, A. M., & Arthur, J. L. (1983). *Troubled families: A treatment program.* Champaign, IL: Research Press.

Golub, J. S., Espinosa, M., Damon, L., & Card, J. (1987). A videotape parent education program for abusive parents. *Child Abuse & Neglect, 11,* 255–265.

Graziano, A. M., & Mills, J. R. (1992). Treatment for abused children: When is a partial solution acceptable? *Child Abuse & Neglect, 16,* 217–228.

Greene, B. F., Norman, K. R., Searle, M. S., Daniels, M., & Lubeck, R. C. (1995). Child abuse and neglect by parents with disabilities: A tale of two families. *Journal of Applied Behavior Analysis, 28,* 417–434.

Henggeler, S. W., & Borduin, C. M. (1990). *Family therapy and beyond: A multisystemic approach to treating the behavior problems of children and adolescents.* Pacific Grove, CA: Brooks/Cole.

Henggeler, S. W., Schoenwald, S. K., & Pickrel, S. G. (1995). Multisystemic therapy: Bridging the gap between university- and community-based treatment. *Journal of Consulting and Clinical Psychology, 63,* 709–717.

Hoagwood, K., Jensen, P. S., Petti, T., & Burns, B. J. (1996). Outcomes of mental health care for children and adolescents: A comprehensive conceptual model. *Journal of the American Academy of Child and Adolescent Psychiatry, 35,* 1055–1063.

Jacobson, N. S., & Revenstorf, D. (1988). Statistics for assessing the clinical significance of psychotherapy techniques: Issues, problems, and new developments. *Journal of Behavioral Assessment, 10,* 133–145.

Jaffe, P. G., Wilson, S. K., & Wolfe, D. A. (1986). Promoting changes in attitudes and understanding of conflict resolution among child witnesses of family violence. *Canadian Journal of Behavioral Science, 18,* 357–366.

Jaffe, P. G., Wilson, S. K., & Wolfe, D. A. (1988). Specific assessment and intervention strategies for children exposed to wife battering: Preliminary empirical investigations. *Canadian Journal of Community Mental Health, 7,* 157–163.

Kolko, D.J. (1996a). Clinical monitoring of treatment course in child physical abuse: Psychometric characteristics and treatment comparisons. *Child Abuse & Neglect, 20,* 23–43.

Kolko, D. J. (1996b). Individual cognitive-behavioral treatment and family therapy for physically abused children and their offending parents: A comparison of clinical outcomes. *Child Maltreatment, 1,* 322–342.

Kolko, D. J. (1998a). Integration of research and treatment. In J. R. Lutzker (Ed.), *Handbook of child abuse research and treatment: Issues in clinical child psychology* (pp. 159–181). New York: Plenum.

Kolko, D. J. (1998b). Treatment and intervention for child victims of violence. In P. Trickett (Ed.), *Violence to children in the family and the community* (pp. 213–249). Washington, DC: American Psychological Association.

Kolko, D. J. (2002). Child physical abuse. In: J. E. B. Myers, L. Berliner, J. Briere, C. T. Hendrix, C. Jenny, & T. Reid (Eds.), *The APSAC handbook of child maltreatment* (2nd ed., pp. 21–54). Thousand Oaks, CA: Sage Publications.

Lundquist, L. M., & Hansen, D. J. (1998). Enhancing treatment adherence, social validity, and generalization of parent training interventions with physically abusive and neglectful families. In J. R. Lutzker (Ed.), *Handbook of child abuse research and treatment: Issues in clinical child psychology* (pp. 449–471). New York, NY: Plenum.

Lutzker, J. R., & Campbell, R. V. (1994). *Ecobehavioral family interventions in developmental disabilities.* Pacific Groves, CA: Brooks/Cole.

Lutzker, J. R., Frame, J. R., & Rice, J. M. (1982). Project 12-Ways: An ecobehavioral approach to the treatment and prevention of child abuse and neglect. *Education and Treatment of Children, 5,* 141–155.

Lutzker, J. R., & Rice, J. M. (1984). Project 12-Ways: Measuring outcome of a large in-home service for treatment and prevention of child abuse and neglect. *Child Abuse & Neglect, 8,* 519–524.

Lutzker, J. R., & Rice, J. M. (1987). Using recidivism data to evaluate Project 12-Ways: An ecobehavioral approach to the treatment and prevention of child abuse and neglect. *Journal of Family Violence, 2,* 283–289.

Lutzker, J. R., Van Hasselt, V. B., Bigelow, K. M., Greene, B. F., Kessler, M. L. (1998). Child abuse and neglect: Behavioral research, treatment, and theory. *Aggression and Violent Behavior, 3,* 181–196.

Mannarino, A. P., & Cohen, J. A. (1990). Treating the abused child. In R. T. Ammerman, & M. Hersen (Eds.), *Children at risk: An evaluation of factors contributing to child abuse and neglect* (pp. 249–266). New York: Plenum.

National Academy of Sciences. (1993). *Understanding child abuse and neglect.* Washington, DC: National Academy Press.

Nelson, K. E. (1990). Family based services for juvenile offenders. *Children and Youth Services Review, 12,* 193–212.

Nicol, A. R., Smith, J., Kay, B., Hall, D., Barlow, J., & Williams, B. (1988). A focused casework approach to the treatment of child abuse: A controlled comparison. *Journal of Child Psychology and Psychiatry, 29,* 703–711.

Nurius, P. S., Lovell, M., & Edgar, M. (1988). Self-appraisals of abusive parents: A contextual approach to study and treatment. *Journal of Interpersonal Violence, 3,* 458–467.

Oates, R. K., & Bross, D. C. (1995). What have we learned about treating child physical abuse? A literature review of the last decade. *Child Abuse & Neglect, 19,* 463–473.

Oates, R. K., Gray, J., Schweitzer, L., Kempe, R. S., & Harmon, R. J. (1995). A therapeutic preschool for abused children: The KEEPSAFE Project. *Child Abuse & Neglect, 19,* 1379–1386.

Sandler, J., Van Dercar, C., & Milhoan, M. (1978). Training child abusers in the use of positive reinforcement practices. *Behaviour Research and Therapy, 16,* 169–175.

Silovsky, J. F., Valle, L. A., & Chaffin, M. (1999, June). *Group treatment for children affected by family violence.* Presented at the 7th Annual Colloquium of the American Professional Society on the Abuse of Children, San Antonio, TX.

Stevenson, J. (1999). The treatment of the long-term sequelae of child abuse. *Journal of Child Psychology and Psychiatry, 40,* 89–111.

Swenson, C. C. (2000, October). Community-based treatment of child physical abuse: Costs and outcomes. In M. Rowland (Chair), *MST Research: University Affiliated Projects.* Symposium conducted at the First International MST Conference, Savannah, GA.

Swenson, C. C., & Brown, E. J. (1999). Cognitive-behavioral group treatment for physically-abused children. *Cognitive and Behavioral Practice, 6,* 212–220.

Taub, H. B., Kessler, M. L., & Lutzker, J. R. (1995). Teaching neglectful families to identify and address environmental and health-related risks. In M. L. Kessler (Chair), *Treating Physical Abuse and Neglect: Four Approaches.* Symposium conducted at the 3rd Annual APSAC Colloquium, Tucson, AZ.

Tymchuk, A. J. (1998). The importance of matching educational interventions to parent needs in child maltreatment: Issues, methods, and recommendations. In J. R. Lutzker (Ed.), *Handbook of child abuse research and treatment: Issues in clinical child psychology* (pp. 421–448). New York, NY: Plenum.

Urquiza, A. J., & Bodiford-McNeil, C. (1996). Parent-child interaction therapy: An intensive dyadic intervention for physically abusive families. *Child Maltreatment, 1,* 134–144.

Wagar, J. M., & Rodway, M. R. (1995). An evaluation of a group treatment approach for children who have witnessed wife abuse. *Journal of Family Violence, 10,* 295–306.

Walker, C. E., Bonner, B. L., & Kaufman, K. L. (1988). *The physically and sexually abused child: Evaluation and treatment.* New York: Pergamon.

Webster-Stratton, C. (1998). Parent training with low-income families: Promoting parental engagement through a collaborative approach. In J. Lutzker (Ed.), *Handbook of child abuse research and treatment* (pp. 183–212). New York: Plenum.

Weisz, J. R., Donenberg, G. R., Han, S. S., & Kauneckis, D. (1995). Child and adolescent psychotherapy outcomes in experiments and in clinics: Why the disparity? *Journal of Abnormal Child Psychology, 23,* 83–106.

Weisz, J. R., Donenberg, G. R., Han, S. S., & Weiss, B. (1995). Bridging the gap between laboratory and clinic in child and adolescent psychotherapy. *Journal of Consulting and Clinical Psychology, 63,* 688–701.

Weisz, J. R., & Jensen, P. S. (1999). Efficacy and effectiveness of child and adolescent psychotherapy and pharmarcotherapy. *Mental Health Services Research, 1,* 125–157.

Weisz, J. R., Weiss, B., & Donenberg, G. R. (1992). The lab versus the clinic: Effects of child and adolescent psychotherapy. *American Psychologist, 47,* 1578–1585.

Weisz, J. R., Weiss, B., Han, S. S., Granger, D. A., & Morton, T. (1995). Effects of psychotherapy with children and adolescents revisited: A meta-analysis of treatment outcome studies. *Psychological Bulletin, 117,* 450–468.

Wesch, D., & Lutzker, J. R. (1991). A comprehensive 5-year evaluation of Project 12-Ways: An ecobehavioral program for treating and preventing child abuse and neglect. *Journal of Family Violence, 6,* 17–35.

Whiteman, M., Fanshel, D., Grundy, J. F. (1987, November-December). Cognitive-behavioral interventions aimed at anger of parents at risk of child abuse. *Social Work,* 469–474.

Whittaker, J., Kinney, J., Tracy, E. M., & Booth, C. (1990). *Reaching high-risk families: Intensive family preservation in human services.* New York: Aldine.

Wilson, S. K., Cameron, S., Jaffe, P., & Wolfe, D. A. (1986, September). Manual for a group program for children exposed to wife abuse. London, Ontario: Ministry of Community and Social Services.

Wilson, S. K., Cameron, S., Jaffe, P., & Wolfe, D. A. (1989). Children exposed to wife abuse: An intervention model. *Social Casework, 70,* 180–184.

Wolfe, D. A. (1994). The role of intervention and treatment services in the prevention of child abuse and neglect. In G. B. Melton, & F. D. Barry (Eds.), *Protecting children from child abuse and neglect: Foundations for a new national strategy* (pp. 224–303). New York: Guilford.

Wolfe, D. A., Edwards, B., Manion, I., & Koverola, C. (1988). Early intervention for parents at risk of child abuse and neglect: A preliminary investigation. *Journal of Consulting and Clinical Psychology, 56,* 40–47.

Wolfe, D. A., Sandler, J., & Kaufman, K. (1981). A competency based parent-training program for child abusers. *Journal of Consulting and Clinical Psychology, 49,* 633–640.

Wolfe, D. A., & Wekerle, C. (1993). Treatment strategies for child physical abuse and neglect: A critical progress report. *Clinical Psychology Review, 13,* 473–500.

4

Conducting a Comprehensive Clinical Assessment

This chapter provides guidelines and recommended instruments for conducting a comprehensive clinical assessment when child physical abuse (CPA) occurs. Earlier chapters have shown that multiple factors relate to CPA and that children are at risk of developing several types of mental health problems. Problems experienced by physically abused children will differ by child, family, and context. Thus, providing a comprehensive assessment that examines multiple variables related to the individual child, parent, family, and context will assist the clinician in developing a comprehensive treatment plan that addresses all key problems.

❏ Assessment Overview

INTRODUCTION

One of the most important ways to improve the relevance and impact of any treatment is to conduct a comprehensive assessment that documents both strengths and weakness of the client (i.e., the child, parent, or family) in an efficient manner. Doing such allows the practitioner to select the most appropriate services, evaluate the nature and extent of client improvements achieved, and document the targets of treatment. In general, the clinical formulation that derives from such an assessment helps the clinician apply the treatment correctly and facilitates an appreciation for the overall complexity or severity of the case.

In discussing comprehensive assessment, we first present issues in the clinical assessment of maltreated children and their families. Next, we discuss areas to consider during the initial intake, and then we review common, state-of-the-art measures for assessing child victims, maltreating caregivers, and the family. Last, through case presentation, we describe the process and results of an assessment. In considering the standardized measures, the reader should note that each measure described is either copyrighted or published via a study described in the literature. Therefore, we will not include any of the measures in the body of this chapter. Furthermore, manuals and articles are referenced for each measure. These detail how the measure was developed, provide psychometric data (e.g., reliability and validity), and describe how to administer, score, and interpret the measure. Some of the measures even have computerized scoring and interpretation programs. Therefore, we will not cover that information detailed in the manuals in this chapter. One caveat that should be considered is that if the reader is a clinician or researcher with no prior experience or training in administering, scoring, or interpreting standardized measures, supervision by an individual with that experience is necessary.

❏ The Clinical Assessment

CLINICAL VERSUS FORENSIC

The clinical assessment is the first key clinical task conducted with the youth and family, and is necessary to determine who to treat, what problem areas should be targeted by treatment, and the nature and implications of these problems. Many practitioners who work in the child maltreatment field make the distinction between a clinical assessment and a forensic assessment. The purpose of the clinical assessment is to determine symptomatology occurring for a given child, parent, or family and to set goals for treatment. The purpose of a forensic assessment is fact finding to determine whether abuse occurred and, if so, the specifics of the abusive events. The forensic process often includes an interview of the child and family, as well as a complete medical examination. In abuse cases, specially trained physicians collect a history of the incident and determine the location, size, shape, and age of the internal and external injuries (see Johnson, 1996).

The assumption followed in this chapter is that when a child and family are referred for treatment following physical abuse, professionals from the systems that forensically evaluate the allegations or associated family circumstances have already conducted their assessment (see Holder & Corey, 1986). After the initial forensic process is complete and child protective systems have made an initial determination whether to indicate the case, the clinical assessment begins.

Initially, a thorough intake interview brings to light primary concerns of the caregiver, teacher, protective services worker, and other involved systems. Next, the use of standardized measures is of value for two purposes. First, standardized measures provide for a comparison of individuals to those on whom the measure was based, allowing a determination of whether the problem being assessed is occurring at clinical levels. Second, use of standardized measures can occur at multiple points in time to help the clinician determine if the child and family are deriving any benefits from the treatment.

It should be noted that the scales to be discussed should be applied only if the practitioner has a thorough understanding of each scale's content, administration guidelines, and limitations. However, with few exceptions, these assessments do not require substantial training or administration only by a psychologist. Most of these instruments reflect self-report questionnaires or interviews with structured or semi-structured questions and response choices, which make them fairly easy and straightforward to administer. Furthermore, scoring and interpretation procedures (e.g., normative data) are available for many of these instruments, which allows the evaluator efficiently to evaluate the measure's characteristics. Accordingly, these instruments rely very little on specialized interpretation methods.

ASSESSMENT OF MULTIPLE SYSTEMS AND MULTIPLE DOMAINS

Many of the same issues and suggestions for enhancing the quality of research on treatment outcome may be relevant to enhancing an assessment conducted by the practitioner. One important suggestion is to expand the scope of assessment to include an evaluation of client functioning in different domains. Hoagwood, Jensen, Petti, and

Burns (1996) described an interactional model for evaluating the outcomes of mental health treatment that has implications for a comprehensive clinical assessment. The model posits five domains that reflect primary outcomes important for the evaluation of treatments administered in diverse settings. The first reflects the severity of symptoms and diagnoses (e.g., fewer posttraumatic stress disorder [PTSD] symptoms, or less serious depressive or aggressive behavior). The second domain reflects the child's functional status or level of impairment (e.g., role efficacy or enhanced social and problem-solving skill), an area not often evaluated in the abuse field. The next domain is concerned with the child's, parent's, or family's functioning in its environmental context, such as the home, school, or other community settings (e.g., appropriate parenting practices and family support, involvement with deviant peers, or school behavior problems). The client's level of consumer satisfaction describes a fourth domain, in which information is obtained about the adequacy of treatment (e.g., acceptability or usefulness). The final domain solicits information about service use (e.g., participation rates or use of inpatient services).

Although few studies actually evaluate the outcomes in all five domains (Jensen, Hoagwood, & Petti, 1996), one can see how important it would be for the practitioner to understand the nature of the client's problems in terms of the presence of specific symptoms or diagnoses, a patient's degree of impairment, and the extent to which obstacles and supports or resources are found in their immediate environment. Furthermore, contemporary practice places considerable emphasis on understanding the client's satisfaction with and impression of treatment, and the types of additional services being received to address existing problems.

One can certainly appreciate the relevance of each domain to assessing the outcome of treatment in cases of child abuse. For example, many evaluations of the outcome of treatment include children's symptoms, such as PTSD, depression, aggression, and anxiety, and certain domains of parental or family functioning. Attention may be paid less often to evaluating the children's level of impairment, school and peer behavior, satisfaction with treatment, and overall service system involvement. Given the possibility of extended system contact, multiple interventions, and a history of multiple traumas and family adversities, an outcome assessment with both depth and breadth seems warranted. Indeed, many evaluations of cognitive-behavioral treatment (CBT) interventions for CPA have documented these diverse outcomes (Brunk, Henggeler, & Whelan, 1987; Kolko, 2002; Wolfe, Sandler, & Kaufman, 1981).

In general, it is helpful to evaluate multiple domains specifically targeted by intervention (e.g., violence/abuse risk, child and parent dysfunction, cognitive-behavioral repertoire, and family functioning). To facilitate this process, it is helpful to collect assessment measures from different sources, notably children, parents, other family members, teachers, and any other clinical resources or service providers. The use of different methods (i.e., self-reports, parent-child observations, client/therapist ratings, and the state abuse registry) may be helpful in providing a comprehensive representation of the family's circumstances and problems, as described in the consent forms. Conducting an assessment across relevant areas of functioning is an important treatment prerequisite with abusive families (National Academy of Sciences, 1993).

Given the availability of numerous measures both in the abuse field, and in other areas more generally, we have included in this chapter a set of tables that describe some of the more common measures in these two areas. This information provides some background information that may help the practitioner become more familiar with the nature and use of these instruments. What follows is a brief overview of some of the instruments used to evaluate individual and family functioning in several key clinical domains. Among the many existing clinical measures, we have identified several standardized instruments with varying degrees of established psychometric adequacy that may be useful for assessment purposes. The measures evaluate domains related to child, parent, or family functioning, many of which are common referral reasons and/or treatment targets for intervention. Other sources may be helpful in locating additional measures on this topic (see Rittner, Smyth, & Wodarski, 1995). We will not cover risk management assessment instruments, as they fall outside the scope of this book; however, the reader is referred to an excellent sourcebook by Dubowitz and DePanfilis (2000) and to other relevant essays (e.g., Hansen, Sedlar, & Warner-Rogers, 1999) for information on this topic.

ASSESSING THE CHILD

As suggested earlier, a comprehensive assessment will include multiple systems, such as the child, parent, parent/child and family, and community/social systems. As shown in Chapter 2, social and emotional difficulties associated with physical abuse can be complex and can involve multiple domains. As such, an assessment of the child will encompass a variety of problem areas. Box 4.1 provides a summary of some potential measures to be included in the assessment of the child.

Box 4.1	Representative Measures for Clinical Assessment of the Child

Domain	Measure
Abuse history	BATE, ADI, ROME
Behavioral difficulties	CBCL, YSR, CHI, CCI, Kiddie-GAS
Anger expression and management	CIA, PAES, CHI, TSC-C
Social competence	SSRS, CBCL, CBS
Trauma-related emotional symptoms	DICA-R, CAPS-C, TSC-C, CDI, RCMAS, STAIC, CAFAS
Cognition and attributions	CITES-R, CAPS
Academic difficulties	WRAT-III, TRF
Other psychiatric disorders	KIDDIE-SADS, DISC-2

NOTE: See text for full names of all measures.

Case Characteristics/Abuse History

The clinical child assessment should begin with a basic child and family intake, psychosocial history, and thorough review of the abusive events and trauma history. A review of records from child protective services, law enforcement agents, and the physician who conducted the initial assessment will help to clarify what happened. An initial intake interview can assist the therapist in discerning how the physical abuse has affected the child and family. Specific "facts" about the case and the youth's and family's perception of what happened—who is responsible, whether the abuse was minimized—along with the family's level of support for the youth may be important information for assessing that impact. Structured interviews, such as the Brief Assessment of Traumatic Events (BATE; Lipovsky & Hanson, 1992a, 1992b), assess the specifics of the physical abuse and determine if other traumatic events were experienced. The Abuse Dimensions Inventory (ADI) provides interview probes and documentation of abuse incident characteristics and severity for both physical and sexual abuse incidents (Chaffin, Wherry, Newlin, Crutchfield, & Dykman, 1997). The ADI is noteworthy for its reliability and construct validity data. In contrast, the Record of Maltreatment Experiences (ROME; McGee, Wolfe, & Wilson, 1997) requests frequency ratings for a variety of behaviors or potential indicators of diverse forms of maltreatment (e.g., sexual abuse, physical abuse, or emotional exposure to family violence) and other related constructs (e.g., constructive parenting practices). This tool may be helpful in documenting a broad range of relevant experiences and the child's overall level of exposure to or involvement in them.

Behavioral Difficulties

To determine the presence of behavioral difficulties, such as aggression, parent and teacher ratings are typically used. Among the many alternative scales currently available, the Child Behavior Checklist (CBCL) may be the most widely used measure that includes child behavior ratings applicable to children aged 4 to 16 years (Achenbach, 1991). The scale yields two broadband scores measuring internalizing and externalizing behavioral difficulties, and eight or nine factor analyzing narrowband problem scales, depending on gender and age. Children older than 11 years of age may complete the Youth Self-Report (YSR) to assess diverse symptom areas that parallel those found in the CBCL (Achenbach, 1991; Achenbach & Edelbrock, 1983). The CBCL also yields similar externalizing and internalizing behavior problems scales, and a social competence scale. The Children's Hostility Inventory (CHI; Kazdin, Rodgers, Colbus, & Siegel, 1987) includes a brief true/false aggression scale that can be completed by parents or children.

The Child Conflict Index (CCI) provides a complementary measure that can be administered on the phone to document the presence of individual parent-child conflict behaviors exhibited by boys or girls within the past 24 hours (Frankel & Weiner, 1990). There are 10 and 8 items for boys and girls, respectively. The measure may be helpful in identifying salient behaviors that might be most worthy as clinical targets for treatment. To obtain a more broad assessment of functioning, the Global Assessment Scale for Children (Kiddie-GAS) is based on Axis IV of the *Diagnostic and Statistical Manual of Mental Disorders* (DSM-IV), and provides an overall index of child adjustment, ranging from 1 to 100, with a score of 60 representing the cutoff for the clinical range (Shaffer et al., 1983).

Anger Expressiveness/Management

In addition to parent ratings of a child's or adolescent's externalizing behavior problems, a measure of the youth's level of anger arousal or responsivity to various situations may be helpful. Representative measures include the Children's Inventory of Anger (CIA; Finch, Saylor, & Nelson, 1987), Pediatric Anger Expression Scale (PAES; Jacobs, Phelps, & Rohrs, 1989), and the Children's Hostility Inventory (CHI; Kazdin et al., 1987). The CHI includes a hostility factor composed of four subscales (e.g., resentment and irritability) and has both good reliability and validity. The Trauma Symptom Checklist for Children (TSC-C; Briere, 1996; Lanktree, Briere, & Hernandez, 1991) also has an anger problems scale that was developed with abused and control children, and it includes normative scoring procedures.

Social Competence/Interpersonal Problems

Given that physically abused children may have difficulties in social competence, an evaluation of social skills should be conducted. Teacher and parent interview and behavior ratings may be initially helpful in pinpointing social skill difficulties. Measures such as the parent-completed Social Skills Rating Scale (SSRS; Gresham & Elliott, 1990) provide standard comparisons on social skills, problem behaviors, and academic competence. From standardized measures and informal assessment, treatment providers will need to determine whether the child (a) has not learned appropriate social skills; (b) has the skills, but lacks motivation or practice in use; or, (c) has the skills, but is unable to use them because of overriding emotional difficulties or problems with self-control (Hazel, 1990). Other useful measures include the social competence section (e.g., social skill and school activities) of the CBCL (Achenbach, 1991) and the Child Behavior Scale (CBS), which provides teacher ratings of children's behavior with peers (Ladd & Profilet, 1996).

Trauma-Related Emotional Symptoms

Symptoms of an internalizing nature that may relate to abuse include anxiety, depression, and PTSD. The Diagnostic Interview for Children and Adolescents (DICA-R; Earls, Smith, Reich, & Jung, 1988) is an interview tool for diagnosing PTSD, although it has not been empirically validated. The TSC-C (Briere, 1996) is one of the few clinical instruments developed to assess the sequelae of abuse in children and adolescents. It includes several clinical scales (e.g., PTSD, anxiety, depression, dissociation, anger, and sexual concerns) and several validity scales (e.g., underreporting bias). A strength of this instrument is the availability of norms and its easy scoring and interpretation. The Clinician Administered PTSD Scale for Children (CAPS-C) is an interview designed to evaluate the presence of a PTSD diagnosis (Nader, Blake, Kriegler, & Pynoos, 1994). The instrument includes a useful interview guide and clear criteria for making the diagnosis. To measure general anxiety, the Revised Children's Manifest Anxiety Scale (RCMAS; Reynolds & Paget, 1983) and the State/Trait Anxiety Scale for Children (STAIC; Spielberger, 1973) are common scales. The Children's Depression Inventory (CDI) is a widely used 27-item measure that assesses affective, cognitive, and behavioral symptoms of depression in children ages 7 to 17 (Kovacs, 1981). Therapists should pay particular attention to the items assessing suicidal ideation and intent. The Child and Adolescent Functional Assessment Scale (CAFAS; Hodges, 1996) measures degree of impairment in a child's functioning across a range of domains and how the child's problems affect the child, his or her family, and other people who interact with the child. The CAFAS has been found to predict youth service utilization (see Hodges & Wong, 1997).

Cognitions and Attributions

Recently, measures have been developed that address children's attributions about their abusive or traumatic experiences. Attributions and cognitions about a given incident of physical abuse—such as beliefs about why adults physically abuse children, whether children cause adult aggression, and more specifically, whether children feel responsible for their parent's aggressive behavior—may bear implications for clinical work.

Measures developed to evaluate reactions to sexual abuse or similar traumatic experiences include the Children's Impact of Traumatic Events Scale–Revised (CITES-R; Wolfe, Gentile, Michienzi, Sas, & Wolfe, 1991), and items specifically designed to measure perceptions of self-blame and stigma (Feiring, Taska, & Lewis, 1998). The CITES-R provides an examination of the severity of various attributions associated with the incident. Certain factors in the CITES-R (e.g., self-blame, dangerous world) have been found to relate to the severity of psychopathology in physically abused children (Brown & Kolko, 1999). The Children's Attributions and Perceptions Scale (CAPS; Mannarino, Cohen, & Berman, 1994) was developed to assess attributions and perceptions relevant to child sexual abuse. This 18-item scale contains four subscales: feeling different from peers, personal attributions for negative events, perceived credibility, and interpersonal trust. The CAPS questions are general (i.e., no questions specifically inquire about beliefs about sexual abuse) and can be used with normative groups as well as with children who have experienced other types of abuse. In the initial study, the sexually abused children scored higher on the CAPS than did a control group (Mannarino et al., 1994).

Academic Difficulties

Some abused children experience school difficulties that are not related to the emotional effects of the abuse but rather are a function of learning difficulties. A formal evaluation of those specific difficulties may be necessary to attain needed remedial services. In some states, school districts require assessments to be completed by a certified school psychologist. Therapists should familiarize themselves with the guidelines of their particular school district to expedite receipt of services for their clients. To assist with the process, some initial academic screening on brief measures such as the Wide Range Achievement Test–III (WRAT-III; Wilkinson, 1993) may be helpful for determining academic weaknesses and skills in need of development. Ratings of children's school behavior, emotional problems, and academic performance can be obtained using the parallel teacher version of the CBCL, the Teacher Report Form (TRF; see Achenbach, 1991). The TRF includes scales that reflect internalizing and externalizing behavior, as well as an adaptive behavior scale. The existence of extensive normative comparison data and clinical cutoffs is a strength of this instrument.

Other Psychiatric Disorders

Physically abused children may exhibit psychiatric disorders that may or may not be related to the abuse. Semi-structured and structured interviews, such as the KIDDIE-SADS (Schedule for Affective Disorders and Schizophrenia; Chambers et al., 1985; Kaufman, Birmaher, Brent, Rao, & Ryan, 1996) and Diagnostic Interview Schedule for Children, Version 2.3 (DISC; Shaffer et al., 1996) are among those that provide a comprehensive assessment of various child and adolescent diagnoses. For example, children who suffer from attention deficit/hyperactivity disorder (ADHD) may benefit from a medical evaluation. Children with long-term behavior problems may need an assessment for oppositional behavior or conduct disorder. Some abused children will experience major depression or an anxiety disorder, which may require additional evaluation and ongoing monitoring. Certainly, a thorough intake coupled with parent and teacher behavioral ratings can assist with identifying symptoms that merit further evaluation. The key to developing appropriate treatment strategies is to identify the behaviors of concern that may be reflected in a child's varied diagnostic profile.

ASSESSING THE MALTREATING PARENT/CAREGIVER

Box 4.2 provides some background information related to parent assessment measures among the many self-report, interview, and observational instruments that have been reported. Many of these measures have been developed for use with other patient populations and, thus, may not have been used extensively with abusive adults.

Box 4.2	Representative Measures for Clinical Assessment of the Maltreating Adult

Domain	Measure
Abuse/trauma history	CANIS-R, MCS, ADI,
Violent behavior and abuse risk	CTSPC, CAPI
Parental dysfunction/adjustment	PSI, BSI
Substance abuse history	DAST, ASI
Depression/anxiety	BDI
Parental attributions/distortions	POQ, PAT
Parenting skill/practices	APQ, PS, PPI, DPICS, MCIS, FIGCS

NOTE: See text for full names of all measures.

Abuse/Trauma History

Parental childhood abuse history may be evaluated using the Child Abuse and Neglect Interview Schedule (CANIS-R; Ammerman, Hersen, Van Hasselt, Lubetsky, & Sieck, 1994). The CANIS-R includes items relating to diverse forms of maltreatment. In contrast to the availability of numerous assessment measures in other domains, there are few well-validated, standardized instruments to assess the child's abuse experiences from the adult caregiver's perspective. Although no single standard exists to evaluate other clinical problems faced by children, a few instruments designed to clarify a child's abuse history and current status have been evaluated psychometrically and are included in some outcome studies. The instruments reflect both case record procedures and interview measures. Examples of these two types of instruments include the Maltreatment Classification System (MCS; Barnett, Manly, & Cicchetti, 1993) and the ADI noted earlier (Chaffin et al., 1997). As these and other related tools are used to describe children's abuse histories, it may be possible to further refine our probes and coding rules for documenting important parameters of children's experiences with abuse. Certainly, multiple informants may be helpful in depicting the nature of the child's maltreatment experiences (Kaufman, Jones, Stieglitz, Vitulano, & Mannarino, 1994).

Violent Behavior and Abuse Risk

Parents may complete the Child Abuse Potential Inventory (CAPI; Milner, 1986, 1994) to evaluate their overall risk for physical abuse. The items aggregate to form an abuse scale that can be interpreted using the recommended abuse-risk cut-off score of 215 to identify cases falling in the high-risk category. The CAPI also includes three validity scales (e.g., lie) as well. The Conflict Tactics Scales (CTS; Straus, 1990a, 1990b) and the revised Parent-Child Conflict Tactics Scales (CTSPC; Straus, Hamby, Finkelhor, Moore, & Runyan, 1998) provide a structured report of parental involvement in various violent behaviors directed to a specific child. Child reports on the CTS have been obtained as well (Kolko, Kazdin, & Day, 1996). Informants indicate the general frequency with which certain violent behaviors (e.g., slapping on the arm, hand, or leg, or threatening with a knife or gun) were used within the past year. The CTSPC contains several factors (e.g., nonviolent discipline and physical assault) and a few additional items related to neglect and sexual abuse.

Another brief measure, the Weekly Report of Abuse Indicators (WRAI) evaluates high-risk parental behaviors within a short time frame, and may be helpful in documenting ongoing clinical course (Kolko, 1996a). The three primary items reflect the severity of parental anger (on a 1–5 point scale), the severity of family problems (on a 1–3 point scale), and parental use of threats or physical force/discipline (No/Yes) during the preceding two weeks. A fourth item reflects parental thoughts about using physical force. Of course, parents can also be asked to identify individual treatment goals prior to intervention (Brunk et al., 1987; Wolfe et al., 1991) that can be rated on Likert scales (e.g., use of abusive punishment and inability to use appropriate discipline; see Kolko, 2002).

Parental Dysfunction/Adjustment

The Parenting Stress Index (PSI; Abidin, 1997) contains 47 child stress, 54 parent stress, and 19 life stress items designed to assess stress in the parent-child system resulting from child behaviors (the Child Domain) or parent-related factors (the Maternal Domain). The PSI has been shown to discriminate between affected and unaffected parent-child dyads in the areas of developmental issues, physical handicaps, risk for parenting problems, and physical abuse (Abidin, 1997).

The 53-item Brief Symptom Inventory (BSI), a shortened version of the Symptom Checklist-90 (SCL-90), can be used to evaluate overall parental dysfunction or psychological distress (Derogatis & Melisaratos, 1983). The measure yields a mean item severity rating reflecting the degree of discomfort caused by various symptoms (e.g., depression, anxiety, or anger-hostility) rated on a 0–2 point scale covering the previous week. Turning to the assessment of more specific constructs, the 21-item Beck Depression Inventory (BDI; Beck, Ward, Mendelson, Mock, & Erbaugh, 1961) evaluates severity of depressive symptoms.

For parents suspected of having substance use problems, the Drug Abuse Screening Test (DAST; Gavin, Ross, & Skinner, 1989) can be used to reflect overall parental involvement in substance abuse. The Addiction Severity Index (ASI; McLellan, Luborsky, O'Brien, & Woody, 1980) is a widely used semi-structured 40-item interview designed to assess problem severity in seven areas commonly affected adversely by substance abuse: (1) medical condition, (2) drug use, (3) alcohol use, (4) employment, (5) illegal activity, (6) social relations, and (7) psychiatric condition. Two types of results are obtained from each problem area: severity ratings (ranging from 0 to 9) and composite scores. The severity ratings and composite scores are significantly related, obtaining average correlations of 0.88 (McLellan et al., 1985). Finally, parents can be rated on the Global Assessment of Functioning scale (found in DSM-IV) to capture some index of overall impairment (see Kolko, 1996b).

Parental Attributions/Distortions

Measures related to abusive behavior are also found in certain scales. The 80-item Parent Opinion Questionnaire (POQ) examines the appropriateness of expectations for child behaviors in six domains (e.g., family responsibility and punishment) that differentiate between maltreating and control parents (Azar, Robinson, Hekimian, & Twentyman, 1984). A parent's unrealistic expectations and distortions in beliefs may be an indicator of change following intervention. The Parent Attribution Test (PAT) may evaluate parental expectations regarding responsibility for failure and success, which have been helpful in distinguishing abusive from control parents (Bugental, Mantyla, & Lewis, 1989). Responses to items reflecting different sources of responsibility (causality) have been used to develop composite scores reflecting a low level of attribution to adult control over failure and a high level of attribution to child control over failure, which are patterns associated with abusive behavior.

Parental Skill/Practices

Several subscales that evaluate such parenting practices as use of positive discipline or follow-through with consequences may be important to evaluate. The Alabama Parenting Questionnaire (APQ; Shelton, Frick, & Wooten, 1996) includes various factors based on responses to individual questions rated along 5-point Likert scales (e.g., monitoring and discipline). Another instrument, the Parenting Scale (PS), evaluates content (e.g., overactivity and verbosity) designed to reflect the use of ineffective parental discipline and other inappropriate or angry responses that may be common among abusive parents (Arnold, O'Leary, Wolfe, & Acker, 1993). Children can complete the Parent Perception Inventory (PPI; Hazzard, Christensen, & Margolin, 1983) to evaluate parental involvement in management and interactional behaviors on positive, severe negative, and net positive (total) subscales.

Behavioral observations provide a supplementary format for examining parental behavior and competence in the context of structured interactions involving one or more children. Systems for orchestrating and then coding such interactions have been used primarily with nonabusive parents, but they evaluate relevant types of parental behaviors and child responses, such as the Dyadic Parent Child Interaction Coding System (DPICS; Eyberg & Robinson, 1983), both the Maternal Observation Matrix and Mother-Child Interaction Scale (MCIS; Tuteur, Ewigman, Peterson, & Hosokawa, 1995), and the Family Interaction Global Coding System (FIGCS; Heatherington, Hagan, & Eisenberg, 1990). These systems provide fairly objective and precise levels of specific behaviors and can be used to help characterize the parent-child interaction on various dimensions of relevance to family interactions (e.g., warmth, support, or use of harsh statements). The FIGCS examines a range of constructs, several general subscales (e.g., anger/rejection, coercion, and authority/control), and both parenting (e.g., authoritative parenting) and child behavior (e.g., prosocial behavior) scales. More information on these measures can be found in Hansen et al. (1999).

ASSESSING THE FAMILY

Box 4.3 shows some of the domains that are important to evaluate when conducting a structured family assessment. The instruments to be covered in this section relate primarily to the evaluation of family environment and functioning, with some attention paid to family structure. Because of the importance of family service involvement, measures relating to treatment history are included in this section.

Family Environment/Functioning

Children and parents can be asked to complete the Family Environment Scale (FES), which includes several scales reflecting on the structure (e.g., rules and control) and relationships (e.g., cohesion or conflict) found in the family (Moos, Insel, & Humphrey, 1974). Each informant may also contribute to evaluations of the family's other processes and general functioning. The Family Assessment Device

Box 4.3 Representative Measures for Clinical
Assessment of the Family

Domain	Measure
Family environment, functioning,	
support, cohesion, warmth	FES, FACES, SOCSS
communication, problem-solving	FAD
Family structure hierarchy,	
dominance, control	FES, FACES
boundaries/rules	FES, FAD,
Family treatment history	TIE, CASA, LUSI, SNACR

NOTE: See text for full names of all measures.

(FAD, Version 3) includes several factors (e.g., problem solving, communication, and affective involvement), as well as a general functioning subscale (Epstein, Baldwin, & Bishop, 1983). The Family Adaptability and Cohesion Scales–III (FACES III; Olson, Portner, & Lavee, 1985), a 20-item self-report instrument, was designed to measure both perceived and ideal family functioning. The items tap two dimensions of family functioning: cohesion and adaptability. Generally, the FACES-III is a reliable and valid scale that is theoretically and empirically sound (Olson, 1986). The Conflict Behavior Questionnaire can be used to evaluate overall level of parent-adolescent hostility and discord (Robin & Foster, 1989). Children may provide an estimate of family, teacher, and peer social support on the Survey of Children's Social Support Scale (SOCSS; Dubow, & Ullman, 1989). Finally, the Children's Life Events Inventory (CLEI; Chandler, Million, & Shermis, 1985) may help to assess level of family stress.

Family Structure

There are few brief self-report instruments for evaluating family structure/hierarchy. Among those with psychometric support, the FAD includes factors related to family structure (i.e., roles and behavior control) that relate to the establishment of patterns or standards of behavior within the family. Other types of family system-maintenance variables include the organization and control subscales in the FES (Moos et al., 1974). The FACES-III also includes subscales to evaluate structural dimensions that are included in its general family adaptability (e.g., leadership and control, roles, and rules) and cohesion factors (e.g., family boundaries and decision making).

Family Treatment History and Service Involvement

There are few measures reflecting treatment involvement that have been used with abused children and their families. Drawing upon other service utilization items (e.g., the National Comorbidity Study; Kessler, 1994), the Treatment History Assessment Items (THAI) was developed to assess the past treatment history of the abused child and adults in the child's home (see Kolko, Selelyo, & Brown, 1999). Four general treatment modalities were surveyed: hospitalization; mental health services; medication for emotional, behavioral, or substance use problems; and medication for medical/health problems. Two questions examined whether the child or adult(s) continued in the service until its scheduled completion (i.e., goals were achieved and termination was mutually determined) and how helpful the services were (0 = *not at all*, 1 = *somewhat*, 2 = *a lot*).

The Child and Adolescent Services Assessment, or CASA, (Burns, Angold, Magruder-Habib, Costello, & Patrick, 1994) provides a structured interview designed to document recent involvement in an array of services and treatment settings, and includes other impressions of the scope, impact, and obstacles of these services. A related instrument, the Local Use of Services Instrument (LUSI; Kolko et al., 1999), was used with children and parents to document which of 32 specific services had been received by the family. The services can be classified into one of six primary categories (e.g., crisis intervention, family, caregiver/adult, child, placement, and evaluation). Both of these instruments may be helpful in examining the specific service delivery experiences of children and their parents.

Practitioners may want some initial understanding of children's and their parent's motivation for treatment. The Service Needs and Concerns Report (SNACR; Kolko et al., 1999) evaluates level of perceived service needs, motivation and interests, goals or expectations, and obstacles associated with treatment. For example, the items devoted to family problems evaluate the perceived severity of child, parent, and family problems on 3-point scales, whereas the service motivation and interests score reflects the respondent's and perceived family's willingness to participate in treatment. Interest in several treatment goals is also examined.

ASSESSING COMMUNITY/SOCIAL SYSTEMS

As noted in Chapter 2, families involved in physical abuse are often interpersonally isolated and view themselves as having little support from others. Measuring changes in perceived social support will assist the therapist in determining whether the family is changing in their perceived connections with others. The Interpersonal Support Evaluation List (ISEL; Cohen, Mermelstein, Kamarck, & Hoberman, 1985) is a brief 40-item, true-false questionnaire designed to measure perceived social support. In addition to providing an overall index of perceived support, the scale includes four subscales: (1) tangible support (perceived availability of material aid); (2) appraisal support (perceived availability of someone to talk to about one's problems); (3) self-esteem support (perceived availability of a positive comparison when comparing self to others); and (4) belonging (perceived availability of people with whom to do things).

ASSESSMENT SUMMARY

In this chapter we have presented methods for a comprehensive assessment of the multiple systems (i.e., child, parent, family, and social systems) that may be treated when CPA occurs. We have described measures that may be used to assess multiple domains within each system. Because the problems that correlate with child abuse and the potential mental health outcomes of abuse will vary across victims and families, a multifaceted assessment is needed to help the practitioner determine what the problems are and where treatment progress has occurred.

❏ Case Presentation: The Comprehensive Clinical Assessment

REFERRAL

Roman Murphy is a 12-year-old male referred along with his family for treatment due to physical abuse. An interview with the Child Protective Services caseworker revealed that the family had been investigated a total of three times for abuse. In each instance, Roman and his mother started an argument that escalated into a whipping with a belt. In the most recent incident, Roman had tried to run from his mother, and the belt buckle struck him on the face, leaving an abrasion on his right cheek. Other belt marks were apparent on his arms and legs. Ms. Murphy is a single parent, and Roman has two siblings who have not been the subject of physical abuse. Roman has a large extended family of 2 grandmothers, 1 grandfather, 4 aunts, 3 uncles, and 15 cousins. A comprehensive clinical assessment was conducted to determine the strengths of the family and areas that should be targeted for intervention.

CHILD DIFFICULTIES

Initially, the BATE was administered and an intake interview was conducted with Roman and his mother. On the BATE, Roman indicated he had not experienced any other form of abuse. He had experienced several losses due to the death of his grandfather and the imprisonment of his father. From the intake, the clinician determined that Roman's chief difficulties were in the areas of anger management, aggression, and depression because of the losses in his life. The anger management difficulties occurred in the home and at school. Although he was doing well academically, the periodic problems managing anger placed Roman at risk of being suspended from school. Standardized measures were used to assess targeted behaviors of concern from the intake. The CBCL parent and teacher forms revealed clinical elevations in the overall externalizing scale. Furthermore, on the TSC-C, Roman indicated anger specific to the abuse. On the CHI, Roman scored within clinical levels on resentment and irritability. The CDI revealed moderate depression with occasional suicidal thoughts. In addition to academic strengths, Roman had drawing skills and often helped with chores around the house.

PARENT DIFFICULTIES

Information gained from the intake and standardized measures indicated that Ms. Murphy was dealing with PTSD from her own childhood history of sexual and physical abuse by her stepfather. The anxiety scale of the BSI was elevated. The interview indicated that conflict with Roman was a trigger for re-experiencing memories of assaults by the stepfather. Ms. Murphy held a great deal of anger toward her mother for not protecting her from the abuse by the stepfather. The APQ indicated that, although Ms. Murphy had a strong capacity to monitor her children, she was low on discipline skills (e.g., providing nonphysical consequences and praise). Despite these problems, Ms. Murphy had several strengths. She was employed, did not use drugs or alcohol, was committed to keeping her family together, and wanted to parent more positively.

FAMILY DIFFICULTIES

The family assessment characterized the family as engaging in high conflict and low warmth. However, there were many strengths that could be bolstered by treatment. Ms. Murphy's many siblings were supportive of her and willing to help with Roman. At this point, she had isolated her immediate family to prevent extended family from finding out about the problems. Everyone in the family had a strong desire for the conflict to end and for the family to become closer.

COMMUNITY/SOCIAL SUPPORT SYSTEMS

Although Ms. Murphy had kept her problems from her family, she perceived herself as having social supports and belonging. On the ISEL, she indicated low appraisal support—the perceived ability of having someone to talk to about problems. The family lived in a small community. Although drug dealing occurred on the streets of the neighborhood, the community center was a safe haven for the youths of the area and host to many prosocial activities.

❏ Summary

The comprehensive clinical assessment included the use of interviewing and standardized measures to assess child, parent, family, and community/social support systems. From each these of areas, targeted behaviors were evident. Also, strengths were noted. In the next chapter, we will show how the assessment is used to develop a comprehensive treatment plan.

References

Abidin, R. (1997). Parenting Stress Index: A measure of the parent-child system. In C. P. Zalaquett & R. J. Wood (Eds.), *Evaluating stress: A book of resources* (pp. 277–291). Lanham, MD: Scarecrow Press.

Achenbach, T. M. (1991). *Manual of the Child Behavior Checklist and 1991 profile*. Burlington, VT: University of Vermont, Department of Psychiatry.

Achenbach, T. M., & Edelbrock, C. S. (1983). Manual for the Child Behavior Checklist and Revised Child Behavior Profile. Burlington, VT: University of Vermont, Department of Psychiatry.

Ammerman, R. T., Hersen, M., Van Hasselt, V. B., Lubetsky, M. J., & Sieck, W. R. (1994). Maltreatment in psychiatrically hospitalized children and adolescents with developmental disabilities: Prevalence and correlates. *Journal of the American Academy of Child and Adolescent Psychiatry, 33*, 567–576.

Arnold, D. S., O'Leary, S. G., Wolff, L. S., & Acker, M. M. (1993). The parenting scale: A measure of dysfunctional parenting in discipline situations. *Psychological Assessment, 5*, 137–144.

Azar, S. T., Robinson, D. R., Hekimian, E., & Twentyman, C. T. (1984). Unrealistic expectations and problem-solving ability in maltreating and comparison mothers. *Journal of Consulting and Clinical Psychology, 52*, 687–691.

Barnett, D., Manly, J. T., & Cicchetti, D. (1993). Defining child maltreatment: The inter-face between policy and research. In D. Cicchetti & S. L. Toth (Eds.), *Child abuse, child development, and social policy* (pp. 7–73). Norwood, NJ: Ablex.

Beck, A. T., Ward, C. H., Mendelson, M., Mock, J., & Erbaugh, J. (1961). An inventory for measuring depression. *Archives of General Psychiatry, 4*, 561–571.

Briere, J. (1996). *Trauma Symptom Checklist for children: Professional manual.* Odessa, FL: Psychological Assessment Resources.

Brown, E. J., & Kolko, D. J. (1999). Child victims' attributions about being physically abused: An examination of factors associated with symptom severity. *Journal of Abnormal Child Psychology, 27*, 311–322.

Brunk, M., Henggeler, S. W., & Whelan, J. P. (1987). Comparison of multisystemic ther-apy and parent training in the brief treatment of child abuse and neglect. *Journal of Consulting and Clinical Psychology, 55*, 171–178.

Bugental, D. B., Mantyla, S. M., & Lewis, J. (1989). Parental attributions as moderates of affective communication to children at risk for physical abuse. In D. Cicchetti & V. Carlson (Eds.), *Child maltreatment: Theory and research on the causes and consequences of child abuse and neglect* (pp. 254–279). New York. Cambridge University Press.

Burns, B. J., Angold, A., Magruder-Habib, K., Costello, E. J., & Patrick, M. K. S. (1994, July). *Child and adolescent services assessment (CASA): Information package.* Durham, NC: Duke University Medical Center.

Chaffin, M., Wherry, J. N., Newlin, C., Crutchfield, A., & Dykman, R. (1997). The Abuse Dimensions Inventory: Initial data on a research measure of abuse severity. *Journal of Interpersonal Violence, 12*, 569–589.

Chambers, W. J., Puig-Antich, J., Hirsch, M., Paez, P., Ambrosini, P. J., Tabrizi, M. A., & Davies, M. (1985). The assessment of affective disorders in children and adoles-cents by semistructured interview. *Archives of General Psychiatry, 42*, 696–702.

Chandler, L. A., Million, M. E., & Shermis, M. D. (1985). The incidence of stressful life events of elementary school-aged children. *American Journal of Community Psychology, 13*, 743–746.

Cohen, S., & Hoberman, H. M. (1983). Positive events and social supports as buffers of life change stress. *Journal of Applied Social Psychology, 13*, 99–125.

Derogatis, L., & Melisaratos, N. (1983). The brief symptom inventory: An introductory report. *Psychological Medicine, 13*, 595–605.

Dubow, E. F., & Ullman, D. G. (1989). Assessing social support in elementary school chil-dren: The survey of children's social support. *Journal of Clinical Child Psychology, 18*, 52–64.

Dubowitz, H., & DePanfilis, D. (Eds.). (2000). *Child protection practice.* Thousand Oaks, CA: Sage.

Earls, F., Smith, E., Reich, W., & Jung, K. G. (1988). Investigating psychopathological consequences of a disaster in children: A pilot study incorporating a structured diagnostic interview. *Journal of American Academy of Child and Adolescent Psychiatry, 27*, 90–95.

Epstein, N. B., Baldwin, L. M., & Bishop, D. S. (1983). The McMaster Family Assessment Device. *Journal of Martial and Family Therapy, 9*, 171–180.

Eyberg, S. M., & Robinson, E. A. (1983). Dyadic Parent-Child Interaction Coding System (DPICS): A manual. *Psychological Documents, 13*, 24.

Feiring, C., Taska, L., & Lewis, M. (1998). The role of shame and attributional style in chil-dren's and adolescents' adaptation to sexual abuse. *Child Maltreatment, 3*, 129–142.

Finch, A. J., Saylor, C. F., & Nelson, W. M. (1987). Assessment of anger in children. In R. J. Prinz (Ed.), *Advances in behavioral assessment of children and families* (pp. 235–265). Greenwich, CT: JAI.

Frankel, F., & Weiner, H. (1990). The Child Conflict Index: Factor analysis, reliability, and validity for clinic-referred and nonreferred children. *Journal of Clinical Child Psychology, 19*, 239–248.

Gavin, D. R., Ross, H. E., & Skinner, H. A. (1989). Diagnostic validity of the drug abuse screening test in the assessment of DSM-III drug disorders. *British Journal of Addiction, 84*, 301–307.

Gresham, F. M., & Elliott, S. N. (1990). *Social Skills Rating System manual*. Circle Pines, MN: American Guidance Service.

Hansen, D. J., Sedlar, G., & Warner-Rogers, J. E. (1999). Child physical abuse. In R. T. Ammerman & M. Hersen (Eds.), *Assessment of family violence: A clinical and legal sourcebook* (pp. 127–156). New York: John Wiley.

Hazel, J. S. (1990). Social skills training with adolescents. In E. L. Feindler & G. R. Kalfus (Eds.), *Adolescent behavior therapy handbook* (pp. 191–209). New York: Springer.

Hazzard, A., Christensen, A., & Margolin, G. (1983). Children's perceptions of parental behaviors. *Journal of Abnormal Child Psychology, 11*, 49–59.

Heatherington, E. M., Hagan, M. S., & Eisenberg, N. (1990). *Coping with marital transitions* (Monographs of the Society for Research in Child Development). Chicago: University of Chicago Press.

Hoagwood, K., Jensen, P. S., Petti, T., & Burns, B. J. (1996). Outcomes of mental health care for children and adolescents: A comprehensive conceptual model. *Journal of the American Academy of Child and Adolescent Psychiatry, 35*, 1055–1063.

Hodges, K. (1996, February). *Utilization of the Child and Adolescent Functional Assessment Scale (CAFAS) for assessing program and clinical outcomes*. Paper presented at the annual System of Care Research Conference, Tampa, FL.

Hodges, K., & Wong, M. M. (1997). Use of the Child and Adolescent Functional Assessment Scale to predict service utilization and cost. *Journal of Mental Health Administration, 24*, 278–290.

Holder, W., & Corey, M. K. (1986). *Child protective services risk management: A decision-making handbook*. Charlotte, NC: Action for Child Protection.

Jacobs, G. A., Phelps, M., & Rohrs, B. (1989). Assessment of anger expression in children: The Pediatric Anger Expression Scale. *Personality and Individual Differences, 10*, 59–65.

Jensen, P. S., Hoagwood, K., & Petti, T. (1996). Outcomes of mental health care for children and adolescents, II: Literature review and application of a comprehensive model. *Journal of the American Academy of Child and Adolescent Psychiatry, 35*, 1064–1077.

Johnson, C. F. (1996). Physical abuse: Accidental versus intentional trauma in children. In J. Briere, L. Berliner, J. A. Bulkley, C. Jenny, & T. Reid (Eds.), *The APSAC handbook on child maltreatment* (pp. 206–226). Thousand Oaks, CA: Sage.

Kaufman, J., Birmaher, B., Brent, D., Rao, U., & Ryan, N. (1996). *KIDDIE-SADS-present and lifetime version (K-SADS-PL)*. Instrument developed at Western Psychiatric Institute and Clinic, Pittsburgh, PA.

Kaufman, J., Jones, B., Stieglitz, E., Vitulano, L., & Mannarino, A. P. (1994). The use of multiple informants to assess children's maltreatment experiences. *Journal of Family Violence, 9*, 227–248.

Kazdin, A. E., Rodgers, A., Colbus, D., & Siegel, T. (1987). Children's Hostility Inventory: Measurement of aggression and hostility in psychiatric inpatient children. *Journal of Clinical Child Psychology, 16*, 320–328.

Kessler, R. C. (1994). Building on the ECA: The National Comorbidity Survey and the Children's ECA. *International Journal of Methods in Psychiatric Research, 4*, 81–91.

Kolko, D. J. (1996a). Clinical monitoring of treatment course in child physical abuse: Child and parent reports. *Child Abuse & Neglect, 20*, 23–43.

Kolko, D. J. (1996b). Individual cognitive behavioral treatment and family therapy for physically abused children and their offending parents: A comparison of clinical outcomes. *Child Maltreatment, 1,* 322–342.

Kolko, D. J. (2002). Child physical abuse. In: J. E. B. Myers, L. Berliner, J. Briere, C. T. Hendrix, C. Jenny, & T. Reid (Eds.), *The APSAC handbook of child maltreatment* (2nd ed., pp. 21–54). Thousand Oaks, CA: Sage Publications.

Kolko, D. J., Kazdin, A. E., & Day, B. T. (1996). Children's perspectives in the assessment of family violence: Psychometric characteristics and comparison to parent reports. *Child Maltreatment, 1,* 156–167.

Kolko, D. J., Selelyo, J., & Brown, E. J. (1999). The treatment histories and service involvement of physically and sexually abusive families: Description, correspondence, and clinical correlates. *Child Abuse & Neglect, 23,* 459–476.

Kovacs, M. (1981). Rating scales to assess depression in school-age children. *Acta Paedopsychiatrica, 46,* 305–315.

Ladd, G. W. & Profilet, S. M. (1996). The Child Behavior Scale: A teacher-report measure of young children's aggressive, withdrawn, and prosocial behavior. *Developmental Psychology, 32,* 1008–1024.

Lanktree, C. B., Briere, J., & Hernandez, P. (1991, August). *Further data on the Trauma Symptom Checklist for Children (TSC-C): Reliability, validity and sensitivity to treatment.* Paper presented at the annual meeting of the American Psychological Association, San Francisco, CA.

Lipovsky, J. A., & Hanson, R. F. (1992a, October). *Multiple traumas in the histories of child/adolescent psychiatric inpatients.* Paper presented at the annual meeting of the International Society for Traumatic Stress Studies, Los Angeles, CA.

Lipovsky, J. A., & Hanson, R. F. (1992b, November). *Traumatic event histories of child/adolescent psychiatric inpatients: What is being done to our children?* Paper presented at the annual meeting of the Association for the Advancement of Behavior Therapy, Boston, MA.

Mannarino, A. P., Cohen, J. A., & Berman, S. R. (1994). The Children's Attributions and Perceptions Scale: A new measure of sexual abuse-related factors. *Journal of Clinical Child Psychology, 23,* 204–211.

McGee, R. A., Wolfe, D. A., & Wilson, S. K. (1997). Multiple maltreatment experiences and adolescent behavior problems: Adolescents' perspectives. *Developmental & Psychopathology, 9,* 131–149.

McLellan, A. T., Luborsky, L., Cacciola, J., Griffith, J., Evans, F., Barr, H. L., & O'Brien, C. P. (1985). New data from the addiction severity index: Reliability and validity in three centers. *Journal of Nervous and Mental Disease, 173,* 412–423.

McLellan, A. T., Luborsky, L., O'Brien, C. P., & Woody, G. E. (1980). An improved evaluation instrument for substance abuse patients: The Addiction Severity Index. *Journal of Nervous and Mental Disease, 168,* 26–33.

Milner, J.S. (1986). *The Child Abuse Potential Inventory: Manual* (2nd ed.). Webster, NC: Psyctec.

Milner, J. S. (1994). Assessing physical child abuse risk: The Child Abuse Potential Inventory. *Clinical Psychology Review, 14,* 547–583.

Moos, R. H., Insel, P. M., & Humphrey, B. (1974). *Family work and group environment scales.* Palo Alto, CA: Consulting Psychologists Press.

Nader, K. O., Blake, D. D., Kriegler, J., & Pynoos, R. (1994). *Clinical-Administered PTSD Scale for Children (CAPS–C).* White River Junction, VT: National Center for PTSD.

National Academy of Sciences. (1993). *Understanding child abuse and neglect.* Washington, DC: National Academy Press.

Olson, D. (1986). Circumplex Model VII: Validation studies and FACES III. *Family Process, 25,* 337–351.

Olson, D., Portner, J., & Lavee, Y. (1985). *FACES-III.* St. Paul, MN: University of Minnesota, Department of Family Social Service.

Reid, J. B., Kavanagh, K., & Baldwin, D. V. (1987). Abusive parents' perceptions of child problem behaviors: An example of parental bias. *Journal of Abnormal Child Psychology, 15,* 457–466.

Reynolds, C. R., & Paget, K., (1983). National normative and reliability data for the Revised Children's Manifest Anxiety Scale. *School Psychology Review, 12,* 324–326, 334.

Rittner, B., Smyth, N. J., & Wodarski, J. S. (1995). Assessment and crisis strategies intervention with suicidal adolescents. *Crisis Intervention and Time-Limited Treatment, 2,* 71–84.

Robin, A. L., & Foster, S. L. (1989). *Negotiating parent/adolescent conflict: A behavioral-family systems approach.* New York: Guilford.

Shelton, K. K., Frick, P. J., & Wooten, J. (1996). Assessment of parenting practices in families of elementary school-age children. *Journal of Clinical Child Psychology, 25,* 317–329.

Shaffer, D., Gould, M. S., Brasic, J., Ambrosini, P., Fisher, P., Bird, H., & Aluwahlia, S. (1983). A Children's Global Assessment Scale (CGAS). *Archives of General Psychiatry, 40,* 1228–1231.

Shaffer, D., Fisher, P., Dulcan, M. K., Davies, M., Piacentini, J., Schwab-Stone, M. E., Lahey, B. B., Bourdon, K., Jensen, P. S., Bird, H. R., Canino, G., & Regier, D. A. (1996). The NIMH Diagnostic Interview Schedule for Children, version 2.3 (DISC-2.3): Description, acceptability, prevalence rates, and performance in the MECA Study. *Journal of the American Academy of Child and Adolescent Psychiatry, 35,* 865–877.

Spielberger, C. C. (1973). *Preliminary manual for the State-Trait Anxiety Inventory for Children ("How I Feel Questionnaire").* Palo Alto, CA: Consulting Psychologists Press.

Straus, M. A. (1990a). The Conflict Tactics Scales and its critics: Evaluation and new data on validity and reliability. In M. A. Straus & R. J. Gelles (Eds.), *Physical violence in American families. Risk factors and adaptations to violence in 8,145 families* (pp. 49–73). New Brunswick, NJ: Transaction.

Straus, M. A. (1990b). Measuring intrafamily conflict and violence: The Conflicts Tactics (CT) Scales. In M. A. Straus & R. J. Gelles (Eds.), *Physical violence in American families. Risk factors and adaptations to violence in 8,145 families* (pp. 29–47). New Brunswick, NJ: Transaction.

Straus, M. A., Hamby, S. L., Finkelhor, D., Moore, D. W, & Runyan, D. (1998). Identification of child maltreatment with the parent-child Conflict Tactics Scales: Development and psychometric data for a national sample of American parents. *Child Abuse & Neglect, 22,* 249–270.

Tuteur, J. M., Ewigman, B. E., Peterson, L., & Hosokawa, M. C. (1995). The Maternal Observation Matrix and the Mother-Child Interaction Scale: Brief observational screening instruments for physically abusive mothers. *Journal of Clinical Child Psychology, 24,* 55–62.

Wilkinson, G. S. (1993). *The Wide Range Achievement Test 3.* Austin TX: PRO-ED.

Wolfe, D. A., Sandler, J., & Kaufman, K. (1981). A competency based parent-training program for child abusers. *Journal of Consulting and Clinical Psychology, 49,* 633–640.

Wolfe, V., Gentile, C., Michienzi, T., Sas, L., & Wolfe, D. A., (1991). The children's impact of traumatic events scale: A measure of post-sexual-abuse PTSD symptoms. *Behavioral Assessment, 13,* 359–383.

5

The Comprehensive Individual and Family Cognitive-Behavioral Therapy (CIF-CBT) Model

This chapter integrates the epidemiological and treatment literature to develop a research-based model for treatment. In Chapter 2, we demonstrated that multiple factors are related to child physical abuse (CPA). These factors include those specific to the child, parent, family, and community or social network. In Chapter 3, we presented current outcome research on the treatment of physically abused children and their families. The literature shows that the majority of treatments address individual systems—child or parent. Given that multiple factors relate to CPA and that the current research literature is pointing to the need for comprehensive models, a gap exists in the transfer of information gained from research and disseminated through practice.

To address this gap, we have combined research-based information on the epidemiology of CPA with empirical findings regarding the treatment of several of these epidemiological factors. The resulting model, Comprehensive Individual and Family Cognitive-Behavioral Therapy (CIF-CBT), demonstrates how practitioners can provide comprehensive, evidence-based treatment to their clients. In this chapter, we first discuss existing models related to the origins of CPA. Second, to demonstrate support for the CIF-CBT model, we discuss the integration of child, parent, and family approaches. Specific to the treatment, we present features of individual CBT and then features of family therapy (FT). Third, we show how individual CBT and FT approaches can be integrated into a comprehensive treatment model. Fourth, we discuss the treatment components that address these multiple factors/systems—child, parent, family, community and social systems—and offer general parameters for the treatment approach. We close by demonstrating a treatment plan based on the assessment presented in Chapter 4 and illustrating the integrated approach.

❑ Models of Child Physical Abuse

CONCEPTUALIZATIONS AND EMPIRICAL SUPPORT

There are few conceptualizations of the origins and maintenance of CPA, and even fewer well-articulated treatment models to guide practice for this population. Still, the importance of these perspectives is their ability to identify specific characteristics worthy of assessment and treatment. For example, the social-situational model has generally emphasized problems in parent, child, and parent-child characteristics as the basis for coercive or abusive parent-child interactions (see Azar, 1991). Specifically, this formulation has examined a broad array of individual and family attributes, including parenting and discipline problems, poor stress management, limitations in general caregiver competencies, and hostile beliefs about the child. Wolfe (1987) provided an early articulation of this perspective, emphasizing various parental functions in the origins of abusive interactions, which he has updated (Wolfe, 1999). Some have suggested that abuse be viewed as an escalated aggressive response (Knutson & Bower, 1994).

Another perspective, considered the ecological model, views CPA from a systemic perspective emphasizing the interrelationships among individual, family, and social support factors (e.g., family communication and extrafamilial contacts; Belsky, 1993). Thus, this model emphasizes the interplay among child, parent and/or family factors, and larger social system issues. Thus far, no specific variables have been identified as necessary and sufficient for the development of physically abusive behavior.

One of the few conceptual models postulated to account for the origins of abusive behavior is the stress and coping model outlined by Hillson and Kupier (1994). This model suggests that parental appraisals may interpret a stressor as a threat, which results in secondary appraisals that elicit internal sources, which may then yield coping dispositions that are influenced by the availability of external supports. The model outlines a number of parental coping responses that may result in various outcomes, such as facilitative caregiver behavior (e.g., active planning and seeking social support), child neglect (e.g., behavioral or mental disengagement), or child abuse (e.g., venting of emotion). Furthermore, the model suggests that these appraisals are influenced by child (e.g., child deviance), parent (e.g., parenting behavior), and ecological (e.g., unemployment) factors.

Greenwald, Bank, Reid, and Knutson (1997) tested a discipline-mediated model with a sample of adolescents and their parents. The authors posited that harsh discipline would result from inadequate discipline tactics and skills. The findings revealed that parental discipline did mediate the relationship between stress and punitive parental practices. Interestingly, parental irritability was not a significant predictor; furthermore, child coercion contributed to parental discipline, but not to punitive parenting practices. The relationship between stress and punitive parenting was completely mediated by parental discipline. In addition to evaluating various aspects of ineffective parenting behavior, the authors suggest the importance of carefully assessing the parent's perceptions of and affective reactions in parent-child interactions to understanding incidents involving physical abuse.

Other empirical studies provide some support for the importance of understanding the role of multiple variables associated with abusive behavior. Christmas, Wodarski, and Smokowski (1996) examined the empirical evidence found for seven abuse risk factors. Consistent evidence was found for a parental history of abuse, depression, single parenthood, low socioeconomic status, isolation, low maternal age, and substance abuse.

Certainly, each of these general models is consistent with the notion that abusive behavior represents an exaggerated aggressive response that occurs within a continuum of parenting practices, that it should be understood within a developmental perspective that can appreciate how the child is affected by and contributes to coercive interactions, and that abusive behavior must be understood in its family-social context. Whereas the social-interactional model seems to emphasize the various processes that occur between parent and child, the ecological model illustrates the importance of understanding the interrelationships among these various domains. Of importance to assessment and treatment is the general emphasis on psychological processes that contribute to a parent's escalation from routine punishment to aggressive behavior, including emotional reactivity, beliefs and attributions about the intent of the child's behavior, parental management skills, and social competencies. Coincidentally, these domains are equally relevant to understanding the extent to which children exhibit various sequelae to an abusive experience. Thus, these and other skill domains and interactional processes are among the key targets noted in our intervention approaches.

❏ The Integration of Child, Parent, and Family Approaches

THE BENEFITS OF INTEGRATION

As shown in earlier chapters, children who experience physical abuse are at risk of varied and multiple mental health problems. Likewise, multiple factors relate to the risk of parents or caregivers physically abusing their child. Considering the multiple correlates and potential outcomes, treatment that focuses on a small part of the problem (e.g., parenting skills only or child anger only) is incomplete and will likely do little to reduce abuse risk or repair the mental health problem. Yet the majority of treatment studies are devoted to the treatment of a single problem with a one-size-fits-all treatment.

The implication of a multidetermined etiology is a treatment model that addresses all known risk factors, including specific child mental health problems. Furthermore, treatment should be tailored to the risks and needs of a specific family. Importantly, intervention strategies used should be those that have some empirical support in the research literature. In cases where abuse has occurred, the treatment should focus specifically on the abuse, the factors that drive abusive behavior, and strategies for reducing risk and repairing family relations.

The model we present in this book is comprehensive and based on an integration of CBT and FT. Initially, as shown in Chapter 4, a multimethod, multisource clinical assessment is conducted to determine child, parent, and family strengths that may help with change. The assessment determines whether the child is experiencing current problems and, if so, the nature of those difficulties. Also, parental and family difficulties that may be occurring and that are contributing to the risk of abuse are determined. A treatment plan is developed to set goals for each need identified, and CBT and FT strategies are implemented toward those goals. Treatment strategies are individualized to address the current strengths and needs of the child, parent, and family.

One of the implications of an integrated model is the need to evaluate the effects of treatment across settings and in multiple contexts. This is, in part, because real-world settings are where we hope to realize the effects of treatment and because more and more services are being administered in the child's ecology.

PRIMARY FEATURES OF CBT

Box 5.1 lists some of the primary features of the CBT approach that are reflected in many of the treatment techniques we describe in subsequent chapters. These features illustrate the emphasis upon helping clients both learn new techniques and "unlearn" certain maladaptive or inappropriate behaviors. The techniques are based on experimental principles of behavior, and have been evaluated in applied research, which sometimes includes different populations. The techniques usually are directed towards behaviors or reactions in three response channels or domains, namely, cognition (thoughts), affect (feelings), and behavior (actions). Assessment often reveals the different domains where a client's primary problems are manifested and how they may work in consort or in contradiction to one another.

The treatment procedures work best when administered by active and directive therapists who can appreciate how to activate the client

---

Box 5.1 | Primary Features of a Cognitive-Behavioral Therapy Approach

1. Focus on learning and "unlearning"
2. Three related response channels
   - Cognition (thinking)
   - Affect (feeling)
   - Behavior (doing)
3. Principles and procedures evaluated in applied research
4. Active therapist
5. Teach relevant skills
6. Step-by-step, structured approach

to learn and apply the skills described in each session. This is not to suggest that therapists are rarely client centered or reflective, but that certain activities require direct instruction, training, and feedback. In many instances, the approach will emphasize training using a structured and sequential approach.

Overall, the research literature indicates that parents respond well to CBT. Specifically, studies show parents learn skills, improve parenting, improve interactions with their child, and reduce abuse indicators through a CBT approach. Likewise, studies on abused children receiving CBT show that child behavior problems are reduced.

PRIMARY FEATURES OF THE FT APPROACH

Box 5.2 lists the primary features of the FT approach that also are reflected in many of the treatment techniques we describe. According to a family systems approach, behavior is understood in terms of patterns of family interactions. Family problems are seen as being affected by how the family interacts. FT models generally share some similarities and differences on several dimensions, such as the participants involved in treatment, family structure or organization, the functioning and interpersonal processes of the family, and family strengths and resources, among other variables. Much of the material incorporated in this manual draws from several sources, including the work of Robin and Foster (1989) on behavioral systems FT, Alexander and Parsons (1982) on functional FT, and Minuchin (1974) on structural FT, and other sources dealing with problem families (Anderson & Stewart, 1982).

The structural content of this intervention usually emphasizes problems in two general areas. The first relates to the level of family cohesion or affiliation shown by family members. Thus, the family's relationships may fall on a continuum ranging from enmeshment to disengagement. Accordingly, the therapist may find that disengaged families generally provide little to no structure to guide the child such that the child is fairly autonomous and independent, whereas enmeshed families may encourage considerable dependence upon parents and offer few opportunities for the child to engage in independent thinking and activity. Other aspects of structure relate to the nature of the family's alignments with one another and their response to efforts to influence one another. Some families have established coalitions in which subsets of family members unite to confront another member. Thus, parental alliances may be weak in the face of a more dominant (or controlling) child, or parental alliances may be fairly controlling or rigid such that the child may feel denied in his or her efforts to influence the family. Abusive families often display aspects of enmeshment within the family, but appear to be fairly disengaged from other families, and they show signs of firm parental alliances, often at the cost of excluding children from the decision-making processes. Occasionally, certain children from abusive families are placed in multiple roles, suggesting that they may be highly involved in family activities and in sharing authority or power on some occasions, whereas on other occasions they are placed in a highly subordinate and powerless position. This ambiguous structural or hierarchical quality often makes it difficult for both the child and parent to interact smoothly and efficiently.

Although studies on family systems treatment with maltreating families are limited, there is some indication that FT increases family cohesion and reduces family conflict, parental distress, and abuse risk (Kolko, 1996).

Box 5.2 | Primary Features of a Family Therapy Approach

1. Behavior is understood in terms of patterns of family interactions.
2. Family problems are seen as affecting and being affected by how the family interacts.
3. Family relationships are considered to fall on a continuum from enmeshment to disengagement.
4. Coalitions within the family are addressed.
5. Interventions aim to change patterns of interactions thought to sustain the identified problems.
6. Interventions also focus on changing the structure of families to be one that is more adaptive.

INTEGRATING CBT AND FT: THE CIF-CBT MODEL

The model we present combines individual CBT with FT. As such, we propose a very comprehensive treatment in which individual strategies are implemented with the child and parent; clarification strategies are implemented specifically to address the emotional impact of the abuse; and, finally, FT occurs. Box 5.3 presents primary features of the CIF-CBT approach.

Box 5.3   Primary Features of the CIF-CBT Approach

1. Focus on solving individual problems through skills training with the child and parent.
2. Understand behavior through three response channels: thinking, feeling, and doing.
3. Tailor individual interventions to child, parent, and family needs identified in the assessment.
4. Implement the clarification process throughout treatment as a means directly to address the abuse.
5. Use the clarification process as a bridge to family work regarding the emotional impact of the abuse.
6. Determine patterns of family interactions and understand how those patterns are maintained.
7. Determine the level of family cohesion and coalitions within the family.
8. Family interventions aim to change patterns of interactions thought to sustain the identified problems.

TREATMENT COMPONENTS

Figure 5.1 provides an overview of the CIF-CBT treatment model. Given the likelihood of overlap among various treatments directed towards the child, parent, family, and community systems, the figure highlights the interrelationships among them. Each of these systems will be described in turn.

Child Treatment

The child treatment strategies used will depend on the needs of the child as determined from the assessment. After the forensic assessment has been completed, the clinical assessment determines the strengths and needs of the child. Doing such allows treatment strategies to be tailored to those strengths and needs. Given that the empirical literature shows that physically abused children may experience a host of clinical problems, therapists must stand ready to treat many potential difficulties.

Regardless of specific child problems, the abuse experience must be dealt with openly. Therefore, in this model, therapists begin by

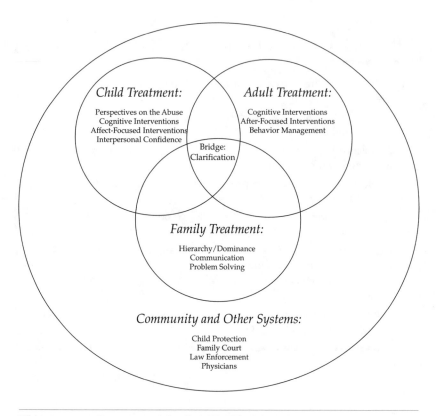

Figure 5.1   Overview of the CIF-CBT Model

addressing perspectives on the abuse experience through under-standing the child's experiences with family violence and teaching children an understanding of antecedents and consequences of behavior in general. Furthermore, cognitive interventions include clarifying the child's views about violence in general and, more specifically, the abuse he or she experienced. In cases where children are experiencing abuse-related anxiety problems such as PTSD or dif-ficulty modulating anger and aggression, affect-focused interventions are used. These may include relaxation techniques with mildly anx-ious children and graduated exposure for those with anxiety prob-lems. Children who have problems with anger are taught empirically validated anger management strategies. Finally, interpersonal com-petence is addressed by teaching children general coping, first aid, safety, support, and specific social skills.

Parent Treatment

Similar to work with the child, assessment of the parent determines strengths and needs. The first order of business in treatment is addressing the abuse. Therapists must determine the parent's view on violence in general and, more specifically, of the abuse that occurred. Early in treatment, the parent begins the abuse clarification process by developing a letter of responsibility that will go to the child and family. In addition, specific mental health problems that affect parenting must be addressed. As with children, the empirical literature shows that multiple parent factors often relate to abuse. Therefore, therapists must be prepared to treat a variety of difficulties.

In addition to addressing the abuse specifically, cognitive interventions for the parent also examine parental expectations of children and offer parents information on child development that can help correct erroneous expectations. From a cognitive perspective, parents' attributions of their children's behavior are addressed. Negative attributions that indicate an expectation that the child is deliberately trying to annoy the parent are corrected. Finally, parents are taught ways to cope with child misbehavior.

For parents having difficulty with anxiety or depression, affect-focused interventions are implemented. Anxiety problems may relate to a parent's own childhood history of abuse and can be managed through the use of relaxation techniques and prolonged exposure. Cognitive and cognitive-behavioral techniques are used to reduce depression by addressing maladaptive thinking and reductions in activity level. Many parents may have difficulty modulating anger and aggression because of skill deficits. Empirically validated anger-management techniques are used to address this problem, and parents are taught to develop a self-management plan. Some parents may experience difficulty managing their child's behavior because of limited knowledge of management techniques. Behavioral strategies that target specific behavioral problems are incorporated into parent-child interactions.

The Clarification Process

The clarification process bridges individual child, individual parent, and family therapy. This process occurs throughout treatment and involves cognitive work by the maltreating parent, preparation of the child, and preparation of other family. The process culminates with a family clarification meeting in which acceptance of responsibility for the abuse is given by the maltreating parent and a family safety and reabuse prevention plan is developed. Although the family addresses the physically abusive actions by understanding family interactions, working to reduce risk factors, and following a safety plan, the clarification can aid the family in processing the emotional impact of the abuse and bring about resolution of emotions that are a barrier to the family getting along well.

Family Treatment

Outside of any individual parent or child interventions, parent-child and/or family sessions that include other family members may be helpful. As noted earlier, FT techniques overall address interactions between family members that sustain problems. After the family clarification meeting, family relations and structure are assessed. Within family relations, the level of family cohesion, ranging from enmeshment to disengagement, is determined. In situations where children and parents are enmeshed, strategies are implemented to foster the child's independence. In situations where parents are disengaged from their children—or vice versa—strategies are implemented to help them reconnect. Another important task during FT is to determine if there are coalitions within the family and whether they are maladaptive, and then work with the family to restructure relations to an appropriate hierarchy. Family interactions are addressed through techniques for communication and problem solving.

Community and Systems Involvement

All treatment, regardless of whether individual, conjoint, or family, occurs within the context of other systems, such as child protection, family court, law enforcement, medical care, and the school system. As such, especially in maltreatment cases, there is interplay between those systems and the family while certainly can affect the course of treatment and the outcome. Therefore, interacting with those systems is important. Within the CIF-CBT model, the multiple systems external to the family are drawn into the treatment. Strategies for doing such are expounded upon in Chapter 16.

GENERAL PARAMETERS OF TREATMENT

Treatment Modalities

In general, the treatment described in this integrated model is designed for use with CPA cases involving children of at least school age and an available parent or caregiver. The population of abuse cases targeted reflects those where physical discipline is no longer being administered properly, but where there is not a high risk for repeated physical injury. Most of our experiences with these techniques have been with children who can understand and apply the various behavior change procedures. Furthermore, most of the procedures can be applied in individual, group, and/or family treatment, but unique procedures in each domain will be emphasized where applicable. Finally, inherent in the approach is the need to apply treatment to several potential abuse-specific problems, more general adjustment problems, and prosocial skill areas that are often relevant in most cases presenting to treatment.

The Treatment Setting

The treatment model presented can be implemented in an office-based or a home-based practice. An important therapeutic development in recent years is the application of clinical services in various community settings, such as the child's home, school, and neighborhood. This programmatic shift has been reported in efforts to deal with a variety of child and family problems, including drug abuse, child conduct problems, and severe emotional disturbance (Henggeler, Schoenwald, Borduin, Rowland, & Cunningham, 1998). Conducting treatment in the natural environment conveys several potential benefits, such as the ability directly to address and target contextual problems that contribute to these problems (Loeber & Farrington, 2000), enhancement of family participation and the use of community resources, and minimization of obstacles to access and ongoing participation. Indeed, in the area of children's conduct problems, favorable outcomes have been reported by studies that have conducted sessions in the natural environment (see Henggeler, Schoenwald, & Pickrel, 1995). In the abuse field, a few noteworthy studies of family-based interventions conducted in real-world settings have reported positive outcomes, although studies have been based on small samples, have been limited in scope, or suffered from other methodological problems (see Brunk, Henggeler, & Whelan, 1987; Lutzker & Campbell, 1994; Nicol et al., 1988; Whittaker, Kinney, Tracy, & Booth, 1990).

Course of Treatment

The treatment model proposed will include strategies for addressing the needs of the child, parent, and family. Generally, the family's overall treatment priorities must first be understood (see Azar & Wolfe, 1998). Efforts to enhance participation and the impact of treatment on abusive families may begin by targeting those settings that influence the level of adjustment and competence of abused children, notably the family, school, and peer context. However, it is possible that parental disorders may require treatment prior to working with the child or family. Likely, treatment of the child and parent will be occurring simultaneously, with individual symptom reduction preceding some of the family strategies. Flexibility will be required to allow the therapist to tailor the treatment and prioritize problems with the greatest need and of the greatest import to the family.

Contraindications of Treatment

Because the CIF-CBT model addresses a large array of mental health problems and risk factors and individualizes treatment to the strengths and needs of a family, the model can be applied to the majority of children and families in situations where physical abuse has occurred. However, several contraindications should be noted. First, in situations where children are not going to remain or reunite with their family, application of a treatment to the parent and family is not indicated. In this case, children may need treatment to help them deal with the loss of their family or to help them reintegrate into another home. Furthermore, in cases where little to no mental health problems are apparent following physical abuse, application of this entire model to the child and family is not warranted. In that case, some work with the parent to reduce risk of reabuse may be needed. As we review each treatment technique, we will discuss when a technique should or should not be used within the context of this model.

The Treatment Plan

Box 5.4 illustrates a treatment plan based on an individualized assessment and treatment approach combining CBT and FT.

Box 5.4	Sample Treatment Plan for the Murphy Family Illustrating the Integrated CIF-CBT Approach

Strengths of Child, Parent, and Family

Child

- Doing well academically
- Draws well
- Helps around the house

Box 5.4   *continued*

Parent

- Employed
- Desire for change in the family
- Wants to parent the child more positively
- No drug or alcohol use

Family

- Strong extended family
- Attend occasional activities together without fighting

Target Problems of Child, Parent, and Family

Child

- Problems with temper in school and at home
- Angry about the abuse
- Moderate depression

Parent

- PTSD from own childhood abuse
- Low parenting skills

Family

- Lots of conflict: mother and child get into screaming matches that end with belt whippings
- Low warmth or closeness in the immediate family
- Grandmother not protective of her own daughter (mother is angry with grandmother for not protecting her in childhood from an assaultive stepfather)

Goals of Treatment

1. Reduce child's use of aggression as a means for handling anger

   Strategy: CBT anger management training; use of academic activities as a reward for positive anger management

2. Process the physical abuse events

   Strategy: Psychoeducation of views on violence, cognitions of abusive events, and clarification

3. Reduce Roman' s depressed feelings

   Strategy: Cognitive reframing, involvement in positive physical activities, and target interactions between mother and son

> **Box 5.4**   *continued*
>
> 4. Reduce mother's PTSD symptoms
>
>   Strategy: CBT techniques for PTSD
>
> 5. Increase mother's parenting skills
>
>   Strategy: Behavioral parent training
>
> 6. Reduce family conflicts
>
>   Strategy: Family systems techniques—identifying interaction patterns that escalate and then stopping the escalation early in the sequence of events
>
> 7. Process grandmother's lack of protection of her daughter
>
>   Strategy: Address the lack of protection through a clarification process

❏ Summary

The model on which this book is based is a comprehensive one integrating CBT and FT to produce CIF-CBT. Although the therapy is comprehensive, not all families will be treated with the same strategies. Tailoring the treatment to the specific strengths and targeted problems of the family is key to efficient treatment. Use of evidence-based strategies is central to obtaining outcomes. The following chapters will elaborate upon evidence-based strategies for treating children, parents, and families. Attention will also be given to the systems with which the family interacts and strategies for including those systems in the treatment team.

References

Alexander, J. F., & Parsons, B. V. (1982). *Functional family therapy.* Pacific Grove, CA: Brooks/Cole.

Anderson, C. M. & Stewart S. (1982). *Mastering resistance: A practical guide to family therapy.* New York: Guilford.

Azar, S. T. (1991). Models of child abuse: A metatheoretical analysis. *Criminal Justice and Behavior, 18,* 30–46.

Azar, S. T., & Wolfe, D. A. (1998). Child physical abuse and neglect. In E. J. Mash & R. A. Barkley (Eds.), *Treatment of childhood disorders* (2nd ed., pp. 501–544). New York: Guilford.

Belsky, J. (1993). Etiology of child maltreatment: A developmental-ecological analysis. *Psychological Bulletin, 114,* 413–434.

Brunk, M., Henggeler, S. W., & Whelan, J. P. (1987). Comparison of multisystemic therapy and parent training in the brief treatment of child abuse and neglect. *Journal of Consulting and Clinical Psychology, 55,* 171–178.

Christmas, A. L., Wodarski, J. S., Smokowski, P. R. (1996). Risk factors for physical child abuse: A practice theoretical paradigm. *Family Therapy, 23,* 233–248.

Greenwald, R. L., Bank, L., Reid, J. B., & Knutson, J. F. (1997). A disciplined-mediated model of excessively punitive parenting. *Aggressive Behavior, 23,* 259–280.

Henggeler, S. W., Schoenwald, S. K., Borduin, C. M., Rowland, M. D., & Cunningham, P. B. (1998). *Multisystemic treatment of antisocial behavior in children and adolescents.* New York: Guilford.

Henggeler, S. W., Schoenwald, S. K., & Pickrel, S. G. (1995). Multisystemic therapy: Bridging the gap between university- and community-based treatment. *Journal of Consulting and Clinical Psychology, 63,* 709–717.

Hillson, J. M. C., & Kupier, N. A. (1994). A stress and coping model of child maltreatment. *Clinical Psychology Review, 14,* 261–285.

Kolko, D. J. (1996). Individual cognitive-behavioral treatment and family therapy for physically abused children and their offending parents: A comparison of clinical outcomes. *Child Maltreatment, 1,* 322–342

Knutson, J. F., & Bower, M. E. (1994). Physically abusive parenting as an escalated aggressive response. In M. Potgel & J. F. Knutson (Eds.), *The dynamics of aggression: Biological and social processes in dyads and groups* (pp. 195–225). Hillsdale, NJ: Lawrence Erlbaum.

Loeber, R. & Farrington, D. (2000). Young children who commit crimes: Epidemiology, developmental origins, risk factors, early interventions, and policy implications. *Development & Psychopathology, 12,* 737–762.

Lutzker, J. R., & Campbell, R. V. (1994). *Ecobehavioral family interventions in developmental disabilities.* Pacific Grove, CA: Brooks/Cole.

Minuchin, S. (1974). *Families and family therapy.* Cambridge, MA: Harvard University Press.

Nicol, A. R., Smith, J., Kay, B., Hall, D., Barlow, J., & Williams, B. (1988). A focused casework approach to the treatment of child abuse: A controlled comparison. *Journal of Child Psychology and Psychiatry, 29,* 703–711.

Robin, A. L. & Foster, S. L. (1989). *Negotiating parent/adolescent conflict: A behavioral-family systems approach.* New York: Guilford.

Whittaker, J., Kinney, J., Tracy, E. M., & Booth, C. (1990). *Reaching high-risk families: Intensive family preservation in human services.* New York: Aldine.

Wolfe, D. A. (1987). *Child abuse: Implications for child development and psychopathology.* Newbury Park, CA: Sage.

Wolfe, D. A. (1999). *Child abuse: Implications for child development and psychopathology* (2nd ed.). Thousand Oaks, CA: Sage.

6

Initial Treatment Considerations

Working with families when abuse has occurred and Child Protective Services (CPS) is involved presents special considerations for a therapist. Not only must the therapist select the appropriate strategy to address specific problem areas, but attention must also be paid to therapeutic issues that may promote or hinder treatment progress. Therapists must begin treatment with an understanding of each of these issues and of how to overcome the barriers with which they are associated. Special issues include engagement, respecting cultural differences, safety, confidentiality and abuse reporting, children in out-of-home placements, child psychiatric disorders, and parent issues that can affect all domains of functioning. Equally important to understanding issues that may become barriers to treatment progress is setting the stage for a collaborative relationship with parents. This may be done not only through showing respect for the parent, but also by providing a proper orientation to treatment.

❏ Preparation and Prerequisites

ISSUES AND TASKS

Engagement

Engaging the family in the treatment process is the first task of the therapist. Without family engagement, even the best treatment strategies will have little value. Cunningham and Henggeler (1999) identify several strategies to facilitate family engagement. These strategies, such as therapist empathy, gift giving, credibility, and scientific mindedness are illustrated below.

Empathy predicts a strong therapeutic alliance (Schaap, Bennun, Schindler, & Hoogduin, 1993). However, in cases where a child has been injured, empathy for the parents may be difficult to develop. Therapists must guard against anger toward and pejorative language about the parent. To increase empathy in the face of child maltreatment, therapists can be asked to consider the level of problems that the parent is experiencing, and to put herself or himself in the shoes of the parent. Doing so allows the therapist to examine the multiple factors that relate to abuse and the many hardships the parent is likely to experience. On the positive side, therapists can be asked to examine fully the strengths of the family, parents, and children. Focusing on these strengths and how they can be used to attain the family's goals may help therapists redirect themselves away from negative views.

Gift giving is defined as strategies that provide the family with immediate benefits during the early treatment sessions (Sue & Zane, 1987). For example, simply having someone to listen to a parent's description of her or his plight and providing some hope that a solution is possible may bring about anxiety reduction. For parents who have abused their children, learning that someone is "on their side" and will advocate for them despite their past behavior may bring about some relief. This is not to say that parents are not held responsible for abusive behavior, but that therapists will not reject them even with their history of family violence.

Therapist credibility can relate to therapeutic outcome (Sue & Zane, 1987). Credibility can be assigned by others or directly demonstrated through skills used in sessions. Credibility assigned by others can be instrumental in initially establishing engagement. For example, most people would be more likely to seek treatment from a therapist who others laud. To retain that initial credibility, therapists must exhibit skill in recommending interventions that are manageable for the family and connected to the goals to which the family has agreed. Credibility can be promoted by being reliable, consistent, and respectful of the family.

Scientific mindedness is a skill that can enhance engagement by developing and testing hypotheses regarding client behaviors rather than endorsing any convenient stereotypes. For example, in abuse cases therapists may look at the multiple factors involved in the abuse (e.g., substance use, financial strain, or lack of social supports) and determine which of these factors apply to a particular family rather than stereotyping the parent as a violent person or one who does not care about the children.

When a family fails to engage despite these initial efforts, potential barriers to engagement must be recognized and overcome. Initially, families may have little trust and may view the therapist as an agent of the Department of Social Services (DSS) whose purpose is to divide the family further. Trust may also be hampered by previous negative experiences with CPS. For example, a parent may have experienced abuse as a child, was not protected by social services, and so harbors anger that becomes associated with any therapists' services. If that anger is met with confrontation, the relationship is likely to become more adversarial. Meeting the anger with support may diffuse the adversarial nature of events (Patterson & Chamberlain, 1988). The therapist should indicate to the family that he or she understands that the family may not feel trusting, which the therapist will work to change. Therapist behaviors should then be sensitive, nonpejorative toward the family, and demonstrative of the desire to earn trust. Therapists must never presume trust, and will need to take a one-down approach to earn trust from the family through respectful interactions.

Engagement can also be hampered by the parents' clinical problems. For example, parents may have difficulty engaging if they are experiencing psychosis, depression, or serious substance abuse. Therapists will need to address these problems directly by treating them or referring the parent to the appropriate expert for consultation or treatment.

For a "9-to-5," office-based practice, practical problems, such as a lack of transportation or an inability to leave work repeatedly to attend treatment during the daytime, may be barriers to engagement. Therapists must be willing to problem solve with families about overcoming these barriers and avoid the pejorative view that the family does not want help if they cannot overcome the barrier on their own. For some families, financial concerns may inhibit their participation in treatment. Therapists should ask about this issue and resolve it at the initial meeting.

At times, engagement is hampered by therapist factors. For example, therapists may experience anxiety over hearing about child abuse and be reluctant to meet with the family. Therapists who are experiencing stress or who fear for their safety may also be unable to engage with the family. Therapist factors should be directly addressed in clinical supervision.

Gaining Cultural Understanding

Crucial to forming a collaborative relationship with children and their families is developing an understanding of the family's language, cultural background and how that background and their experiences influence their view of the world and approach to problem solving. Abney and Gunn (1993) term this ability to share the client's worldview *cultural competence*. Often, therapists make the mistake of assuming they are culturally competent with a family from a background different from their own when they are aware of the typical customs of that family's race. However, therapists should not mistake race for culture or assume that people with the same skin color are from the same culture. Consider the following scenario:

> Tina and Theresa were two women with many similarities and differences. Tina was tall, blonde, of German descent, and reared in the northern United States. Theresa was tall, blonde, of Dutch descent, and reared in the southern United States. Although the two women had the same skin, hair, and eye color, and could pass as biological sisters, their cultural backgrounds gave them very different views of the world. Such different views and understanding of language in a different way could potentially lead to misunderstandings and different perceptions of the same experience. To overcome potential cultural misunderstandings, the two women spent time listening to each other tell of their background, family, growing up, and perceptions of life experiences. Both had to be open to hearing of the other's perceptions of situations and show a willingness to inquire about each other's actions in the context of their cultural background. As a result, each came to understand the other's culture and individual view of the world.

In this scenario, neither woman was a client or therapist to the other: They were simply friends. Developing cultural understanding in a therapeutic relationship is similar to developing any other interpersonal relationship. Doing so takes respect and a desire to understand another person's beliefs or views, a skill critical to sound clinical practice.

Even though cultural background may differ for two people from the same race, some studies have shown that clients prefer counselors who are racially and ethnically similar to them (Ponce & Atkinson, 1989; Terrell & Terrell, 1984). Research evidence also shows that a cultural match is important to treatment outcome for some populations. For example, S. Sue and colleagues (Sue, Fujino, Hu, Takeuchi, & Zane, 1991) conducted a large ethnic-match study of African Americans, Asian Americans, Mexican Americans, and white clients in the Los Angeles County Mental Health System. When Asian Americans were matched culturally or linguistically with a therapist, they attended more sessions and evinced better outcomes, and fewer cases dropped out of treatment. Similar findings were shown for Mexican Americans. Ethnically matched whites and African Americans attended more sessions, but the match was not related to treatment outcomes.

This research suggests that the content of treatment, as well as an ethnic match, may contribute to more positive outcomes for some populations. Of course, the capacity of the therapist to communicate with family members in their own language also may enhance treatment. Thus, whenever possible, treatment teams should reflect the racial and ethnic makeup of the population that is served. At the very least, individuals providing an office-based practice should try to incorporate symbols (e.g., decorations) that are welcoming to the backgrounds of the people they serve.

To enhance the welcoming of clients further, therapists from a different background must recognize the importance of addressing trust issues that often influence therapist-patient relations. When the therapist and client are from different races, ethnicities, or sociocultural backgrounds, historical events or the client's individual life experience may lead him or her automatically to distrust the therapist. Therapists should not be afraid to ask the client how his or her background, different as it is from the therapist's, might affect the client's view of and participation in treatment. Together, client and therapist can devise ways to overcome the negative effects of these differences and to understand each other. Also, therapists should always inquire whether a behavior is connected to the person's culture, rather than assume negative intent. For example, a therapist who understands that some African American people do not make eye contact with the therapist as a sign of respect might ask if the lack of eye contact is due to respect or some other reason, rather than assuming lack of interest. Finally, understanding another's worldview is not a goal that can be attained in a single session, but is a process that occurs throughout the course of treatment and takes continuous work. To obtain further information on cultural issues and child maltreatment, the reader is referred to such sources as the work of Fontes and Volker (Fontes, 1995, 1998; Fontes & Volker, 1996).

Safety

Child, family, and therapist safety is a primary consideration in situations where violence has occurred. In all cases, agencies should have a written safety plan to curb violence potential or for handling potentially violent clients. In general, the therapist in an office-based practice should not see any clients without other personnel somewhere in the office complex. This is especially true if the client is a family or individual who has engaged in violence. Furthermore, therapists should be vigilant of escalating irritation, aggression by the parent toward the child, or increases in identified risk factors. Any references to violence should be taken seriously, and concerns about child safety should be explored and reported if abuse is suspected.

For therapists who provide in-home treatment, attending to safety issues is of paramount importance. First, in-home therapists have a greater potential for detecting increased risk for violence simply by being in the family home. Observations of increased risk can be addressed directly and rapidly. Second, away from the confines of the office or clinic, therapists must be watchful of risks to their own safety. For example, when approaching a family's home, therapists should avoid large groups of people who may be engaging in any deviant activities (e.g., substance use). In some communities, being an unknown person creates a situation of risk and the therapist may need the family to let neighbors know that it is okay for the therapist to be coming into the community. In unfamiliar neighborhoods, therapists should not be afraid to speak to people with a greeting and should always walk with a purpose so that they appear to belong in the neighborhood.

Within a family's home, the therapist should avoid situations where the parent is drunk, high, or handling a weapon. Furthermore, therapists should be careful where they sit and look for potentially dangerous equipment or materials (e.g., hypodermic needles), which are more difficult to see on soft furniture or that might be covered by blankets or sheets. If a situation is at all precarious, the home-based therapist should simply not go into that situation or, alternatively, should use a phone to call the family to assess the situation or call the police for protection.

Confidentiality and Abuse Reporting

Confidentiality and abuse reporting can be an intimidating issue for therapists dealing with physical abuse. Foremost, therapists should have an in-depth knowledge of the reporting laws of their state, province, or country. This law, plus the limits of confidentiality, should be made clear to the child and family at the start of treatment. In fact, the therapist may want to provide this description in writing. In general, if the therapist suspects new abuse by the parent, those suspicions should be reported to a child protection agency. Different states in the United States have differing policies and laws around reporting alleged abuse by individuals other than the parent. For example, in South Carolina, abuse allegedly committed by a sibling would be handled by law enforcement officers rather than protective services workers, and therefore would not be reported to DSS.

Abuse reporting can be confusing for parents and children, and they may fear that they will have to experience future investigations on old abuse. Therapists should make clear that the abuse that has already been investigated will not be reported again. Of course, if the therapist suspects a new incident of abuse and plans to report that alleged abuse—given that it is safe to do so—he or she should inform the parent of the report in advance. Doing so may initially hurt the alliance with the parent, but chances are that the parent will know who made the report and be able to work through any implications of this report. In such instances, silence may be viewed as deception, irreparably harming the alliance. If informing the parent of the report will place the child in danger, then the therapist should not discuss this with the parent until the child is safe.

In addition to abuse reporting, confidentiality limits mandate reporting homicidal intent and monitoring of suicidal intent. Families should be clear about these mandates at the start of treatment. Per the 1976 decision handed down in the case of *Tarasoff v. Regents of the University of California* (see Truscott, 1993; VandeCreek & Knapp, 1993), warnings regarding homicidal intent should be given by the therapist to the appropriate police jurisdiction and the intended victim. If the child reports suicidal intent, the parent or caregiver should be informed and a decision made regarding whether the family can monitor the child until he or she is stabilized or if psychiatric hospitalization is required. Similarly, if the parent reports suicidal intent, monitoring of that parent and stabilization are necessary.

Given that the family is likely to be involved in the court process during or after treatment, confidentiality around records should be spelled out for the family. Specifically, the therapist cannot guarantee that the notes in the chart are confidential. A judge may subpoena the chart requiring the therapist to relinquish therapy notes. Therefore, therapists should keep notes up to date, take care that notes are written clearly, and see that no pejorative references are made to the family or anyone else. Nothing can be as disconcerting to a therapist as having to read his or her notes on the stand in front of the parent and reading a negative, judgmental comment about that parent.

Out-of-Home Placement

In some abuse cases, children will be living in an out-of-home placement. The reasons for such may be for the protection of the child or because the child needs an intense level of treatment. When the child lives away from the family but the plan with DSS is reunification, the therapist must work closely with the foster parent or other caregivers. For children in foster care, work with the foster parent can focus on adjustment to the foster home and how the foster parent can assist with both helping the child deal with abuse issues and preparing the child to return to the family. Children with externalizing behavior problems may be at risk of disrupting the foster care placement. Helping to stabilize the child to avoid multiple placements is important to his or her recovery.

Foster parents can be an important partner in the treatment process and a model or support for the original family. Therapists may need to help the foster parent overcome anger toward the parent for abusing the child and to facilitate a positive relationship between the two families. For example, in one recent case, children were removed from their mother following partner violence and physical abuse of the children. The foster mother became an important support person for the mother who visited the children with the foster mother. They shared stories and strategies about the children. After the children returned to the mother, the foster mother continued to have contact and the children occasionally visited her for the weekend. This provided respite for the overtaxed mother, who had no extended family. The foster mother, in effect, became extended family.

For children in institutional care, the family's therapist may be able to form a team with the providers in the residential facility to assure that everyone is working toward the same goals. Together, everyone can determine how quickly the child can safely return to the family.

Child Psychiatric Disorders

Although certainly not unique to therapists working with children who have been abused, one of the overarching issues for treatment relates to whether a child or adolescent suffers from any psychiatric disorders. Certainly, abused children may experience psychiatric dysfunction before, during, and/or after an abusive event. Children referred by CPS may or may not have received a formal evaluation for psychiatric disorders, prompting the clinician to determine whether further assessment is warranted. When such assessments have been conducted, it is important to understand the nature of the interview procedures or methods, the quality and rigor of the interviews, whether full diagnostic criteria were examined, and whether parents and children participated in separate or joint interviews, among other questions (see Azar & Wolfe, 1998). Such an assessment may reveal multiple disorders (some of which may be quite surprising to the clinician), a single expected disorder, or the absence of any disorder despite reports by either informant of certain types of symptoms. It is possible that children may report or exhibit behavioral and emotional problems (e.g., depressive symptoms) without meeting the full criteria for a given psychiatric disorder (e.g., major depressive episode). At the same time, clinicians may learn about psychiatric disorders that bear significant implications for further evaluation and/or treatment.

There are obviously numerous treatment approaches and alternatives to addressing the many psychiatric disorders with which abused children present during intervention. These treatments vary in conceptualization, technical procedure, scope, complexity, duration, level of parental involvement, potential side effects, and likely outcome (see Kazdin, 2000). Some of the more common approaches are mentioned here to assist the clinician in selecting or requesting the most appropriate course of treatment for a given child or adolescent. In some instances, understanding how a child's clinical symptoms may reflect the presence of a full-blown disorder and how to target these symptoms most efficiently may contribute to the application of a shorter and more effective treatment regimen.

As an example, a child with attention deficit/hyperactivity disorder (ADHD) may benefit from an initial evaluation using standardized forms for documenting the severity of these symptoms at school and home (see, e.g., Schachar & Ickowicz, 1999). For those children displaying high levels of ADHD symptoms, both behavior management (e.g., clear rules and consequences) and stimulant medication (e.g., methylphenidate or Ritalin) have been found to be effective in the short- and long-term (Pelham & Waschbusch, 1999). Generally, the use of structure and behavioral contingencies may be necessary in order to establish some decorum for more intensive skills-based intervention.

Children who present with oppositional defiant disorder (ODD) or conduct disorder may respond to many of the cognitive-behavioral techniques described in this book, including anger control, social problem solving, and other cognitive-social skills training procedures (see Kolko, 2000). Parent management training and related parent effectiveness interventions are among the most effective interventions for these disorders that have been administered in varying clinical contexts for a long time (see Schoenwald & Henggeler, 1999). In general, such treatment has involved teaching self-regulation and prosocial skills to the children, appropriate discipline and self-control skills to parents, and effective problem-solving strategies to families.

In contrast, internalizing disorders have been reported among physically abused children, including major depressive disorder (MDD; Brown, Cohen, Johnson, & Smailes, 1999) and anxiety disorders, especially posttraumatic stress disorder (PTSD; Pfefferbaum, 1997; Ackerman, Newton, McPherson, Jones, & Dykman, 1998). Children presenting with MDD may experience symptoms that interfere with the administration of treatment and its motivation (e.g., dysphoria, anhedonia, hopelessness, isolation, or withdrawal). Common treatments emphasize methods to modify depressogenic cognitions or distortions, establish positive activity routines and personal goals, and validate negative affect. Likewise, there are effective medications, such as Luvox® and Wellbutrin®, which have few side effects. Indeed, some children presenting with both internalizing and externalizing symptoms may benefit from a combination of psychosocial and pharmacological interventions. Such combinations may be designed to enhance the breadth of treatment, but must be carefully monitored to both ensure safety and enhance efficacy (Steiner, 1997).

ISSUES AFFECTING PARENTAL FUNCTIONING

Parental Substance Abuse

Parental substance abuse is targeted for treatment when it is identified as contributing to risk for reabuse and when it interferes with parenting or the family moving forward (i.e., when it is a barrier to the family making needed changes). Information regarding the parent's substance use should be gathered from the parent and other family members. The parent may deny substance abuse, and therapists will need to gather enough information from enough different sources to be sure that this is a contributing problem. If treatment for substance abuse is warranted, therapists may make a referral for the parent to receive appropriate treatment or provide the treatment, if competent to do so.

The number of substance abuse treatment programs has grown in recent years, but research regarding their effectiveness has lagged behind. Current evidence does not indicate that restrictive programs, such as hospitalization or residential centers, are more effective than outpatient programs. Among outpatient treatments, behavioral therapies have shown more success than such other treatments as support groups or group treatment (Henggeler, Schoenwald, Borduin, Rowland, & Cunningham, 1998). Multicomponent behavioral therapy, in particular, has been shown to be effective for treating cocaine dependency (Higgins & Budney, 1993).

Partner Violence

In some situations, parents cannot effectively parent their children because of partner violence. For the physically abused child, partner violence presents a double whammy. That is, the child victim is affected by his or her own abuse and by witnessing the abuse of a parent. When a therapist discovers partner violence, even if it is not reported to be occurring at present but has happened in the recent past, the focus of treatment is immediately placed on safety. To set up a safety plan, an assessment is rapidly made regarding the safety of the children and the parent who is the victim. If partner violence is currently occurring, the therapist works with the victim and involved agencies to do whatever is necessary to keep the family safe. The situation may necessitate someone moving out of the house to establish safety. In some states, partner violence falls under the mandatory reporting law. That is, professionals are required to report to CPS the threat of physical harm to children. Therapists must know the laws in their particular state and the mandates for abuse reporting. If required to do so, a report will need to be made to CPS. Then, the therapist can work with this agency, law enforcement, and the parent who is the victim to determine the terms of the safety plan (e.g., moving out, obtaining a restraining order, or having extended family help).

Once safety is established, the therapist can move on to determining what interventions need to take place to reduce the risk of partner violence. First, the therapist must understand all factors that are related to the violence. Some of the same factors that relate to partner violence will relate to physical abuse. For example, does the violence occur when the offending parent has been using substances? Are there financial difficulties? Does the parent have a problem with anger management or impulse control? Once the therapist and parents understand the factors related to the abuse, interventions can be designed. For example, if the major factor relating to abuse is substance use, treatment for this problem should begin.

Limited Social Support and Low Use of Resources

Decreasing social isolation is imperative for reducing risk for reabuse. Enhancing parents' social supports can serve a number of purposes. Support systems can help parents manage the stress of parenting by providing emotional support, such as a listening ear. In some cases, social supports can provide resources needed to manage financial or instrumental tasks (e.g., help with household tasks or childcare needed for respite). Social supports can also provide social outlets for parents to interact with other adults so that they can refocus energy and attention on positive aspects of life.

People who are socially isolated become that way for a variety of reasons. Psychiatric difficulties, such as substance abuse or even health problems, may make reaching out to others difficult. Isolated parents may have difficulty trusting others and may have given up on life getting better. Some parents will have low skills for connecting with people because they have had so little practice and do not know where to begin.

To move parents toward being more socially connected and making better use of existing resources, the therapist will take the family through a number of steps. First, the therapist starts by determining if the family currently accesses any resources or social supports and what skills they may have for doing so. Next, the therapist helps the parent determine what supports or resources are needed. Third, the therapist works with the parent to determine supports that are already available to them within their family or the community. Last, the therapist and parent make a plan to access supports and resources, and that plan should make use of existing strengths currently held by the parent (see Spratt, 1997).

Although therapists can be viewed as an initial formal source of social support for parents, supports from the natural environment of the family are best because they are accessible after treatment is over. To empower families to gain their own support systems and access their own resources, therapists will need to guide them through the process but not take over the task. Guiding through the process will differ according to the needs, skills, and experiences of the family. Therapists should never assume that parents are empowered to do for themselves by the therapist telling them what to do. Making social connections can be intimidating, and initial efforts to link families with social supports may require a lot of "hand holding" and direct guidance, especially if parents are low in skills for linking with people and resources. For example, to link with formal supports to obtain funds to pay utilities, parents can be guided toward a written resource to gain numbers, provided with a role play to prepare for interactions, and be assisted through the phone call or face-to-face conversation. Little by little, therapists should fade out of the picture to allow families to do for themselves.

Although informal supports in the natural environment are best, while the family is involved with CPS, the therapist can be instrumental in helping the family view this agency as a resource. The family may be reluctant to let CPS know of needs that they have because of fears of having their children removed. The therapist may be a liaison between the family and the agency, working with both to foster communication and encouraging the agency to provide for some instrumental needs of the family. For example, Ms. Tanner stopped coming to treatment because she could not afford gasoline for her car. CPS, in an effort to help her comply with court-ordered treatment and to make progress, provided a certificate that would allow her to purchase enough gas to get to the session and back home.

❑ Overview of Treatment

In this section, we will discuss a general overview of treatment. Specific suggestions will be given for proving an orientation for parent, child, and family treatment.

SAMPLE ORIENTATIONS

An Orientation for Parent/Family Treatment

Therapist Background. By way of background, it is helpful to briefly describe who you are, your background, and what you do as a therapist before discussing the nature of the treatment. Such information includes the therapist's degree, level of experience (i.e. *"I have worked before with children who have behavioral problems and their parents and families"*), and specific functions (e.g., *"I work with parents; another staff member works with the child"*).

Several issues or reactions that may be important to the parent may be worth noting at the outset of treatment. Certainly, parents may feel frustrated and overwhelmed by the need or mandate for treatment. Thus, try to reassure the parents that they are not "bad" or "wrong." Emphasize that you are here to help them learn better ways of managing their child's behavior so that they will have a better quality of life with their child.

> *We are therapists and counselors, and our job is not to tell you that you are bad or wrong. We are not here to say that you are a poor parent. Our job is to work with you and to help you and your family get along better and interact more positively.*

It may also be helpful to remind the parent what she or he is likely to receive from the therapist: (a) We advocate—we help the client or family reach the goals they want; (b) we help parents who have a lot of conflicts with their children; and (c) we teach, give suggestions, and set up programs at home that help parents manage their children more effectively.

Getting to Know You: Begin to Build Trust. Parents may be reluctant to discuss much early in treatment because of feelings of guilt or anger. It is important to begin to build rapport, gain trust, and create a safe environment that facilitates open discussion. Parents need to be open to exploring what happened and how they can change. A sample script describing this introduction is shown in Therapist Example 6.1. The spirit and overall theme of this material is intended to reduce the parent's defensiveness and enhance the likelihood that some aspect of individual or family improvement could be achieved through participation in treatment.

THERAPIST EXAMPLE **6.1**

Sample Treatment Rationale for Parents

"We understand how it is sometimes easy for things to upset someone or upset that person's family. There have been incidents where you *[the therapist uses information he or she has regarding the incidents]* lost control, became very angry at least once with your child, or used force, or may have used harsh punishment. Maybe you hurt your child's feelings by saying mean things, or hurt him *[or her]* by hitting, slapping, pushing, or throwing things. A pattern of negative behavior began between you and your child. This has led to more problems.

"Sometimes, even when parents and kids aren't fighting, they're not very nice or respectful to each other. Maybe they're mad at each other, or sad, about all the fighting. Maybe they just gave up trying to talk to each other because every time they did they got into another fight. This is understandable. By the time a pattern gets established, people sometimes feel little hope that things will ever change. So, a lot of times parents and kids don't talk to each other much, or, when they do, they're not too nice to each other. No one, including parents, is saying 'please' and 'thank you,' or asking about each other's day; no one knows how to ask for something nicely or how to discuss a problem calmly. As the situation gets worse between parents and their kids, they each start avoiding each other as much as possible—they don't spend time together doing fun things . . . they even avoid doing things together that they each do with their own friends or neighbors. Often, the only time the parent and child interact is when the child has caused trouble and the parent reacts.

"Some families fight a lot. Some families may not fight as often. But, no matter how often it happens, most parents probably wished that it never happened . . . or, more realistically, that it happened a lot less. Parents wish that a disagreement or a frustrating incident could be handled more constructively, and that they had a better relationship with their child."

Other statements, like those following, may prove useful in providing parents with a positive orientation to treatment:

- *"Many, if not all, families have arguments, conflicts, and real disagreements at one time or another. Some families, though, have arguments, conflicts and disagreements that are expressed in a destructive way and someone usually ends up getting emotionally or physically hurt."*

- *"There are some members of a family who mistakenly believe that they are solving problems, especially with their child, by using force, by hitting, threatening to hurt, or using harsh ways to make their child obey."*

- *"Lots of things can hurt children, such as ignoring them when they want to talk to us, treating them with disrespect* [this idea may surprise some parents; remind them that their child is a person], *using physical force— slapping, hitting, pulling, or dragging them—or using harsh words, insulting them, calling them names, or humiliating them. These things may make kids feel bad about themselves."*

- *"Sometimes, things we don't do can be harmful, like not protecting our child, not being supportive or helpful when this is needed (being neglectful or uninvolved), or not getting help if we need it ourselves."*

- *"You and your family may be having problems right now. This does not mean that your family is crazy, hates you, or cannot change, and it doesn't mean that you're crazy, a bad person, or that you've done something so wrong that you can never change things for the better."*

It is important to reassure parents (e.g., *"We'll help you and respond to your needs. You are here. That's the first step"*) and tell them that they are not alone (e.g., *"I am here to help parents like you"*).

Treatment Motivation and Preparation

Why Should You Do Anything? Ask the parent to consider the following statements and to suggest what a person saying each statement might be thinking and feeling. Note that there are no right or wrong answers, but there is another way of thinking and another way of saying these things:

1. *"It's not my problem—it's my kids! They've got the behavior problem. Let them do the work!"*

2. *"I'm doing all I can under the circumstances. My kids are supposed to know how to act. I don't have time to be watching them 24 hours a day. I have other responsibilities."*

3. *"I don't care anyway. I don't get along with my kids. They don't respect or like me. They just cause trouble. I'm through with them. Let them do what they want."*

After asking the parent to consider the preceding statements, the therapist can then prompt the parent: *"Okay, now I want to read to you some different responses, which show how people can change the way they think and then change the way they feel. See if you can tell what the difference is and how you think a person who thinks this way might feel."*

1. *"I know that problems aren't things in people. If we cut open a person, we wouldn't find a thing in there that says 'problem.' Problems are things that people experience, and they can come* between *people. They, then, share the problem. My child and I need to find a better way of dealing with our problems. I need to understand what causes my child to behave this way, and then learn how to help him [or her] change that destructive behavior."*

2. *"I can do more and change how I treat my child. He [or she]* is, *after all, a child who needs my love, guidance, and support. I can learn to manage my time better so I do* have *time for my child."*

3. *"I spend too much time now being negative and angry over my child's behavior. We're in a rut. I may not always feel good about how my child behaves or reacts to me, but there are times when I do feel good about my child. I'm going to focus on the positive from now on, not on the negative."*

The therapist should try to have a brief discussion of the differences in thinking and feeling states accompanying each statement.

Benefits of Participation in Treatment

The parent may be wondering about the benefits of being in treatment. A few possibilities are listed here:

- *"It's helpful to talk with another person because, then, one does not feel as frustrated, guilty, or alone."*
- *"It's a chance to learn better ways to cope with difficult family experiences or serious problems because, then, there are new ideas, support, and encouragement. You are not by yourself with the problem."*
- *"It's a chance to learn positive and healthy ways to solve family and personal problems, which will influence what happens in your family and change the way you, your child, and other family members interact."*

Once these ideas are presented, it may be helpful to ask the parent to think of one or two other benefits of being in treatment.

How We Provide Treatment

To give an orientation to the specific treatment used with parents and family, the therapist may offer a statement like the one presented in Therapist Example 6.2.

THERAPIST EXAMPLE 6.2

Sample Orientation to Treatment for Parents

"When we provide counseling here, we very much consider parents, children, and families to be on a team with us. We know from our experiences with other families that it takes every member of a team to make things work. So, we will start by meeting with you and your child to get right to work on some of the issues that got Child Protective Services in your life and the things that you want to change about yourself, your child, and/or your family. After you, your child, and I finish our work, we will then begin to meet with all of you together as a family. The family meetings will involve talking about what happened and learning a new way to solve problems and talk about conflicts that you have at home. For this, I will also be asking you to do some tasks at home. We will also be working on some ways to get rid of some of the stresses your family has. The counseling we will use is called cognitive-behavioral therapy and family therapy. We use this kind of counseling because there is some evidence from research studies that it can help families. As we work more together, I will show you what cognitive-behavioral therapy is."

Treatment Goals

Therapist Example 6.3 provides an introduction to the general goals and procedures that will be addressed during treatment. Of course, this overview is intended as a guide rather than a specific contract.

THERAPIST EXAMPLE 6.3

Sample Introduction to Treatment Goals for Parents

"Before we set out on any journey, we need to have an overall goal. If I want to go to the beach, I wouldn't just drive all over the place and hope I end up at a beach somewhere; I would decide on a particular beach. It would be my long-term goal, and I would set out on my trip, following the short-term goals of the rules of the road and points on my map. I would eventually reach my long-term goal of, say, Miami, Myrtle Beach *[therapist should name a familiar beach]*, or Yosemite Park *[pick a relevant location]*. It's the same here. We are going on a journey to learn new ways of thinking and dealing with issues in our lives. And we need to know what our long- and short-term goals are going to be. So, what do you see as long-term goals about your child and family you want to achieve? Here are some goals that I would like you to consider working towards.

"First, I want to help you improve self-control and appropriate feelings—help you learn how to stay in control and to make it less likely that your reactions and interactions at home could end up making you feel frustrated, angry with your child's behavior, or hurting your child in an effort to control his *[or her]* behavior.

"Second, We'll work on change. We can help you practice more effective ways of managing yourself and your child, improve your relationships with your kids, and learn new and/or effective parent skills to help your child change his *[or her]* behavior.

"Third, we'll work on problem solving: There are some ways to cope that allow you to solve problems and develop social supports."

Review Goal-Setting

It should be explained to the parent why goal setting is helpful and how to identify goals for the family. Generally, the parent will be asked to narrow down the goals to include those that are most important. The therapist can help by drawing upon what is known about the child and family from the assessment. Understandably, this discussion is facilitated to the extent that the therapist has shared information with the parent from the assessment. The goals should be written down on a goal-setting form so that, at the end of treatment, it will be easier to learn whether these short- and long-term goals were achieved. Parents can be asked to pick three long-term goals relating to an individual and/or the family. These goals should be practical and reflect what the parent wants to achieve by the end of the program. Then, the therapist should attempt to break these long-term goals down into short-term goals with the parent.

Next the therapist should clarify the current status of this long-term goal. The parent may find it easier to describe something happening right now that concerns him or her in specific terms, such as how often it happens or how much of a problem it is. Giving an example may be helpful (e.g., *"I get very mad and lose control when my child talks back to me"*). The short-term goals described by the parent could be as follows: (a) *"to learn to recognize when I begin to get mad"*; (b) *"to learn to recognize what I'm thinking that leads me to get mad"*; (c) *"to learn options to dealing with my anger"*; and (d) *"to learn positive parenting skills to manage my child when he or she talks back to me."*

The therapist should be sure that the long- and short-term goals are realistic for the parent. The therapist may need to provide help to the parent in deciding which goals are appropriate. This exercise is important in two ways: (a) it begins the process of helping parents feel less isolated as they realize that the difficulty they are having with their children is not uncommon, and (b) it establishes reasonable expectations for the parent. After development of the goals and a review of the goal setting form, the therapist can end the session as shown in Therapist Example 6.4.

THERAPIST EXAMPLE 6.4

Sample Ending for the Parental Goal-Setting Session

"Your involvement and commitment to participating in the program is the critical first step toward reaching these goals and making things better at home. My goal is to do all I can to make this happen. My job is to help you to feel more confident about yourself, be more effective as a parent, and have more options to use in solving problems that will come up at home. I'm here to help you reach the goals we just discussed. Do you have any questions about the goals or my role?"

Sample Targets/Domains to Be Covered During Treatment

Participants in treatment generally wish to know what is to be covered during treatment and how this information will be of use to them. Therapists should provide parents with an overview of the content areas to be discussed in treatment. A few examples of the skill domains to be examined in this book can be found in Therapist Example 6.5.

THERAPIST EXAMPLE 6.5

Sample Overview of Parental Skill Domains

"The first topic we'll cover is how to recognize and then minimize stress. We know that it is more difficult to be effective and act appropriately with children if parents are always feeling tense and stressed. This section will go through specific things that a parent can do to feel better even under the most stressful or anger-producing situations.

"The second topic covered is child development. This is important because, if you have higher expectations for your child than what your child can do at her [or his] age, then you have set yourself and your child up to fail. For example, I say to a two-year-old, 'Now go in your room and pick up all your toys, then put on your pajamas and go to bed.' This is beyond that child's ability because of her age, so when I get angry with her because she has disobeyed, it is really not fair to her.

"The third topic involves becoming more aware of what you think, how those thoughts affect how you feel, and ways to modify your negative thoughts and resulting feelings. Sometimes, we experience very intense emotions and find it hard to control these feelings; or, we think in ways that do not really help the situation, like when we blame others or see others as doing things purposely to bother us. Here, we will review ways to get calm—to chill-out—and to challenge our ideas or beliefs if they seem distorted—too negative or inaccurate.

"The fourth topic is effective child management. We will discuss nonviolent ways of helping your child listen better and behave. The fourth topic is, in a sense, problem solving. You will learn how to go through a step-by-step approach to solving child-rearing problems, which you might even use in other areas of your lives in which you have a problem.

"In addition to these topics, we will look at other things going on in your life that you may need help with. Also, I will be asking you right away to begin writing a letter of responsibility and apology to your child. This may feel uncomfortable at first, but once you begin working on it, you will want to do it because it allows you to stand up, take responsibility, and show the strength you have inside. Typically, we find that children respect their parents' taking responsibility for things they have done that have hurt the child. We will work together on this letter for a while, and then you can read it to the family in a family session when it is ready."

An Orientation for Child/Family Treatment

Therapist Background and Introductions. The therapist can start with the child by giving his or her name, position, and where he or she grew up, and by describing some interests. As the therapist describes his or her role, it is important to make sure the child knows that the therapist is not a part of CPS and that he or she works with many children. The role of the therapist can be explained as that of a helper, teacher, or friend: *"As your counselor I will meet with you every week and we will talk about you, your family, or how you are feeling about things, and I will be here to help you with things that may worry you about your family, school, friends, or other things you can decide on."*

To begin to get to know the child, the therapist can ask simple, nonthreatening questions. The therapist should also try to identify some similar interests, as well as some unique differences. Suggested topics include the child's age; where she or he lives; the number of siblings in the family and the family size; the child's school and grade; his or her interests or likes—hobbies or favorite food, sports, or TV shows; or unique characteristics or special history of the child.

Why You Are in This Program. To help the child gain an understanding of why he or she has been brought in for treatment, the therapist might use some of the following probes:

- *"Do you know why you are here, talking with me?"*
- *"It sounds like there are things at home that you would like to change. Let's talk a little about why you are here."*
- *"Sometimes, it is helpful for me to understand what happened in order to get to know you better and to really help you."*

At this point, the therapist should keep in mind that children might have different reactions to what happened. The child should be allowed to describe how she or he felt in reaction to the violence—therapists should not probe or push at this point for details. This particular topic is also addressed in more detail in a subsequent chapter.

Treatment Motivation and Preparation

Why Should You Do Anything? Some children may be hesitant to engage in treatment. To address this, the therapist might offer examples of what "some kids might say," and then respond to those comments, as in the following dialogue:

Child: It's not my problem, they've got the problem! Let them do the work!

Therapist: Your parents are learning things like this in their sessions, too.

Child: But I'm the kid, they're the adult and they're supposed to know how to act.

Therapist: You can influence how you're treated by your parents [and brothers/sisters]—help to change things for the better.

Child: I don't care anyway. I don't like them, don't care what they do to me, and don't want to spend any fun time with them.

Therapist: You may not feel good about what they've done or are doing to you, but this is a chance to change that and have better feelings about them and yourself.

Overview of the Program

In further addressing why the child is in treatment and how she or he might benefit, the therapist gives a rationale indicating that the child is not alone and acknowledging the home situation and the child's feelings. Therapist Example 6.6 offers an example of such a rationale applied in a group context.

THERAPIST EXAMPLE 6.6

Sample Treatment Rationale for Children

"What do you think you have in common with other children whose parents sometimes have arguments or fights with them? You might have already found something that you have in common with other children. If so, can you tell me what you've learned?

"There are a lot of children who are like you.

"There are many children from different families who have had similar experiences: That experience is having a parent who often seems angry with us, yells at us, fights with us, and sometimes may hurt us. They might hurt our feelings by saying mean things, or they might hurt us by hitting us, slapping us, pushing us, or throwing things at us. You may have experienced a lot of hurt at home. In some families, it may happen a lot; in other families, it may not happen very often. But, no matter how often it happens, most of you in this room probably wish that it happened less often."

"Another thing that sometimes happens at home is that even when you and your parents aren't fighting, you may not be real nice to each other. Maybe they're mad at each other or sad about all the fighting, or maybe they just gave up trying to talk to each other because every time they did they got in another fight, which is understandable. So, a lot of times parents and kids don't talk to each other much or, when they do, they're not too nice to each other. They forget to say 'please' and 'thank you,' or to ask about each other's day, or they forget how to ask for something nicely or how to discuss a problem calmly. They might not spend much time with each other doing nice stuff that parents and kids might do with their friends or neighbors, but don't do with each other."

The major points that the child should gain are that all families have disagreements and arguments, and that some families learn to solve those problems with force—by hitting or making threats to hurt—but the child's family can learn to handle their disagreements in a different way that does not involve hitting or hurting.

How We Provide Treatment

To give an orientation to the specific treatment used with children and families, the therapist may offer a statement like the one provided in Therapist Example 6.7.

THERAPIST EXAMPLE 6.7

Sample Orientation to Treatment for Children

"When we provide counseling here, we very much consider parents, kids, and families to be on a team with us. We know from our experiences with other families that it takes every member of a team to make things work. So, we will start by meeting with you and your parent to get right to work on some of the things that you want to change about yourself, your parent, or your family, and we'll begin to make sure you are safe and are not hurt again. After we finish our work with you and your parent, we will then begin to meet with all of you together as a family. The family meetings will involve talking about what happened and learning a new way to solve problems and talk about problems that you have at home. For this, I will also be asking your whole family to do some homework. The counseling we will use involves talking, teaching skills, and doing family work. We use this kind of counseling because there is some proof in research that it can help kids and families. As we work more together, I will show you what cognitive-behavioral therapy is.

"Now, for your part of the counseling, one of the things you will do is learn some new skills that will help you at home. I'll ask you to practice some of the things I'll teach you. These may be new ways to handle being angry, or what to say when your parents are upset with you. We will talk more about that soon.

[Next, the therapist reviews treatment session rules.]

"It is helpful to have rules we agree to so we can get everything done. This helps us know what we have to do and to get our work done easily. First, What we talk about here together is private. I may talk with other staff members about what we do in our sessions, but I won't tell your parents what you've said unless I feel you are in danger of getting hurt or of

hurting yourself or others. The law says that I have to do this when someone is in danger. I will talk to you first before I tell your parents about anything you've said.

"Sometimes when you come here, I'll ask you to answer some questions about how things are going—this might be information you can put
down on a piece of paper. If you need help, I'll help you. I'll ask you questions about how you and your parents got along that week. This information is also private. But you can share information about what we do
here with your parents.

"Second, it is really important to attend all the sessions. I can help you
better if you attend all of the sessions. Most of the time, we will talk
about something and then have a follow-up session or lesson the next
time. If you miss sessions, we'll fall behind in our lessons and work. Even
though it is your parents' responsibility to bring you here, you can still
encourage them to bring you to the sessions.

"Your parents are counting on you to work together with them on
making things better at home. Being here regularly will make it easier to
achieve this goal."

Goal Setting

Here, the therapist works with the child to set goals for treatment
as a way to check progress. The therapist should discuss the benefit of
having goals and tracking progress. We often ask the child initially
about current problems with others, parenting practices at home, and
what the child would "want to change" about his or her interactions
with parents. (See Therapist Example 6.8 for an example.)

THERAPIST EXAMPLE 6.8

Sample Goal Setting for Children

"For now, let's talk about the kinds of things you'd like to see different in
your home. Think about the kinds of things that bother you or make you
feel unhappy. If you could do anything you wanted to, what kinds of
things would you like to see change?"

[The child then fills out the goal-setting form with the therapist.]

"We go over this form so that when our sessions are over, we'll be
able to measure whether or not our goals have been achieved. Think
about this so that we can review your own ideas about what should be
improved."

Next, the therapist asks about problems with the child's own behavior. Are there any behaviors the child would change? (e.g., *"If you had a magic behavior wand and could wave it over your head and change any of your behaviors, which behavior would you change first (second, third)?"*)

We then discuss with the child some of his or her goals for treatment. Once identified, the therapist should summarize these goals (see Therapist Examples 6.11 and 6.12). In addition, the therapist reassures the child and parent that their involvement is one of the best steps toward helping make things better at home. The staff will do all they can to make this happen.

THERAPIST EXAMPLE 6.9

Reviewing the Child Goal-Setting Form

"How would you like to see each of these problems change? What would you like to have happen?

"It is helpful for us to know what you'd like to see happen at the end of these sessions—how you would like things to be different. This form helps us understand your goals—what you want to have happen."

THERAPIST EXAMPLE 6.10

Sample Ending of the Child Goal-Setting Session

"You have mentioned some goals you have—some ways that you would like your family life to be. Let me tell you some of my goals for you, things that I hope will help you reach your goals: I want (a) to help you learn ways to improve your safety at home; (b) to help you and your parents change so they can improve your relationships with each other; and (c) to teach you how to handle a crisis—emergencies."

The orientation ends with a recap of the session and overview of homework (e.g., *"On some days, we will end with a practice assignment. These are important. We have tried to make them simple and short, and I expect the homework to be done. We'll go over any homework at the start of the next session"*), along with several points that participants will learn in treatment, namely, that (a) other children have had or are having similar experiences—the child is not the only person to ever have these experiences and it is okay to talk about these experiences;

(b) there are ways to cope with difficult family experiences or serious problems, such as danger; and (c) there are new ways to influence what happens in the family—the child can change ways in which he or she interacts with family for the better.

Application, Comments, and Caveats. This goal-setting exercise is an important one, but its outcome may be hard to predict. An example of one of the more unusual but revealing products of this session derives from the treatment notes for a 7-year-old girl who was asked to identify some potential benefits to treatment. What she wrote down on paper were 10 different possible improvements or changes in her life that she desperately sought; she stated that these were the reasons she would participate in treatment. Here are a few of her "10 wishes":

- *"She* [the mother] *and I watching movies together that are for kids, so they are funny."*
- *"Me and her going to parks together when she's happy, because when she says no, she's too tired to go wherever I want to go."*
- *"When me and my mom go on rides that we both like."*

❏ Summary

In summary, the issues outlined above are important considerations for initiating clinical work with families where child maltreatment has occurred. Although discussed at the outset of treatment, these issues often require attention throughout the course of treatment. Doing so will help to form a solid base for implementing evidence-based treatment strategies.

References

Abney, V. D., & Gunn, K. (1993). A rationale for cultural competency. *APSAC Advisor, 6,* 19–22.

Ackerman, P. T., Newton, J. E. O., McPherson, W. B., Jones, J. G., & Dykman, R. A. (1998). Prevalence of Post Traumatic Stress Disorder and other psychiatric diagnoses in three groups of abused children (sexual, physical, or both). *Child Abuse & Neglect, 22,* 759–774.

Azar, S. T., & Wolfe, D. A. (1998). Child physical abuse and neglect. In E. J. Mash & R. A. Barkley (Eds.), *Treatment of childhood disorders* (2nd ed., pp. 501–544). New York: Guilford.

Brown, J., Cohen, P., Johnson, J. G., & Smailes, E. M. (1999). Childhood abuse and neglect: Specificity of effects on adolescent and young adult depression and suicidality. *Journal of the American Academy of Child and Adolescent Psychiatry, 38,* 1490–1496.

Cunningham, P. B., & Henggeler, S. W. (1999). Engaging multiproblem families in treatment: Lessons learned throughout the development of multisystemic therapy. *Family Process, 38,* 265–286.

Fontes, L. A. (1995). *Sexual abuse in nine North American cultures: Treatment and prevention.* Thousand Oaks, CA: Sage.

Fontes, L. A. (1998). Ethics in family violence research: Cross-cultural issues. *Family Relations: Interdisciplinary Journal of Applied Family Studies, 47,* 53–61.

Fontes, L. A., & Volker, T. (1996). Cultural issues in family therapy. In F. P. Piercy & D. H. Sprenkle (Eds.), *Family therapy sourcebook* (2nd ed., pp. 246–282). New York: Guilford.

Henggeler, S. W., Schoenwald, S. K., Borduin, C. M., Rowland, M. D., & Cunningham, P. B. (1998). *Multisystemic treatment of antisocial behavior in children and adolescents.* New York: Guilford.

Higgins, S. T., & Budney, A. J. (1993). Treatment of cocaine dependence through the principles of behavior analysis and behavioral pharmacology. In L. S. Onken, J. D. Blaine, & J. J. Boren (Eds.), *Behavioral treatments for drug abuse and dependence* (National Institute on Drug Abuse Research Monograph No. 137, NIH Publication No. 93-3684, pp. 97–122). Rockville, MD: National Institute on Drug Abuse.

Kazdin, A. E. (Ed.). (2000). *Encyclopedia of Psychology.* New York: Oxford University Press.

Kolko, D. J. (2000). Conduct disorder. In A. E. Kazdin (Ed.), *Encyclopedia of Psychology* (pp. 256–260). New York: Oxford University Press.

Patterson, G. R., & Chamberlain, P. (1988). Treatment process: A problem at three levels. In L. C. Wynne (Ed.), *The state of the art in family therapy research: Controversies and recommendations* (pp. 189–223). New York: Family Process Press.

Pelham, W. E., & Waschbusch, D. A. (1999). Behavioral intervention in Attention Deficit/Hyperactivity Disorder. In H. C. Quay & A. E. Hogan (Eds.), *Handbook of disruptive behavior disorders* (pp. 255–278). New York: Plenum.

Pfefferbaum, B. (1997). Posttraumatic stress disorder in children: A review of the past 10 years. *Journal of the American Academy of Child and Adolescent Psychiatry, 36,* 1503–1511.

Ponce, F. Q., & Atkinson, D. R. (1989). Mexican-American acculturation, counselor ethnicity, counseling style, and perceived counselor credibility. *Journal of Counseling Psychology, 36,* 203–208.

Schaap, C., Bennun, I., Schindler, L., & Hoogduin, K. (1993). *The therapeutic relationship in behavioral psychotherapy.* New York: John Wiley.

Schachar, R., & Ickowicz, A. (1999). Pharmacological treatment of Attention Deficit/Hyperactivity Disorder. In H. C. Quay & A. E. Hogan (Eds.), *Handbook of disruptive behavior disorders* (pp. 221–254). New York: Plenum.

Schoenwald, S. K., & Henggeler, S. W. (1999). Treatment of oppositional defiant disorder and conduct disorder in home and community settings. In H. C. Quay & A. E. Hogan (Eds.), *Handbook of disruptive behavior disorders* (pp. 475–493). New York: Plenum.

Spratt, E. G. (1997, April). *Joining hearts, hands, heads, and halos: Strengthening a community outreach child protection team through adoption of a Department of Social Services worker.* Collaborative community meeting, Mt. Pleasant, SC.

Steiner, H. (1997). Practice parameters for the assessment and treatment of children and adolescents with conduct disorder. *Journal of the American Academy of Child and Adolescent Psychiatry, 36,* 122S–139S.

Sue, S., Fujino, D., Hu, L., Takeuchi, D., & Zane, N. (1991). Community mental health services for ethnic minority groups: A test of the cultural responsiveness hypothesis. *Journal of Clinical and Consulting Psychology, 59,* 533–540.

Sue, S., & Zane, N. (1987). The role of culture and cultural techniques in psychotherapy: A critique and reformulation. *American Psychologist, 42,* 37–45.

Terrell, F., & Terrell, S. (1984). Race of counselor, client sex, cultural mistrust level, and premature termination from counseling among Black clients. *Journal of Counseling Psychology, 31*, 371–375.

Truscott, D. (1993). The psychotherapist's duty to protect: An annotated bibliography. *Journal of Psychiatry and Law, 21*, 221–244.

VandeCreek, L., & Knapp, S. (1993). *Tarasoff and beyond: Legal and clinical considerations in the treatment of life-endangering patients.* Sarasota, FL: Professional Resource Press.

7

Treatment of the Child Victim
Understanding the Child's Experiences and Behavior

The objectives of this chapter are threefold: (1) to describe how hostility and violence can be harmful and/or hurtful to children, (2) to elicit a dialogue about some of the more common causes of hostility and violence from a child's perspective, and (3) to provide a context for learning and practicing ways of coping with hostility and violence. We suggest the use of a few supplementary materials, described herein, that may help to introduce the topic and to minimize the child's reluctance to discuss these experiences.

❏ Perspectives on the Child's Experiences With Family Hostility and Violence

PROCESSING THE ABUSE EXPERIENCE

Background and Overview

When abuse has occurred, an essential part of treating children and families is directly addressing the abuse by talking about it, determining what led up to the abuse, assessing and correcting distorted cognitions about the abuse, and making a plan to prevent reabuse. In some cases, children do not have extreme anxiety about the abuse, but talking about it is stressful and they may benefit from both support from a family member and skills training to help them manage the stress and process the abuse. In addition, children may need skills training regarding how to cope with general problems that may not specifically relate to the abuse. Most of the techniques described in this section can be used with any child to assist in the therapeutic process of talking about the abuse and to enhance general coping skill. A later chapter reviews the use of graduated exposure with children who have extreme anxiety related to the abuse. Of course, any such discussion requires good rapport with the child and a sensitivity to the child's willingness at the time to divulge what are sometimes very upsetting details of an abusive experience.

Description of Procedure

Children who have experienced physical abuse often need an opportunity to discuss what happened to them, and to address their feelings and thoughts about the abuse. This context may allow them to view physical violence in a different light, for example, that it serves as an inappropriate form of child discipline. Our approach is to have a general discussion on family violence and physical abuse before the therapist directs the child to discuss what happened at the time of the abuse. Therapists should keep in mind that the child may not be traumatized from the abusive event and may not even view it as abuse. If the child has not experienced the event as traumatic, the goal for the therapist is to help the child view physical violence as a less desired alternative to solving problems during parent-child interaction and to come to some closure on the experience.

Therapeutic work may set the stage for the child openly to discuss with the parent his or her feelings about conflict in the family and alternatives to physical aggression for managing family conflict. General processing of the abuse experience includes a review of what happened during the abusive event, the child's belief about culpability, and other cognitions about the abuse and feelings the family may have toward the child. The therapist should be clear regarding specific events that the child would like the parent to include in an apology letter, what the child would like the parent to know regarding how he or she feels about the abuse, and any questions the child has for the parent. All of this information will be brought into the clarification family meeting. In our experience, the first aspect of this process involves eliciting information about the child's general and specific experiences with conflicts.

Describing Family Problems and Feelings About Them. Abused children vary in their willingness to acknowledge, disclose, and describe abusive and other distressing experiences. Thus, some children will be quite forthcoming in their reports during the early portion of treatment, whereas others may be reluctant to discuss what happened to them for some time. To make this discussion easier to initiate, children should first be reminded about the different types of family problems they have reported or experienced by referring to them in a clear, reassuring manner, as suggested by this brief statement:

> *The safety and happiness of all children is everyone's responsibility because we want you to grow up to be happy, healthy adults. If you are hurt and learn not to like yourself, this won't happen. So, that's why you and your parents are getting help. We are all working together to make things better for you and for them.*

An initial approach to eliciting these difficult details is to talk to children about events that have hurt their feelings as a prelude to a discussion of more traumatic experiences. A sample introduction to the topic that may help to legitimize the discussion of this issue and their experiences during treatment is found in Therapist Example 7.1. One important point to emphasize is that many of the children seen in a therapeutic setting have experienced different types of family problems and that these may be quite common in some families (e.g., saying things that bother us and doing things that hurt us).

THERAPIST EXAMPLE 7.1

Sample Introductory Script to Eliciting Family Problems

"Sometimes, family members or other close friends say things that bother us and do things that hurt us—these can be very common in a lot of families. Now, lots of things can make us feel very bad (words) or hurt us (acts). For example, some children are being emotionally hurt, like when others use words to be mean or critical. Some children are being physically hurt—hurt, like when they get hit or pushed. There are some families where this occurs from parent to child and from child to parent. At times, different family members have done things that have hurt others in their own family.

   "Parents sometimes do things that may hurt a child—like, hitting (or getting out of control, hurting others, or using physical force or violence). Some kids may then copy this kind of behavior and imitate this. What usually happens in a family like this? Sometimes, parents may forget to protect others or they may have trouble being supportive or helpful when this is needed. Maybe something like this has even happened to you or someone in your family."

Identifying Unpleasant Parent-Child Interactions. It is then important to relate these statements about family problems to something
that the child has said (e.g., some form of punishment the child mentioned or a statement about being ignored). This provides a context in
which to discuss the various experiences involving emotional or physical mistreatment to which the child has been exposed. Although not
all children will be willing or able to provide this information, some
children may be ready for it and may even believe that it was "about
time" that they did so. One approach to this task is simply to request
that the child describe what parents (or caretakers) do that hurts or
upsets the child. The following paragraph may be helpful as a summary of this routine:

> *Just because these things have happened at home doesn't mean that your
> parents are crazy, hate you, or cannot change (i.e., that you should feel hope-
> less), and it doesn't mean that there's something wrong with you or that
> you've done something wrong either. Don't forget we are here to help you
> and your family—we'll be available to you if you need us (if you have spe-
> cial needs), and you are not alone.*

Reading and Discussing Background Materials. There are several
examples of materials that can be read and discussed to illustrate some
of the ways in which children have been verbally and/or physically
mistreated, and to model some of the responses made to these types of
experiences. One book, *Mama, Don't Hurt Me* (Stanek, 1987), provides
a story that was read as part of the Project IMPACT (Interventions to
Maximize Parent and Child Togetherness) outcome study (Kolko,
1996a, 1996b). The book can be read at home or aloud during the session before asking the child to comment on the story. For example, the
child can be asked to explain what happened and what kinds of things
made the child in the story feel upset, hurt, or worried. The child can
also be asked if any of these things have happened to him or her. In
this case, it is important to try to get some details of the situation while
showing support for the child's experiences. Other questions to be
addressed with the child include situations that made life hard for the
parent (e.g., the spouse left, or the parent had no money or no job).

Communication and Feeling: What People Say and Do Can Hurt.
One initial probe can simply suggest that the therapist and child talk
a little about what people say to each other and whether the child has
heard people say certain things. If the child seems amenable, one
way to understand a child's experience is to ask questions about what
people close to him or her say or do *"in ways that may hurt, bother, or
upset you."* It may be useful to emphasize that these behaviors can be

ones that hurt their feelings or their bodies, and may take a variety of forms (e.g., people saying, *"Hey, stupid, bring that over here"*; *"I wish you were never born"*; or *"You are disgusting. . . . Just get out of here"*). One related approach to eliciting this information is to give the child a piece of paper with a large circle on it (*"Imagine this is a whole pie, like the kind you would buy in a store"*) and to ask the child to create pie slices that reflect different types of parental acts that fit this description of things that can hurt. Each slice should represent the approximate frequency with which the child has experienced that action. Box 7.1 shows an example of the unpleasant experiences reported by one of the children seen in the Project IMPACT outcome study. The pie chart shows the often typical pattern of experiencing considerable emotional or psychological forms of mistreatment, with some experience of physical discipline or coercion. At times, children will prefer to compose the pie chart themselves before providing the completed outline to the therapist.

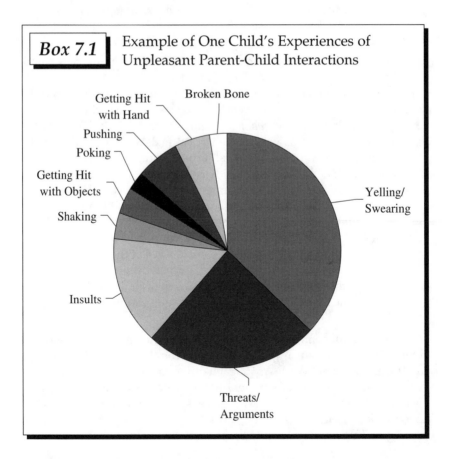

Box 7.1   Example of One Child's Experiences of Unpleasant Parent-Child Interactions

Once the child is amenable to discussing personal circumstances, various questions may be asked relating to a specific situation or event (i.e., what, who, when, how, and why). For example, the child can be asked how people usually feel when this happens (e.g., *"We feel hurt, sad, scared, bad, angry, and mad. No one likes to be put down or criticized"*). Other questions include how a person might respond or react when this happens to them (e.g., *"We tend to believe things these people tell us; we may act this way, say the same things to others, try to hurt others, run away or be afraid, or stop trusting others"*).

Alternatively, stories can be read to children of different ages to provide a context for this discussion, especially if they are reluctant to disclose these types of details. The older child could read one or more stories in *Emotional Abuse: Words Can Hurt* (Brassard & Hart, 1987, pp. 5–10) or the special edition of the *Spider-Man* comic book devoted to verbal abuse (Marvel Comics, 1987) and its accompanying *Teacher's Guide to Spider-Man on Emotional Abuse* (National Committee to Prevent Child Abuse, 1988). The younger child may find it helpful to read *The Hurt* (Doleski & McNichols, 1983). For those children who need an even more direct discussion of these types of interactions, other materials may be helpful (e.g., *About Emotional Abuse and Neglect of Children*, 1996). Sometimes, it may be useful to ask the child to discuss and learn about the reasons why an adult may hurt his or her feelings (e.g., *"They are stressed and feeling badly themselves"*; *"They think this will help get you to do something"*; *"They, too, were hurt this way as children and they are used to it"*).

Specific questions can be used to guide an understanding of the child's perceptions of the critical or coercive interactions contained in these stories or, perhaps, their own lives. The therapist can ask the child to review the featured child's behaviors in one scenario and to identify which, if any, apply to his or her family. Then, the child can be encouraged to indicate the degree to which each behavior depicted in the story is problematic or upsetting, as some may be especially common and bothersome. It is helpful to write down the behaviors that are of most concern on a sheet of paper for later reference.

Other questions to address include how the child usually feels about people when mistreated by them in this way (e.g., *"They don't care about me"*; *"They're really angry and mad at me"*; *"That's the way all adults act"*). Some physically abused children appreciate their contribution to a given disciplinary event and, perhaps, even request suggestions on what they can do when a similar situation involving parental escalation occurs.

At these times, it is important to remind the child that there may be opportunities to demonstrate appropriate behavior, but that, regardless of the child's behavior, it is not the child's responsibility to contain the parent's coercive behaviors. When pressed for these types of suggestions, we have occasionally found it helpful to describe several potential responses, such as the following:

- *"Stop and think about what's going on with this person."*
- *"Ask yourself if there's some reason why this person would be saying hurtful words."*
- *"Take a break and get away from the person for awhile, until things calm down, then talk to the person later to find out what they might have been responding to."*
- *"Tell them how the things they say make you feel"; "Show your willingness to help them and help yourself."*

There will be many times when the situation has nothing to do with what the child said or did, such that the child may be able to understand that the person was upset about something else.

❏ Contributors to Coercive or Stressful Interactions

This section is designed to help the child learn (a) how to appreciate the various contributors (or "causes") of a problem, (b) why some situations can cause problems, (c) how behavior can affect these problems, and (d) positive behaviors that may minimize the effects or impact of these problems.

STRESS MANAGEMENT FOR CHILDREN

Background and Definition

Discussions of the child's exposure to problem situations, not just an abusive experience, may raise questions about the reasons for what happened and, in particular, the nature of the child's role in such events. Because what the child believes about the abusive experience and his or her ability to determine what really happened may be unclear, we find it helpful to teach the child some basic behavior (i.e., functional) analysis (see Kazdin, 2001; Paniagua, 2001). Simply telling the child that others are responsible for the abuse, although correct, may not be sufficiently instructive or helpful with some children.

Description of Procedure

Identify potential contributors (antecedents) to problems. The first aspect of this behavior analysis formulation to be covered is one of the most difficult concepts to grasp. It is important to help the child understand what is meant by the concept of an antecedent without actually using the term *antecedent*—for example, by saying, *"What happens before something may influence the outcome of that event."* One can introduce the exercise by reminding the child that what happens *before* they argue or get hurt by their parents can help to determine whether or not they will argue with or get hurt by their parents, or how bad the argument will be.

One way to illustrate this topic is to play the "What Things Cause Problems" game. In this activity, therapists should identify antecedents with younger children by asking them to generate a list of potential precursors of any recent negative parent-child interactions. When needed, help the child generate the list by providing word cues from the game and getting the child to discuss them. For example, with respect to money, the child could be asked, *"Can money affect how someone feels? Why or how?"* If necessary, more direct probes could be issued, such as, *"Could anything happen with money that could give your parents unhappy feelings?"* A sample description of this activity can be found in Therapist Example 7.2.

THERAPIST EXAMPLE 7.2

Sample Activity for Identifying and Discussing Antecedents to Parental Problems

"Let's say you come home from school, and as soon as you walk in the door, you get into a fight with your mom. Well, all the stuff that happened to your mom all day long while you were at school probably influenced the way she felt and whether you two were going to fight. Things that happen to parents, who might not always be able to cope easily with the things that put them in a bad mood or give them unpleasant or unhappy feelings, sometime make them more likely to get into a fight with or hurt their kids.

"What kinds of things could happen to your parents that might put them in a bad mood or give them unpleasant (sad or angry) feelings?" *[Have the child list several antecedents.]*

"Are these things fun/good/positive or unpleasant/negative/difficult? Unpleasant things that give people unhappy feelings are called stressors."

Identify stressful events or problems that parents experience. As illustrated in Box 7.2, one follow-up exercise involves dividing a list into three columns labeled *Me, My Parents,* and *Outside of My Family.* The child can be asked to identify stressors (i.e., contributing problems) associated with each source. This exercise can show that there are multiple stressors in different domains, which might not otherwise be identified by the child. The therapist should indicate that many of these stressors can occur at the same time (i.e., that they can combine in several ways). It may help to depict these concepts visually by combining the antecedent pictures in sequential fashion.

Box 7.2 Results of an Exercise to Identify Stressful Events in One Family

Me	My Parents	Outside of My Family
disobedient	alcohol or drugs	financial problems
nag, pester	short temper	got fired
push limits	in a bad mood	Child Protective Services worker yelled at mom
fight with sister/brother	fighting with each other	school problems
bored	tired, ill	
talk back, yell	busy trying to do something	
clumsy, have an accident	make a mistake	
friends rejecting me		

Once the events are described, the therapist can discuss the child's degree of control over the *Me* versus *Parent* versus *Outside of My Family* list (e.g., asking *"Which can you change?"*) in an effort to highlight that only those circumstances directly involving the child can be controlled by the child. In this context, it is helpful to emphasize that control means *"what you can change, what you can do differently, or what you can fix."* For each item on the list, the child can be asked, *"If you tried something different, would the stressor go away?"* Then, one can discuss the child's control over each item in the three lists (focusing primarily on the *Me* list), and then order the items by the degree to which the child exercises control over them. The therapist can also help the older child understand the potential role of different contributors to conflictual situations. That is, one can distinguish between stressful events (e.g., working two jobs or having a bad day) and other circumstances that may mediate or influence these events (e.g., drinking alcohol, feeling sad, or having a child who is fighting or being defiant).

Comments and Caveats

The therapist should appreciate the difficulty that some children will have in recognizing how much control they can exert over certain events. Furthermore, some events will appear to relate to all three of the columns because each is, in part, a source of influence. The overall theme to bear in mind here is that the child should begin to better understand the events for which others are generally responsible.

❏ Understanding How We Respond to Different Problem Situations

IDENTIFYING OUR REACTIONS TO INDIVIDUAL EVENTS

Background and Definition

The preceding section emphasizes that problem situations are often affected by different events or behaviors shown by several individuals, rather than being influenced primarily by a single person's behavior. This section seeks to help the child understand his or her own reactions to a given event or a series of events, highlighting the fact that she or he may exhibit different reactions and that these responses may not always be compatible (or "in sync") with one another. What is important to understand at this point is the fact that children respond very differently to similar events and that an understanding of how they respond to these events may help them be better prepared to address them in the future. This includes common cognitive, emotional, and behavioral reactions shown by abused children following exposure to violence.

This can be illustrated using any recent situation the child is willing to discuss. The clinician should attempt to identify the nature and extent of the child's various reactions to an everyday event, followed by a similar discussion in response to his or her exposure to a conflictual, coercive, or abusive event. It may be helpful simply to document each response and then to ask details about each one for comparison purposes.

Description of Procedure

Overview of the Cognitive-Behavioral Model. The clinician should make an effort to explain the importance of this model for understanding how the child has responded to the abusive experience and other conflicts she or he has experienced. The following paragraph in Therapist Example 7.3 serves as some introductory comments.

THERAPIST EXAMPLE **7.3**
Introduction to the Cognitive-Behavioral Model

"Different situations or things that happen may affect each of us differently. You may react to them differently, too. We have different experiences, and these experiences help us learn how to respond to things. Sometimes, we're prepared for something, but at other times we're not. It is important to be able to identify stressful situations and how you respond to them, especially the really upsetting ones. This helps us to change our thoughts about the situation, our feelings, and then our behavior. This can sometimes make the situation better. The goal is to keep ourselves in control of our thoughts, our feelings, and our behavior, and get relaxed, not more upset."

The child should be given an explanation of the basic components of the cognitive-behavioral model, which are outlined in Box 7.3 (e.g., *"Feelings are just one of the ways we react to things that happen. We also have certain thoughts or we may do different things when something happens to us"*). The therapist should write down and explain each of the terms in the model before attempting to elicit details of a recent situation that can be used to illustrate it.

Box 7.3   Basic Cognitive-Behavioral Model

                    Thoughts
Situation →   Feelings   → Consequences (Other Reactions)
                Actions (Behavior)

Simple language should be used to introduce both this topic and the notion that we may respond in different ways to a situation. Briefly, we offer the following descriptive explanations: (a) thoughts (*"These include what pops into your head, what you say to yourself, and your beliefs or ideas about yourself, people, and things"*), (b) feelings (*"How you feel at the moment about something, like feelings about yourself or your behavior"*), and (c) behavior (*"What you do or say"*). The clinician should simply list carefully each response for use elsewhere in the discussion.

The purpose of obtaining some details about a recent incident is simply to provide the child with an understanding of the terms in the model and some practice in identifying any of the specific reactions made in response to a given situation. Once the child understands the model, the therapist can begin to examine various responses to different events, especially those that have been difficult or challenging for the child.

Case Application

Susan was a 9-year-old girl who was very talkative about different aspects of her life, including the stressful circumstances to which she was exposed and which were related to her physical mistreatment. During a discussion of these events, she proceeded to draw some pictures depicting several recent interactions in which her parents exhibited conflictual or unpleasant behaviors. Some of these pictures are included in Box 7.4. In one case, for example, Susan's illustration showed her crying after being yelled at by her mother for having earlier damaged her mother's vase. In another situation, the father was shown raising his fist towards Susan's mother; this event occurred after the father had returned home from a local bar.

Box 7.4	Examples of Depictions of Stressful Circumstances Associated With Family Violence/Force

❏ Summary

This chapter has addressed the task of identifying the nature and extent of the child's experience of a range of both emotional and physical violence. In our experience, just eliciting this information can be very difficult for many children, so it is important to approach this session systematically but carefully. Although it is important to understand the child's experiences, it is also important to try to follow the child's lead and to avoid forcing the child to articulate these experiences. Thus, the therapist may be able to directly inquire into these experiences or use stories and other third-person probes to gain access to this information. Once such information is obtained, the child may give evidence of various contributors and responses to these situations, which may prove useful in influencing the specific techniques selected for use later in therapy. Such information may provide some initial understanding of the risks for and consequences of the child's involvement in physically abusive behavior.

References

About emotional abuse and neglect of children (1996). South Deerfield, MA: Channing L. Bete.

Brassard, M. R., & Hart, S. N. (1987). *Emotional abuse: Words* can *hurt.* Chicago, IL: National Committee to Prevent Child Abuse.

Doleski, T., & McNichols, W. H. (1983). *The hurt.* New York: Paulist.

Kazdin, A. E. (2001). *Behavior modification in applied settings* (6th ed.). Belmont, CA: Wadsworth.

Kolko, D. J. (1996a). Clinical monitoring of treatment course in child physical abuse: Child and parent reports. *Child Abuse & Neglect, 20*, 23–43.

Kolko, D. J. (1996b). Individual cognitive behavioral treatment and family therapy for physically abused children and their offending parents: A comparison of clinical outcomes. *Child Maltreatment, 1*, 322–342.

National Committee to Prevent Child Abuse. (1988). *Teacher's guide to Spider-Man on emotional abuse.* Chicago, IL: Author.

Marvel Comics. (1987). *Spider-Man* [Special issue on verbal abuse, Vol. 1, No. 1]. New York: Marvel Entertainment.

Paniagua, F. A. (2001). Functional analysis and behavioral assessment of children and adolescents. In V. H. Booney & A. Pumariega (Eds.), *Clinical assessment of child and adolescent behavior* (pp. 32–85). New York: John Wiley.

Stanek, M. (1987). *Mama, don't hurt me.* Niles, IL: Albert Whitman.

8

Treatment of the Child
Cognitive Interventions

This chapter describes cognitive interventions that may be used with a child to address thoughts and feelings related to violence and physical abuse. We will discuss first how to gain an understanding of the child's views and experiences with violence in general, as well as within families in particular. Next, we address the child's perception of the impact of violence on him- or herself. Finally, we present ways to educate the child on misattributions and misperceptions that sometimes occur with physical abuse.

❏ Clarifying and Changing the Child's View of Violence

A DEFINITION OF VIOLENCE

A next logical step in discussing problem situations is to examine the child's views about the abuse experience that served as a referral for treatment and violence in general. This section expands upon the prior section, which sought to elicit information about the child's level of exposure to hostility and abusive behavior, by attempting to understand how these experiences influence the child's overall impression of role and utility of these events. It can be explained to the child that family members or close friends . . .

> *"may do things that hurt one another, like when they hit or hurt others (or get out of control, use physical force, or threaten to hurt us—for example, by raising a fist, making a face, yelling, or screaming). This is like what happens in all kinds of recent situations* [here, the therapist may use appropriate recent examples of movies or news events, like, for example, the Terminator or Bart Simpson]. *This is sometimes what others mean when they use the words* force *or* violence."

The therapist should carefully consider what language to use in describing the abusive acts to which the child has been exposed (e.g., being hit or faced with a raised fist, having faces made at him or her, or being yelled at); obviously, the terms should be ones that the child seems to prefer or has used to represent these experiences.

DESCRIPTION OF PROBES FOR EVALUATION AND DISCUSSION

Because aggression or violence is perhaps the most common or robust consequence of child physical abuse (CPA), it is important to extend the dialogue on exposure to family conflict, force, or violence by discussing the child's own views about such events and about the general use of force or coercion to influence others. One method for promoting this discussion is to ask the child to respond to some questions about the role and impact of aggressive behavior. A series of relevant questions on this topic were reported originally with adult victims by Sinclair (1985) in the context of a counseling program for victims of domestic abuse.

These questions were modified for use with physically abused children in the Project IMPACT (Interventions to Maximize Parent and Child Togetherness) outcome study to elicit their views on violent behavior (Kolko, 1996, 2002). Where possible, we found it helpful to ask the child to answer each question with a yes/no response and then to discuss the answers to elicit their views on violence. Each question was designed to evaluate a topic for discussion regarding the child's attitude toward violence and the degree to which she or he accepts it as a self-control or conflict resolution technique. Box 8.1 lists the questions and the responses from one of the children in the Project IMPACT study. It can be seen that the child endorses certain views or beliefs that seem supportive of the use of aggressive behavior and protective of the individual who exhibits the behavior. Such information may provide a glimpse into one of the potential mechanisms by which coercive behavior is transmitted across the generations.

| **Box 8.1** | Questions for Probing a Child's Perceptions of Family Violence |

Parents and Children

Here are some statements about how parents react to their children. Check off whether you agree or disagree with these statements by checking *Yes* or *No*. There are no wrong or right answers. We will then discuss your answers.

	Mother	*Son*
Parents who hit their children are "crazy."	No	Yes
Alcohol causes parents to beat their children.	Yes	Yes
Only poor children get beaten.	No	No
Children do things that make their parents angry, so they deserve to be hit.	Yes(?) (Don't know)	No
Children need to be beaten to help them learn how to behave properly.	Yes (Smacked once in a while)	Yes
If children really didn't want to be hit, they would tell the adult to stop, or they would tell another adult.	Yes	No
Parents who beat their children are a danger to others in the community.	No	Yes

SOURCE: Adapted from Sinclair (1985). Reprinted by permission.

APPLICATION EXAMPLE

Once this first specific set of questions is completed, the child can be asked more generally what she or he thinks about the use of force, hitting, and/or violence between people (e.g., *"I think it would be important for us to discuss what you think about the use of force, hitting, and/or violence between people"*). Any and all types of coercive or violent behavior raised by the child is appropriate for discussion. The child's statements may be helpful in determining whether his or her views are likely to conflict with the "system's" views of aggressive behavior or with the ultimate goals of treatment. Furthermore, this discussion provides the therapist with an opportunity to examine individual differences in the child's general values and beliefs, which may provide some direction for treatment. For this discussion, we draw upon questions adapted from the work of Sinclair (1985) with victims of domestic violence, as well as the work of Alessi and Hearn (1984) and Jaffe, Wolfe, and Wilson (1990) with children of battered women. The questions that were modified for use in the Project IMPACT outcome study are listed here:

- *"Do you like action shows, fighting, or violence on TV?"*
- *"Is it okay for a man to hit a woman (and vice versa)?"*
- *"Is it okay for parents to hit their kids—to use some type of physical force or punishment?"*
- *"Is it okay for children to hit their siblings or parents?"*

The clinician should look for supportive views towards aggression in the statements that children make in response to these probes and incorporate them as much as possible in a summary of responses designed to challenge the child's views of aggressive behavior (see Therapist Example 8.1). Such information may be helpful in understanding the impact of abusive behavior on child victims.

THERAPIST EXAMPLE 8.1

Children's Views on Family Violence and Responses to Them

View: Violence is an okay form of conflict resolution.

"But, does it work in the long run?"
"Doesn't it require lots of physical and emotional energy?"

View: There are few consequences if violence is reported.

"What happens if you get hurt?"
"Is this a crime? Can you go to jail/court?"

View: Inequality of power (sexism/racism) is encouraged.

"If we see others as not as good as us, don't we do or say things that upset their feelings and make them feel bad about us?"
"If we say hurtful words and put down someone, how will they feel?" (e.g., sad, worried, afraid, etc.)
"How will they treat others?" (e.g., do the same thing to other people, etc.)

View: Victims should just tolerate this behavior and see themselves as responsible (victims deserve what happens to them).

"But, is that usually what happens?"
"Sometimes we feel responsible for people acting mean toward us and we feel, 'What's the use?' Sometimes we feel angry, or sad, or mad or worried, or afraid. These feelings keep us from enjoying our lives and the people we care about. That's why it's important not to feel responsible and not to let ourselves just sit and tolerate this behavior. It's important for you and your parents to get help so this will stop happening."

SOURCE: Adapted from Sinclair (1985). Reprinted by permission.

❏ Normalization of the Child's Abused-Related Feelings and Reactions

DESCRIPTION AND EXPLANATION OF PROCEDURE

The therapist should focus next on understanding the child's perceptions of the impact of being exposed to individuals or incidents associated with violent or aggressive behavior. A general probe, like the one following, may be useful to introduce the topic: *"How might a person respond when this happens to them?* [The therapist waits for the child's reactions.] *We tend to believe things these people tell us. We may act this way by doing similar things, say the same things to others, try to hurt others, run away or be afraid, or stop trusting others."*

A child can be asked questions about what might happen to children who live in families where violence is used, allowing the child to draw upon personal experience if she or he is comfortable doing so (e.g., *"So, how do you think this type of experience affects kids? How about you?"*). This is often necessary to help the child feel more comfortable about having various experiences related to his or her history of being abused and to encourage the child to be able to ask questions about the nature and course of these experiences. Some children will be able to suggest several plausible reactions; others will need therapist prompting to guess or make suggestions.

APPLICATION EXAMPLE

With this diversity in responses in mind, several possible outcomes of such exposure could be covered, as listed in Box 8.2, by asking the child about the kinds of experiences that children who have been exposed to CPA may have.

Box 8.2 | Potential Consequences Experienced by Child Physical Abuse Victims

A good chance that the child will be hurt more

Possibly taken out of the family and placed in another home for safety

May become very sad, depressed, and unhappy

May become very angry, and yell, scream, and hit others

May see him- or herself as a bad person who caused the violence and blames him- or herself for all the family's problems

---

Box 8.2   *continued*

May not like him- or herself very much and may feel that they can never be a loveable person (may have low self-esteem)

May see him- or herself as having no control over anything and being powerless to do things to make their lives better (i.e., may see self as externally controlled → dependent → overly compliant, anxious to please others)

May have little patience, reduced frustration level, and an inability to cope with things in a positive way

May become very worried, nervous, and unable to relax (e.g., hypervigilant)

May feel confused, betrayed, or outraged by what happened

May feel she or he deserved to be hurt

May withdraw from other people and not talk (be uncommunicative)

May be in denial and/or very defensive about what happened

May be stoic (neutral) and willing to tolerate pain or suffering

---

Certainly, some children come to perceive themselves as problematic or defective and, ultimately, as being too strange or disturbed to be helped by a counselor. What may be even more subtle, but potentially more worrisome, are those children who give evidence of being stoic in the face of parental or family adversity, especially harsh punishment or violence. This is of clinical concern because such children may not make their angry or anxious feelings known to others, may not seek assistance or help, and may actually tolerate levels of pain or abuse that could be dangerous. Thus, it is important to be somewhat skeptical of those children who appear to suggest that what happened to them "was no big deal." For example, in one of our case discussions, a child had to be reminded of the referral incident and the fact that his mother had hit him in the head with a metal stick that caused bleeding and a visit to the hospital. In a second case involving a young girl, the therapist learned of a strong desire to please or be appropriate when she was asked to talk about the things she liked to do with her mother. The activities she reported without hesitation were sweeping floors, cleaning her room, and cleaning her bed, because she felt that she needed to be "considerate" of her mother.

Comments and Caveats

The list in Box 8.2 is not meant to be exhaustive, but, instead, to reflect some of the more common types of reactions shown by physically abused children, in our experience. Upon noting these types of consequences, the therapist may also wish to help the parent understand the child's clinical presentation and to gain some perspective on how such an experience has affected other children. Of course, it is not necessary to place all of the child's reactions into this framework; indeed, one would not want to encourage the parent to be hypervigilant in monitoring and examining the child's everyday behavior and activities. The fact that children do show similar reactions to similar circumstances may be comforting enough to the parents as they seek to navigate the intervention process.

❏ Psychoeducation About Physical Abuse

DEFINITION AND EXPLANATION OF WHAT THE LAWS SAY

We have found it useful to help the child understand something about the child's and maltreating parent's involvement in the Child Protective Services (CPS) system and any resulting intervention program. Even more than their maltreating caregivers, most children have no appreciation for the existence and functions of these systems. Thus, the therapist can provide information on this topic to the child that may be comforting and instructive.

The first point is that there are laws in this country specifically designed to keep caregivers from inflicting injuries or hurting children. This statement is a revelation to some children, as they have always been led to believe that the parent's abusive behavior is both justified and socially appropriate. Furthermore, it may help a child recognize that the parent's possibly mandated involvement with the system and any ensuing interventions is simply due to society's efforts to comply with these laws. Such information may help the child to recognize that all such incidents are illegal and in violation of social norms, and that the parent's involvement with CPS does not simply imply that this parent was singled out for punishment or is being unfairly treated. In essence, it is important to convey that these laws are designed primarily to protect children and, ultimately, their families.

The second point is to help the child disaggregate discipline and harm. One of the circumstances that often underlies a child's minimization of the seriousness or concern surrounding an abusive experience is the child's belief that punishment is conveyed by inflicting harm or injury on someone. Many children come to believe, because of parental declarations, that discipline needs to be harsh or hurtful. Thus, they do not perceive their experiences of physical punishment as inappropriate or undesirable. In these instances, then, the therapist may wish to emphasize that discipline is both legitimate and useful, but is not synonymous with inflicting pain.

The third point is that the therapist and, when relevant, the caseworker have a genuine concern regarding the child's and the family's welfare and safety. Insofar as the processing of many such cases eventuates in considerable confusion and hostility directed towards the system (which includes the therapist), the child may not perceive the therapist as serving an honorable and beneficial role. Therapists are encouraged to underscore their desire to be helpful to the child and to promote the child's personal needs, which may serve to counter this initially adversarial perspective.

CHILDREN'S ATTRIBUTIONS OF RESPONSIBILITY FOR VIOLENCE

One of the more important consequences of CPA is that some children perceive themselves as responsible for the violence that occurs in their lives, such as the violence between their parents or when their parents are violent towards them. For example, one of the children in the Project IMPACT outcome study noted, almost in passing, *"that if I hadn't called my dad a bum, he would never have hit me."* This brief statement highlighted this child's perception of the cause of the abusive experience and his belief that he could have stopped any such incident from happening in the first place. Although one can appreciate how these views may develop following some circumstances, they are often inaccurate explanations of the reasons for these events. Therapist Example 8.2 provides an introduction for a responsibility discussion.

THERAPIST EXAMPLE 8.2

Who Is Responsible for the "Violence" (Hitting, Hurting, etc.)?

"Some children may see themselves as responsible for the violence that occurs in their lives, such as the violence between their parents and when their parents are violent toward them. Although children may do things their parents really don't like, they need to be reminded that parents are responsible for the ways they treat (and respond to) their children. This is true, even if children do or say things to their parents. All children misbehave and do things that can make parents upset; they may even do and say hurtful things to their parents. But, no matter how they feel or what they do or say, children should understand that they are not responsible for their parents' or any adult's behavior. No child is responsible for how these adults decide to behave. You are only responsible for yourself and how you decide to behave."

As responsibility for the abuse is discussed, the therapist can let the child know that the parent is preparing a letter for the child and family in which the parent takes responsibility for the abuse, and that, after the letter is complete, the family will be meeting to discuss the letter and what happened. (See Chapter 14 for information on preparing the child victim for the clarification meeting.)

CHILDREN'S INVOLVEMENT IN AGGRESSIVE BEHAVIOR

Although children are not responsible for the violent acts directed at them, it may be helpful to encourage them to consider the offender's situation in order accurately to depict this responsibility and to show the potential similarity between the parent's behavior and any child aggression. Comments, such as the following, may facilitate this discussion: *"If a parent uses violence, how do you think they might be feeling? . . . Are they always happy? No—they have different types of feelings. Sometimes they feel sad, angry at themselves, disappointed, worried, frustrated, or nervous."*

The therapist may also find it helpful to ask the child about his or her own likelihood of using force and violence in managing his or her own relationships or in trying to influence the outcomes of various interpersonal situations (e.g., *"Do you think you'll grow up to be violent— to hit or use angry words—or to accept violence, like letting someone hit you, as an adult?"*). In certain instances, children may come to prefer the use of force as a general survival strategy or coping skill.

In addition to discussing the likelihood of using force, the therapist can discuss whether the child is currently using force or aggression with other people and the function of doing so (i.e., as a way to get back at someone, to express anger, or to relieve boredom). The therapist might then add, *"Although you are using aggressive ways or force with others, there are other ways to solve problems. As we work together, you can learn ways to handle your anger, ways to make friends and handle conflicts with peers or family, and ways to communicate without having to use force."*

Comments and Caveats

This section on psychoeducation about abuse is intended to initiate a didactic and therapeutic process in which the child's abusive experience is placed in the context of adult behavior and responsibility. At the same time, it does so by highlighting child behaviors that may have occurred in close proximity to the incident. This task of balancing an appreciation for the child's behavior and the overall responsibility of parents in responding to their children is certainly a delicate one, and it needs to take into consideration the child's own developmental sophistication. The clear message should be that children are not responsible for parental reactions, especially harsh or abusive interactions. This may be difficult for the child to accept initially.

❏ Summary

One of the critical functions of this chapter is to elicit children's perspective on their experiences in an effort to understand both their beliefs or views about what happened and their role in it. A review of the child's general beliefs about force and violence may reveal various misperceptions or distortions about the benefits and disadvantages of using these behaviors, which the therapist may decide to target in this or a later session. Of particular concern is the view that the child believes she or he is responsible for an adult's violent behavior. Whenever feasible, the therapist should provide alternative explanations and feedback regarding the legitimacy of these views and provide alternative suggestions for the child's consideration.

References

Alessi, J. J., & Hearn, K. (1984). Group treatment of children in shelters for battered women. In A. R. Roberts (Ed.), *Battered women and their families* (pp. 49–61). New York: Springer.

Jaffe, P. G., Wolfe, D. A,. & Wilson, S. K. (1990). *Children of battered women*. Newbury Park, CA: Sage Publications.

Kolko, D. J. (1996). Individual cognitive-behavioral treatment and family therapy for physically abused children and their offending parents: A comparison of clinical outcomes. *Child Maltreatment, 1,* 322–342.

Kolko, D. J. (2002). Child physical abuse. In: J. E. B. Myers, L. Berliner, J. Briere, C. T. Hendrix, C. Jenny, & T. Reid (Eds.), *The APSAC handbook of child maltreatment* (2nd ed., pp. 21–54). Thousand Oaks, CA: Sage Publications.

Sinclair, D. (1985). *Understanding wife abuse: A training manual for counsellors and advocates.* Toronto, Ontario: Ontario Government Bookstore, Publication Services Division.

9

Child Treatment
Affect-Focused Interventions

This chapter focuses on techniques for helping children manage various emotional feelings in general, and more specifically those emotions related to the abuse experience. The three areas covered are teaching children (1) to identify the emotions they feel and how they express them, (2) to manage stress and anxiety, and (3) to regulate responses to anger.

❏ Affect Identification and Expression

BACKGROUND AND DEFINITION

Cognitive-behavioral therapy (CBT) addresses thinking, doing, and feeling. Each of these areas is targeted in our interventions. This section presents techniques that help alter feelings. The first step in teaching children to manage various emotional feelings is identification of their own and others' feelings. Once they identify how they are feeling, specific techniques for managing the type of feeling identified can be taught. Sometimes, discrimination of the different types of feelings associated with a situation (e.g., anger vs. fear) is difficult. Developing the capacity to discriminate those feelings can affect one's cognitions and subsequent behavior. Additional sources can be consulted for further information on feeling identification and expression (see Borba & Borba, 1978; Cohen, 1985; Jaffe, Wolfe, & Wilson, 1990).

DESCRIPTION OF PROCEDURE

One of the themes used to explain how one can identify and discriminate between different feeling states involves the "Feeling Detective." Specifically, the child has to conduct an investigation and function like a detective, paying attention to various clues and other signs in order to determine how he or she or another person feels (*"A feeling is on the inside of your body, so you can't see it. So, how do you know how you're feeling?"*).

The "investigation" begins with searching for clues by looking at our own bodies. Common clues can be found in the following ways: (a) *looking* at one's face, hands, and posture; (b) *listening* to one's voice tone and volume, to what one is saying to oneself (e.g., *"I'm going to get him!"*); (c) *thinking* about how one's head, stomach, chest, neck, and shoulders feel; and (d) *asking* oneself, "How do I feel?" Thus, the child can be encouraged to pay attention to these clues in order to discriminate his or her own or someone else's feelings.

Some of the more common emotions children report are *glad, mad, sad,* and *scared/worried* (see Alessi & Hearn, 1984). In general, these emotions reflect happiness, anger, hurt, and sadness. Related, albeit more complex, emotions include feeling confused (e.g., confusion over staying together or not, experiencing love vs. hate towards a parent), embarrassed (e.g., that people are hearing about something that makes one feel funny), and lonely (e.g., wanting closeness, but thinking maybe it's better to be apart).

A related tool to elicit feeling states is to ask the child, *"How would you show this emotion—what would you do?"* or *"How would you look if you felt that way?"* As the child answers this question, it is helpful to emphasize recognition of physical clues (e.g., *"My head hurts," "My face burns"*), behavioral clues (e.g., *"My voice gets loud and I clench my fist"*), cognitive clues (e.g., *"I say to myself, 'You jerk, I hate you'"*), and verbal clues (e.g., *"My voice becomes loud when angry, soft and weak when scared"*). To help children learn how they look or sound when they have these feelings, the therapist might use the teaching activities shown in Box 9.1. Additional teaching activities to clarify the child's own feelings or discriminate emotional states are shown in Box 9.2.

| **Box 9.1** | Teaching Activities for Feeling Identification |

1. Have the child look at a magazine or other pictures and identify the feeling states of the people in the pictures via facial or postural clues.
2. The therapist models a feeling state. The child guesses the therapist's affective state and is asked to state a reason that someone might feel that way (e.g., "A boy might feel sad because _____"). This activity can be conducted through role play or by having the child listen to tape-recorded statements and identify the affective state of the speaker. This exercise emphasizes vocal clues of affective states.
3. Have the child pantomime an affective state and make a video or audiotape after engaging in role plays, or take Polaroid™ snapshots of the child in an affective pose.
4. Have the child read a statement with intonation and volume for different affective states (e.g., have the child read the statement once in an angry voice, and then in a sad voice).

| **Box 9.2** | Teaching Activities for Discrimination of Emotional States |

1. Ask the child whether and how often he or she has special feelings like these. Then ask the child to identify them, stating, "Okay, now what would make you feel [pick each emotion]? . . . And, how would you show this—what would you do or look like if you felt that way?
2. Ask the child to complete some incomplete sentences, such as (a) "I feel sad when _____" ; (b) "When I feel mad, I _____"; or (c) "I don't usually feel _____."
3. Have the child construct pictures that emphasize the physical sensations experienced during negative emotions. Make the pictures as concrete as possible (e.g., draw butterflies in the stomach, draw a thermometer near the head, draw bands around the back and chest).
4. Describe several physical sensations (e.g., "My stomach is churning," or "I feel hot") and have the child identify the affective state.
5. Have the child pantomime an affective state, and have the therapist guess the actor's feeling. The child can describe an experience and then the therapist can label the feeling associated with the experience (e.g., "When X happened, I felt Y").
6. Ask the child to identify the physical sensations associated with *his or her* own negative feelings (e.g., "How do you know when you're _____?" or "When I'm mad, my head gets _____").

The therapist should consider asking the child to practice specific concepts learned in the session at home, which the parent may be encouraged to support and then review. To follow up on the assignment, the therapist can bring into the session something for the child to discuss, such as a poem, or ask for a brief description of two specific feelings that the child experienced and the situations in which they occurred.

CASE APPLICATION

Eight-year-old Ryan was physically abused by his uncle who had been his caregiver for 7 years. The abuse left Ryan with a broken arm and fears of telling people about what his uncle had done. He was removed from his uncle's care and placed with a cousin. In discussing feelings regarding the abuse, Ryan initially only recognized anger. By videotaping what he reported as anger and discussing how he felt physiologically, Ryan discovered that he also felt tremendous sadness over the loss of his uncle. Work to identify and discriminate feelings led the therapist, Ryan, and his caregiver cousin to intervene with relaxation when Ryan felt anger over a situation and to intervene with supportive listening and reassurance when the emotion was sadness over loss.

COMMENT AND CAVEATS

When discussing feelings, therapists should take care to help children go through the exercises necessary to label how they feel instead of showing an expectation that they will feel a certain way. Some children are hesitant to express certain feelings (e.g., suicidal feelings), because they fear that they will be viewed as different. It may be helpful to have children guess what kind of feelings other physically abused children experience, and then determine if they are having similar feelings to their peers.

❑ **Management of Stress and Anxiety**

BACKGROUND AND DEFINITION

As noted earlier, some physically abused children may experience anxiety disorders, such as posttraumatic stress disorder (PTSD), which includes core symptoms of avoidance of reminders of the abusive events, hyperarousal (e.g., sleep difficulties), and cognitively re-experiencing the abusive event (American Psychiatric Association, 1994). More likely, children experiencing anxiety following child physical abuse (CPA) will exhibit PTSD symptoms rather than the full-blown disorder. Anxiety increases or decreases are related to cognitions and physical arousal. When an individual who has experienced a trauma encounters reminders of the trauma, the body's sympathetic nervous system may initiate physical arousal to activate a fight-or-flight response for survival. Indeed, in the past, certain sights, sounds, or smells may have signaled the occurrence of abusive behavior toward the youth. Those sights, sounds, and smells could continue to signal danger although danger is not present. Therefore, the individual experiences anxiety over those reminders of the abuse. The purpose of using anxiety management techniques is to break the link between the signal for abuse and anxiety.

When abuse-related anxiety is evident, such symptomatology can be treated with several evidence-based CBT techniques. The research supporting CBT techniques for anxiety is found in general child clinical research for anxiety disorders (Kendall, 1994) and more recently in the research for treatment of sexually abused children who have PTSD (Cohen & Mannarino, 1996; Deblinger, McLeer, & Henry, 1990). Here, we present CBT techniques for anxiety management, including controlled breathing, relaxation training, and graduated exposure. Each of these techniques addresses the three channels through which children— as well as adults (see Craske & Barlow, 1993)—experience fearful situations, namely, through feeling, thinking, and doing.

DESCRIPTION OF PROCEDURES

Controlled breathing and relaxation are techniques used to help the body reduce physical arousal to reminders of the abuse or any cue that elicits anxiety. Controlled breathing teaches diaphragmatic breathing that slows the breathing rate, thus helping to bring about a relaxed state. Relaxation training teaches individuals how to relax groups of muscles to achieve a relaxed state. As shown in Therapist Examples 9.1 and 9.2, several rationales might be given for the value of learning relaxation techniques.

THERAPIST EXAMPLE **9.1**

Sample Rationale Given to Older Children for Relaxation Training

"Our bodies get tensed up or stressed naturally when we are faced with fearful or stressful situations. Certain sights, sounds, or even smells are going on at the time of the event. Later, even when we are not in a scary or stressful situation, we come across those same sights, sounds, and smells and they are like a signal or a clue for danger, even when there is no danger. *[The therapist elicits examples.]* Breathing and relaxation techniques can help get rid of the scared or stressful feelings that the sights, sounds, or smells cause us to have because they remind of the abuse."

THERAPIST EXAMPLE 9.2

Alternate Sample Rationale Given to Older Children for Relaxation Training

"What happens to you when you feel stressed? *[The therapist prompts for physical symptoms, such as 'my heart races,' or 'my stomach feels funny.']* What do you think you are like when you're stressed? What happens to you when you feel stressed? *[The therapist prompts for acts, such as being more emotional or not thinking things through.]* What can we do when we feel tense or upset? One thing we can do is to relax our bodies. If you learn to relax your body when you feel stressed or upset, how do you think that might help? Now, I am going to teach you some ways to get your body to relax. We will start with learning a special way of breathing, and then go to work on getting your muscles to relax."

Controlled Breathing

Breathing retraining has been described and scientifically evaluated for adults with anxiety disorders (Craske & Barlow, 1993). Specifically, breathing retraining has been used for adults with panic disorder to manage the overbreathing that occurs, and the type of breathing that is learned can be referred to as controlled breathing. Individuals who learn controlled breathing basically learn to breathe diaphragmatically. Controlled breathing can contribute to a relaxed physiological response, but adult techniques need modification for children (Swenson & Kolko, 2000). Photograph 9.1 shows a model receiving instructions from his mother on conducting controlled breathing. Parental involvement is essential in that it increases the likelihood that the parent will learn the technique and help the child use it outside the session. Photograph 9.2 shows the parent encouraging the child to breathe diaphragmatically so that the cup rises up to her hand. The child is in the process of managing anxiety and receiving encouragement from the parent, thus reinforcing his use of this strategy. Therapist Example 9.3 provides a transcript for teaching controlled breathing with children. This exercise can be done individually with a child, but to increase the likelihood of generalization, a family member should attend and participate in the session. Also, the therapist can audiotape the session as a guide for the child to use for practicing outside of session.

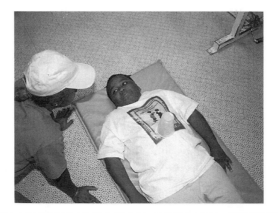

Photograph 9.1 A child receiving instructions from his mother on conducting controlled breathing.

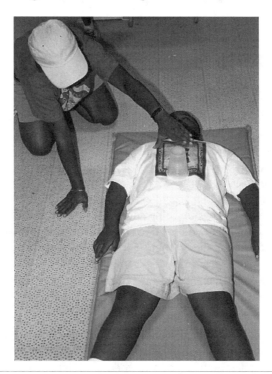

Photograph 9.2 A parent encouraging her child to breath diaphragmatically
so that the cup rises up to her hand.

THERAPIST EXAMPLE 9.3

Sample Transcript for Controlled Breathing Exercise

Therapist: Today, we are going to talk about how to get your body to relax—about what to do when you get scared, upset, or nervous. Maybe you can tell me first a little bit about how you feel when you get scared, upset or nervous. How do you know? How does your body feel?

[If there is no response, the therapist should prompt for such changes as increased heartbeat.]

Child: I start kind of sweating. I get weak in the knees. I stutter a lot and feel like I have a big heat in my chest.

Therapist: All of those things you described are normal things that happen to people when they are scared, upset, or nervous about things. The reason they are normal is because your body has things it does when you are scared, upset, or nervous that protect you, get you ready to get out of there or fight to protect yourself.

For example, if you were walking down the street and somebody came up to you and pointed a gun at you, what would you do?

Child: I'd run.

Therapist: Right. Your body gets all geared up to give you the amount of energy you need to get out of there or fight to protect yourself. The body has a system called the *sympathetic nervous system.* Have you heard about that in science class? That's the system in your body that gets you geared up to get out of there, or fight to protect yourself, or do something about it when you are scared, nervous, or upset.

But you can't be geared up all the time, or be upset or nervous, or feel that weight on your chest or your heart beating fast all the time. So your body has another system that gets you calmed down, and that is called the *parasympathetic nervous system.*

What I am going to teach you is how, when your sympathetic nervous system gets you geared up to protect yourself and you don't really need to protect yourself but you need to calm down to help, you can take control and get your parasympathetic nervous system going and get yourself calm. So, this would be like when something reminds you of something bad that happened to you and you get scared or upset, but you don't need to be scared, you can do the things I will teach you and get calm.

[The therapist asks the child for examples.]

The first skill I will teach you is how to breathe in a way that helps get your body to relax. This is a special way of breathing called *controlled breathing* and I'll show you how it works. First, let me give you a balloon and have you blow it up. Once you get it blown up, just hold on to it.

[NOTE: The therapist should select balloons that can be blown up easily.]

Now, with this kind of breathing that we're going to do, your stomach will be like a balloon. When you blow air into the balloon, what does it do?

Child: It gets bigger.

Therapist: Good, it gets bigger or expands. Now let's see what happens when you let air out of the balloon. Let just a little bit out. What happens to the balloon?

Child: It gets smaller.

Therapist: Right, it gets smaller or goes in. That is exactly what your stomach is going to do when we practice this special kind of breathing, controlled breathing.

Now, maybe we should talk about how fast or slow to let the air out. What if you let the air out slow? What do you think? Try it. Is that kind of nervous or kind of relaxed?

Child: That's relaxed.

Therapist: Right. Now, what if you let the air out fast—is that nervous or relaxed? Try it.

Child: *[Lets the balloon fly around the room.]* That's nervous.

Therapist: Right. Now, as we do this breathing, if you let the air out really fast you won't be as relaxed as if you let it out really slow. Okay, so remember that your stomach will be like a balloon. You will see your stomach move out when you take a breath in or inhale, and you will see your stomach go down when you let the breath out or exhale.

Okay, any questions?

[If the child has no questions, the therapist states, "Let's practice."]

First, put your hand on your stomach with your little finger right above your belly button. When you inhale, you will feel your stomach go out, and when you exhale, you will feel your stomach go in. To help you do the breathing a little slower, what I will say is, "Baalloooon Out," and I will mean you are inhaling and your stomach is going out like a balloon. You are inhaling the whole time I am saying "Balloon Out."

Then, I will say, "Baalloooon In," and I will mean that you are exhaling and your stomach is going in like a balloon. You will be exhaling or letting the breath out the whole time I am saying "Balloon In."

Now, let's try it.

[The therapist leads the child through the exercise while the child is sitting up in a chair. The therapists notes any progress and states, "Now we will do a little test to see how this is working." The child then moves to a mat on the floor and the therapist gives the child a lightweight paper cup to

place on his or her stomach. The therapist and child note if the cup moves up when child inhales and down when the child exhales. Family members who may be present can monitor the movement of the cup and give feedback. The therapist can also have family members try out the exercise.]

Relaxation Training

The rationale behind deep muscle relaxation is that tensing followed by relaxing of certain muscle groups will result in a physiologically relaxed state. Ollendick and Cerny (1981) provide a detailed and widely used description of deep muscle relaxation. Therapist Example 9.4 provides a description of a deep muscle relaxation exercise based on their work.

To enable the child and parent to practice this technique, the therapist should consider audiotaping the exercise as it is conducted. The therapist first points out the different muscle groups that the child will work to relax. The child identifies his or her hands, forearms, biceps, neck, chin, throat muscles, chest, back, and legs. Once the therapist is sure that the child is familiar with the body terminology, the deep muscle relaxation procedure is introduced. For younger children, deep muscle relaxation may be woven into an interactive story (see Therapist Example 9.5).

THERAPIST EXAMPLE 9.4

Transcript for Administering a Muscle Relaxation Exercise

"This exercise teaches you how to help your muscles relax so that you can better handle situations or times when you are worried, tense, or nervous. Can you think of a situation that makes you feel worried, tense, or nervous? *[If child is not forthcoming with a situation, the therapist prompts with something like, 'How about when you have a big test?' 'How about when an adult yells at you?' 'How about when you are really, really mad?' or 'How about when you think about the physical abuse that happened to you?']* These are all times when you can use deep muscle relaxation."
"To do the deep muscle relaxation, you will

1. Take a deep breath.
2. Tense each muscle group for 5 seconds.
3. Say or think the word 'relax.'
4. Let the deep breath out.
5. Let go of the tension in your muscle.

"Now, let's do this together. I'll show you how. Let's start with you left hand and arm.

"Take a deep breath. Tense your left hand and arm by making a fist. *[The therapist praises the correct response.]* One one thousand, two one thousand, three one thousand, four one thousand, five one thousand. Think or say 'relax.' Let your deep breath out. Now, let go of the tension in your left hand and arm.

"Feel that relaxed feeling in your left hand and arm. They may be warm or tingly. Now, let's tense and relax that same muscle group again." *[The therapist leads the child through the exact same process with the left hand and arm.]*

[Then the therapist leads the child in two sets of deep muscle relaxation of the following muscle groups, in this order: (a) right hand and arm, as above; (b) arms and shoulders, by stretching the arms out in front and then over the head; (c) shoulder and neck, by pulling the shoulders up to the ears and the head down into the shoulders, much like a big shrug; (d) jaw, by biting down hard on the teeth; (e) face and nose, by wrinkling the nose; (f) stomach, by tightening it very tight and making the stomach very hard; and (g) legs and feet, by pushing down on the floor hard with toes spread apart.]

THERAPIST EXAMPLE 9.5

The Turtle Exercise

[This exercise starts by introducing a turtle puppet to the child.]

Therapist: The exercise that we are going to do now is called "The Turtle Story." This is a turtle, as you can see. When he goes in his shell, what do you think he can hear?

Child: Nothing.

Therapist: Well, he can probably hear something. But he may not be able to hear the outside sounds. What can he hear inside the shell?

Child: He hears himself?

Therapist: Exactly; he hears himself breathing. When he comes outside the shell, he probably doesn't hear himself breathing as well and he has to really concentrate.

What we'll do together is tell a story that is about how to get your body to relax. You get to be the turtle in the story. Let's think of a name for the turtle.

Child: Al.

Therapist: Okay, Al it is. Now, let's think of two kinds of animals.

Child: A cat and a dog.

Therapist: A cat and a dog. Now, let's think of names for the cat and dog.

Child: The cat is Sugar and the dog is Godzilla.

Therapist: Okay, so we have Al, Sugar, and Godzilla. Now, remember in this story you are Al, the turtle. So, let's get going.

One day, Al was inside his shell. *[The therapists prompts child to "go inside your shell."]* Inside his shell it was very quiet. All he could hear was himself breathing. Just listen. *[The therapist gives the child 10 seconds to listen to herself breath and get quiet and calm.]*

All is quiet and Al is very calm, listening to himself breath.

Then Al gets an idea: I think I'll go for a walk. So, he stuck his head out of his shell and said, "Wow! It's a beautiful day," and he rolled his head around *[prompt the child to do head rolls]* to get a good look at the sky and he rolled it back the other way to get another good look at the sky. He said, "Wow! The sun is so bright," and he had to scrunch his eyes really tight *[the child to tenses eyes for 3 seconds]* because the sun was so bright. Then he let his eyes go and thought how relaxed they felt.

He said, "If I'm going to take a walk, I guess I had better get my legs out." So, out comes one leg, and it feels really tight. So, he has to hold it tight and then stretch it really good. *[The therapist demonstrates tensing and relaxing the leg].* Then, here comes the other leg. He has to hold it tight and then stretch it out really good.

He said, "Okay, my legs feel good and I'm ready to take my walk." All of a sudden, a cat comes up to him and Al says, "Who are you?" The cat says, "My name is Sugar. Where are you going?" Al puts his chin to his chest and raises his shoulders to his ears as high as he can get them and says, "I don't know." *[The therapist prompts the child to demonstrate the tensing that takes place with the shoulder shrug.]*

Sugar says, "Well if you're going for a walk, maybe I can go with you." Al said, "Okay." Then, he figured out that when he stopped to talk to Sugar he got stuck in the mud. To get out, he had to hold his stomach in really tight and push down really hard with one leg and release. Then, he had to push down really hard with another leg and then release. He had to hold his stomach in again really tight and get real skinny and, voilà, he was able to get himself out of the mud.

Al and Sugar walked along, and the next thing you know, here comes a dog. They stop and Sugar says, "What's your name?" And the dog says, "I'm Godzilla. Where are you going?" Al puts his chin to his chest and raises his shoulders to his ears as high as he can get them and says, "I don't know." *[The therapist prompts child to demonstrate again the tensing that takes place with the shoulder shrug.]* Godzilla says, "Where do you want to go?" and Al puts his chin to his chest and raises his shoulders to his ears as high as he can get them and says, "I don't know." So, Godzilla says, "Well, it's a good day to walk. The sun sure is bright—see it in the sky?" Al rolls his head around to see the sun and rolls it around again. The sun is so bright he has to again scrunch his eyes really tight [child scrunches eyes for 3 seconds] and then open them. He invites Godzilla to go along, and guess what happened? Stuck in the mud again.

To get out of the mud, this time he picked up a handful of the mud with his left hand and squeezed it really hard and opened his hand. Then, he picked up a handful of mud with this right hand and squeezed it really hard, and then opened his hand. Then, he had to push down really hard his left leg and let go, and then push really hard with his right leg and then let go. He had to hold his stomach in again really tight and get real skinny and, voilà, he got unstuck again.

They continued walking and came to the end of their journey. Godzilla and Sugar said, "Al, what do you want to do now?" And what do you think Al said? [The therapist prompts child to put chin to chest and raise shoulders to ears and say, "I don't know."]

Godzilla and Sugar decide to go home, and Al decided to relax a bit. He went back into his shell. He closed his eyes. It was really quiet. He could hear himself breathing. He felt really good. He met new friends and had a good journey. His body felt really relaxed. He could still hear his breathing. He was really, really calm. Now, you can open your eyes. You are very relaxed.

Guided imagery is an additional relaxation technique. In this exercise, the therapist works with the child to understand visual images that are relaxing to that individual (e.g., floating, lying in the sun, or sitting by a mountain stream). Subsequently, a transcript of a scene using those images is used to guide the child to become relaxed. Therapist Example 9.6 provides an example of a guided imagery transcript using a beach scene. Therapist Example 9.7 provides a guided imagery transcript using color, rather than a particular scene to help relax various muscle groups. As with other relaxation exercises we describe, we recommend audiotaping the actual session and giving the audiotape to the child for a guide in practice and for the parent to hear and understand the techniques used.

THERAPIST EXAMPLE 9.6

Transcript of a Guided Imagery Exercise

"Take a minute to get relaxed in your chair.
"Uncross your legs and arms.

"Take a few seconds to listen to yourself breathe." *[The therapist should take the child through controlled breathing.]*

"Now we are going to pretend that you are at the beach—a very relaxing place.

"Close your eyes.

"You can see yourself walking toward a white sand dune. There are yellow, red, and purple wildflowers on the trail. You walk over the white sand dune and you see the ocean. The waves are slowly coming in and the color of the water is a beautiful green.

"You take your yellow raft and go to the edge of the water. You can see through the water because it is so clear. You see white sand on the bottom of the ocean. You see your feet standing on the white sand.

"You lie on your raft, paddle out a short distance, and begin to float.

"The waves are very gentle and this is a very safe place. The waves slowly lift your raft just a little and then lower you. Slowly lift, then lower; up then down, up then down, up then down.

"You feel very relaxed. The sun is shining and it feels warm on your face, arms, and legs.

"You feel so relaxed that you are about to fall asleep, but you know that the waves keep lifting you up a little and then lower you down.

"You float away from the shore, and then the tide brings you back in. You can see your yellow raft coming onto the shore.

"When I count to three, you can open your eyes. You will still be relaxed.

"One . . . you are feeling very calm; two . . . your body is very relaxed; and three . . . open your eyes. Now, how do you feel?"

THERAPIST EXAMPLE 9.7

Transcript for a Guided Imagery With Color Exercise

[This exercise should be conducted in a quiet, soothing voice. The speed at which the exercise continues depends on the child and how fast he or she is able to move and actually relax the muscle groups.]

Therapist: For this exercise, we are going to use color. What is a calm, relaxing color for you?

Child: I think blue.

Therapist: What kind of blue—light? dark? Can you show me that color on anything in the room?

Child: It's light baby blue, like on that picture on the wall there.

Therapist: Ah. Okay, now I understand what color you would like to use. As I guide you, you will imagine each muscle group we cover turning light baby blue. First, we will start by taking a few deep breaths using controlled breathing. So, relax in your chair, uncross your legs and arms. Put your hand on your stomach with your little finger above your belly button. *[Therapist guides child through controlled breathing exercise, taking five deep breaths.]*

Now, I would like you to close your eyes to help you imagine the color better. Are you ready? *[When the child is ready, the therapist starts.]*

Let's start with the toes on your left foot. Just concentrate on your toes for a minute and think about how relaxed they feel. As your left toes relax you will see a beautiful, light baby blue relaxation liquid start to come into your toes, and they become light baby blue. The light baby blue relaxation liquid moves on up your left foot, and you can see it move up. As it moves up your foot, your foot becomes a beautiful, light baby blue and feels completely and totally relaxed. Now, you see the relaxation liquid move into your right toes, and they become a beautiful, light baby blue and start to feel totally relaxed. The light baby blue liquid moves on up your foot. Now, both of your feel are light baby blue and are very, very relaxed.

Now, the light baby blue relaxation liquid is beginning to move up your left leg. It circles around and around the bottom part of your leg, relaxing your calf muscles, moves up to your knee, continues up the top part of your leg, all the way to where your leg joins with your hip. Now, your whole left leg is light baby blue and really, really relaxed. Now, the light baby blue relaxation liquid is beginning to move up your right leg. It circles around and around the bottom part of your leg, relaxing your calf muscles, moves up to your knee, continues up the top part of your leg, all the way to where your leg joins with your hip. Now, your whole right leg is light baby blue and really, really relaxed. You can see that both of your legs and feet are light baby blue and they feel great, really relaxed.

Now, the light baby blue relaxation liquid is moving up your stomach and hips, moving back and forth unlocking tense muscles. It moves up to your belly button. You can see the beautiful, safe, light baby blue relaxation liquid move up your lower back. It just moves back and forth, taking away the tension from your back. Now, the light baby blue relaxation liquid moves all the way up your chest and back to your neck. You can see it moving up your shoulders and it goes back and forth, back and forth, letting the muscles in your shoulders relax. Now, your body from your neck down and your legs and feet are a beautiful, light baby blue and are very, very relaxed.

Now, you see the light baby blue relaxation liquid begin to move in the fingers of your left hand. Light baby blue moves up your fingers and your hand. You see it begin to move in your wrist, up your forearm, all the way to your elbow. Now, the beautiful, light baby blue relaxation liquid moves up the upper part of your arm and joins your blue shoulder. Your entire left arm and hand is light baby blue and is very relaxed.

Now, you see the light baby blue relaxation liquid begin to move in the fingers of your right hand. Light baby blue moves up your fingers and your hand. You see it begin to move in your wrist, up your forearm, all the way to your elbow. Now, the beautiful, light baby blue relaxation liquid moves up the upper part of your arm and joins your blue shoulder. Your entire right arm and hand is light baby blue and is very relaxed. From your neck all the way to your toes is a beautiful, relaxed, light baby blue color. It feels very good; you feel very peaceful.

Now, the light baby blue relaxation liquid begins to move up your neck. This can be a really tense area, and the light baby blue moves back and forth safely relaxing your muscles. On muscles that are really tight, the light baby blue relaxation liquid circles around and around letting the tension go.

You see the light baby blue relaxation liquid move up the back of your head and over the top of your head, and here it comes to your forehead. It goes back and forth, from side to side, relaxing your forehead. You see the light baby blue move down your left cheek, down your right cheek, circle around your left eye, and circle around your right eye. Now, your eyes and forehead feel totally relaxed and every area of your face is light baby blue except your nose, mouth, and chin. Here comes the beautiful light blue relaxation liquid moving down your nose to the tip of your nose, around your mouth—it feels so relaxed that it just wants to fall open. You can let your mouth fall open. Now, the light baby blue liquid moves to your chin and the final spot that wasn't blue is now blue.

You can see that your whole body from your head to your toes is light baby blue. Your whole body feels so relaxed. I will count to five to give you a chance to get ready to open your eyes. When you open your eyes, you will still be relaxed. One . . . two . . . three . . . four . . . five. Now, slowly open your eyes.

How do you feel? You did a great job taking control and getting your body relaxed.

Graduated Exposure

Graduated exposure is a technique used to break the link between anxiety and reminders of the abuse. This technique involves recapitulation of the abuse, and is often referred to as *gradual exposure* because children are gradually exposed to reminders of anxiety provoking situations regarding the abuse and then anxiety management techniques are used to reduce the anxiety. Graduated exposure has been validated with sexually abused children (Deblinger, McLeer, & Henry, 1990; Stauffer & Deblinger, 1996), and applied in individual (Smith, Swenson, & Hanson, 1995) and group (Swenson & Brown, 2000) treatment programs for physically abused children. Graduated exposure should be used only in cases where the child is experiencing intense anxiety related to the abuse. Before graduated exposure is used, children should have mastered controlled breathing and other relaxation techniques.

To conduct graduated exposure, first a rationale is given to the child and parent. For the parent, therapists should assure them that research has confirmed the usefulness of this technique in helping children reduce problems with anxiety. Parents or caregivers should know that discussion of the abuse can be so anxiety provoking for some children that they may have bad dreams at first and may not want to come back to see the therapist. Such a reaction should be normalized for the parents, and the therapist should elicit their help in getting the child through the difficulty he or she may face when exposure begins.

For the child, the rationale should be developmentally appropriate and therapists should not indicate to children that this process will be easy. A summary of a rationale used by Deblinger (1999) in her workshops on treatment of PTSD with sexually abused children and described in her recent book (Deblinger & Heflin, 1996) is shown in Therapist Example 9.8.

THERAPIST EXAMPLE **9.8**

Sample Rationale for Exposure Treatment Exercise

"Have you ever been swimming in a pool and the water was cold? How would you go into the pool? Some people jump right in all at once, but a lot of people stick their toes in the water and let them get used to it. Then, they go in a little bit more and get used to the cold water, then a little bit more, and then more till their whole body is under the water and they are used to it. This is similar to what we will do when we talk about the abuse. We will talk about a little and let you get used to talking about it, then a little more, and a little more, until you are able to talk a lot about it and feel okay."

Second, the therapist should review anxiety management techniques to be sure that the child has mastered those skills. Third, detailed recapitulation of the abusive incident(s) begins. Lower-anxiety-provoking situations (e.g., where they were during the abuse) are approached first. Eventually, higher-anxiety-provoking situations (e.g., the actual physical abuse) are discussed. During the recapitulation, the child is asked to talk about specific sights, sounds, or smells remembered from the abuse. Anxiety is countered by performing relaxation techniques.

The method for recapitulation of the abuse depends on the developmental level of the child. For older youths, simply discussing the abuse may be possible. For younger and some older children, telling about the abusive experience may be done by talking, drawing, use of puppets, and any other method that works for the child. Some children have such extreme anxiety that pairing a fun, anxiety-reducing activity may be necessary to help them talk about the abuse (e.g., playing a videogame during the recapitulation of the abuse). Following an exposure session, time should be devoted to calming activities, such as drawing, playing games, or listening to music.

CASE APPLICATION

Eleven-year-old Harvey and his 7-year-old sister Fredricka were having difficulty with anxiety. Harvey's anxiety was related to reminders of physical abuse and Fredricka's to sexual abuse. The children both lay on their back on an exercise mat and placed lightweight cups on their stomach. Harvey was able immediately to watch the cup rise when inhaling and lower when exhaling. Fredricka had difficulty because she used her muscles to push her stomach up and was breathing shallowly. When she placed her hand on her chest, she was able to feel her chest move on its own and then get her stomach to move on its own.

COMMENTS AND CAVEATS

When abuse happens to children, care should be taken to help protect boundaries and body space. When a hand needs to be placed on a child's chest to check for shallow breathing, the therapist needs to make sure that neither he or she nor another child places a hand on the chest, but that the child does it himself or herself. Furthermore, placing the cup on the stomach should be done by the child and not the therapist. Parents should be shown the procedure so that they understand what it is about and how it is conducted.

❏ Management of Anger

BACKGROUND AND DEFINITION

Difficulty managing anger and aggression is strongly associated with a history of physical abuse. When children have limited skills for modulating and managing anger, CBT techniques for anger management are called for. Studies evaluating existing models of anger control training have shown some success in reducing adolescents' disruptive and aggressive behaviors (Feindler, Ecton, Kingsley, & Dubey, 1986; Feindler, Marriott, & Iwata, 1984; Kolko, Dorsett, & Milan, 1981; Swenson, Butler, Kennedy, & Baum, 1988), verbal aggression (Dangel, Deschner, & Rasp, 1989; Feindler et al., 1986) and impulsiveness (Feindler et al., 1986). CBT school-based anger management group treatment programs evaluated with school-aged, aggressive children have been related to increases in self-esteem and reductions in aggression (Lochman, Burch, Curry, & Lampron, 1984).

DESCRIPTION OF PROCEDURE

Work on anger management begins with helping the youth recognize the negative consequences of not handling anger appropriately and the benefits of better management (e.g., staying out of trouble at school, keeping friends, helping the family, and avoiding a reputation as someone who is easy to set off). Therapists can approach these tasks through several methods, such as explaining the importance of anger control and addressing the potential thinking error that the youth may gain pride and status through the use of aggression.

An introduction to anger management training may then follow, as shown in Therapist Example 9.9.

THERAPIST EXAMPLE **9.9**

Sample Introduction to Anger Management Training

"Being angry to the point of being out of control and aggressive—pushing, yelling, and hitting—can lead to trouble with people you know. It can also lead to trouble in how you feel about yourself. There will always be some amount of trouble between people, because we are different in many ways. How much trouble depends on how you or other people handle angry feelings. There will be times when there will be trouble and you didn't start it or you couldn't keep it from happening. You can't always control situations or what other people say and do. That is why you need to be able to control how you act when you get angry. *[The therapist emphasizes the importance of anger control with positive examples of people such as Martin Luther King Jr. or Rosa Parks, who were angry over an injustice but remained calm and did not lose control.]* It is okay to be angry, but not okay to lose control, and there are lots of things you can do rather than lose control."

For some children, a pattern of aggression toward others is associated with strong feelings of pride and power. It is important not to discount the youth's occasional need for self-defense (e.g., when attacked by others), but excuses for aggression should be dispelled early on. For example, statements like, *"Everyone in my neighborhood fights,"* can be countered with, *"It may seem that way, but there are people in your neighborhood who get along day to day without fighting. Help me by thinking of who those people are and what they do to handle their anger."* Another possible excuse for aggression is, *"My mom was investigated by the Department of Social Services for hurting me. If you were in my family, you'd fight, too."* Statements like this can be countered with,

> *I know that the things you have experienced must be difficult to feel inside, but there are some other ways to handle them without fighting. Some other children who have been through difficult experiences similar to you have found ways to stop the fighting, and I know you can too.*

One way to address the aggression-equals-pride-and-power thinking is through a fishing analogy role play. A transcript addressing pride, power, and aggression is provided in Therapist Example 9.10.

THERAPIST EXAMPLE 9.10

Sample Transcript Addressing Aggression, Power, and Pride

Therapist: Have you ever been fishing? *[If not, the therapist can ask, "Have you ever seen anyone fish?" or "Do you know about fishing?" Depending on the region in which the youth lives, knowing about fishing is highly likely.]*

Child: Yep. I went once with my grandpa and a lot of times with my homeys.

Therapist: What kind of pole do you use for fishing?

Child: I use a cane pole.

Therapist: Explain for me step by step what you do when you go fishing with a cane pole.

Child: I put the bait on and catch a fish.

Therapist: Wait, help me understand. What do you do first?

Child: Man, you don't know anything about fishing. I get the pole and then I put it in the water.

Therapist: What's on the pole?

Child: Well, it's got a line and a hook at the end, and I put a cricket on the hook.

Therapist: Then what do you do?

Child: I throw the hook out in the water.

Therapist: What happens next?

Child: The fish bites on the cricket and I yank the pole and catch the fish.

Therapist: Then what?

Child: I bring it in and put it in a bucket.

Therapist: Who is in control—the fish or the fisher?

Child: Me, the fisher.

Therapist: Who wins—the fish or the fisher?

Child: Me, 'cause I clean it and take it home, cook it and eat it with a big ol' plate of red rice.

Therapist: How is the fishing that you have just told me about like anger?

Child: I don't know.

Therapist: You said when the fish takes the hook, he loses control and doesn't win. Bad things happen to him. You told me earlier that somebody saying, "I'm gonna bust you up" is a hook for you. What happens when someone throws out that hook for you or when they say to you, "I'm gonna bust you up"?

Child: I gotta box [hit] em.

Therapist: Thinking about the fish that took the hook, when you take the hook—meaning you hit someone because they said, "I'm gonna bust you up"—do you win?

Child: No, if I take the hook, I don't win.

Therapist: And how do you know if you have taken the hook?

Child: I hit the boy.

Therapist: And who is in control—the person who threw out the hook or the person who took the hook?

Child: The person who threw the hook.

Therapist: Good job! You got it. When someone tries to hook you and you allow it by arguing or fighting, you lose and you stop being in control of the situation. We're going to work more now on how to be in control and prevent yourself from getting hooked.

The next step in anger management training involves understanding what situations usually provoke anger in the youth and how he or she typically handles the anger through teaching youth how to conduct a functional analysis. That is, teaching the youth how to identify antecedents, behaviors, and consequences. To identify antecedents, the therapist helps the youth write out any possible situations, people, or verbalizations that seem to make him or her angry. These are identified as triggers. Reviewing with the youth things that other people say or do that makes the youth "hookable" (by "hookable," we mean the youth can be provoked to lose control by another youth or adult using a known trigger, such as name calling) may help identify potential triggers (Swenson & Brown, 2000).

Next, the therapist has the youth describe how he or she typically handles being in those situations, with those people, or faced with those provocations. Finally, the therapist asks the youth to list all positive consequences for aggression as a response to anger and then all negative consequences. For negative consequences, the therapist asks the youth to give specific examples in his or her life rather than accepting vague answers, such as, *"I might get in trouble."* Therapist Example 9.11 provides an example of conducting a functional analysis.

THERAPIST EXAMPLE 9.11
Sample Functional Analysis

Therapist: I am going to teach you how to do a functional analysis to help us understand what happens when you get angry and lose control, and what we might do about it. We will be looking at the ABCs of behavior. A stands for antecedents, or things that happen before you act. B stands for behavior, or what you do. C stands for consequences, or the things that happen as a result of your behavior. Consequences can be positive or negative.

Let's start with A, antecedents. What kinds of things happen that usually make you feel really mad—mad enough to fight?

Child: Well, people talk about my mama and say she hits the pipe *[refer-ring to smoking crack cocaine].*

Therapist: That's a good example. Let's look at some of the things you said make you "hookable." Let's see, you said "when my mama yells at me and says she's gonna hurt me" and when you are with Rodney, because he fights everybody and you've got to fight when you're with Rodney. I think you have some really good ideas about what things come before you get into a fight or argument. We'll call those situations or people *triggers,* because being with those people or hearing those things said get you all geared up to get into a fight.

Now let's go to B, behavior. What do you usually do when someone talks about your mama?

Child: Well, I say something back about their mama.

Therapist: And then what happens?

Child: They say, "Your mama smoke that crack, she's a crack head."

Therapist: Then what?

Child: I hit 'em as hard as I can.

Therapist: Okay, I have a good understanding of what you do when people talk about your mama. You did a great job helping me. *[The thera-pist then goes over other triggers to determine if the behavior is simi-lar for those triggers.]*

Therapist: Now, let's talk about the last letter—C, consequences. Do you know what I mean by the word *consequence*?

Child: You get in trouble.

Therapist: Exactly, a consequence is what happens to you because of how you behave or act. Getting in trouble is a good example of a conse-quence. Now, for you, what consequences happen when you hit peo-ple as hard as you can?

Child: I get in trouble.

Therapist: What do you mean? How do you get in trouble?

Child: I get suspended from school. My mama beats me.

Therapist: What about with the other kids? What do they learn that you will do if they just talk about your mama?

Child: That I will fight.

Therapist: Exactly, and when your classmates know that you are easy to "hook," you get a hookable reputation. They know if they want to see a good fight, they just have to talk about your mama. Then, they can go on about their business and you are in the principal's office, in trouble or even arrested. When people say things to you to hook you and you fight, do they usually get in trouble?

Child: No, because they didn't hit me first.

Therapist: So, you're telling me when someone says something to you that gets you mad, you lose control and you are the one with the negative consequences!

Child: Yep.

Therapist: As we continue to work on controlling anger, we will do lots of functional analyses. The next step is to figure out what you can do instead of losing control and fighting.

Assessing Inside Anger Cues

After teaching the structure of the functional analysis and addressing the role of pride or power in aggression, additional work is done to strengthen the functional analysis. First, an assessment of inside anger cues, including physiological and cognitive cues, is added to the functional analysis. These cues are the initial signal that it is time to use an alternative strategy to de-escalate the child. The child is asked to help make a list of how his or her body feels when he or she gets really angry, before a fight. The therapist or child writes down physical cues on a piece of colored paper. This page will be placed on the wall or desk at subsequent sessions, and additional cues may be added to the list. If the child is unable to determine physical cues, the therapist prompts with a question, such as, *"Does your heart beat fast, do your eyes water, does your jaw feel tight?"* If the child cannot report any physical cues, observation of physical cues becomes the homework assignment. Next, the child is asked to tell what he or she usually thinks when he or she starts to get angry. For example, what does the child feel when another child calls him or her a name or makes a negative comment about his or her mother? These responses are cognitive cues, and they are recorded on the same sheet with physical cues. In later sessions, additional cognitive cues can be added to the list. Physical cues and cognitive cues are rank ordered by asking the child, *"What do you feel first, . . . then next?"* and *"What do you usually think first, . . . then next?"* Understanding what comes first physically and cognitively gives the therapist knowledge both of when to substitute responses that deescalate the child physically and what cognitions need to be replaced to help with the de-escalation process. Box 9.3 shows an example of a physical and cognitive cues worksheet.

Box 9.3 | Anger Cues Worksheet

My Anger Cues

Physical Cues

1. Eyes water
2. Feel butterflies in my stomach
3. Emotional hurt, in my left shoulder [referring to tension]
4. Ball up my fist

Cognitive Cues

1. "I'm gonna get him."
2. "I just want to die."
3. "I just want to flip him off."
4. "That bastard."

Assessing Outside Anger Cues

Outside anger cues refer to what others may see in the child that indicates to them that he or she may be escalating in anger whether or not this is so. For example, the therapist can poll the family or teachers to understand how they know the youth is escalating. They may be observing behaviors that indicate anger when none is intended (e.g., the rolling of eyes or sucking of teeth). The therapist can point out to the youth that these nonverbal behaviors may provoke angry responses from others and have the youth become cognizant of these behaviors. For analyzing a situation that has occurred and understanding outside anger cues, the Hassle Log can be used (see Feindler & Ecton, 1986, for an original copy). On the Hassle Log, the youth, parent, and therapist can take an actual conflict situation and specify both the situation and his or her behavior in response to the situation. Children completing the Hassle Log rate themselves on how they handled the situation and how angry they were. Hassle logs can also be used to document progress in managing anger over time.

Substitution Procedures

After determining inside and outside anger cues, specific procedures for substituting positive for negative behaviors are introduced. One way to introduce substitution procedures is to ask the child if he or she can tell what a substitute teacher is. Most children are familiar with this term and respond with a definition of substitute that involves somebody who comes in when the teacher is out, or someone who takes the teacher's place. The therapist emphasizes that a substitute is something that takes another thing's place and that the child will be learning things he or she can substitute for fighting when he or she recognizes the physical or cognitive cues—that is, things that will take the place of getting madder and madder and then fighting. Two types of substitution procedures are taught: physical and cognitive. When physical cues of anger are recognized, the child can immediately begin to use one of the relaxation skills taught earlier. The child should decide in the session which skill is most meaningful to him or her, and that particular skill should be used in all role plays. Next, the child will need to develop a cognitive substitution, a coping statement he or she can tell him- or herself that will help de-escalate. For example, when the child catches herself thinking, *"I'll get him for this,"* she can replace that statement with a coping statement, such as, *"I need to just chill."* This statement may require multiple repetitions to help de-escalate.

A second substitution response involves thinking ahead to the consequences. Children make a list of all potential consequences that may occur following a conflict situation. The list of consequences is then arranged in a descending order, from *worst* to *not so bad*. The probability that these consequences will occur is reviewed with emphasis on the predictability of negative consequences if the child has been in trouble a lot. The think-ahead procedure involves substituting a negative cognition with a reminder to the self of the consequences early in the chain of escalating behaviors. Many role plays will need to be conducted to give the child the opportunity to practice new skills. Role plays can be taken from actual situations that are recorded on the Hassle Logs completed each week. Alternatively, the therapist, child, or parent can make up a situation to be used in the role play. Some sample role plays are shown in Box 9.4.

Box 9.4 | Sample Role Plays

1. You go to the store and buy a lot of stuff. At the counter, you realize you don't have enough money. The cashier complains in a loud voice about "people like you" wasting his time.
2. You come home from school with a black eye. In response to your mom's questions, you say that you were hit by a kid while in

---

Box 9.4 | *continued*

school and that it was witnessed by teachers, but you were still suspended and nothing happened to the other child.

3. Your bike won't work because the chain has fallen off and this makes you late for an important game in the neighborhood.

4. You go over to your friend's house to hang out. She tells you to go home and she doesn't want to be your friend anymore.

5. You are walking home from school. A group of kids is standing on the corner and yell at you and call you names.

6. You are playing baseball. It's your turn at bat. You strike out and the other team laughs at you.

CASE APPLICATION

Twelve-year-old Boo participated in anger management training. He identified physiological cues of fist clenching, feeling hot in his face, and feeling as if his stomach were a volcano erupting. The "volcano" feeling was identified as occurring first. Boo determined that when he felt the "volcano" in his stomach, he would immediately begin controlled breathing. In his role plays he successfully demonstrated the substitution technique, and his mother reported she saw him using the technique at times when he was angry.

COMMENTS AND CAVEATS

The anger control training described above is to be used with youths who have difficulty managing anger in that they act impulsively with aggression. This training is not meant for those youths who carry out instrumental aggression, such as strong-armed robbery as part of a gang activity or other planned acts of aggression.

❏ Summary

CPA may result in poor management of affect. The types of affect problems children may experience include reactions to general stressors, abuse-related emotional difficulties, such as anxiety, PTSD, and anger. In this chapter, we have presented some techniques for identifying emotions that children feel and how those are expressed. Such recognition sets the stage for then identifying the children's emotions related to the abuse and the management of those emotions. In that process, the management of stress and anxiety is first presented. The majority of physically abused children will not likely be diagnosed with PTSD, but may experience some anxiety related to the abuse or to processing the abuse. Core techniques presented are controlled breathing, relaxation, and graduated exposure. We note that exposure techniques should be used only in cases of extreme anxiety. More likely, physically abused children will benefit from anxiety management techniques that address daily stressors and worries.

Second, techniques for management of anger are presented. For aggressive children who associate power and pride with aggression, a case for managing anger and avoiding aggressive tactics will need to be made. Then, anger management skills introduced will build on each other. For example, children are taught to recognize internal and external anger cues. These are incorporated into an understanding of when CBT techniques should be used to divert an escalation of anger or aggression. The importance of role playing to practice skills as they are taught cannot be overemphasized. Much practice will be needed to change an automatic behavior of anger escalation and aggression to one of management of that emotion. In the next chapter, we address coping and interpersonal competence, thereby adding to the skills presented in this chapter. The combination of stress and anger management with interpersonal relationship skills will provide children with many options for diverting problematic externalizing behavior.

References

Alessi, J. J., & Hearn, K. (1984). Group treatment of children in shelters for battered women. In A. R. Roberts (Ed.), *Battered women and their families* (pp. 49–61). New York: Springer.

American Psychiatric Association. (1994). *Diagnostic and statistical manual of mental disorders* (DSM-IV, 4th ed.). Washington, DC: Author.

Borba, M., & Borba, C. (1978). *Self-esteem: A classroom affair*. San Francisco: Harper & Row.

Cohen, M. A. (1985). *Feel safe*. Racine, WI: Western.

Cohen, J. A., & Mannarino, A. P. (1996). A treatment outcome study for sexually abused preschool children: Initial findings. *Journal of the American Academy of Child and Adolescent Psychiatry, 35*, 42–50.

Craske, M. G., & Barlow, D. H. (1993). *Therapist's guide for the Mastery of Your Anxiety and Panic (MAP) program*. Albany, NY: Graywind.

Dangel, R. F., Deschner, J. P., & Rasp, R. R. (1989). Anger control training for adolescents in residential treatment. [Special issue: Empirical research in behavioral social work]. *Behavior Modification, 13*, 447–458.

Deblinger, E. (1999, October). *Cognitive behavioral treatment with sexually abused children.* Annual Fall Training Meeting of the South Carolina Professional Society on the Abuse of Children, Columbia, SC.

Deblinger, E., & Heflin, A. H. (1996). *Treating sexually abused children and their nonoffending parents: A cognitive behavioral approach.* Thousand Oaks, CA: Sage.

Deblinger, E., McLeer, S. V., & Henry, D. (1990). Cognitive behavioral treatment for sexually abused children suffering post-traumatic stress: Preliminary findings. *Journal of the American Academy of Child and Adolescent Psychiatry, 29,* 747–752.

Feindler, E. L., & Ecton, R. B. (1986). *Adolescent anger control: Cognitive behavioral techniques.* New York: Pergamon.

Feindler, E. L., Ecton, R. B., Kingsley, D., & Dubey, D. R. (1986). Group anger-control training for institutionalized psychiatric male adolescents. *Behavior Therapy, 17,* 109–123.

Feindler, E. L., Marriott, S. A., & Iwata, M. (1984). Group anger control training for junior high school delinquents. *Cognitive Therapy and Research, 8,* 299–311.

Jaffe, P. G., Wolfe, D. A., & Wilson, S. K. (1990). *Children of battered women.* Newbury Park, CA: Sage.

Kendall, P. C. (1994). Treatment of anxiety disorders in children: Results of a randomized clinical trial. *Journal of Consulting and Clinical Psychology, 62,* 100–110.

Kolko, D. J., Dorsett, P. G., & Milan, M. A. (1981). A total-assessment approach in the evaluation of social skills training: The effectiveness of an anger-control program for adolescent psychiatric patients. *Behavior Assessment, 3,* 383–402.

Lochman, J. E., Burch, P. R., Curry, J. F., & Lampron, L. B. (1984). Treatment and generalization effects of cognitive-behavioral and goal-setting interventions with aggressive boys. *Journal of Consulting and Clinical Psychology, 52,* 915–916.

Ollendick, T. H., & Cerny, J. A. (1981). *Clinical behavior therapy with children.* New York: Plenum.

Smith, D. W., Swenson, C. C., & Hanson, R. (1995, June). Reducing trauma-related emotional symptoms through individual treatment for physically abused children. In M. L. Kessler (Chair), *Treating Physical Abuse and Neglect: Four Approaches.* Symposium conducted at the 3rd Annual APSAC Colloquium, Tucson, AZ.

Stauffer, L. B., & Deblinger, E. (1996). Cognitive behavioral groups for nonoffending mothers and their young sexually abused children: A preliminary treatment outcome study. *Child Maltreatment, 1,* 65–76.

Swenson, C. C, & Brown, E. J. (2000). Cognitive-behavioral group treatment for physically-abused children. *Cognitive and Behavioral Practice, 6,* 212–220.

Swenson, C. C., Butler, A. C., Kennedy, W. A., & Baum, J. G. (1988). *Group treatment for anger control with institutionalized adolescent offenders.* Paper presented at the annual conference of the Florida Association of School Psychologists, Tampa, FL.

Swenson, C. C., & Kolko, D. J. (2000). Long-term management of the developmental consequences of child physical abuse. In R. M. Reece (Ed.), *The treatment of child abuse* (pp. 135–154). Baltimore, MD: Johns Hopkins University Press.

10

Promoting Children's Effective Coping and Social Competence

This chapter addresses children's coping, social support, and social competence. First, we focus on cognitive and behavioral coping with problems in general, as well as with violence and the occurrence of medical emergencies. Next, we address social supports broadly, and the use of those supports to help with emergencies and personal problems. Last, we present some skills-training suggestions for improving children's relationships with their friends and family.

The first section deals with helping the child learn how thoughts affect feelings and how negative choices cause negative consequences. An additional focus is on helping the child understand the difference between things we can change and things we cannot change, as well as the options available for each one. The material includes discussion of some of the child's coping responses to common situations.

❏ Children's Coping Skills

COPING WITH PROBLEMS, INCLUDING VIOLENCE: IDENTIFYING
NEGATIVE REACTIONS OR RESPONSES

Definition

One of the therapist's most difficult tasks is figuring out how well
the child handles everyday stressors and in what ways she or he commonly responds to or copes with them. This information is relevant to
determining whether or not certain responses increase the risk of further coercive behavior or other negative consequences, either self-
inflicted or administered by others.

Description

A few general probes might be used to introduce this topic and to
elicit information about the child's behavior and temperament in various circumstances: *"What are you like at school (at sports, at home, with
your friends, in the community, etc.)?"* or, *"What would others say about
you—or your behavior—there? How about other places where you usually
are?"* These questions are designed to provide a neutral context for
understanding what the child is like and how she or he may be perceived by others.

Next, the therapist should attempt to elicit information about
some of the problematic ways in which the child responds, which can
be introduced as follows:

> *I'm sure you've had to handle some difficult situations involving your fam-
> ily, friends, or others you've met but don't know well. Kids do different
> things when they're upset. Have you ever done anything like this?* [The
> therapist should mention a few coping responses as a basis for dis-
> cussion.] *How do you usually solve problems? . . . What things do you do
> to deal with problems? . . . What things usually help? . . . What things usu-
> ally don't help?*
>
> *Thinking for a moment about some of the more challenging and upset-
> ting ones, can you tell me some of the things that you or other kids should
> really avoid doing when you have problems or feel uptight or upset? Are
> there some things that you've done that might not have been helpful.*

Once these questions are answered, it may be helpful to discuss the
child's preferences for responding to these situations. It is important to

help the child focus on alternative, positive ways of coping (e.g., *"What can we do that is helpful or good for us?"*).

Comments and Caveats

The therapist should try to understand some of the reasons that these behaviors were selected as a way of understanding the child's motivation and current repertoire. Based on this discussion, the therapist may be in a position briefly to describe some of the negative consequences of these choices, including any potential, likely, or actual ones. Box 10.1 shows types of coping responses or reactions, among others, that the child may have exhibited in these problem situations and for which it may be useful to look.

Box 10.1 | Common Coping Responses or Reactions Reported by Children

Younger Child:

1. Not listening/following rules or doing what you're told
2. Breaking or taking things that don't belong to you
3. Fighting or hurting others
4. Not telling the truth
5. Hiding or staying by yourself
6. Not wanting to do anything
7. Talking like a baby
8. Screaming and yelling when you don't get your way

Older Child:

1. Seeking out delinquent friends; criminal or destructive behavior
2. Using drugs or alcohol
3. Engaging in self-injury or withdrawal
4. Running away instead of getting help
5. Daydreaming
6. Eating or sleeping too much or too little
7. Have problems with police or the courts (vandalizing)
8. Skipping school; poor grades
9. Fighting or hurting others
10. Stealing

Certainly, some children will be forthcoming and appreciative of this effort, whereas others may be uninterested in such a discussion. Therefore, it may be necessary to ask directly those children who acknowledge few behaviors whether they have ever found themselves "doing any of these things" in order to identify their involvement in typical problem behaviors. Each individual behavior then can be reviewed.

CHARACTERIZING AND ENHANCING THE CHILD'S RECENT COPING EFFORTS

Description

Once the child has begun to discuss the different ways that he or she copes with difficult situations, the therapist should be in a position to formulate an impression of the overall nature and efficacy of these coping efforts. An existing rating scale designed to evaluate the general use and impact of various types of coping behaviors is the KIDCOPE (Spirito, Stark, & Williams, 1988). The KIDCOPE asks the child to describe how he or she responded to a few common recent stressors (e.g., breaking curfew or doing poorly in school) and includes a prompt to elicit an individualized scenario reflecting something that bothered the child during the past month. Of course, the instrument can be adapted to address any type of problematic situation, such as involvement in a conflictual, hostile, or physically punitive interaction. For each situation, the child is asked whether one of several coping responses was used and, if so, the extent to which it was helpful.

Application

We have used the KIDCOPE to assess the specific types of coping responses commonly used by individual abused children and to determine whether any specific changes may be needed to their coping repertoire. In some instances, the specific situation selected for evaluation was highly idiosyncratic to the child. For example, Joe was asked to respond to the questions on this scale with reference to the standard situations, but was also asked about a recent incident in which he was involved in a fight at home. This situational analysis revealed that he had engaged in a broad range of coping responses, some of which were found to be potentially destructive (e.g., the use of drugs, driving fast, and staying away from school).

The KIDCOPE was used by clinicians in the Project IMPACT (Interventions to Maximize Parent and Child Togetherness) outcome study to elicit children's coping responses, which were examined on at least two dimensions that pertain to the ways in which children cope. First, the responses may be characterized as *behavioral* (e.g., tried to feel better by spending time with others, did something like watch TV, or blamed someone else) or *cognitive* (e.g., tried to fix problem by thinking of answers, tried to see the good side of things, or blamed self for causing the problem). This dimension reflects the domain in which the child prefers to cope. Second, the responses may be characterized as reflecting *active* (e.g., being assertive) or *passive* (e.g., taking drugs) coping strategies. These responses reflect different types of coping strategies (e.g., distraction, cognitive restructuring, problem solving, or social support). When crossed together by clinicians in that study, these two dimensions yielded a grid with four cells, into which the therapist classified the child's coping responses (see Box 10.2). The therapist may learn that the child's responses constitute a more general coping style, reflecting a consistent type of response across situations. Such information may be helpful to point out to the child, especially if it emphasizes the reliance upon a less than effective coping style.

Alternatively, one can simply discuss the different strategies or responses that the child prefers and any problems that ensue from these strategies, including the actual benefits and costs of these strategies. Some children may be inclined to use avoidance (e.g., leaving the room, distracting themselves, or getting busy); others may prefer more active strategies (e.g., dealing with problems directly or getting help).

Box 10.2	Grid Showing Examples of Different Types of Coping Responses

	Active	*Passive*
Behavioral	assertion	withdrawal
Cognitive	self-talk	distraction, denial

Finally, the clinician should help the child recognize the benefits and risks or disadvantages of these coping responses, and then discuss responses that might be more effective—that is, more likely to get the outcome the child wants or needs (*"So, is there something else you could do or try that will get you what you want when that happens?"*). Of course, the purpose of this routine is to encourage more resourcefulness and helpful coping efforts when the child has shown helpless, ineffective, and/or destructive coping responses, and to provide suggestions on how to respond in a more useful manner when these situations occur again.

Comments and Caveats

The therapist should be prepared for the child to need considerable prompting and examples in order to determine how she or he typically responds to a stressful or conflictual situation. It is possible that the child responds in several different ways and that certain aspects of the situation dictate which type of response is actually made. The lack of any consistently demonstrated style in this review is as important as determining whether the child, to paraphrase songwriter Paul Simon, leans on "old familiar ways."

COPING WITH PAIN AND MINOR INJURIES

Description

One of the more obvious threats to the welfare and coping of children who have been physically abused is their not so uncommon experience of physical injury or pain. To further enhance the theme of empowerment and active coping in this population, we often review with the child suggestions for responding to mild physical injuries or pain, regardless of whether this is due to an abusive experience or not. Box 10.3 provides a handout used in the Project IMPACT outcome study containing recommendations for children that are based on the advice of a nurse practitioner. These suggestions are intended to promote active coping efforts that may also minimize the child's pain or suffering, even over minor injuries such as a scratch or cut. Thus, the overall purpose for this exercise is to promote an awareness of the child's needs and the importance of addressing any physical problems or injuries through the child's own attempts to himself or herself, as well as efforts to elicit the help of others.

Box 10.3	Initial Suggestions for Handling Medical Concerns or Emergencies

EMERGENCY NUMBERS: If you or someone else needs help.
If it is a medical emergency and you need help right away, **DIAL 911**

State Childline: _____

Emergency Room: _____

Box 10.3 | *continued*

MEDICAL CARE AT HOME:

Minor cuts and bruises can be cared for by someone who is not a doctor or nurse. Ice can be put on a bruised area. Minor cuts and scrapes should be cleaned with plain water and covered with a band-aid.

Serious cuts that will not stop bleeding need to be looked at by an adult. If your parent is unavailable, call a neighbor or adult friend. If no one is available, **DIAL 911** and tell them what is wrong.

Burns can be caused by matches and cigarettes, hot water, or placing skin next to something hot. Run cold water or put ice on the burned area immediately. If your skin blisters or swells, have an adult look at it.

Broken bones are present when the area is painful to touch, or when there is pain, swelling, an unnatural position of the limb, and the sound of breaking. Try not to move the broken limb and call an adult for help. If you can't, **DIAL 911.**

If you are hurt and you are not sure if it is serious, always have an adult look at it. You could ask parents, a neighbor, teachers, a school nurse, or one of us.

❏ Social Support

SOCIAL SUPPORTS TO HANDLE EMERGENCIES AND PERSONAL PROBLEMS

This section deals with helping the child to learn about the benefit of having and using social supports, how to handle an emergency and determine from whom to ask for help, and constructive ways to feel better when stress becomes unbearable. Some materials to be explained later in the section are intended to promote the application of these techniques.

The Benefits of Social Support: Orientation and Definition

The child can be reminded that they have talked before about people who can help us when we need them. These people can be called our *social supports*. A general probe may elicit some initial discussion of this topic (e.g., *"Did you think about the people who help you since we talked last time? Everybody needs people who help and care for them. We also need friends who do things with us, like play with us in the neighborhood, go places together, or play games together"*).

Description

It is important for the child to understand that children can make things better for themselves. The child first can be taught that self-disclosure is possible by using modeling, rehearsal, shaping, and reinforcement. One of the first steps in this teaching process is to have the child brainstorm and generate a list of ways to feel better. Common examples of these behaviors including talking to a friend, sibling, counselor, neighbor, relative, or peer. One of the details to doing this exercise successfully involves discussing how to decide to whom the child should or could talk. As found in the Project IMPACT outcome study, many of the children needed some helping figuring out the "right" person (e.g., *"This person will listen to what you have to say. They won't ignore you, tell on you, or make fun of you. Perhaps it is someone who's also had this experience, someone you trust, and/or someone you have a long-standing friendship with"*).

Next, the clinician can ask the child to identify and be prepared to use a support system. The following considerations are relevant to a discussion of social supports: (a) who helps you, and (b) who doesn't seem to help you. Encourage the child to identify some different individuals who can serve as supports (*"Who can help you?"*)—friend, family member, or community person, for example. It is important to assess the child's fears or concerns about talking to another person about family violence. Reassure the child about the benefit of being protected—having a relative or friend to help out.

HANDLING CONFLICTS OR CRISES USING SOCIAL SUPPORTS

Description

Although cases of injury or being placed in a situation where injury is likely may be relatively infrequent, it seems prudent to understand what the child might do in these situations. There may be different reasons for discussing this topic with the child, but it may be useful to offer a general rationale initially (e.g., *"All children should know how to get help or assistance and how to deal with emergencies"*).

A few instructions may be helpful to review with those children who may be able to appreciate and follow them, and only when the therapist believes that they would not jeopardize the child's welfare or family situation further. First, the clinician can provide a business card and discuss medical emergency information (i.e., whom to call). If necessary, the child may be encouraged to leave home if there is an emergency (i.e., if someone is likely to get hurt). Although some children may find it difficult to understand, emphasize that it is important not to argue with a volatile or violent adult. In such instances, the child should be encouraged to find someone to contact or talk to when this is possible (e.g., a neighbor, relatives, a friend, the clergy, or a counselor). Other sources of potential help also could be reviewed (e.g., 911, an abuse hotline, the caseworker, or the local mental health clinic). Sometimes, it may be necessary to remind the reluctant child not to try to solve the parent's arguments, if an argument happens, and not to get caught between them. Instead, their efforts would be better spent trying to concentrate on solving their own problems and getting help if they need it. Box 10.4 shows a form adapted from the work of Wilson, Cameron, Jaffe, and Wolfe (1986) that can be used to identify and prepare supportive individuals for their inclusion in a child's safety plan or call.

| **Box 10.4** | Sample Form for Identifying Potential Social Supports for the Child |

"If I Need Help" Form

There may be times when I may need someone to help me. If I need help, some of the people to whom I could turn are listed here.

I could get help from these people at my school: Phone:	I could get help from these members of my neighborhood (or church/synagogue): Phone:
I could get help from these friends: Phone:	I could get help from my these members of my family: Phone:
I could get help from my caseworker at the Children & Youth Services agency: Phone:	I could get help from you, my counselor: Phone:
If there is an emergency, I could call the emergency room at this clinic/hospital: Phone:	If there is a medical emergency and I need help right away, I could get help from: **DIAL 911**

SOURCE: Adapted from Wilson et al. (1986). Reprinted with permission.

Comments and Caveats

It is important to note a few caveats and considerations in using this procedure. First, the child must be comfortable with the notion of contacting the identified support person and have adequate self-disclosure skills in order to make this useful. Second, the support person certainly needs to be alerted to and be comfortable with being placed in this helping role. Failure to make contact with this individual may invite basic apathy at best and outright hostile responses at worst. Third, it is helpful to review the procedure in advance with the parents and to ensure that they are comfortable with the use of this procedure and the child's identified support person. Certainly, parental approval may make it possible in some cases for a child actually to use the procedure. Finally, children ought to be reminded that even though all of these plans may be in place, there will be times when a support person cannot or will not be helpful to them with a particular problem.

OTHER ATTEMPTS TO ENHANCE SELF-DISCLOSURE AND FEELING BETTER

Description

An initial difficulty that children experience when this material is reviewed is the discomfort at the thought of talking to others about their family problems and going outside of the family for assistance, because they have often been told, "We don't talk about our business with others." Thus, some children may not be very amenable to discussing their problematic experiences or family circumstances with others. We have occasionally suggested to these children that they make an effort to document some of these experiences in a simple format, such as keeping a diary or journal, making audiotapes, or making a scrapbook. The clinician can model a constructive journal entry in a small diary or paper in order to stimulate the development of one of the important skills underlying this task, namely, a self-disclosing repertoire. Asking specific questions (e.g., "*What happened? How did I feel? Can I do anything different next time?*"), may be helpful to initiate this discussion. There are times when it will be necessary to examine the child's entries and to contrast a constructive versus a destructive entry whenever relevant.

The therapist may also ask the child about other ways to feel better that were not covered earlier (e.g., "*Do you ever do something like . . . ?*"), and to suggest some alternative activities when a difficult situation requires some reflection, a break, or another's perspective (e.g., listening to music, exercising, drawing, writing in a diary, talking with friends, writing stories, playing sports, or telling a friend). In modeling a constructive (vs. destructive) communication, the therapist may provide a destructive example (e.g., *"Leave me alone! I hate talking to you or anyone. I can take care of myself and I don't need anyone's help!"*), or a constructive example (e.g., *"I feel very angry and scared because my parents were fighting again and blamed it all on me"*). The therapist should reinforce the benefits of constructive communication, such as building healthy relationships with others (*"If you're talking to others and you're not in a good mood, it is helpful to tell them, 'I feel X because of Y'"*). Then, it would be useful to have the child practice having a constructive conversation.

Finally, there may be some children who need to develop some personal and family interests as a way of providing exposure to others and to practice new skills. One of the other ways to help children is to teach them how to encourage quality family time, to learn strategies and options for overcoming obstacles to positive family time, and to review and apply new skills to daily situations. A few simple questions may be helpful in discussing the child's personal interests or hobbies (e.g., *"What do you like to do now—artwork? Music? Sports?"*). Similar questions might be asked to determine how to get the child involved in positive activities with family members (e.g., *"What activities do you like to do as a family? What do you not like to do?"*). Likewise, the child may be able to discuss various problems that make it difficult to do things together or to enjoy each other's company. The situations may vary in terms of whether the situations relate to parental or family events (e.g., marital fighting, conflicting loyalties, or not having any time or money).

Comments and Caveats

Before concluding this discussion, the therapist may wish to review the child's progress and consider any follow-up plans, such as what the child learned that seems important to his or her family situation (e.g., what skills or supports the child learned), what plans were made (e.g., *"We call and may schedule a few visits, as needed"*), and what expectations the therapist has of the child (e.g., try hard, use skills, and call if necessary).

❏ Enhancing Children's Social Competence and Developing Relationships: Getting Along With Friends and Family

This section introduces the concept of social skills to the child. Part of this lesson seeks to show and practice with the child the effective use of social skills in various situations at home and with friends. Of course, learning these skills first requires that the therapist and child discuss some of the potential rewards to engaging in positive social interactions. In many instances, the skills can be construed and appreciated as alternatives to some type of aggressive or passive behavior by the child. For further information, an excellent resource can be found in Michelson, Sugai, Wood, & Kazdin (1983).

THE BENEFITS AND COSTS OF HAVING FRIENDS

Although there are many reasons why having friends can be beneficial, having friends also can create problems or conflicts. To understand some of the peer or social problems commonly reported among physically abused children, it is important to appreciate the child's perspective on both of these considerations. The therapist first can introduce the topic by pointing to some of the more common reasons why children have friends, as suggested by Therapist Example 10.1.

THERAPIST EXAMPLE **10.1**

Introduction to a Discussion of Children's Friendships

"Almost everyone has at least one friend, although some children and adults have lots of friends. We realize that having friends can be a wonderful thing because we sometimes get to do fun things with others, learn things from them, or just simply spend time with them when we don't have much to do. Some of us may need friends who do things with us, like play with us in the neighborhood, go places together with us, or play games with us. Of course, it may not always be easy to make friends, keep friends, or like all of the things they say or do. So, it might be hard to have friends all of the time and to want to be with them."

Description

An attempt should be made to ask the child about his or her own friends and the ways in which the child interacts with these friends (e.g., *"Maybe you can tell me about some of the ways that having friends can be or is good? How can having friends be helpful or fun? Okay, now, are there some ways in which having friends can be hard or difficult for us? How can having friends be a problem for us?"*). Be attentive to the quantity and quality of friends with whom the child has contact. Box 10.5 provides a list of the some of the interview probes we used to elicit information about the child's friends and friendships. These probes are meant to be general and fairly neutral to minimize how challenging or upsetting this initial discussion could become.

| **Box 10.5** | Initial Probes to Understand the Child's Friends/Friendships |

Who are your friends?

What do you like about them?

What do you think they like about you?

How often do you do things with them?

What do you usually do together?

What do you usually talk about?

What would you like to do differently with them?

How could you get this to happen?

SOCIAL SKILLS AND FRIENDS

Description

The therapist can describe to the child what social skills are and provide a rationale for their use in the following way:

> *You know that there are some good ways and not so good ways to talk to or interact with others, like our friends or our family. If you talk in certain ways, it will be easier for you to make and keep the friends that you care about. We call these 'good' ways to get along with others social skills. These are ways to act, like sharing toys and not fighting, and things to say that will make others enjoy playing and being with you.*

Discussion Questions to Understand the Child's Concept of Social Skills

Because a child's level of sophistication on this topic is not easy to determine in advance, an initial dialogue may be helpful and can be stimulated by the following questions: (a) "Why is it important to have social skills—that means, where you say things in a way that is nice or friendly?"; (b) "Can you give me examples of situations where it is good to have social skills? Why?"; and (c) "Can you give me examples of situations where it is important to be careful what you say and how you say it? Why?"

Rationale for Social Skills

The child should be asked about the potential benefits to having and using good social skills. The therapist can look for and review several potential benefits:

- *"You can communicate better with others."*
- *"You may make more friends and get to know them better."*
- *"It is easier to join in on fun activities"* (e.g., clubs, games, etc.).
- *"You may be better liked by others, including adults."*
- *"You may be a happier person."*
- *"It's easier to keep the friends you already have."*
- *"You may be more successful in getting what you want from others."*

It is also reasonable to ask the child about potential problems or risk associated with not using social skills, as this may be part of his or her experience (e.g., *"When you don't have or even show good social skills, you may have other problems"*). A few of the more common problems children may identify are listed here: (a) one could end up being left out of important or fun things that are happening (e.g., conversations, activities, etc.); (b) one may get lonely, lose friends, or get into trouble with adults; and (c) one might not be able to communicate one's needs or feelings to other people very well. The therapist can emphasize that children with good social skills usually have more friends and better friendships, and they know how to get along better with their friends.

BASIC SOCIAL SKILLS THAT CHILDREN USE WITH THEIR FRIENDS AND FAMILY

Some of the more important skills that children use with friends or family, which they may actually take for granted, involve being polite, starting or opening conversations and taking turns, making requests and getting help, and standing up for themselves. It is helpful to introduce some of these basic skills, as follows:

> One way you make friends is by talking to people. If you want to start a conversation or an activity, you have to think of something to say that another person can easily understand and respond to—we call this an opener because it helps to open a conversation.

Openers are short, easy to understand, generally not likely to make someone upset or angry, and something people probably know about (e.g., where we live, school, sports, or the weather). Typical examples might include *"Want to see the picture I drew?"* or *"Guess what happened at school."* The child can be asked related questions to discuss this skill area (e.g., *"So, while you talk to your friends, how do you play nicely with them?"*). Several points might be made about what happens during this type of activity: (a) it is done without fighting; (b) one asks for things instead of grabbing them; (c) one answers questions; (d) one takes turns, shares, and follows the rules; and (e) one accepts responsibility for what one says and does and for the consequences.

Certainly, there are many other suggestions the therapist can make about what to say when initiating a conversation, but, in general, it should be explained to the child that we often feel good when we say nice things to others and when someone says something nice to us (e.g., *"Most children like to have their friends talk nicely to them. Now, you can say something nice about your friend and say why you said it, like something they did, something about them, something you did together"*). The therapist should offer a few examples of typical responses, such as (a) *"That was fun"*; (b) *"You're really good at basketball"*; (c) *"That was a great idea—look, it worked"*; or (d) *"That's a neat watch (shirt, game, etc.)."*

It may also be possible to encourage being helpful to others and providing social support to friends when they may need it (e.g., *"Now, you can also try to show that you really understand and support your friend when they really need your help. What are some different ways you can show support to another person?"*). Potential responses that might be discussed include the following:

- *"You can help them in some way."*
- *"You can support them by saying nice things, compliments."*
- *"You can say things that make them feel better or understood by telling them you see their point of view."*
- *"You can give them a gift."*
- *"You can give them a hug."*

A final aspect to this discussion involves helping the child appreciate the impact of a child's negative behavior on his or her friends' reactions to the child. Accordingly, one may continue with the following questions designed to promote this discussion:

Now, do you want to be nice to someone who yells, pushes, takes your toys without asking, fights, and isn't nice? Or, do you want to be nice to someone who talks in a regular voice, doesn't push, asks if he or she can play with your toys, doesn't fight, and says nice things to you?

Clearly, the message to be conveyed here is that when one is nice to others, they generally will be nice in return, and this will make it easier later on when one asks for their assistance or needs help (e.g., *"Could you help me with this? This is confusing—I don't understand"*).

Next, the child should be asked about his or her use of these social skills in order to understand whether they are actually in the child's current repertoire (e.g., *"So, which of these skills can you do? Which of these skills do you use?"*). If the child is forthcoming in responding to these questions, it seems reasonable to discuss the types of skills the child will use and how she or he could apply them (i.e., with whom, when, why, etc.). Offering some specific suggestions for use or practice of these skills at home may be instructive and informative.

SOCIAL SKILLS AND THE FAMILY/PARENTS

Rationale and Implications for Skill Use

A similar rationale for the use of social skills with friends may be given for the importance of their use with parents. However, it is important not to make the assumption that this has worked well in the past and to ask questions to determine whether social skills have been helpful (e.g., *"If you do these nice things at home, do you notice a difference in how you and your parents get along?"*). Examples might be given to determine the nature of these interactions—for example, by asking the child if she or he says "thank you" or "please" at home and how his or her parents respond to these statements when they are said.

Some children may experience frustration with this section because they feel they are not responsible for the problems and harm they have experienced, and they see their positive efforts to use social skills as being punished rather than reinforced. Indeed, this situation appeared to be true for some of the children in the Project IMPACT outcome study. Still, these children may benefit from statements that highlight that they are responsible only for their own behavior and that they do not need to do more if they already do nice things and do their part to get along with their parents. It is important to reiterate the goal of meeting parents "halfway" in this regard. We certainly do not want to create the wrong message or a situation where the child feels it is his or her responsibility to change or make everything all right because most of these children already feel responsible for the chaos or conflicts they experience at home. Instead, the focus here is on encouraging the child's prosocial behavior that, in turn, may enhance positive attitudes and impressions from the parents and family members. It is also important to emphasize that the parents may be learning many of the same skills and are being encouraged to do similar things in order to make things better at home (e.g., *"The things you learn here will help you get the things you want, have a better relationship with your parents, be treated better"*). So, just like children, parents, too, want to know when their children like something they are doing or something about them. There are many simple statements that children could use to reward their parent's positive behavior, including the following: (a) *"I like playing with you, mom/dad"*; (b) *"Thanks for helping me, mom/dad"*; or (c) *"Now I get it. Thanks!"*

SPECIFIC SOCIAL SKILLS

Skills for Home Use

There may be several skill areas worth discussing with the child that the therapist should explore and identify as relevant. Some common examples for discussion are listed in Box 10.6. It is most helpful to determine with the child which behaviors she or he is more likely to use and to encourage those behaviors initially. This list can be given to the child to serve as a reminder and to provide the specific language suggested for each skill.

Box 10.6 | Examples of Social Skills Domains and Responses

Getting Parent's Attention

"Take a look at this!" (to parent); "Now, how was that?" (asking for feedback)

Morning Statements

"Did you sleep well, mom/dad?"; "Have a good day"; "Good morning"

Evening/After School

"Hi! I'm home"; "How was your day, mom/dad?"

Nighttime

"Good night"; "Sleep well"

Remembering Special Occasions

Younger child: Make a holiday or birthday gift/card; leave someone a note saying something nice about the occasion

Older child: Mark special dates (e.g., birthday, anniversary, mother's/father's day, etc.) on a calendar and do something nice for a parent or sibling

---

Box 10.6 | *continued*

Being Supportive of Your Parents

Younger child: Be excited and show it when your parents tell you about something good; leave your parents alone when they are talking privately about something serious or upsetting

Older child: Be enthusiastic about the good news your parent shares with you ("Wow! That's great!"); be sensitive to their feelings about bad news or their complaints ("That sounds scary/upsetting/frustrating"; "Can I do anything to help?")

In-Session Activities for Practice

Besides describing the specific content skills to be learned, the therapist may wish to practice some of the skills with the child during the session. The opportunity for the child to rehearse the execution of these skills and receive feedback on their application may encourage their use outside of the session. The following scenarios may be read and used for role plays. Afterwards, the interaction can be discussed.

- *"Mom comes home from work. She looks tired and is yelling about the house being a mess. How is she feeling? How could you help?"*
- *"Dad is on the phone. He hangs up the phone, kicks the chair over, and swears. He tells your mom that he just got fired from his job. How is he feeling? How could you help?"*
- *"You come home from school. Your baby sister is crying and your mom is yelling at her. How is mom feeling? How can you help?"*

BEING ASSERTIVE/MAKING REQUESTS

There are three objectives to this section: (1) to learn the differences between assertive, passive, and aggressive behavior; (2) to understand how to identify aggressive or passive behavior, and (3) to use assertive behavior more effectively.

Assertive, Passive, and Aggressive Responses

There could be great diversity in the child's social repertoire and style of interacting with others. The therapist will briefly review the three interpersonal styles or responses—being assertive, passive, or aggressive—but first should discuss differences among them (see Michelson et al., 1983). One can introduce this topic with the following terms:

> There are different ways to do things when you're with others—you can be aggressive, which involves using force or control to make something happen; you can be passive, which means not doing a thing, letting someone else take control, just accepting whatever happens; or you can be assertive, which means doing something specific to change a problem, but without hurting others in any way.

We illustrate the impact of these different response options by highlighting their definitions in the context of some examples. The therapist can define what it means to be assertive. Being assertive may mean that someone is more likely to listen to us and to do something that we want him or her to do. Use an example, such as when we request a favor, which is something everyone does, to illustrate how being socially skillful may actually improve one's chance of getting what one wants from another person.

> Sometimes, we want other people to help us or we want to be treated in a good way. When you make requests in a nice way, like asking nicely or discussing something without getting loud or angry—the assertive way—then you really have a better chance of getting what you want.

Therapist Example 10.2 presents situations where children might request favors.

THERAPIST EXAMPLE 10.2

Sample Interpersonal Situations for Discussion

Situation #1: When asking a friend to help you with homework

Wrong (aggressive) way: *"You have to help me with my homework!"* This is demanding their help, ordering others around, which is bossy.

Wrong (passive) way: Say nothing and wait for someone to realize that you need help.

Right (assertive) way: *"Please help me with my homework."*

What is the difference in these responses? Politeness and respect for others, making a clear request without making others angry or feeling pressured.

Situation #2: When asking your parent(s) for something

Wrong (aggressive) way: *"I want that! Get that for me! You never give me what I want!"* This is bossy.

Wrong (passive) way: Sit and wait for your parent(s) to notice that you want something, then feel hurt that they didn't notice.

Right (assertive) way: "I want to earn an allowance so I won't have to bug you for stuff. Will you have time on *[name a day and time]* to sit down and work out a list of things I can do, and what I will earn if I do them?" So, ask yourself: "Will asking this way get me what I want." Remember, there are several skills you can use here: (a) ask nicely ("Please," "Excuse me,")—be positive; (b) make eye contact, use a calm inflection, and make a clear request with reason; (c) pick a good time and place (wait until later if necessary), and (d) be reasonable—compromise if you need to.

The parenthetical example offered in the previous paragraph provides an illustration of the types of statements that can be reviewed with the child. Some probes for use in eliciting the child's understanding of this section and some final suggestions or caveats on their use include the following questions and comments:

- *"Which way is the better way to ask for something? Why?"*
- *"How do you feel when someone asks you for a favor in a rude way, or when people are pushy?"*
- *"What can you do if someone refuses your request?"* (e.g., do not be mean or sarcastic, and try to listen carefully to and then understand the other person's reason).
- *"If you didn't make your request clear the first time, it's okay to ask the person again and to try to make it clearer by explaining the importance of the favor. If the answer is still no, leave that person alone and drop the issue for awhile. If you continue to ask, the person may become angry and may not want to talk with you for awhile."*

Box 10.7 provides several examples of role-play situations relating to the skill of making requests that can be practiced during the session. The therapist can provide feedback and suggestions on the child's use of the skills, as well as on when these skills are most relevant. In addition, the child should be encouraged to practice these skills at home. She or he should be encouraged to remember what requests were made and what the results were. To make this practice most relevant, the child should identify in advance some type of activities that he or she would like to do at home or with friends.

Box 10.7 | Role-Play Situations Related to Making Requests

You would like to borrow a friend's new videogame.

You would like to ask your father if you can stay overnight at a friend's house.

You would like to ask a neighborhood friend to play a sport with you.

As you board a bus to go downtown, you realize that you need to borrow a quarter.

You would like to go home with some friends who are getting a ride home from school.

You would like to work with a classmate on a project.

You are contacting the local recreation center to learn about an upcoming tryout.

You stop by a few neighbors' homes to learn if they have seen your bike.

You see some friends playing ball down the street and would like to play with them.

You want to ask a classmate if they have the homework assignment for today.

STANDING UP FOR YOURSELF: SAYING WHAT'S ON
YOUR MIND

Rationale

Among the many personally challenging social situations faced by an abused child are those that involve responding appropriately to others' complaints or to put-downs, which may be especially important given the frequency that critical or hostile interchanges may occur in the home. The therapist can explain the rationale and potential benefits of using the procedure described in Therapist Example 10.3. It is important to understand that the child may not appreciate the benefits of being assertive in the event his or her experiences using this skill have been less than successful. Thus, discussing both the benefits and some disadvantages may be a more realistic approach to addressing this skill (see Michelson et al., 1983, for additional material on this topic).

THERAPIST EXAMPLE 10.3

Example of Rationale for Using Assertion

"Being assertive sometimes means that you let other people know what's on your mind and how you feel when you need to, but in a way that doesn't hurt or bother others. Sometimes, what's on our mind is something positive and nice that we want to share about something we like; and, at other times, we may have something to say about someone or something that we don't like. The best (fastest) way to correct a problem we may not like—or whatever bothers us—is to let the person or people responsible know we are unhappy. We let people know this to make things better, not to hurt others or make them feel bad.

"For example, say you go to the store to buy a can of soda or a candy bar and the cashier ignores you or tells you to get out because kids aren't allowed in the store. It's your right to buy these things at a public store. If you are behaving and respecting others, then you have a right to buy your items. If you don't stand up for yourself, not only will you be pushed around or taken advantage of, but it might also happen to someone else—or even to you again. So, it's important to stand up for your self."

Benefits of This Skill

Why is it important to stand up for one's rights? A few answers to elicit from and discuss with the child are listed here: (a) *"You are a good person: you respect yourself and deserve to be treated fairly"*; (b) *"You make sure you get what you want"*; (c) *"You make sure that others know more about the real you"*; and (d) *"It will help to keep you from being mad or upset at others."*

Furthermore, certain statements may minimize any further problems, arguments, or conflicts that standing up for oneself may generate. The therapist coaches the child to role-play the use of some of the following skills: (a) state how you feel about it: *"I feel X about Y"*; (b) ask for clarification: *"Do you mean . . . ?"*; (c) accept "no" for now, and discuss it later; (d) suggest a compromise: *"If you help me with X, then I'll do Y"*; and (e) do not complain a lot, *"otherwise people will think you are a complainer and they won't pay attention to you. If others complain to you, listen and ask them how they are feeling about their complaint"* (e.g., sad, upset, or frustrated). The child can be told that it is important to listen to other people when they say something assertive to them: At times, this can help them save a friendship, prevent making mistakes, and show how others are respected by them. A child can learn a lot about him- or herself—or about others who are being assertive—by listening and thinking about what the other person has to say.

That said, one needs to follow these instructions with some points for review that provide the child with a context for appreciating what has just been said. First, the therapist can tell the child, *"You'll get what you want when you make a positive, constructive complaint; and you won't if you don't."* Second, the therapist can remind the child to think of someone who complains a lot and then consider how she or he feels when around this person (e.g., *"What does this tell you about how to use complaints?"*).

Description

There are many situations in which it would be good for a child to stand up for him- or herself. Here are a few examples for session role plays:

- *"You and your friend are playing a board game. Your friend says to you: 'You can't do that! I don't think you can move that way.'"*
- *"You are in a store looking for a gift for a friend. One of the store clerks come up to you and says, 'If you're not buying something, you are going to have to leave.'"*
- *"You are watching one of your favorite TV shows. Your dad comes in, changes the station without saying a word to you, and starts watching something else."*

Once these situations are acted out, the therapist can ask the child for a critique with recommendations on making a more competent response. Other examples of relevant role plays for children and adolescents can be found in Box 10.8

Box 10.8   Role-Play Situations Related to Standing Up for Oneself

Someone borrowed a record from you a while ago. You've already asked for it back once.

You just bought a slice of pizza and got the wrong amount of change.

While standing in the check-out line at a local store, someone cuts in front of you.

Someone in class unfairly accuses you of talking while the teacher stepped out.

You bought a new computer game and notice that it doesn't work properly. You go back to the store.

Your sister tells you that it is your turn to wash the dishes. You washed them yesterday and you know that it is not your turn.

You've worked for your allowance. When you ask for it, your mom says that she didn't see you do your chores.

Comments and Caveats

For home practice, the child can be asked to think of at least one situation at school and at home where she or he could or should have been more assertive, like standing up for one's rights or making a complaint (see Michelson et al., 1983). The therapist should consider the following questions for discussion of the outcome of this home practice exercise: (a) *"Did you do what you wanted to do?"*; (b) if the answer is yes, *"How hard was this to do?"*; (c) if the answer is no, *"Why didn't you?"*; (d) *"How could you have said something?"*; and (e) *"What would be the assertive way to handle this situation?"* Other situations for practice can be found in Box 10.9.

Box 10.9 | Role-Play Situations Related to Making Complaints

You have been punished by a teacher for something you did not do.

You purchase a shirt from a store that you later decide isn't the right color.

You're involved in a serious and close basketball game, but your friend isn't taking the game seriously.

You family starts to laugh at something you worked hard to make for a friend.

A good friend of yours begins to criticize another good friend.

You are talking to a friend while another friend is trying to distract you and get you to leave.

You are late for a sporting event because your friend forgot to tell you that the arrangements have changed.

You get home from the video store and find that the movie you rented is ripped.

You are watching television and your sibling or friend keeps changing the channel.

❏ **Summary**

The techniques in this chapter seek to enhance the child's coping skills primarily through the implementation of efforts to enhance the child's social support and social skills. As is generally true of most children, abused children may vary considerably in their coping skills and responses, so it should not be surprising to find that many children are coping just fine. What may be more complicated for the therapist is to elicit and understand the very subtle ways in which abused children respond to their circumstances and to determine whether any particular coping responses are problematic or dangerous. Furthermore, the nature of these coping responses may have implications for the use of various treatment techniques (e.g., withdrawal vs. aggression) discussed in the following chapters.

The therapist also should recognize that any efforts to change a child's problematic behaviors must be initiated at the appropriate time. This is equally true with the use of a social support individual, which must be monitored for some time in order to determine the nature of any assistance provided by such individuals. Likewise, parents may wish to know about any social skills taught to their children, especially if they are amenable to promoting such skills at home.

References

Michelson, L., Sugai, D. P., Wood, R. P. & Kazdin, A. E. (1983). *Social skills assessment and training with children: An empirically based handbook.* New York: Plenum.

Spirito, A., Stark, L. J., & Williams, C. (1988). Development of a brief coping checklist for use with pediatric populations. *Journal of Pediatric Psychology, 13,* 555–574.

Wilson, S. K., Cameron, S., Jaffe, P., & Wolfe, D. A. (1986). *Manual for a group program for children exposed to wife abuse.* London, Ontario: Ministry of Community and Social Services-Family Violence Unit.

11

Adult Treatment
Cognitive Interventions

❏ **Parental Perspectives on Violence, Expectations, and Distortions**

This chapter highlights cognitive-behavioral treatment (CBT) techniques for understanding how stress in the family and the stress inherent in parenting can affect behavior. Furthermore, we address ways to manage stress other than through the use of harsh talk or physical force. Finally, we look at situations when parental expectations are out of line with reality, as shown through misattributions about the child and limited understanding of developmental level.

❏ **Stress Management and Family Characteristics**

CHILD AND PARENT CHARACTERISTICS, AND THEIR
RELATIONSHIP TO PROBLEMS

Background and Definition

To introduce techniques for addressing stress in the family, we find it helpful to remind the parent of the goal of treatment and the material that may be covered (e.g., *"It is helpful to understand how families behave or get along—especially the specific ways in which you and your children interact on a regular basis"*). This means looking at different reasons for why children or parents behave in certain ways. All families have different characteristics that may make them more likely to feel stressed; in some cases, it may be useful to mention that parents may get overwhelmed, not only by their child's behavior, but also by the other stressors that can affect their daily life. Consequently, any parent may find himself or herself doing things that are not good for either the parent or the child, and this may not help to improve their child's behavioral or emotional problems.

Description of Procedure

Objective instruments or measures incorporate a number of common circumstances in different families. Clinicians can use these instruments to ask parents to articulate some of the problems or stressors they have experienced. For example, we have administered the Profile of Child and Parent Characteristics (Barkley, 1990) to identify problems. A rationale for examining this information can be given emphasizing the potential benefits to thinking about different reasons for why children and parents behave in certain ways. The parent should understand the kinds of events that may influence children and what happens in their homes. Therefore, the therapist can encourage the parent *"to look at these and other types of characteristics that may influence your child's behavior,"* which are listed on the profile sheet. One might ask the parents to determine which, if any, sound like they describe the child or themselves, and how these characteristics have affected what has happened at home. Examples of the domains that can be discussed and of what is included in those domains can be found in Box 11.1.

Box 11.1 | Sample Domains and Their Components

Child: For example, what is inherited (traits), difficult temperament, activity level, attention span, impulse control, emotionality, sociability, response to stimulation, developmental abilities (e.g., limited language, health problems), and physical characteristics (e.g., cute/fair). The parent should be reminded that children who are more extreme in these ways may be harder to manage, may show more problem behaviors, and may need more attention or involvement from their families—these may increase stress and conflict.

> # Box 11.1 | *continued*
>
> **Parent:** Includes all of the factors noted above, as well as the ability to tolerate frustration and to show self-control. Concerns related to health or physical status, and behavioral, emotional and cognitive functioning, deserve mention.
>
> **Situational:** Anything that is going on in the situation, including the reasons why people do things, like getting something or avoiding something (i.e., the consequences), or what is happening when a particular behavior is initiated (e.g., angry situation, who is around).
>
> **Family:** Includes marital and health problems, problems with family members, parental availability, and how siblings get along.
>
> **Community:** Noise, crime, violence, resources, supports.

Parents can be guided to relate these characteristics to the types of stressors they have experienced. For example, the parent can think of individual characteristics in each family to better understand how they may contribute to any family burdens:

> *All of these characteristics may cause problems, because they affect how well you, as a parent, (and other members of your family) can function or how well you feel, and how you view your children and their adjustment. So, think about some of the different types of characteristics of your family. Here are some questions for you consider: (1) Do you see your child's behavior affecting you or others at home? (Draw upon child stressors); (2) What other things happen in your family that make things difficult?; that increase or decrease stress? That increase or decrease coping?; that increase or decrease violence or anger?*

APPLICATION EXAMPLE

A profile form completed by the mother of a 6-year-old boy identified the following characteristics: having a lot of energy, being inattentive, having problems making friends, and getting into many fights. Interestingly, she answered negatively to a question that asked if she thought there was anything in her behavior that contributed to any of these problems. In this case, the therapist sought further information about both parental and teacher responses to these behaviors.

Comments and Caveats

It is important to try to relate these circumstances to the referral incident when discussing this information with the parent (e.g., *"Do you see the incident that led to your coming here as being related to any of these kinds of things? Could they have influenced your behavior? Which ones may have influenced your behavior?"*). Likewise, the clinician should support the parent's reasonable (understandable) reactions and try to be empathic (e.g., *"I could certainly understand someone getting that upset about a child fighting with a younger sibling; this could be very dangerous"*).

UNDERSTANDING PARENTAL REACTIONS TO FAMILY OF
ORIGIN ISSUES

Review the Parent's Early Family History

Some effort should be made to determine how the parent views his or her own parents and siblings, and their current relationships in an effort to learn how well they got along. We often include questions about the use of discipline and control of the children (i.e., *"How much discipline was used in your home and what did it look like?"*). Try to get an idea as to whether the parent was abused or mistreated in some way and, if so, how this made the parent feel. An example of a discussion along these lines is shown in Therapist Example 11.1.

THERAPIST EXAMPLE **11.1**

A Discussion of Family of Origin Issues

"You said that you see yourself as using a lot of physical punishment *[or a lot of criticism, etc.]*. How does that relate to how you were raised—how you were treated by your family? Did you have many losses of people who were close to you or any separations from them? If so, were any of them early in your life? Did you have any special role in your home growing up?" *[e.g., child acted like parent; child was problem; or the child was frail, weak, or sick.]*

In conducting this brief interview, the clinician should try to help the parent gain some perspective on and appreciation for his or her own early history of abuse or mistreatment, if there was any, and the parent's existing behavioral repertoire (e.g., *"Do you ever have questions about your family life and how it influenced you—for example, 'Am I crazy?' 'Am I a bad person?' 'What will happen to my kids?'"*). Give the parent an opportunity to discuss/describe his or her life and personal difficulties (e.g., *"Do you ever think about your own situation as a parent? Are there certain things that you think about and are concerned about a lot? Are there things about your life or your family now that still upset you or worry you?"*). Try to give a simple explanation as to why the parent may think or behave in a certain ways. Highlight certain characteristics (e.g., training from the parent's early upbringing/modeling, the parent's personal stressors, or available resources or assistance from others), if relevant.

It may also be helpful to review the child's developmental history and get other details about the parent's early experiences with the child (e.g., *"Tell me about some of the difficulties you had as a parent—for example problems in pregnancy, developmental milestones on time, prematurity, temper tantrums, or learning problems"; "Was the child seen as difficult?"; "Was this child wanted?"*).

OVERVIEW OF A SIMPLE MODEL OF STRESS

The parent can be shown the same cognitive-behavioral model included in Chapter 7 on child treatment to illustrate its relevance for understanding situations and how they respond to them. For the parent, we suggest the following introduction as outlined in Therapist Example 11.2.

THERAPIST EXAMPLE **11.2**

Introduction to and Rationale for a Simple Model of Stress

"It is important to be able to identify stressful situations and how one responds to them in different ways, especially the extreme forms. This helps us to change our behavior, as well as the situation. We respond to a situation in different ways; sometimes, one of our responses may not be helpful and can create other problems. When we manage stressful situations well, we maintain self-control over all of these responses and, therefore, can accomplish our goals. When people lose control, they are less likely to accomplish their goals and may even create new problems.

"This model is meant to show that we can respond to a situation in different ways. Different situations may affect each one of us differently— you may have to deal with your own special ones regularly. Now, how we respond may vary because we each have different experiences, a different history, and unique characteristics, and we are exposed to different situations, similar to those we just reviewed. Some of these we're prepared for, but others we're not. Now, some people may have extreme reactions of a certain type in response to one type of situation."

Stress and Warning Signs

Review Common Stressors. It is important to help the parent be able to identify events that make him or her feel stressed and his or her individual reactions to stress and anger. This is important, because when one is very stressed or angry, it is harder to think before acting. If the parent acts before thinking, she or he sometimes may do things that will be regretted later. An example of this, as suggested in Therapist Example 11.3, can be helpful in making this point.

THERAPIST EXAMPLE **11.3**

Example of Contributors to a Stressful Situation

"Let's take an example of a person who comes home from work with a headache. His child spills milk as soon as he walks in the door and, because he is not feeling well, he really yells at the child. The child feels ashamed for an accident that he did not do deliberately. The father feels angry that the child has done something that adds to his headache and reacts as if it was a deliberate act. If the father had been aware of his warning signals—in this case, a headache—he could have said to himself, 'I'm really mad that the milk was spilled, but it was only an accident and I'm overreacting because of my headache, so I won't yell at my kid.' This ability to recognize the warning signal would have resulted in a different outcome for both of them."

The parent then can be asked to describe some individual stressors and an experience with warning signals that includes those stressors. In the examples provided in Therapist Example 11.3, it is reasonable that anyone might overreact and be angry. Certainly, each person has things that are his or her own personal signs of stress. Next, it would be helpful to learn whether the parent has noticed that certain things really make him or her feel stressed, and how the parent knows that he or she is at-risk for blowing a situation out of proportion? (e.g., *"What are your touchy situations and what are your personal warning signals?"*).

Here's another example:

> I've been working hard all day and am very tired. I come home, and the first thing I see is a mess in the living room and my family looking at me and asking what I'm going to make for dinner. That in itself is annoying, but the degree of anger I am going to feel is related to my being physically tired.

The therapist can ask the parent if she or he has had this kind of experience. Also, it is helpful for the therapist to indicate that he or she will discuss some things that can help when the parent feels very stressed and angry. The goal will be to help the parent feel more in control of his or her emotions during interactions in stressful situations with a child or partner.

Homework

The parent can be asked to complete the Profile of Child and Parent Characteristics sheet (Barkley, 1990), taking into consideration the characteristics of his or her family that increase stress and make it more likely that family interactions may be strained or harsh.

❏ Views on Hostility and Violence

OVERVIEW

This section deals with the same topic addressed with children in Chapter 7. Many of the same background materials discussed in Chapter 7 may be helpful to review with parents (e.g., Brassard and Hart's *Emotional Abuse: Words Can Hurt* [1987] and the *Teacher's Guide to Spider-Man on Emotional Abuse* [National Committee to Prevent Child Abuse, 1988]). Indeed, it is important to help parents understand the nature and impact of emotionally abusive comments as well as physically abusive or coercive behaviors in order to help reduce the child's risk of either form of maltreatment. Virtually all of the content of Chapter 7 is relevant for discussion with parents, albeit from their unique perspective. We include in this section just a few comments on this material in order to highlight key issues for the use of these procedures with parents. The rationale in Therapist Example 11.4 may be given to initiate the discussion.

THERAPIST EXAMPLE **11.4**

Introduction to and Rationale for Understanding Harsh or Violent Talk

"Now, we are going to talk about words. Certain words and how we use them can and do hurt. They hurt our feelings, our perceptions of ourselves, our perceptions of how others view us, and so forth. This is very true between parents and children. How we talk to our children can be as powerful and as violent as a physical slap. I'm talking about words and tones that emphasize hostility, insults, and humiliations. Words that don't help. Words that hurt. So, the first thing we'll review is how you talk to your child."

Many of the topics in the child's section merit review with the parents, including providing examples of words that hurt, how children or parents may feel or respond when this happens, and reasons why adults say these things. It would be important to ask each parent for examples of statements she or he has made that fit this description and to learn what the circumstances were and the reasons for making them in the first place. Parents should also be asked to identify any reactions shown by their children to these interactions.

Each parent also should be asked to discuss alternative comments or statements to any examples she or he has made of recent coercive verbal or physical behaviors, and ways to reduce the likelihood that such behaviors are exhibited again (e.g., stopping to think about what is going on with this person, taking a short break, or talking to the person later).

VIEWS ON PHYSICAL FORCE AND ITS IMPACT

As noted in Chapter 7, it is important to assist parents in clarifying and understanding their views on violence and its impact on their child's behavioral and emotional functioning. One goal of this section is to help parents recognize how harsh parenting affects their relationships with their children.

Salient issues for discussion with parents include potentially influential opinions or views they may hold that could support their use of coercion and specific types of physically abusive behavior, like those that follow: (a) force is useful, even necessary, at times to influence or control children when alternatives have failed; (b) there are benefits to the use of force that outweigh its costs or adverse consequences; and (c) force is not likely to harm children. Each of these viewpoints may be important to discuss in order to understand a parent's justification for each perspective. Furthermore, they may need to be challenged by the therapist in an effort to help parents rely less upon physically harsh methods of discipline.

DISCUSSING SOURCES OF VIOLENCE IN THE PARENTS' LIVES AND IN THEIR FAMILIES

We try to inform parents that they are participating in treatment because of their concern about their children's adjustment and the ways in which they interact with their children. It is often equally important to mention that they may or may not agree that there is really much to be concerned about, but that it may still be helpful for them to discuss their views regarding the use of physical force or their disciplinary styles.

It is helpful to use general probes, such as the following, to clarify the nature and impact of parental discipline without conveying a particular preference or concern about it from the start: (a) *"How would you describe your ways of managing and disciplining your child? (What do you usually do?)"*; (b) *"How important is physical discipline or punishment?"*; or (c) *"Should parents use physical punishment with their children?"*

Summarize Parental Views on Violence

To avoid any misinterpretations, the therapist is encouraged to summarize the prior discussion by incorporating the parent's views of violence in it (e.g., *"Having heard you talk about your views, I think I can summarize them in general terms. Tell me if I've got these right"*).

HARSH OR VIOLENT INTERACTION PATTERNS

Impact on Children

Understanding the Effects of Violence on Children. Parents may have widely discrepant views regarding what they expect are the effects of exposure to violence and harsh discipline. Therefore, it is useful to learn their impressions of these effects, which can be elicited through a few simple probes:

> *Have you thought about how you or your child have been affected by the ways in which you both interact or relate, especially in terms of the physical force or discipline in your family? For example, what might happen to children in families that use these methods (e.g., violence)?*

Sometimes, it may be easier to ask the parent a more direct question about these effects, such as, *"How has your child been affected by being exposed to physical discipline? For example, has your child gotten hurt or have you lost control?"*

It is important to help the parent recognize and understand the many possible consequences of exposure to violence, harsh discipline, or other forms of physical punishment on children. Certain common reactions include the following:

- Getting injured or hurt on other occasions
- Getting angry, oppositional, or aggressive
- Showing signs of being depressed, withdrawn, uncommunicative
- Expressing denial about what happened or being defensive

- Showing greater frustration or being less able to cope with things
- Showing signs of being hypervigilant to cues related to the abusive experience
- Seeing oneself as negative (feeling that one deserves blame/victimization role) or that they "caused" the violence or low self-esteem

Other more general reactions may be worth mentioning to highlight the potential long-term consequences of exposure. These include the following:

- Seeing oneself as being externally controlled or doing things to correct one's "badness" (e.g., being overly apologetic, compliant, or anxious to please others)
- Thinking one is bad, awful, and/or ungrateful
- Failing to try to achieve or do well in life, perhaps feeling hopeless or helpless
- Being placed out of home

Responsibility for Violence

The clinician is encouraged to provide the parent with an explanation as to the responsibility for violence in the home and the child's role in conflicts that result in such an outcome (e.g., "Who is responsible for violence in the home and for what happens to the child?"). It is important to convey that children, depending on their age, may not understand what violent behavior means. They may even blame themselves for the violence between parents or toward themselves. Although a child's behavior may contribute to an increase in conflicts, parents need to understand that the child is not responsible for the adult's choices and resulting behavior. Rather, this responsibility rests with adults, who are older, more experienced, and have the ability to comprehend what is and is not the best option for dealing with conflicts (e.g., "When adults act before thinking and use violence, they are the ones responsible"). Furthermore, it is important to help the parent appreciate that when parents use physical discipline or control techniques at home, the child's safety (and that of siblings) becomes a community responsibility.

A few questions can be administered, in part, to learn how the parent views the use of violence and whether it will be used in relationships or as a survival skill: (a) "How might you as a parent feel when this occurs?" (common reactions include feeling sad, angry, disappointed, and relieved); (b) "How do you think your child's views will be shaped by the use of violence in the home?"; (c) "How will your child view the use of force later on?"; and (d) "Will your child accept or use physical force?"

❑ Expectations of Our Children

In this section, we seek to assist parents in clarifying their attributions about or expectations of their children. In addition, an effort is made to enhance parents' understanding of their role in mediating their interactions with their child. To facilitate this discussion, we draw upon the use of several materials, including the Denver Developmental Screening Test form (Frankenburg, 1969; Frankenburg & Dodds, 1967), a child development handout, and a list of some common safety precautions.

PERSONAL ATTRIBUTIONS

Introduction and Orientation

An overview of personal attributions is provided in Therapist Example 11.5.

THERAPIST EXAMPLE 11.5

Introduction to Understanding Expectations of Our Children

"We all have certain thoughts or ideas about different situations that have happened to us. This includes the thoughts we have about our friends and family. Many times, these thoughts involve strong beliefs (or ideas) about what others are like—for example, what they'll do or how they'll behave. These are called *attributions.* Attributions are often based on our experience with similar people in similar situations and on the other person's actual behavior. Parents come to have expectations of their children. Now, most often, they are probably accurate and fair. But, sometimes, they can be too high or too low. Expectations should be based on a child's level of development. Knowing about normal child development may help us understand more about our own child's behavior—about why they do or can't do things. Let's discuss children's development as it relates to the ways in which parents view their children."

Developmental Stages

Children at Different Ages (Stages). The parent can be asked to indicate the ages of his or her children. Then, the therapist can introduce the issue of developmental stages (e.g., *"As you know, kids do different things at different ages. And we look for different skills—or abilities—and* *problems at each age. Kids show their skills in different areas of ability"*). Ask parents to indicate some of these different areas. Parents might name the following areas: physical, social, motor, speech, cognitive (i.e., intellectual), play, emotional, moral, sexual, and identity (i.e., self-image). There are different stages or periods of development for each of these areas, and the therapist should help the parent to realize that (a) stages are related and affect each other; (b) one stage helps to determine what happens at the next stage; and (c) there is a range to so-called normal development—of what most kids can do. To begin a dialogue regarding the parent's developmental concerns regarding his or her child, the therapist might ask a few probes: *"Are there certain stages that are easy—or hard—to identify?"*; *"What are the stages that you worry about the most? The least?"*; *"Can you think of specific ways to help your child with this particular problem?"* The therapist should pay close attention to the types of behaviors and circumstances about which the parent is concerned and provide guidance accordingly.

Factors That Influence Child Development. Discuss with the parent various factors that may influence how children develop, some of which are listed here:

- How family interacts on regular basis
- The parent's own development and role models
- The extended family environment
- Schools, churches, or community organizations
- The child's peers

Parental Feelings About Unusual Development. The parent can be asked a few questions about the child's development (e.g., *"How do you see your own children's development?"*). Discuss their feelings of helplessness, guilt, anger, or being out of control. Support parents who are being too hard on themselves when they make a mistake or cannot relate as well to a child in one stage as in another.

Guidelines to Support Children's Development. Suggest to the parent the importance of being supportive of the child's existing abilities and upcoming developmental tasks, in part through the following activities:

- Being a good role model
- Providing consistency and structure
- Providing nurturance and acceptance
- Being sure the child feels listened to and valued in the family

- Loving oneself and put oneself in a good support system
- Providing the child with community supports
- Assisting the child to identify and accept his or her feelings
- Giving the child constructive feedback about how he or she interacts with the family
- Allowing the child to make some decisions
- Ensuring that the child trusts you and feels secure with you before he or she can move on to more healthy development
- Knowing the child's special interests, goals, dreams, and desires, and helping to reach his or her potential (not your agenda for them)
- Helping the child to learn in a supportive relationship

In general, the parent should be reminded of the importance of being tolerant (i.e., understanding) of the child's developmental status.

NORMAL CHILD DEVELOPMENT

Parental Expectations About the Timing of Developmental Tasks

This section involves discussing the timing of various developmental tasks. To do so, we have used different tasks included on the original Denver Developmental Screening Test form (Frankenburg, 1969; Frankenburg & Dodds, 1967) to determine the likely age at which most children master a variety of developmental tasks. (A revised version of this test is also available; see Frankenburg, Dodds, Archer, Shapiro, & Bresnick, 1992.) The screening form for the Denver Developmental Screening Test has shaded areas indicating the seventy-fifth percentile for mastery of each task on the form (e.g., motor skills and language). The following rationale can be given for this exercise:

> It isn't always easy to know what to expect about a child's behavior. To show you what I mean, let's try to figure out when most children would show a few common behaviors. I'm going to read to you a behavior, and I'd like you to tell me when you think a majority of children—that is, more than 75% of children—would show this behavior.

The aforementioned instruction is intended to elicit parents' judgments or beliefs regarding the age at which most children master various developmental milestones or tasks. The therapist will quickly learn whether the parent believes that most children will master the task at an earlier age than what has been documented in the general population. Such a view may reflect high or exaggerated expectations for reaching common developmental milestones. For illustrative purposes, what follows are the approximate ages for a few of the tasks on the Denver Developmental Screening Test form:

- Plays peek-a-boo (9 mos.)
- Throws ball overhand (2 yrs.)
- Drinks from cup (16 mos.)
- Balances on one foot (5 yrs.)
- Gives first and last name (3½ yrs.)
- Says "dada" or "mama" (9 mos.)
- Copies a "+" sign (4 yrs.)
- Plays pat-a-cake (1 yr.)
- Follows 2 out of 3 directions given (2½ yrs.)
- Can walk backward, heel to toe, 2 out of 3 times asked (6 yrs.)

Review Child Development: Birth to 10 Years

The clinician is encouraged to examine several background sources that provide information regarding the child's developmental stages and needs (see Davies, 1999; Dixon & Stein, 2000; Gemelli, 1996; Greenspan, 1991; Schor, 1999). Each of these sources offers a somewhat unique perspective on the child's development and on key tasks that both children and parents should master. A summary of relevant information appears in Therapist Example 11.6, and that information can be used to introduce the handout in Box 11.2, which explains some basic information on children from ages 1 to 10. The material was developed in consultation with a pediatric nurse practitioner (Joanne Moser, RN, CRNP) who collaborated with David Kolko on a pilot project designed to provide group treatment for abusive parents of psychiatrically hospitalized children. Material was drawn from some several existing sources (e.g., Brown & Murphy, 1975; Chinn & Leitch, 1979). During the session, the therapist should cover some background information on each age range or period. The parent could be encouraged to review this information with a fresh perspective in light of the wide differences in developmental status found among different children at these ages.

THERAPIST EXAMPLE **11.6**

Developmental Information: From Birth to 10 Years

"Do you remember what it was like to have a newborn child? As you know, newborn babies need to have most everything done for them by parents. Some babies cry all the time and won't calm, no matter what is done, while others seem to be calm and happy all the time. Neither is abnormal and neither is indicative of a serious problem, although the latter is much easier to live with. The parents' task during the first year is to provide all the physical needs of the child in a calm, loving way.

"By the time the baby is reaching his or her first year of life, he or she will be trying to walk or stand, will be making talking noises or even saying words. The year from 1 to 2 years of age is a year of tremendous growth and development, but is frustrating for parents because at some point during this year the 'terrible twos' begin. The parent's task during this year is to help the child learn new things and to allow the child enough room to do things for him- or herself, to bring out the child's natural intelligence and curiosity, while making sure that the child is safe.

"Two-year-olds struggle with figuring out how far they can go. This is an important part of personality development, and the two-year-old child who never says 'No' to the parent is not as healthy as the one who often says 'No.' They are testing their boundaries and they are testing their parents to determine what is appropriate and what is inappropriate behavior. The parent's task is to allow the child some freedom while not giving the child the message that he or she can do whatever he or she likes without any consequence.

"Three-year-olds have developed speech and bowel/bladder control (accidents are normal, however). The child is concerned with seeing him- or herself as 'not a baby anymore' (especially if there are older siblings). Because the turmoil of the two-year-old child has passed, parents find three-year-old children more open to displays of affection. Three-year-old children have a desire to learn about the world around them. The parent's task is to provide enriching experiences and explain how things occur.

"Four-year-olds may be ready to begin doing specific tasks. While children should be taught to pick up after themselves from the time they are toddling, it is at this age that small household chores can be assigned. Instead of expecting the child to do the chore without any help, the parent should expect to supervise and assist the child in doing the chore, as needed. The parent's task is to start seeing the child as a child, not a baby, and making sure expectations are reasonable (this is not the age for perfection).

"Five-year-olds are discovering the outside world as they begin kindergarten. They need reassurance from parents that they can still be nurtured and get affection, but they need support for trying new things and taking chances. Some five-year-old children go through a phase when they test limits and don't listen. It is important to set limits and explain the reasons for them.

"Now, there's a lot that happens during these few years. And almost all of us would appreciate the differences between what a one-year-old and what a four-year-old can do. The rest is more variable; to understand the older child, you can finish reading the handout at home."

Box 11.2	**Parent Handout**
	Child Development: Birth to 10 Years

A baby's first year is all growth and change. At this stage, a baby is very demanding and helpless. Parents cannot expect to control a young baby through any kind of punishment or discipline.

1 Month: Starts to sleep more regularly. Cries when hungry, when wants to be held, or when physically uncomfortable. Totally unaware of self and others.

By 4 Months: May like to be propped up or held, instead of left lying down. Watches everything with interest. Will begin to go to sleep more easily. May start to smile back when smiled at and become aware of surroundings.

6 to 7 Months: Very social age. Grabs objects. Likes to *bang* things. Can amuse self, but will cry when mother leaves. Likes to be held standing up and to bounce.

9 to 10 Months: Working at standing and may walk a step or more. Some begin to say "da-da" or other short words. Can understand the meaning of "No" at some time around 10 months. Loves to crawl and will grab at anything—is into everything. Begins to like games like peek-a-boo.

By 1 Year (52 Weeks): Becomes more sociable. Likes to stand. Crawls quickly and doesn't keep still for long. May be walking and talking.

2½ Years: A difficult age. Stubborn. Demanding. Can't make decisions and stick to them, so it's best to make decisions for the child. Lots of energy. Once started on something, it's hard to get a two-and-a-half-year-old to stop.

3 Years: Begins to like to share, to say "Yes" as often as "No." Likes to make friends. No longer so demanding. New words are fun for her or him. Enjoys learning. Can begin to dress self a little and to try to help around the house. Motor development increases greatly to riding tricycles, jumping, and throwing balls. The desire to please and conform is great, and preschool begins.

3½ Years: Again, a more demanding stage. Insecure. Becomes more awkward physically. May be very shy one minute and very bold the next. Needs extra understanding and affection—kind of an awkward age of growing and changing.

4 Years: "Out of bounds" behavior. Moods change quickly. Hitting, kicking, throwing, yelling, swearing, and loud silly laughing. Tells lies

---

Box 11.2 | *continued*

because she or he does not yet understand difference between lying and pretending. Boasting and bragging are common. Parents have to control the most unreasonable behaviors, but the four-year-old child needs to test her or his independence, too. Needs some things she or he can mess up or destroy with all her or his extra energy (e.g., newspapers, clay, etc.).

4½ Years: Begins to question what is real and what is pretend. Most like to talk about things more than before. They want to know about all sort of things. Begins to be less defiant of the parents' efforts to control her or him. Pictures and drawing, building with blocks, can interest a four-and-a-half-year-old child for long periods of time.

5 Years: A calmer, friendlier stage. Less out-of-bounds than at four. Accepts directions from parents. Plays quietly, likes to stick close to home. Going to school for the first time can be fairly easy for most five-year-olds because kindergartens are planned for this age. But, some children are less mature than others, and may be in the four-year-old phase of out-of-bounds behavior even at five.

6 Years: Very emotional age. One minute, the child seems to love, the next to hate. Demanding of mother. Needs lots of praise. Reacts badly to blame or criticism. Will do what he or she is told only slowly and with resistance. Some six-year-olds have problems adjusting to first grade; they may not yet be ready to concentrate on the work with all the other children there to distract them. The parents' task is to support the child's separation from them while not making the child feel rejected. This age child needs help with homework.

7 Years: Another calmer age. Likes to spend time alone, watching TV, reading, daydreaming. A seven-year-old tries hard and tires easily. Sometimes less happy for a while, pouting, saying nobody loves him or her. Lots of complaints about teachers, brothers and sisters, and life in general; feeling sorry for self. Needs a little sympathy, but a lot of encouragement and praise for things done well. The parents' task is to encourage and praise this age child. Consider having the child join Cub Scouts or Brownie Scouts. These children can do simple tasks with only one prompt.

8 Years: Begins to be aware of relationships with family and friends. Concern with what other people think of her or him. May try things much too hard for self, starting with a great deal of enthusiasm and ending in tears. Sensitive about failure and criticism. Friendships and school are a big part of the child's life. The parents' task is to support the child's out-of-family activities. Perhaps time for child to go to day camp or an organized sport activity, such as little league.

9 Years: By nine, some children starting to have body changes of pre-teens—more aware of their bodies, more self-conscious. Aware of and interested in words or TV shows dealing with sex, even if in an immature or

---

Box 11.2   *continued*

"silly" way. Independent, interested in friends more than family. Already showing signs of how the teenage years might be. The parents' task is to be supportive of the child's worries about new things. May be the time in some early maturing children to talk about what they can expect from puberty. This is not necessary if the child isn't asking for this information.

10 Years: Complains and worries a lot. Physical symptoms—stomach aches and other aches and pains—are common, along with general preoccupation with body, especially in girls, who mature physically a little earlier than boys. The parent's task is to continue to set firm limits so that this preteen feels secure in the family. Child may begin some rebelling, but this is normal. If parents anticipate this, it doesn't seem like defiance.

Children's Developmental Needs and Parental Efforts to Address Them

The therapist can use this material to highlight important developmental achievements that children of different ages or stages need to make and how parents can help them do this. Borrowing from the work of Justice and Justice (1990), the therapist can help the parent to appreciate a few concepts and issues on the handout related to each age period:

- At 0–6 months, contact is important.
- From 6 months to 1.5 years, children need opportunities to learn about the world—which means they get into everything.
- From 1.5 to 3 years, parents should provide consequences that are fair and predictable.
- From 3 to 6 years, the parent should teach the child how to do things and understand things or situations.
- From 6 to 12 years, the child can reason and seeks fairness.
- From 12 to 18 years, parents must try to be consistent in their decisions and interactions, and to be patient.

Homework

Responding to Children's Development. The parent should be encouraged to review this background information to more fully understand and explain the child's behavior as consistent with a specific developmental stage. Thus, one may ask about the timing of a specific type of behavior and what impact the timing has on how the parent would handle or already has handled the behavior. For example, the therapist might ask the following:

> *Assume that the age periods might be one and four years. Here a couple of other behaviors—they could occur at different ages and you might deal with them differently at each age: (a) hitting, (b) crying,(c) initiating hugs and kisses with lots of people, and (d) whining. Can you tell me how you've dealt with them at different ages in the past?*

Safety Precautions. The parent might also be provided with a list of general safety precautions (see Box 11.3), which might be helpful in preventing any types of accidents (e.g., *"Here's a handout that shows some different things that all of us with young, or even not so young, children might need to use at one time or another to keep them safe or to handle some kind of emergency"*). The therapist should address any questions parents may have regarding their child's or their own safety.

Box 11.3	**Parent Group Handout** Safety Precautions for Parents

Once a child is one- or two-years-old, he or she can climb and reach high, "safe" places in a home—cabinets, shelves, and medicine chests. As children venture out into the neighborhood, their world expands rapidly and the danger of accidents generally increases. They ask "why" to everything, and instructions in safety should begin. They begin to understand what is dangerous. Here are a few general suggestions to promote home safety:

1. Take another look at where you store poisons—drugs, harmful household substances, garden insecticides, and fertilizer should be locked up! Even if you must leave the room for only an instant, remove the container to a safe spot.
2. Get rid of poisons (rat poison, roach paste or powders) as much as possible.
3. Warn small children not to eat or drink drugs, chemicals, plants, or berries they find without your permission, and insist on it.
4. Have ipecac at home.
5. Follow all previous suggestions.

General Rules

1. Get rid of old unused medicine and hazardous substances by pouring down the drain; then rinse and throw away the container out of reach of children and pets.

Box 11.3 | *continued*

2. Do not take medicine from an unlabeled bottle; transparent tape can be applied over the label to protect it. Replace all torn labels.

3. Read all labels for directions and caution statements before giving medicine.

4. Never give medicine in a darkened room, and when measuring drugs, pay close attention to what you are doing.

5. Always shake the bottle thoroughly before measuring liquid medicine.

6. Give medicine only to the person it was prescribed for and only in the amount directed.

7. Mark each drug carefully with the name of the person it was prescribed for, and date all drug supplies when you buy them.

8. Clean out the medicine cabinet periodically and weed out leftovers, especially any prescription drug that your doctor ordered for a particular illness.

9. When purchasing drugs, ask your pharmacist for child-resistant safety closures. Do the same with your grocer when buying household cleaning and polishing supplies; ask which ones have safety packaging.

10. Learn to use the special child-resistant packaging and be certain to resecure the safety feature after use.

11. Do not take medicines in front of children.

12. Remove cleaning aids, polishes, kerosene, lye, etc. from under the sink and lock up.

13. Read all labels on such supplies and carefully follow "caution" statements. Even if a chemical is not labeled "poison," incorrect use may render it dangerous.

14. Be sure all poisons are clearly marked by sealing with adhesive tape or using a special marker.

15. Household chemicals in aerosol spray cans or bottles with very small openings are safer because less of the harmful substance can get out at one time.

16. Do not allow food or food utensils to become contaminated when using insect sprays, aerosol mists, rat poisons, weed killers, or cleaning agents.

17. Follow the directions for protecting eyes and skin when using insect poisons, weed killers, solvents, and cleaning agents. Be sure to wash thoroughly after using these things and remove contaminated clothing.

Box 11.3 | *continued*

18. Use cleaning fluids in adequate ventilation only—never in baby's room—and avoid breathing vapors.

19. Never eat or serve foods that smell or look abnormal, and remember that they may also poison animals.

20. Remove all poisonous plants from your home.

21. Check your yard to see if there are any plants with poisonous leaves or berries and remove them.

22. Have ipecac at home and remember to call your doctor, hospital, or poison control center immediately before using in the case of an accidental poisoning.

SOURCE: Joanne Moser, RN, CRNP.

❏ **Thinking in Negative or "Distorted" Ways**

This section is designed to assist parents in clarifying their thinking style, teach parents the relationship between thoughts and feelings, and show parents how to change thoughts and feelings. We draw upon some existing clinical materials, such as the Sample Thought Menu and the Hassle Log (see Feindler & Ecton, 1986).

STRESSFUL THINKING

Distortions and How They Happen

Rationale. The therapist might provide the following as a rationale for the need to clarify thinking:

> *One consequence of being in a stressful situation is that we may begin to have negative thoughts. Negative thoughts may make things worse, especially if they distort the situation—if they make us think in a way that isn't accurate with what's happening.*

The therapist should review different types of negative thoughts, such as when we think in ways that are not quite accurate or when we have unrealistic expectations of what is appropriate behavior.

Example of Distortions. There are many examples of common distortions. First, we may exaggerate or misrepresent some explanation for an event, as when we think that children are deliberately trying to annoy or disturb us. We may misunderstand the child's motive and see the child as deliberately trying to do something negative or intentionally annoying his or her parents (e.g., *"She's trying to get me"*). Alternatively, we may blame our children for problems we have in caring for them or ourselves: We see them as the cause of the problem. We see them as trying to make our lives miserable—as trying to make us fail as parents. In addition, we may overstate how limited our abilities are, seeing ourselves in a negative way by being critical of our skills (e.g., *"He must think I'm stupid"*). Finally, we may think that we are at the end of our rope (e.g., *"I can't take it anymore"*).

Impact of Having Distorted and Negative Thoughts

The parent should be asked about the consequences of having distorted thinking (e.g., *"What usually happens when we think this way—when we don't expect to succeed in managing or raising our children well?"*). A few notable consequences are worth mentioning here: (a) Parents may be more likely to lose control when children misbehave, may become less tolerant and willing to exert effort to change a situation; and (b) parents may "leak" to children just how annoyed they are, sometimes communicating in a negative way, even if the children are behaving acceptably. When this happens, a child may respond by being even more negative, possibly because he or she thinks the parent simply does not care.

Box 11.4 provides an illustration of two different situations (panels A and B), each of which is associated with two alternative interpretations of the same incident. In each case, the thoughts in the top panel seem more distorted or exaggerated than those in the bottom. The therapist should review the thoughts and their implications with the parent to help the parent appreciate how these cognitions may lead to different reactions and, ultimately, to different child outcomes.

Tasks for Identifying and Challenging Thoughts

A few specific steps for addressing and confronting the parent's distorted or exaggerate beliefs should be described by the clinician. First, the therapist should remind the parent that thoughts clearly can affect behavior and feelings. Then, the therapist should ask the parent to discuss incidents and to report on the following: (a) what the parent

Box 11.4	Samples of Distortions and Alternative Cognitions in Two Situations

	Cognitive	Affective	Behavioral
Panel A Child Spills Milk	He's so clumsy He's trying to annoy me He is bad	Anger Disgust Impatience	Hurt Child Refuse to give more milk
	It was an accident	Displeasure Patience	Help child clean up Refill milk

	Cognitive	Affective	Behavioral
Panel B Child comforts crying baby brother	He's so jealous He's trying to hurt the baby He is mean	Anger Impatience Displeasure	Pull child away Yell at child Hit child Take baby
	He's trying to help He loves his brother He's nurturing	Pleasure Pride Happy	Give child a chance to be successful Praise child Assist child

says to him- or herself, and whether she or he is talking or thinking negatively; and (b) how these statements would (or did) affect his or her behavior. If the parent has trouble coming up with information, set up a role play, based on previous information provided by the parent, where they have to think aloud so you can hear what they would say to themselves. After the role play, ask how the parent feels about the situation. Then, conduct another role play, this time using a different theme (e.g., *"Think about any recent feelings of intense anger. What would make you feel that way—what would have to happen? Why would it affect you that way?"*). This should help to elicit how they are thinking about the situation.

If the thoughts seem distorted or exaggerated, try to provide a mild challenge to some of their irrational beliefs. Therapist Example 11.7 provides an example of a series of statements designed to challenge them.

THERAPIST EXAMPLE 11.7

A Few Suggestions on Statements to Help Challenge Cognitive Distortions

"You know, you were saying that when *[name the child and a behavior: e.g., 'John screams at you after dinner']*, that means to you that he *[name the outcome: e.g., 'doesn't think that you're doing a good job' or 'doesn't really appreciate how much you've done for him']*, and this gets you very angry and, perhaps, sad. But, I'm wondering whether it could also mean some other things. Do you think it could? . . . What might it mean? . . . Does that thought about him not appreciating you help or hinder you? How so? . . . Can you replace it with a more appropriate statement or idea that will help to explain the situation—one that might be more positive or constructive?"

Once this discussion is well underway, offer some suggestions for how the parent can challenge his or her thoughts. These include the following: (a) step back and try to think clearly; (b) ask if this is accurate or based on all that has happened; (c) try a test—ask if the thought is really correct (check it out); and (d) revise the thought, asking how else this action could be interpreted.

COPING SELF-STATEMENTS

Homework

The parent can be provided with some material that gives examples of upsetting thoughts and calming thoughts. It is helpful to ask the parent to write down on the bottom of the paper examples of upsetting thoughts that she or he had during the week and to identify calming thoughts that might be used in these situations:

> *We're going to try to do a few things to help you think about this problem so that you can work on changing it at home. First, write down two upsetting thoughts. Next, identify a positive alternative thought—something that you think of that would be more helpful to have in mind.*

The clinician may also give the Hassle Log to help capture this information, explaining how to use the log (e.g., *"Think of a situation where you became angry or acted in a way that you regretted because you were not aware of your warning signals"*).

❏ Summary

In this chapter, we have addressed the role of cognitions in parents' behavior toward their children. These cognitions include thoughts related to stress, attributions about the child, beliefs about child development, and beliefs about violence and its impact on children. From a cognitive-behavioral perspective, thinking is one aspect of behavior that must change to reduce the risk for reabuse. In the next chapter, we move on to addressing feelings through affect-focused interventions.

References

Barkley, R. A. (1990). *Attention deficit hyperactivity disorder: A handbook for diagnosis and treatment.* New York: Guilford.

Brassard, M. R., & Hart, S. N. (1987). *Emotional abuse: Words* can *hurt.* Chicago: National Committee to Prevent Child Abuse.

Brown, M. S., & Murphy, M. A. (1975). *Ambulatory pediatrics for nurses.* New York: McGraw-Hill.

Chinn, P., & Leitch, C. (1979). *Child health maintenance.* St. Louis, MO: C. V. Mosby.

Davies, D. (1999). *Child development: A practitioner's guide.* New York: Guilford.

Dixon, S. D., & Stein, M. T. (2000). *Encounters with children: Pediatric behavior and development* (3rd ed.). St. Louis, MO: C. V. Mosby.

Feindler, E. L., & Ecton, R. B. (1986). *Adolescent anger control: Cognitive-behavioral techniques.* New York: Pergamon.

Frankenburg, W. K. (1969). The Denver Developmental Screening Test. *Developmental Medicine and Child Neurology, 11,* 260–262.

Frankenburg, W. K., & Dodds, J. B. (1967). The Denver Developmental Screening Test. *Journal of Pediatrics, 71,* 181–191.

Frankenburg, W. K., Dodds, J. B., Archer, P., Shapiro, H., & Bresnick, B. (1992). The Denver II: A major revision and restandardization of the Denver Developmental Screening Test. *Pediatrics, 89,* 91–97.

Gemelli, R. J. (1996). *Normal child and adolescent development.* Washington, DC: American Psychiatric Press.

Greenspan, S. I., (1991). *The clinical interview of the child* (2nd ed.). Washington, DC: American Psychiatric Press.

Justice, B., & Justice, R. (1990). *The abusing family.* New York: Plenum.

National Committee to Prevent Child Abuse. (1988). *Teacher's guide to Spider-Man on emotional abuse.* Chicago: Author.

Schor, E. L. (1999). *Caring for your school-age child: Ages 5–12.* New York: Bantam.

12

Treatment of the Maltreating Adult
Affect-Focused Interventions

❏ **Self-Management and Affect Regulation of Abuse-Specific Triggers**

BACKGROUND AND DEFINITION

Many parents who cross the line from corporal punishment to maltreatment have trouble with self-management and affect regulation. Self-management refers to the day-to-day skills one uses to manage behavior and maintain control over impulses. Such management skills often fall within the domains of "thinking and doing." Affect regulation, or the process of managing one's emotional reactions, relates to the "feeling" domain. Within their repertoire of self-management skills, parents need to be able to modulate flexibly their affect so that they do not allow their anxiety, anger, frustration, or other feelings to escalate to the point where they resort to disorganized, dangerous, or violent behavior. Most of the self-management and affect regulation techniques available for adults are similar to those described for use with children in the preceding chapters. As is true with children, therapists should ensure that any techniques used are developmentally appropriate and clear to the parent.

Description of Procedure

The first step in learning self-management and affect regulation of abuse-specific triggers is understanding the concept of risk. That is, specific situations, events, or other cues that elicit stressful reactions may serve as risk factors or triggers for harsh, punitive, or violent behavior. To understand the precursors to violence and develop a management plan targeting those precursors, a functional analysis is conducted with the parent. Therapist Example 12.1 gives directions for conducting a functional analysis of physically harsh or abusive discipline used by the parent. These suggestions reflect modifications from the work of Higgins and Budney (1993) in their protocol for treating substance abuse. The functional analysis components can be written out on the Functional Analysis of the Use of Physical Force or Aggression Form shown in Box 12.1.

THERAPIST EXAMPLE **12.1**

Suggestions for Using Functional Analysis

"Sometimes, parents become so frustrated or angry that they cross the line separating physical discipline from more harsh discipline. Parents who do this can certainly change how they handle themselves with their children. It is important for you to understand that you can learn ways to handle situations with your child in such a way that they do not result in using force or getting someone hurt.

"Now, if you lose your temper with your child during the time we work together, don't think you have failed. As you learn to manage your own feelings you may have slip-ups. We will talk about them and try to understand what happened so that you can stop slip-ups from happening. It is really important when you slip and lose your temper or get frustrated that you do not hurt your child or yourself, or both.

"So, we are going to talk about what typically happens before you physically discipline your child—things you think and feel, and what happens after you physically discipline.

"First, we need to figure out triggers or things that happen before you hit. The kinds of triggers we are talking about are circumstances that make one use force or be aggressive—that is, things that happen to you, places where you are, or things you do that might push you toward hitting or other physical discipline.

"Triggers might be a lot of things, such as your child not doing his chores, having a fight with your partner, or using alcohol or drugs. Triggers can lead to certain thoughts and feelings that push you toward harsh punishment—thoughts like, 'That kid never does his chores; he's just trying me and I am not going to let him try me.' Think about some things that have happened before you hit or used other physical punishment, ones that might be triggers, including your thoughts and feelings. . . .

"Now, you have given me triggers, thoughts, and feelings that may lead to hitting or other physical punishment. So, let's think about consequences or things that happen after you lose control and begin to use force. Some people talk about feeling good after they have hit someone because the tension is over and they get rid of their anger. Tell me about any similar good reactions you have felt after using force with your kids. Let's make a list. . . .

"OK, many people talk about bad things that happen after they hit or are aggressive toward their kids, like they feel badly that their child is hurt, they get arrested, their children are taken away. Let's think about any negative or bad things that happen after you lose control and use force with your child. Let's make a list. . . ."

Box 12.1	Functional Analysis of the Use of Physical Force or Aggression Form			
Trigger	_Thoughts and Feelings_	_Behavior_	_Positive Consequences_	_Negative Consequences_

After the functional analysis is complete and the therapist and parent have a good understanding of triggers, a self-management plan should be made (see Budney & Higgins, 1998). This plan depends on the triggers identified, the parent's skills, and the skills the parent needs to learn. The therapist introduces the parent to self-management planning, as shown in Therapist Example 12.2.

THERAPIST EXAMPLE 12.2
Sample Introduction to Self-Management

"Now that we understand some of the triggers, together we need to figure out how to handle those triggers. To do this, I would like to review with you a self-management plan. Let's choose a trigger from your list and write down some ways to manage that trigger—that is, what you will do differently the next time you are exposed to this trigger. *[Depending on the trigger, the therapist may then conduct skills training and new skills will be incorporated into the self-management plan]*. This plan may also require continued refinement as additional incidents involving the use of force are described."

Case Application

The Burch family was referred for treatment after Ms. Burch, a single parent, left belt marks on 10-year-old Mario. The therapist conducted a functional analysis with Ms. Burch, who initially had difficulty engaging because she objected to child protection using the term *abuse*. Once the therapist began to assure the mother that she, the therapist, was not there to judge but to figure out how to help Ms. Burch improve her relationship with her son and move to the point that child protection was out of her life, and once the word *force* was used to replace the word *abuse*, Ms. Burch participated. She and the therapist determined that the trigger was Mario's refusal to follow his mother's directive about completing his household chores. She experienced anger and felt a lack of respect when he did not comply with her directive. Her cognitions were, *"He doesn't respect me. He's just like his father; he thinks he can do what he wants and can be in charge of me. I'll show him who is in charge."* Her thinking and level of anger led to negative comments towards her son, who returned those comments, and the escalation resulted in hitting. After the hitting, she felt power in the relationship, felt that Mario knew she was in control, but felt bad about leaving marks and cuts on him. Treatment with the mother then focused on managing the triggers and finding a different strategy for getting Mario to comply.

Comments and Caveats

In some cases, parents will not be able initially to participate in the functional analysis because they have not acknowledged engaging in what they perceive to be abusive behavior. It really is not necessary for a parent to use the words *physical abuse*, but the words *harsh punishment* or *force* may better enable them to engage in the functional analysis. In cases where it is difficult for the parent to conduct the functional analysis, another family member or extended family may help with the functional analysis, or the parent can be asked to consider a related (alternative) incident for this analysis.

❏ Self-Management and Regulation of Anger

BACKGROUND AND DEFINITION

Anger may be a major trigger for an escalation of verbal and physical aggression. Poor management of that anger can then lead to physical violence toward the child. Novaco (1975) has nicely articulated a cognitive-behavioral therapy (CBT) approach to anger problems in adults. The initial treatment consists of cognitive techniques, relaxation, and graduated exposure to provocation. Subsequent studies of anger management revised the treatment techniques to include a stress inoculation framework, cognitive restructuring, arousal reduction, and coping skills (Novaco & Chemtob, 1998). Current techniques included in adult approaches are:

1. Education regarding anger, stress, and aggression.
2. Self-monitoring of anger frequency, intensity, and situational triggers.
3. Constructing an anger provocation hierarchy.
4. Arousal reduction.
5. Cognitive restructuring.
6. Behavioral coping.
7. Rehearsal of skills through graduated exposure.
(Novaco & Chemtob, 1998)

Description of Procedure

Treatment starts with a discussion on the nature and functions of anger, what causes anger, and when it becomes a problem. For physically abusive parents, education regarding anger, stress, and aggression may include situations outside the family in which the parent has anger difficulties (e.g., work or sports events), but is generally focused on anger and harsh parenting practices. When the therapist starts anger management training, the functional analysis regarding the abusive behavior will already have been conducted and the therapist and parent will have an understanding of the role that anger plays in the sequence of events that occur around physical abuse. Parents should be told that every parent experiences various levels of anger or frustration in relation to performing the many parenting tasks they face. Children are a tremendous responsibility and, as they grow and test out their independence, situations can be frustrating and anger-provoking for parents. Anger management training is designed to help parents manage their children in a different, self-controlled manner, but is not intended to diminish parental authority or control. It is essential to inform the parent that the therapist recognizes that the parent is still in charge of the child. The task is just to use a different method for discipline while they are in charge.

Therapists should assure that parents can identify persons and situations that trigger anger and signs of cognitive and physiological signs early in the provocation sequence. Similar to the anger management procedures discussed earlier for youth, parents should be asked to identify and then monitor both inside and outside anger cues (i.e., cognitions and physiological cues that signal an escalation of anger).

Next, skills for de-escalation should be taught. These include cognitive restructuring, such as changing the appraisal of the situation or giving self-instructions that de-escalate. The client is taught how to develop an alternative view of a situation where they are provoked that will change the exaggerated importance attached to events. Self-instruction guides coping behavior. Clients give themselves instructions to use coping techniques, such as substituting a cognition or reducing physical arousal. To reduce the arousal physiologically, relaxation techniques may be used. As shown in Chapter 9, relaxation may include controlled breathing, deep muscle relaxation, or guided imagery. Also, parents may be taught how to maintain a sense of humor as a competing response with anger.

Role plays provide the parent a chance to practice CBT techniques that decrease arousal early in the process and skills for responding appropriately to people who provoke or irritate them (e.g., assertiveness vs. aggressiveness). Role play should include actual events the client has experienced so that he or she is exposed to manageable doses of anger stimuli.

Case Application

Ms. Burch indicated in the functional analysis that management of anger was a factor in the escalation that led to physical abuse. The therapist identified with her the role her cognitions played. To de-escalate, she replaced her cognitions about the child disrespecting her and being like his father with a more adaptive cognition. She determined that saying to herself over and over, *"Just let it go; he's not his father,"* was effective in de-escalating. She also set up a behavioral system around household chores and felt comfort that she could fall back on those consequences rather than getting into hitting.

Comments and Caveats

Therapists should keep in mind that substitutions used should be those that are meaningful to the parent. Cognitive substitutions should be developed by the parent. Also, role play of the situation discovered in the functional analysis is essential to carrying out the substitution plan.

❏ Self-Management, Regulation of Anxiety, and Posttraumatic Stress Disorder

BACKGROUND AND DEFINITION

Psychiatric difficulties, such as anxiety, depression, posttraumatic stress disorder (PTSD), or other victimization-related symptoms, can be major barriers to managing stress and carrying out the tasks necessary to parent children. For parents with a childhood abuse history, current involvement with the protective services system may serve as a reminder of their own adverse childhood events and exacerbate existing psychiatric symptoms. When depressive and anxiety symptoms appear to contribute to heightened reabuse risk, therapists must first assess the severity of the problem and determine whether addressing these problems is a clinical priority. If the parent is suicidal, safety measures should immediately be put in place (e.g., enlisting the help of other adults for monitoring, or initiating hospitalization because of significant suicidal intent). For parents who are more emotionally stable, evidence-based techniques for depression, anxiety, PTSD, and victimization-related anxiety can begin immediately. In addition, a psychiatric consultation may be helpful to consider the use of effective pharmacological treatment as an adjunct to psychosocial intervention.

Parental PTSD or anxiety symptoms may result from an array of victimization experiences, such as a history of physical or sexual abuse or other crime-related events. Treatment for PTSD is supported by a wealth of research. The reader is referred to several texts for a comprehensive review of treatment techniques for these problems (Follette, Ruzek, & Abueg, 1998; Meichenbaum, 1994; Resick & Schnicke, 1992). Common components of CBT for PTSD and anxiety include systematic desensitization, flooding, prolonged exposure, and cognitive processing. Following is a brief discussion of each of these techniques, but the manuals listed above should be consulted for a more in-depth presentation.

Description of Procedures

Systematic Desensitization (SD). In implementing SD techniques, the first step is developing with the parent a graduated hierarchy of anxiety-provoking scenes related to the anxiety-producing problem. The first scene is designed to elicit minimal anxiety. Subsequent scenes are rank ordered by the amount of anxiety they provoke. The next step involves helping the client establish a deeply relaxed state, typically using such techniques as deep muscle relaxation (see Therapist Example 9.4) and imagery (see Therapist Examples 9.6 and 9.7). After establishing a relaxed state, the client is asked by the therapist to imagine each of the scenes in the hierarchy, starting with the least anxiety-producing scene. The anxiety-provoking scene is paired with the relaxation repeatedly until the scene no longer elicits anxiety. Then the next scene is introduced and the same procedure is followed. This continues until the client no longer feels anxiety elicited by the scenes.

Flooding. Similar to SD, the flooding technique begins when the therapist and client develop a hierarchy of anxiety-provoking scenes from the anxiety-producing events (e.g., sexual assault). Again, scenes are rank ordered from lowest to highest anxiety producing. Next, the client is asked to imagine all aspect of the trauma and is directed to the highest anxiety-provoking scene as quickly as possible. This technique departs from SD in that with flooding there is no attempt to minimize anxiety at the outset of exposure or to gradually increase the client's ability to tolerate it. Rather, the technique is designed to have the client experience the fear response and maintain it at a moderate level of anxiety from the start, until it subsides. Flooding has not been proven superior to SD in reducing symptoms of PTSD (Meadows & Foa, 1998).

Prolonged Exposure (PE). Based on data indicating that longer exposure is more effective than short exposure and that actual (in vivo) stimuli brings about greater change than imagined stimuli (Meadows & Foa, 1998), PE has become more widely used than SD. A number of studies have supported PE as a superior treatment for PTSD in combat veterans (Boudewyns & Hyer, 1990), mixed trauma groups (Marks, Lovell, Noshirvani, Livanou, & Thrasher, 1998), and rape victims (Foa, Rothbaum, Riggs, & Murdock, 1991). To conduct PE, the therapist and client first develop a hierarchy of anxiety-provoking scenes from least to most anxiety producing. Exposure sessions begin with the scene that is least anxiety producing (thus it differs from flooding). The exposure can be imaginal (e.g., reliving trauma memories) or in vivo (e.g., confronting a feared situation). The more anxiety-producing scenes are described repeatedly over several sessions until habituation is achieved. Sessions generally last from 1 to 2 hours.

Cognitive Restructuring. Based on the assumption that interpretation of the event determines an individual's emotional state and that dysfunctional thoughts may lead to dysfunctional emotional states, cognitive restructuring is a common component of CBT with adult victimization. Three basic steps are involved: (1) identification of dysfunctional thoughts; (2) evaluation of the validity of the thoughts and challenging those that are erroneous; and (3) replacement of the dysfunctional thoughts with more helpful ones.

Cognitive Processing Therapy (CPT). CPT combines exposure and cognitive therapies and has been validated for the treatment of rape victims (Resick & Schnicke, 1992, 1993). The basic assumption is that when someone experiences a traumatic event, his or her basic beliefs about the world are shattered. Therefore, the meaning that the individual gives to the event is important to moving forward. When an individual's core beliefs are inconsistent with information from a traumatic event, two processes may occur: accommodation and assimilation. These processes can be adaptive or maladaptive. On the maladaptive side, in the first process, accommodation, the individual alters preexisting core beliefs to be able to make sense of the traumatic event (e.g., moving from a belief that the world is a safe place to the idea that there is no safety in the world). In the second, assimilation, the individual distorts aspects of the traumatic event to be consistent with prior beliefs (e.g., the world is a safe place so this must not have really been a rape). The goal of CPT is to provide corrective information and experiences regarding the faulty thinking and intense feelings that often can occur as a result of a traumatic event. Thus, treatment techniques help the individual face the trauma for what it was (rather than going to extremes in belief system), integrate it, and move forward. Much of the cognitive restructuring work is done around five areas of functioning affected by victimization: safety, trust, power, esteem, and intimacy. Corrective information is provided through challenges to maladaptive beliefs and the presentation of alternative ways of making sense of the traumatic event. The exposure part of treatment is designed to help individuals overcome fears when they are exposed to stimuli regarding the traumatic event while in a safe environment and given sufficient opportunity to habituate (i.e., the individual experiences a decrease in fears). Over 12 treatment sessions, the major components of CPT are as follows:

1. Exploring what it means to have had the traumatic experience, beliefs about safety in the world, and what caused the event. Clients are asked to write about the meaning of the event they experienced.

2. Understanding the relationship between cognitions, feelings, and behavior. Clients are taught to differentiate thoughts from feelings and to see the connection between thinking and feeling, and the impact of thinking and feeling on behavior.

3. Exposure through writing about the traumatic event and reading the account repeatedly. Clients are asked to write an account of the traumatic event to include feelings, thoughts, and sensory details. Writing about the event and experiencing the emotions are conducted over two sessions.

4. Challenging thinking, "stuck points," that involves beliefs prior to the victimization (e.g., the world is safe) that do not match with beliefs resulting from the victimization. To address "stuck points," the concept of faulty thinking patterns is presented. Clients are then taught to identify maladaptive thoughts and given a list of questions to ask themselves to challenge those beliefs.

5. Challenging thinking about five areas: safety, trust, power, intimacy, and self-worth. These five themes are discussed and analyzed. Clients are asked to look at how prior positive beliefs in these areas are disrupted and how prior negative beliefs are supported. Suggestions for resolution of maladaptive beliefs in these areas are included. Near the end of treatment, clients are asked to write again about the meaning of the traumatic event they experienced.

Case Application

As the therapist worked with Ms. Burch, the therapist discovered that part of the anger related to Mario's father was a result of physical assaults she endured from him. At one point, Ms. Burch had felt that he was going to kill her. The feeling of lack of respect and anger triggered re-experiencing some of the incidents she had experienced at the hands of her former husband. To reduce the re-experiencing, the therapist conducted prolonged exposure with Ms. Burch. Ms. Burch discussed the abuse in detail and stopped at times that she was feeling highly anxious. At those times, relaxation exercises of her choosing were used. Cognitive restructuring around the physical assaults was also conducted, and Ms. Burch began to move away from the view that the physical assaults happened because she was a bad mother.

Comments and Caveats

As with children, therapist should keep in mind that exposure work may be contraindicated if the individual is still in an unsafe situation where abuse or the threat of harm is going on. As soon as is feasible, the therapist should bring in other people in the adult's ecology to understand the abusive experience that adult has had and help support the healing.

❏ Self-Management and Regulation of Depression

BACKGROUND AND DEFINITION

When a parent is showing clinical levels of depression, formal treatment for depression may be needed. Several resources (Hollon & Beck, 1994; Leahy & Holland, 2000) provide in-depth information on Cognitive Therapy and CBT for depression. This section is not intended to be the only resource to consult for treating depression, but instead provides brief guidelines for using a few existing CBT techniques that have been empirically validated.

Cognitive therapies work under the assumption that depressed people have negative views of themselves and maladaptive beliefs about situations, and that these beliefs, rather than the situation, give rise to negative emotions. Therefore, any improvements in a person's optimistic thinking may result in a decrease in depressive feelings. CBT adds to that assumption that a change in thinking *and* doing will decrease depression (Leahy & Holland, 2000).

Description of Procedures

Identifying Thinking Errors. To alter a person's thinking, the therapist should assist the individual in identifying the beliefs she or he holds that may reflect distortions or exaggerations (i.e., thinking errors) that contribute to the maintenance of depression. Beliefs can be treated as specific hypotheses, which can be examined by conducting an experiment to test out the hypothesis. The client and therapist's role, then, is that of a scientist. Examples of errors in thinking to be examined include negative mind reading, ignoring the positive, overgeneralizing negative labeling, and magnifying the intensity of an event. The therapist works closely with the client to look for examples of these thinking errors that might occur when thoughts pop into his or her head, sometimes referred to as "automatic thoughts." Automatic thoughts can reflect an accurate account of the situation, but they can also include thinking errors. For example, one client's automatic thought about not getting an answer from her spouse after being asking a question was, *"He is ignoring me because he doesn't love me; it's hopeless."* This thought may serve to stimulate negative emotions. As part of the "scientific experiment" and to challenge potential thinking errors, the therapist asks various questions, such as, *"What is the evidence in favor of this explanation?"*; *"What evidence is contrary to this interpretation?"*; *"Is there an alternative explanation for the spouse's behavior?"*; and *"Are other motives possible?"* A second strategy to address the thinking errors involves identifying rational alternatives to any illogical beliefs. Here, the client and therapist brainstorm other possible alternatives. For example, the spouse in our example may not have responded for several reasons: He may not have heard her asking a question; he may have been trying to think of an answer; he may have been angry; or he may have been asleep. This effort to examine the basis and accuracy of likely distortions in one's interpretation of events can be directed to a variety of beliefs and attributions.

Use of Diversion Strategies. When thinking errors are identified, clients may need diversion strategies to control or manage those thoughts. For example, a thought-stopping technique can help to prevent rumination over the automatic thought. Clients identify the thought, tell themselves to stop, and then substitute a rational alternative belief for the distortion. Alternatively, clients can use thought stopping, and then distract themselves with a different issue, such as the weather or what people around are wearing. Finally, another strategy is to take the thinking error and reframe the negative view of the situation by labeling it as neutral or positive.

Changing Doing. Another strategy for combating depression is to increase the rate of activities and events that provide reinforcement from the environment and engender pleasure and a sense of mastery (Lewinsohn & Gotlib, 1995); that is, increasing activities that bring about positive mood states. Depressed individuals may not report any activities that are pleasurable, so therapists can explore with them activities that may have been pleasurable in the past. Also, family members may recall activities that the client used to do that were enjoyable. Clients may keep a weekly activity schedule to keep track of activities in which they participate. These activities can be rated on a 10-point scale to reflect the parent's level of pleasure during the event. Therapists can prescribe increases in the selected activities and role-play social skills to be used in activities that require uncomfortable or complex interactions with people. In addition, clients may keep a daily mood diary in which they rate their general mood and the level of depression experienced each day. This diary may help reflect changes in mood and any correspondence with increases in activity.

Case Application

In addition to the cognitive restructuring of the abusive events that was taking place, the therapist gave Ms. Burch homework to help reduce depressive symptoms. She began to keep a daily mood diary that documented improvements in mood. In addition, she began to take walks in the neighborhood. This exercise enhanced her mood and led her to meet some neighbors with whom she came to have positive interactions.

Comments and Caveats

When a client is experiencing clinical levels of depression, the therapist should always recommend a thorough medical examination to rule out any medical causes. Furthermore, if physical activities are assigned, the therapist should make sure that there are no medical contraindications.

❏ Summary

Affect regulation is a skill in which many physically abusive parents may have deficits. Developing that skill is essential to managing the emotions that influence aggressive behavior toward children. In this chapter, we have reviewed some of the major affective problems experienced by physically abusive parents, although the list is not exhaustive. First, we addressed identification of abuse-specific triggers and development of a plan to manage those. Second, we reviewed current approaches for adult anger management. Skills in this section are intended not only for use in general life situations, but also for when abuse risk rises. Included in this protocol are skills similar to those used with children, such as identifying internal and external cues for escalation. With adults, there may be more emphasis on cognitive techniques because adults have a greater capacity for cognitive processing than do some children.

Third, we presented techniques for managing anxiety and PTSD in adults who may be experiencing these problems due to childhood abuse. These methods include systematic desensitization, flooding, prolonged exposure, and cognitive processing. Resick and Schnicke's (1993) CPT model for rape victims was highlighted. We briefly reviewed techniques for managing depression, especially cognitively oriented techniques, such as identifying thinking errors and the use of diversion strategies.

As with the child's treatment, there may be considerable variability in the extent to which parents acknowledge cognitive and affective problems worthy of intervention. Certainly, these techniques are more relevant for the parent who shows evidence of heightened anxiety, anger arousal, and/or cognitive distortions. Such parents may be prone to losing control and, thus, may benefit from additional training in the self-control skills mentioned in this chapter. In such instances, it is important to monitor carefully the parent's level of anger to provide immediate assistance when necessary to prevent any further aggressive or abusive behavior. As the reader reviews the brief description of the CBT techniques used for each problem area, we caution that to use these techniques adequately, therapists should consult the manuals and texts cited. In the next chapter, we move to behavioral approaches for managing children's behavior.

References

Boudewyns, P. A., & Hyer, L. (1990). Physiological response to combat memories and preliminary treatment outcome in Vietnam veteran PTSD patients treated with direct therapeutic exposure. *Behavior Therapy, 21*, 63–87.

Budney, A. J., & Higgins, S. T. (1998). *A community reinforcement plus vouchers approach: Treating cocaine addiction.* Washington, DC: National Institute on Drug Abuse.

Foa, E. B., Rothbaum, B. O., Riggs, D. S., & Murdock, T. B. (1991). Treatment of posttraumatic stress disorder in rape victims: A comparison between cognitive-behavioral procedures and counseling. *Journal of Consulting and Clinical Psychology, 59*, 715–723.

Follette, V. M., Ruzek, J. I., & Abueg, F. R. (1998). *Cognitive-behavioral therapies for trauma.* New York: Guilford.

Higgins, S. T., & Budney, A. J. (1993). Treatment of cocaine dependence through the principles of behavior analysis and behavioral pharmacology. In L. S. Onken, J. D. Blaine, & J. J. Boren (Eds.), *Behavioral treatments for drug abuse and dependence* (National Institute on Drug Abuse Research Monograph No. 137, NIH Publication No. 93-3684, pp. 97–122). Rockville, MD: National Institute on Drug Abuse.

Hollon, S. D., & Beck, A. T. (1994). Cognitive and cognitive-behavioral therapies. In A. E. Bergin & S. L. Garfield (Eds.), *Handbook of psychotherapy and behavior change* (4th ed., pp. 428–466). New York: John Wiley.

Leahy, R. L., & Holland, S. J. (2000). *Treatment plans and interventions for depression and anxiety disorders.* New York: Guilford.

Lewinsohn, P. M., & Gotlib, I. H. (1995). Behavioral theory and treatment of depression. In E. E. Beckham & W. R. Leber (Eds.), *Handbook of depression* (pp. 352–375). New York: Guilford Press.

Marks, I., Lovell, K., Noshirvani, H., Livanou, M., & Thrasher, S. (1998). Treatment of posttraumatic stress disorder by exposure and/or cognitive restructuring. *Archives of General Psychiatry, 55*, 317–325.

Meadows, E. A., & Foa, E. B. (1998). Intrusion, arousal, and avoidance: Sexual trauma survivors. In V. M. Follette, J. I. Ruzek, & F. R. Abueg (Eds.), *Cognitive-behavioral therapies for trauma* (pp. 100–123). New York: Guilford.

Meichenbaum, D. (1994). *A clinical handbook/practical therapist manual for assessing and treating adults with post-traumatic stress disorder (PTSD).* Waterloo, CT: Institute Press.

Novaco, R. W. (1975). *Anger control: The development and evaluation of an experimental treatment.* Lexington, MA: D. C. Heath.

Novaco, R. W., & Chemtob, C. M. (1998). Anger and trauma: Conceptualization, assessment, and treatment. In V. M. Follette, J. I. Ruzek, & F. R. Abueg (Eds.), *Cognitive-behavioral therapies for trauma* (pp. 162–190). New York: Guilford.

Resick, P. A., & Schnicke, M. K. (1992). Cognitive processing therapy for sexual assault victims. *Journal of Consulting and Clinical Psychology, 60*, 748–756.

Resick, P. A., & Schnicke, M. K. (1993). *Cognitive processing therapy for rape victims.* New York: Guilford.

13

Treatment of the Maltreating Adult
Behavior Management Techniques

The focus of this chapter is on reviewing basic child management techniques with the parent. Several procedures will be discussed in this section, along with some suggestions for maximizing their potential impact. The first general approach deals with teaching the parent how to use planned attending/ignoring. Other approaches involve the administration of reinforcing consequences and their removal contingent upon a specific behavior. In each case, we describe key components of the technique and some recommendations for using it. Where applicable, we have noted a few references for further discussion of each technique.

❏ Parenting and Behavior Management

BACKGROUND

Child management techniques are generally the focus of behaviorally oriented parent training programs. A number of manuals and books are available to teach management skills (see Clark, 1985; Fleischman, Horne, & Arthur, 1983; Munger, 1993; Patterson, 1976). In general, techniques include limit setting and rules, use of praise and rewards, loss of privileges, use of time-out, use of contingencies, and setting up and implementing contracts. Although most parents, including parents who have been involved in physical abuse (Walker, Bonner, & Kaufman, 1988; Wolfe, Kaufman, Aragona, & Sandler, 1981), are often taught behavior management skills in the office setting, actual practice in the home may improve the generalization of these skills (Wolfe, Sandler, & Kaufman, 1981).

PARENTING STYLE AND ITS IMPACT ON CHILD BEHAVIOR

Description and Considerations

It is our preference to introduce the topic of parenting influences on child behavior before trying to teach child management skills to parents. That way, the parent can have a more conceptual appreciation for this relationship and the likely utility of learning and administering alternative management techniques. Therapist Example 13.1 provides a sample introduction to this topic. Before proceeding, it is important to consider whether the expectations noted in Therapist Example 13.1 are reasonable for this parent and try to convey this to the parent.

THERAPIST EXAMPLE 13.1

A Sample Introduction to Parenting Style and Its Impact

"There often is a relationship between your style of parenting (how you interact, what you choose to respond to, and when you respond) and your children's behavior. They observe and imitate you, and come to do many of the things that you have done or told them to do. Of course, each parent, like yourself, has a unique style of raising, teaching, and managing a child, and this style may affect which behaviors your child will use when she or he is an adult.

"We're going to talk about some of the ways in which you parent your child. Think for a moment about how you would like your child to grow up and how you would like him or her to be when he or she is older. . . . What types of parenting activities do you find helpful and important to use? . . . Are there any behaviors you see yourself changing or modifying? Are there some skills or techniques that you want to learn more about?"

Once the parent seems amenable to discussing parenting behavior and his or her specific management skills, the therapist should mention the skills that are likely to be discussed during treatment. In this chapter, we cover the following topics: (a) attending/ignoring, (b) praise, (c) giving commands, (d) using reinforcers or rewards, (e) setting up a token economy, and (f) using time-out if the child is younger. Begin this discussion with an understanding of the importance of parenting consistency.

CONSISTENCY IN SETTING LIMITS

Description and Considerations

It is important to help parents first understand the importance of being consistent in setting limits and the impact of consistency on children's responses to limit-setting efforts. There are several aspects to limit setting that merit consideration, and they are discussed below. The first deals with knowing when and how to set them.

When do parents start setting limits? Obviously, this varies by age group. For infants, effective limits involve keeping them on the bed, feeding them, and making sure they sleep properly. For toddlers, these activities include monitoring stairs, doors, and electronic sockets to assure safety. For the latency-aged children, appropriate limits might include designating where they play, when they eat, and when they go to bed. Finally, for teenagers, limit setting may involve establishing a curfew or a policy on places they are able to visit and their peer group.

The purpose of setting limits is also important to discuss. Common reasons include the following: (a) child protection and safety, (b) teaching the child responsibility at home, and (c) teaching the child responsibility to help society, more generally. From the child's perspective, consistency makes the child feel safe (the world is predictable) and helps the child learn, because there are clear signals over what is appropriate and inappropriate.

Obstacles to maintaining consistency are sometimes easy to identify in each family's situation and merit some discussion with the parent. Common obstacles include (a) parents being tired, not having time, or being burdened with other responsibilities; and (b) children being defiant or inappropriate. Of course, it is important to appreciate that children quite naturally push parental limits to learn about growing up and that it is equally natural for parents to try to reinforce limits whenever possible. Indeed, children engage in numerous behaviors that may seem irrelevant to a situation or that actually test the parent's authority or response. Such behaviors include arguing, pleading, throwing tantrums, giving excuses, doing only a part of a task or expectation, and saying "I hate you." Parents can be encouraged to handle these behaviors by using several methods: (a) ignoring the child, (b) encouraging and then guiding compliance, or (c) using natural or logical consequences for behaviors that the child exhibits.

This chapter outlines basic behavior management techniques to help parents manage many common behavior problems. In cases where the child is showing aggression, it is possible that several management techniques will need to be implemented in a coordinated way, and the parent may need a great deal of support from the therapist and other people in the ecology to modulate his or her own affect. In accord with this approach, the parent or caregiver will need to establish a home rule or expectation of no aggression. Furthermore, the parent and child should determine some rewards that the child may earn for responding to situations without aggressive behavior. Similarly, the parent should decide on appropriate consequences—that is, those that fit the misbehavior (e.g., parent would not want to ground the child for a month for breaking a toy) and are developmentally appropriate (e.g., parent would not want to use time-out for a 15-year-old). In cases where the child has carried or used weapons, parents are encouraged to conduct regular searches of the child's room to remove any objects that the child might use to hurt others. For teens, parents may need to determine what types of aggressive situations warrant a call to the police. As supported by the use of good behavior management techniques, developing parental skills in preventing any escalation to violence through changes in interaction patterns is a key element of intervention for aggressive behavior.

❏ Specific Techniques and Guidelines for Rewarding Behavior

ATTENDING/IGNORING

Background and Definition

The Rationale. Parents often may benefit from hearing a rationale for the judicious use of attending and ignoring with their children. Such a rationale is found in Therapist Example 13.2.

THERAPIST EXAMPLE **13.2**
Introduction to the Impact of Parental Attention and Ignoring

"When you are with your child, your attention may be one of the most powerful rewards and a source of motivation for your child to change his or her behavior. We call this *attending*. When parents use attending, they also have to use ignoring, or the attending is not effective. The way all people learn how to behave is by receiving feedback from others. This is a constant process throughout our lives. If you can attend more to your child's positive behavior, the amount of negative behavior should go down while the amount of positive behavior should go up.

"Here are some examples: Early on, children learn quickly that other children play with them when they ask nicely. This is a pleasant experience. Now, children also learn that they can quickly get parental attention by having tantrums. For example, if a child asks to go out and his mother says, 'No,' he may whine for a while, but the mother is firm. He then throws himself on the floor, screams, cries, and kicks. Because the mother wants to stop the tantrum before it gets even more annoying, she may say, 'Okay, you can go out.' The child has just gotten the message that if he throws a tantrum, he will get his way. Now, that same situation could be different. A mother may state that the child can't go out because the family is to have dinner, and then may leave the room when the tantrum begins. The child realizes he has no audience, so the tantrum ends relatively soon. After dinner, the mother may say, 'You sat and ate so nicely. You may go out now.' So, what message did the child get? We could discuss other examples of how parents can use their attention to influence their children's behavior—for example walking away, turning the head away, making eye contact, using praise, or giving a physical hug."

Parents should understand the benefits or reason for using this skill. Certainly, behavior is affected by its consequences; if there is a certain payoff, a behavior may be increased in the future. Children get feedback from what gets them attention: for example, if they smile and laugh, their mothers smile, which may make them smile again. However, children can also use attention negatively: for example, a child may learn to throw a tantrum to get a cookie (giving the cookie may stop the behavior for the moment, but it may occur again in order to get another cookie); soon, bad behaviors (e.g., punch brother) get attention.

Attention also helps parents relate to a child at the child's level; this improves the quality of the relationship with the child. Children certainly learn a lot through attention; therefore, parents can try to promote good behavior and discourage inappropriate or unwanted behavior by changing how they give attention and for what behavior they give it. Help the parent to identify the behaviors that the parent would want to attend to or ignore. If help is needed, try to use this time to show some examples while the parent "misbehaves."

Description of Procedure

There are several suggested steps to consider when using attending and planned ignoring. These steps are included in Box 13.1. It is important to review what these steps mean and how the parent will apply them. Parents can be reminded of some suggestions for using planned ignoring effectively. They should be explicit about the reason for using ignoring by asking if this is a behavior that they want to ignore. The parent should also understand how to ignore properly and to be proficient in attending to alternative behaviors they wish to increase. One aspect of this technique involves providing praise or social reinforcement, sometimes accompanied by physical affection, when the child is behaving appropriately. This is perhaps the most common method for socializing children, so the parent should be encouraged to use praise frequently, but judiciously.

Box 13.1 | Considerations in Using Attending and Planned Ignoring

1. Never ignore a dangerous behavior (i.e., when there is a likelihood of injury or other serious complication).
2. Ignore the same behavior consistently.
3. To ignore the behavior, actively avoid eye contact and turn away from the child.
4. The behavior may increase (get worse) initially, which is common.
5. Remember why you are ignoring, so that you won't feel guilty and stop prematurely.
6. Always attend to the behavior you want to increase.
7. Be specific when using praise, so that the child knows the positive behavior she or he did.
8. Make eye contact and smile when attending to a behavior.
9. Use a pleasant voice [therapist should demonstrate the voice] when attending to a behavior.

Application and Comments

Role plays provide some practice in the proper use of each parenting skill. The therapist can help the parent identify positive and negative behaviors to incorporate in the exercise. Review the rationale for using behavioral techniques with children and answer all questions the parent has about the benefits of using this procedure. When the questions have been answered, ask the parent to role-play different attending experiences for each of the identified positive and negative behaviors. Try to demonstrate attending and ignoring for each one.

Here are five sample scenarios:

- The child cleaned a room when asked.
- The child got angry and didn't hit a sibling but did yell.

- The child hung up his or her coat after school.
- The child is in a bad mood, but is not throwing a tantrum.
- The child got an A on his or her test.

It may be helpful to ask the parent to practice some of these skills at home. The therapist should discuss how the parent will use attending/ignoring with the child over the next week. In addition, it is important to build into this exercise frequent use of praise and other social rewards. In one treatment case, a father was asked to identify behaviors to be managed using attending/ignoring and how he was to ignore his daughter. He returned the following session having identified her nagging (e.g., *"When she calls me and doesn't want a thing"*) and whining (e.g., *"Complaining about simple things, like when she's told to clean her room and do her homework before going outside"*) as the behaviors. His initial suggestions for ignoring her involved trying to talk on the phone, washing dishes, going to the bathroom, or actually going onto the porch that adjoined his bedroom.

Some parents also benefit from an explicit review of their use of praise. One mother of a very young boy needed considerable encouragement to state in a genuine and convincing fashion her approval of his behavior. She settled on the following praiseworthy statements: *"I'm really glad that you did your job on time today. Thanks, son; I appreciate it when I don't have to remind you again to do this."* The therapist can provide helpful feedback as to whether the parent's language is likely to feel positive and supportive.

Comments and Caveats

Do not forget to remind the parent that a misbehavior may appear to get worse as ignoring is used consistently. This "extinction burst," as it was originally described, often frustrates parents and leads them to discontinue the procedure even though it is an indication that the procedure is beginning to work. Furthermore, the therapist should ensure that the parent has picked behaviors that are generally mild in severity and, thus, are appropriate targets for this procedure.

Equally important is the need to evaluate the parent's comfort level in using praise. Some parents find this especially awkward or artificial. This reaction probably reflects some significant discomfort either with the procedure itself or with the notion of being reinforcing to the child. In some cases, parents simply do not feel comfortable saying nice things to their children. Because that reaction may reflect a fairly basic difficulty likely to affect the parent-child relationship and their communication, the therapist may need to spend additional time on this particular aspect of the attending/ignoring procedure.

ISSUING INSTRUCTIONS

This section is designed to help the therapist teach the parent how to use positive instructions and communication skills. Some adjunctive materials are noted later in the section.

Background and Definition

The therapist should encourage the parent to discuss how they give directions and ask the child to do things (e.g., *"Let's talk about how to give your child commands or instructions in order to increase the chance that he* [or she] *will listen to you. Here is each of the steps for giving clear instructions"*). Each of the skills listed in Box 13.2 should be briefly mentioned and explained to the parent.

| **Box 13.2** | Components to Issuing Clear Instructions |

Make eye contact.

Use a loud firm voice.

Be clear about what you would like the child to do.

State an instruction (command) as such, not a request or question.

Only give one command at a time.

Always praise and/or reward the child as soon as the instruction is followed.

Administer an appropriate consequence if the child is noncompliant; then repeat the instruction.

Description of Procedure

Make eye contact. Parents should look at the child, not their shoes or the window. Whenever possible, parents should try to use physical gestures to encourage the child to look at them, but should avoid using these gestures to get the child's attention by force. This should be done calmly.

Use a firm loud voice. If parents sound as if they expect to be listened to, they need to give the child fewer chances to disobey, argue with, or ignore them. Here, the tone should be firm and somewhat louder than usual, conveying the parent's authority, without being angry or tense. The therapist should demonstrate this.

Be clear about what you want the child to do. Let us say that the parent wants Sally to clean up her room. The parent can say, *"Sally, clean your room,"* or can say, *"You are such a pig, how can you sleep in a room like that?"* This first example accomplishes two things: first, it tells the child exactly what the parent is asking him or her to do; and second, because the parent is giving a direct instruction, it is more difficult for the child to ignore the parent.

State the instruction as an instruction. Mary's parents say, *"Would you like to take out the garbage?"* The problem in doing this is that the child can say "No." Sometimes, parents feel guilty or anxious as they give an instruction (i.e., a command), so they make it sound less like a requirement than a request. It is more effective to give the child clear (vs. vague) instructions. When parents issue a question command or a tentative instruction, they tell their children that they can refuse to follow them.

Only give one command at a time. If a parent says, *"Do the dishes, then put your laundry away, then clean your room, but don't forget to do your homework,"* the parent is only confusing the child. The parent may also increase the chance that the child will be overwhelmed (i.e., the child may just tune the parent out).

Always praise/reward as soon as the child responds to an instruction. There are two reasons why a parent should always respond with praise or a reward when the child responds to an instruction. One reason is to increase the likelihood that the next command will be listened to each time. The other is to make the experience of listening a more pleasant one for the child.

Administer a consequence if the child is noncompliant and repeat this sequence. When the child does not respond to the instruction within an adequate period of time, even after repeating the instruction and giving the child ample opportunity, the parent is encouraged to issue an appropriate and suitable consequence. The child should be informed of the consequence before it is administered, and it should be fairly benign and easy for the parent to use.

Application

Give examples of effective and ineffective commands. Have the parent give an ineffective, and then an effective, command for each of the following scenarios:

- The child is watching television, but needs to do his or her homework.
- The child needs to take the garbage out.

- The child needs to pick up the coat that he or she dropped on the floor, which the child does everyday when he or she comes home from school.
- The child needs to go to the store for food.

One mother we treated was asked to identify positive commands that she could use to improve her son's compliance. She picked the following: *"Son, put your toys away and then we can go to your hockey game."* She also suggested using the following when the child objected to her: *"So, do you always have to scream at me—can't you talk to me like a normal kid?"* Certainly, it is important to examine carefully the specific language the parent may wish to use and its appropriateness to the situation.

Comments and Caveats

The parent should be encouraged to follow certain guidelines to promote child compliance and to consider some additional steps when the child does not follow the instruction. These guidelines include doing the following: (a) giving a reminder; (b) if the child is noncompliant, administering any stated consequences; (c) restating the instruction; (d) using gestural or physical guidance, if necessary; and (e) repeating the process.

USING REWARDS (REINFORCERS)

Background

The purpose of this section is to teach the parent to reinforce a child's positive behavior, demonstrate different methods of reinforcement, identify and address the parent's concerns about using reinforcers, and discuss different methods of changing the child's behavior that can be used in the home. Several materials relevant for this lesson are drawn upon and cited herein (see Fleischman et al., 1983; Walker et al., 1988; Wolfe et al., 1981). Certain aspects of these procedures are briefly mentioned for illustration below.

The Rationale. Some of the reasons why parents can and should use rewards are listed in Therapist Example 13.3.

THERAPIST EXAMPLE 13.3

A Sample Introduction to Using Rewards

"There are ways for us to support our children when they solve problems or behave better. One way to do this is by using rewards, and we discussed praise as one type of reward. Most of the children we work with like to earn or receive things as they start to behave appropriately. It helps them understand that their improvements are good and encouraged.

"Sometimes, we need to use special rewards to motivate the child to do things, especially when praise doesn't seem to be quite enough. Most of the time, this is done to help get a new behavior started. However, once the behavior has been going for a while, the reward doesn't seem to be as necessary. Other things become more important than the reward itself. Let's go through different ways you can do this, and you can let me know which ones sound best to you."

A reward can be a powerful motivator for children; it may help to shape desired behavior and clearly tell the child what is good, it can make a parent feel better, and it may increase the child's self-esteem and identity. Of course, there are also obstacles to using rewards. First, there is a sense that it is a form of bribery. However, bribery involves getting children to do something that is not in the child's best interest (e.g., hurting others, stealing, or lying about something), whereas we use these consequences to promote positive or desired behavior for the child. Furthermore, a reward (reinforcer) is similar to equal pay for equal work, and it may not simply teach "only do something if you get something."

Description of Procedure

There are different types of reinforcers for the parent to appreciate: (a) social statements (e.g., receiving praise, a smile, or a hug), (b) material things (e.g., getting new possessions), (c) activities (e.g., playing games or with toys, watching TV, or being given privileges), and (d) symbols (e.g., being given coupons, stars, or points).

There are some general rules to follow if parents want to make these special rewards really count (see Fleischman et al., 1983; Walker et al., 1988). Some of the basic rules that parents should follow are listed in Box 13.3.

Box 13.3 | Components to Using Effective Rewards

Pick a reward that is truly desired by your child—verify this through observation of his or her behavior. It's important to use different ones because sometimes they lose their effectiveness, even if only temporarily.

Give the reward only *after* the desired behavior has occurred; it must be earned.

Box 13.3   *continued*

Give the reward consistently.

Label the behavior when you reward it—be descriptive. So, for example, say "thank you for doing your chores right after you came home from school."

Reinforce the child frequently. It is often necessary to reward effort rather than a given product or outcome.

Don't reinforce any undesirable behavior in the process. Certainly, withhold the reward for any undesired behavior.

Make sure the child doesn't already have separate access to the reinforcer; you must control access to it in order to enhance its potency.

Shape the child's behavior to what you want it to be. Reward behaviors that come close to the overall behavioral goal.

Always include praise.

Use age-appropriate rewards.

Avoid saying, "Yes, but . . ." or giving mixed messages, which can create confusion (e.g., avoid saying, "You did a good job on that housework, now why couldn't you do that before? You must be lazy").

Comments and Caveats

Positive consequences are helpful in getting a desired behavior to occur when it does not occur much at all. Of course, over time, other natural consequences will probably maintain behavior. For older children and teens, receiving rewards can be thought of as similar to working a job. That is, they earn rewards only when they do their job (follow the parent's rules), just as their parent earns a paycheck only for working a job. Therefore, it is important to convey to teens that they are earning the reward: It is not being given to them. It will make sense to them that they receive the reward only when the job is done (e.g., when they have three days of going to school without a fight).

HOME CONTINGENCY PROGRAMS

Background

The parent may be asked to discuss some of the things she or he would want the child to do differently (e.g., *"Try to think about some of the things that you want your children to do. What do you think should be included—what are you really concerned about? What about rewards that you might be able to use?"*).

The therapist can briefly mention certain options for the design and implementation of home programs (e.g., *"Here are a few methods that you could use to try and change some of your child's behaviors"*). For example, one could use an allowance program where the child earns money for completing a few specific tasks or doing things other than inappropriate behaviors the parent wishes to reduce. The parent could set up a point system where the child earns points that are exchanged for different types of rewards; points are earned for doing several things that the parent seeks. Or, the parent could set up a short contract in which she or he does something for the child if the child does something first that the parent would like.

Description of Procedure and Options

Reinforcing Behavior Using "Grandma's Law." The parent should become familiar with the components of "Grandma's Law" (i.e., *"Before you get dessert, you have to finish your meal"*). This can be explained as saying that before the child receives a reward, she or he has to perform some required behavior. One easy way to help motivate the child to do things is to set up a simple agreement—some kind of contract—in which the child can receive access to things she or he wants or likes after doing something else she or he is supposed to do (see Fleischman et al., 1983). The therapist can help the parent set up this kind of agreement—that is, if the child does something desirable, she or he can get to do or have something as a reward. It is important to emphasize the contingent relationship here between these two events (e.g., *"So, what this says is that if you do this, then you get [or get to do] that"*). The child could earn any type of reward that the parent is willing to provide. In some instances, it may be useful to offer the child an array of possible rewarding activities by having a grab bag or a list of desired things or activities. Ask the parent for suggestions to ensure she or he understands the concept.

Allowance Programs. A second option for rewarding the child involves using an allowance program. Discuss this procedure if the parents are interested. Such programs are especially useful if chores, jobs, or responsibilities are being targeted. A useful description of this type of program, called "Allowances," is especially relevant for the older child and can be found in Fleischman et al. (1983).

Contracts. Contracting is a related option that specifies a certain outcome for a certain type or level of performance by the child. This procedure is generally facilitated by using a form to set up a contract and reviewing the program with the child (e.g., *"So, this is to help you* [the child] *do things at home, show better self-control, be helpful, keep from doing* [something unacceptable], *and so forth"*). Here, the parent simply specifies what the child needs to do (a desired behavior), what the child would then receive (a desired outcome), and when the child will earn the reward. It is also helpful to identify in advance any potential problems and to try to prevent them.

Using a Point System or Token Economy. An alternative program involves the use of point systems (for further information, see Fleischman et al., 1983; Walker et al., 1988). Here, the child can earn points for completing certain tasks, following certain rules, or for avoiding doing things the parent does not like, and can lose points for not doing these things. This method may help the child become more willing to do things and less involved with or interested in negative things. In using this procedure, one should determine target behaviors, their point values, any rewards to be exchanged for points, and the timing or criteria for this reward. A record of progress should be monitored each week. The parent should understand each of these components, clarifying each one as needed (e.g., *"Why do you keep a chart? To monitor and record performance; to see physical evidence of earned rewards—points—because they are reinforcing; and to make sure there is no confusion about what happened"*).

Box 13.4 shows the steps to setting up a point system (see Fleischman et al., 1983; Walker et al., 1988; Wolfe et al., 1981). The therapist should explain each one and give an example.

Box 13.4 | Steps to Developing a Point System or Token Economy

Identify the target behaviors (positive and negative behaviors).
Explain earnings and/or loses.

 • The child should know how to earn and/or lose points or tokens.

State criteria for earnings or losses—the exchange rate.

 • The child should know when she or he is entitled to (or actually forfeits) the reward and how frequently it can be earned or lost.

Select an appropriate item or event to be earned or lost.

Make sure that child knows why she or he has earned or lost points.

 • Describe the behavior (e.g., "Bob, you just earned 1 point for doing *X*").

 • Review performance and give feedback on earnings and losses regularly.

Box 13.4 | *continued*

Praise performance: "Wow! You earned 10 out of 10—that's great!"

Evaluate the program with the child. If it is a contract, tally the points with the child at the end of the contract period.

Consider renegotiating the contract or point system, and select a time for doing so.

Application and Role Plays

Guide the parent to use these steps to develop a point system or contract using a point card. Give the parent sample contract forms for review and consideration. The parent can be encouraged to select one that she or he prefers, and to begin to develop a basic contingency of targets and consequences (e.g., *"Please take a careful look at these forms in order to decide which types of reinforcers you would like to use. Then, next week, we can talk about the ones you like"*).

The parent should think about some targets and be prepared to learn how to place them in a contingency. The therapist might introduce this activity as follows:

> *Make up a sample contract you would like to institute with your child. Include your desired outcome and your potential problems. Even if you think you would never do it, bring one in and include what you dislike about the technique and skill. Give some thought to the kinds of things that your child does or doesn't do that you would want to change.*

The therapist should then ask the parent to identify potential rewards that could be used for a given behavior (e.g., *"Also, think about the types of rewards that you think would be helpful in changing these behaviors. What could you use initially? Regularly?"*).

Comments and Caveats

Several potential problems may interfere with the successful application of a home contingency. First, the parent may forget to give (or to remove) points. Regardless of the parent's mood or what has just happened that minute or that day, the parent has to be consistent in giving or removing points. Whatever the child has earned (either punishment or reward) should be given. The second problem is setting up a system that is too extensive. The parent should not set something up that is too big or too hard to manage. Third, do not offer a reinforcer that is too big (or, perhaps, too small). Big rewards are not very helpful because they cannot be used often. Instead, parents should try to use small to moderate rewards that can be used more often. The parent might not have a desirable reinforcer; sometimes it is hard to find an effective reward, one that the child will really work to get. Finally, parents are sometimes poor monitors of their children's performance. It is important to notice how a situation changes and to be consistent, regardless of outcome.

❏ Specific Techniques and Guidelines for Punishing Behavior

Punishment refers to the use of techniques designed to decrease the occurrence of a behavior. The parent should consider carefully what types of consequences are appropriate and consistent with his or her philosophy. In discussing such options, the therapist can help the parent select a general sequence of appropriate punishments for different behaviors. For example, for some behaviors, disapproval is adequate; for others, removing privileges is more appropriate. Still others may require a time-out. In the context of the goals for this treatment program, each option is preferable to the use of harsh physical punishment (for general punishment recommendations, see Walker et al., 1988).

USING LOGICAL CONSEQUENCES

Definition and Description of Procedure

The parent should understand that this approach also seeks to help the child change his or her behavior using special consequences. The therapist might, for example, tell the parent,

> *Sometimes, we need to discourage children from doing things we don't like—things that are inappropriate, manipulative, dangerous, or just plain annoying. One way to do this is to let children experience the natural or logical consequences that occur when they do them. Sometimes, natural consequences may be sufficient. At other times, however, you may need to select a logical consequence that is appropriate for the particular behavior it is designed to change. These consequences teach children a good lesson and help them learn about responsibility; so, they can be effective.*

Natural consequences are the outcomes that would naturally happen without adult intervention. For example, a child who does not wear a coat would probably catch a cold. Or, someone who spends all of his or her money probably cannot go out to a movie. Similarly, logical consequences are the results that occur when a rule is broken—consequences that make sense in a particular case. A child who comes home late may not be able to watch television for the evening. Or, someone who is not dressed and ready for the school bus may need to leave without being fully dressed. In administering logical consequences, simply ask the parent to select two or three target behaviors and then to identify some of the more logical consequences that might ensue if those behaviors occur. Discuss with the parent how the consequences selected are related to the nature and severity of the problem behaviors. Certainly, the number of times when the child's behavior can adequately be managed using logical consequences may be limited.

RESPONSE COST: WITHHOLDING PRIVILEGES OR IMPOSING FINES

Definition and Description of Procedure

In this procedure, the parent removes some activity, privilege, or object contingent upon a specific child misbehavior. Usually, it is helpful if the item or activity is related to the child's misbehavior, which makes it easier for the child to make sense of the consequence. The therapist should provide the parent with a rationale for the use of this procedure. The parent should understand that losing a privilege or object will help a child learn to stop engaging in the undesirable behavior leading to that loss. Here, the child would be expected to lose a previously earned (or soon to be earned) item, activity, or other privilege (possibly even a new reward) after doing something specific that the parent did not want him or her to do. If the child knows in advance that a specific behavior will result in a specific consequence that includes the loss of privileges or of a highly prized personal possession, she or he may be more motivated to listen or behave appropriately. We will focus on the removal of privileges in a subsequent section, although similar procedures apply to the removal of possessions or objects the child already owns.

Here are some examples that might be reviewed with the parent:

- The child throws a tantrum. → So, take away something fun (e.g., a videogame) for a period of time.
- The child hits someone. → So, she or he loses opportunity to visit a friend for a day.
- The child breaks a toy. → So, the toys may be removed for one day/week.
- The child breaks someone's toy. → So, the child has to pay for it out of his or her allowance.

The last example reflects a form of restitution to the victim. When deciding on consequences, it is important for parents to tell the child in advance about the consequences that will ensue.

Description of Procedure

The therapist should review each component in using this skill and emphasize a few key ideas about the procedure (see Fleischman et al., 1983; Walker et al., 1988). The skills are listed in Box 13.5. An important decision in using this procedure is whether the parent will remove something temporarily or permanently. Generally, it is preferable to remove something for a brief period of time. In many instances, the item or privilege is not something that the child should be without on a permanent basis. However, there may be times when the child actually experiences a permanent fine or loss of something. Clearly, the parent needs to make sure that this aspect of the procedure is clearly worked out in advance and is, ultimately, done for the good of the child. In the event that a privilege is to be removed, it should be one that the child likes and often gets, and one that can be easily removed by the parent.

Box 13.5 | Components to Removing Privileges

Identify the behavior to be targeted and what is to be withheld or lost.

If some item or activity is be withdrawn temporarily, determine for how long. In most cases, the loss should be brief.

Clarify the specific criteria for imposing the withdrawal or loss and for the return.

Be fair and quick (no extra nagging, etc.).

The privilege (e.g., an activity) or item to be removed should be one that the child likes.

The loss should be imposed by stating the child's name, then, "If you do X, then you lose Y." Later, the child should be told, "You have lost Y because you did X."

If the child continues to misbehave after losing for the first time, mention the possible loss of a second privilege or item.

Comments and Caveats

Besides ensuring that the child is aware when this contingency is in effect, it also critical for the therapist to ensure that the consequences are indeed reasonable or in some other way appropriate. If they are unreasonable, they are likely to be limited in effectiveness. For example, if the parent takes a child's favorite toy away for a month, the child may forget about it after several days, in which case the toy or other consequence loses its meaning. Thus, consequences should relate to the behavior, be reasonable, and mean something to the child.

TIME OUT FROM POSITIVE REINFORCEMENT (NONPHYSICAL)

Background and Rationale

We introduce this topic with a brief rationale. Simple forms of punishment can help children unlearn undesirable behaviors. A child may learn to throw a tantrum in order to get the parent to give a cookie. To change this habit, it may be necessary to refrain from giving a cookie when the child throws a tantrum the next time. It may also help to remove the child from being in a position to receive or experience other desirable consequences when this behavior occurs.

Description of Procedure

The steps that need to be considered in using time-out are listed in Box 13.6.

Box 13.6 | Steps in Using Time-Out

1. Discuss the type of undesired behaviors and the procedure in advance with the child.
2. Pick a neutral (i.e., a relatively boring) place, but it must also be safe.
3. Designate a specific time period for the length of the time-out.
4. Impose the consequence immediately contingent upon the designated behavior.
5. Time-out starts when the child is quiet and may start over if the child is noisy or leaves.
6. Ignore mild misbehavior while the child is in time-out.
7. Return the child if she or he leaves area. Consider issuing a warning about the loss of privileges if the behavior continues.
8. If the child was placed in time-out for noncompliance, reissue the instruction and repeat the procedure.

Application

Basically, the child should be told to go into time-out for a short time (e.g., 5 minutes) for a specific reason. If the child argues or fails to go, she or he can be told that the time-out will be increased by another 5 minutes (depending on the age of the child, limit the minutes because young children have little conception of time). The parent can add 5 minutes to a time-out for disruption during the time-out. If the child receives an increase to 20 minutes, she or he should lose a privilege. Use a timer to keep track of the time-out length. Remain calm and monitor the child closely—do not leave the child unattended. The parent may use a "sit out" for younger children (e.g., a 2-year-old).

Box 13.7 provides examples of a few sample role plays to practice with the parent. It is important to use these examples to get more relevant situations from the parent.

Box 13.7 | Sample Role Plays and Guidelines for Using Time-Out

1. Your child asks, "Mommy, can I have a cookie?" and you reply, "No, we will be eating dinner shortly." Your child then starts to throw a tantrum; you try to ignore the behavior, but child gets louder and starts to throw toys. You state your child's name and say, "Please stop throwing the toys." Now, go through each step in the time-out sequence.

2. Johnny and Billy are quietly playing with their toys in the room. As soon as you leave, they begin to fight. You [the parent] say _____. [the parent fills in the blank].

3. You ask John to stop yelling at you. He refuses. You then do what?

4. Your child is watching television and is asked to go do his or her homework. He or she ignores the request. Go through the warning you would give, then role-play the time-out.

Comments and Caveats

The parent should be encouraged to discuss with the child the use of time-outs in the home, including the reasons for using it, the setting where the time-out area/chair will be, and how long it will last. After using a time-out, the parent should discuss how well the procedure was applied and identify any potential difficulties in using the procedure regularly. In general, it is important to review the rules, any applications, and all questions or obstacles to this procedure.

It is also useful to discuss with the parent the length of time that the child should be asked to be in a time-out. In general, there is probably little reason or, in fact, empirical evidence to suggest the need to keep the child in time-out for a long period, such as an hour. A brief period of time may be equally effective, and provides the child with many more opportunities to engage in appropriate behaviors and, if applicable, to earn reinforcement. Of course, one can always modify the length of time based on the parent's initial experiences.

❏ A General Review of Behavior Management

A FEW LESSONS LEARNED

Recent Applications

An effort should be made to discuss parents' success or failure with the rewards and consequences they have used. In doing so, provide guidance and make any adjustments to each program they have used. Praise the parent for their successes and encourage them to maintain consistency, especially if they are struggling with these procedures. Also, other aspects of the parent's repertoire might be worth reviewing at this point, such as their own rationale for using these techniques instead of physical discipline and any personal objectives for using these new skills.

Therapist Example 13.4 provides an overview of the use of attending/ignoring as a management technique. Other techniques may need to be reviewed in this manner to ensure that the parent fully appreciates their application and likely impact.

THERAPIST EXAMPLE **13.4**

Summary and Review of Behavior Management

"As we have talked, we have learned how much of your child's behavior is learned and influenced by what you do. What we think, feel, and then do—how we respond—is the way in which our children learn what is expected of them and learn what is appropriate for our culture. This is important to know, because it helps you feel less frustrated and angry when your kids continue doing a certain thing even after you have told them not to. That's why you have to look at what is reinforcing the behavior, and then try to change that, which will in turn help change the behavior. We talked about how a parent can try to change a child's behavior by changing the consequences for that behavior—to use attending or ignoring, to give a reward for any behavior that is appropriate, to withhold a reward, and to use a time-out. So, using these skills helps parents to develop effective, nonviolent ways in which to deal with their child's behavior.

"One of the most important skills we discussed involves using attending and ignoring with your child. Attending is the skill of paying intense attention to a child, and ignoring is the opposite. What is the most important thing about attending?" [Being positive and really focusing on the child.]

"Any behavior that is appropriate should be reinforced with positive attention. Using positive attention with your child is the most important skill you can have if your goal is to ultimately change or shape your child's behavior. If you do nothing else but increase the amount of positive attention (e.g., praise) you use with your child, then you will effect change in your child's behavior. Any questions or comments?

"Also, keep in mind that the opposite of attending is ignoring. You should be using ignoring when the behavior your child shows is behavior that is not serious or dangerous but is one that you'd like to decrease. An example of a behavior to ignore is your child whining when you ask him or her to do something and he or she doesn't want to do it. Can you tell me the rules about ignoring? How do you do it? Let's role-play the following situation: I'm the child and you're the parent. Now, we're eating dinner. [The therapist should make some annoying movement or noise while in the role play, but should be very appropriate except for that one thing.] What behavior should be ignored?"

A Parenting Self-Assessment

By this point, the parent should be thinking about his or her unique situation and should have some ability to apply the types of skills she or he needs to use more often or more effectively. One way to examine this is by having the parent write down this plan. Finally, invite the parent to ask any questions about these skills, programs, or any other aspect of parenting.

❏ Summary

In this chapter, we have reviewed some of the basic behavior management techniques that parents may use as an alternative to physical discipline or harsh punishment of their children. Hopefully, the therapist has been able to illustrate to the parent that these procedures are best applied under conditions of low anger arousal and in the absence of hostile or irrelevant comments. Equally important is the provision of appropriate rationales highlighting the functional nature of these procedures and the importance of appropriate timing in maximizing their effects (e.g., time-out is a function, not a place). This is necessary in order for some parents to feel comfortable with the idea of reinforcement and the nonphysical use of punishment, especially when such procedures may not have been used when they were children. Indeed, a common obstacle to be addressed is the fact that many parents do not believe in the role of reinforcement. Thus, therapists should remember that these techniques may not feel natural to parents and that parents will need a lot of reinforcement themselves for the behavior management to become part of their automatic parenting repertoire.

Also, therapists need to keep in mind the use of developmentally appropriate techniques. For example, time-out would not be appropriate for a 14-year-old; loss of privileges may be a better technique. Therapists will need to work with parents and children to assure that the techniques are implemented consistently and that rewards are updated as needed. In fact, therapists must ensure that parents use social and material consequences commensurate with the child's needs, insofar as many parents have preferences to use large rewards and punishments when these magnitudes may be unnecessary. One reason for this is that parents, especially when highly frustrated, may feel reinforced by the use of harsh punishment, even though they may recognize that severe punishment has limited educational or corrective value. This "big bang" theory of punishment—that is, that the bigger the bang or punishment, the bigger the effect or benefit—needs to be addressed whenever it surfaces. Now that we have covered techniques to use with parents, we move in the next chapter to bridging individual and family work.

References

Clark, L. (1985). *SOS! Help for parents.* Bowling Green, KY: Parents Press.

Fleischman, M. J., Horne, A. M., & Arthur, J. L. (1983). *Troubled families: A treatment program.* Champaign, IL: Research Press.

Munger, R. L. (1993). *Changing children's behavior quickly.* Lanham, MD: Madison Books.

Patterson, G. R. (1976). *Living with children: New methods for parents and teachers.* Champaign, IL: Research Press.

Walker, C. E., Bonner, B. L., & Kaufman, K. L. (1988). *The physically and sexually abused child: Evaluation and treatment.* New York: Pergamon.

Wolfe, D. A. Kaufman, K., Aragona, J., & Sandler, J. (1981). *The child management program for abusive parents: Procedures for developing a child abuse intervention program.* Winter Park, FL: Anna Publishing.

Wolfe, D. A., Sandler, J., & Kaufman, K. (1981). A competency-based parent training program for child abusers. *Journal of Consulting and Clinical Psychology, 49,* 633–640.

14

From Individual to Family Treatment
Bridging Through Clarification

Openly discussing the abuse is important to bringing closure to the family and planning ways to prevent reabuse. To talk about the abuse without being negative and blaming the child requires a review of the maltreating parents' and other family members' attributions (i.e., beliefs about causes of behavior) about the abuse and culpability. Addressing victims' attributions is important because self-blame has been shown to relate to such internalizing problems as lowered self-esteem, anxiety, and depression (Frazier, 1991; Morrow, 1991; Wyatt & Newcomb, 1990). Changing maltreating parents' attributions is important because doing so may serve a preventive role. For physically maltreating parents, attributions of child responsibility for physical abuse relate to increased risk for physically abusive behavior (Bradley & Peters, 1991; Bugental, Mantyla, & Lewis, 1989; Feshbach, 1989). Thus, changing these attributions may help reduce risk for further abuse. For family members, viewing the parent rather than the child as responsible for the abuse may contribute to support of the child's disclosure. Thus, a positive, supportive family reaction to the event may contribute to the child's psychosocial adjustment (Conte & Schuerman, 1987; Everson, Hunter, Runyon, Edelsohn, & Coulter, 1989).

The abuse clarification is a process that provides a structure for the family to talk directly about the abuse (for a more thorough discussion, see Lipovsky, Swenson, Ralston, & Saunders, 1998; Ralston, 1982, 1995, 1996). Importantly, this process is a bridge from individual work to family work, and it begins in the course of individual work and brings the family together to address the main reason they are in treatment—child physical abuse. This process is similar to the family meeting described by Furniss (1987) and the apology session described by Trepper (1986) and Trepper and Barrett (1989). The abuse clarification addresses attributions of the abuse by the maltreating parent, child victim, and other family members, and culminates with a plan for safety and reabuse prevention. The overall goals for the abuse clarification include the following:

1. Change individual and family cognitive distortions about the abuse

2. Focus responsibility for the abuse occurring on the maltreating parent

3. Focus treatment on the needs of the child victim and family

4. Set up a safety and reabuse prevention plan

❏ The General Structure of Clarification

Clarification involves all family members or individuals important to the family or child and appropriate to have involved in such family work (e.g., extended family or a minister may be involved). The process begins with individual work with the parent centering on the construction of a responsibility letter; simultaneously, preparation of the child victim occurs. Following completion of the parent's letter, an evaluation of that letter and approval by the nonoffending parent or another key adult is conducted. Once the therapist is sure that the letter speaks generally to the events that have occurred and, more specifically, to issues the child requests be addressed, and once the letter is approved, a family meeting occurs. The meeting's purpose is to discuss openly the abuse, read the letter, and set up a safety and reabuse prevention plan.

PREPARING THE MALTREATING CAREGIVER

Altering parental cognitive distortions goes hand-in-hand with accepting responsibility for the occurrence of the abuse and prevention of further abuse. For maltreating parents, this therapeutic work begins after the intake assessment and occurs simultaneously with work to complete other therapy goals, such as building anger management skills. A structured format for addressing parental attributions and responsibility is through the writing of an apology and responsibility letter to the child and family.

At the outset of treatment, maltreating parents are given the expectation that an apology and responsibility letter will be written and a family clarification meeting will occur. Parents may be fearful of prosecution if they take responsibility for their actions in writing. Therapists will need to communicate with Child Protective Services and the parent's attorney about the clarification expectation. It is essential to ensure that this technique serves as a therapeutic and not a prosecutorial tool. Therapists must give a rationale for the clarification that makes sense to the parent, family, and attorneys involved. For a rationale example, see Therapist Example 14.1.

THERAPIST EXAMPLE 14.1

Sample Rationale for Participating in the Abuse Clarification Process

"This process is being conducted to give the family an opportunity to discuss openly what happened and make a plan to prevent physical abuse in the future. The clarification is for the victim and family, and not for an agency. So, the main purpose is to help the child and family heal and move forward. For healing to occur, the discussion around the abuse and the plan must not include any blaming of the child or other family members. We are asking the mom or dad (i.e., the maltreating parent) to stand up in her or his family, be strong, and take responsibility. This is a process, so it takes some time. We will be asking the maltreating parent to write a letter to the child and family, and we will work on this letter together. Many drafts of the letter will be written. A family member or person important to the family (e.g., a minister or rabbi) will read the final draft and approve the letter or point out changes. Then the letter will be read in the family clarification session."

STARTING THE CLARIFICATION PROCESS

After the rationale is given and everyone involved is clear about the importance of the clarification, the parent is given an outline of what should go in the letter (see Box 14.1). The parent may begin the letter on his or her own and bring it to the next session. Subsequent sessions involve a review of the letter, challenging distortions (e.g., *"I'm sorry you made me hit you because you acted up"*), encouraging full acknowledgement of all abusive behaviors, and understanding the sequence of events that occurred and the triggers that occur before loss of control. Edits are recommended to the letter, and the parent is allowed to make those changes outside of the session. Box 14.2 shows two drafts of a sample letter. The letters do not include their real names. As noted earlier, in addition to focusing on attributions and the clarification process, all other factors that are related to the abuse (e.g., poor anger management, drug use, and limited knowledge of behavior management) are targeted.

Box 14.1 | Contents of the Clarification Letter

1. State the purpose of the letter.
2. Describe the abusive behaviors.
3. Take full responsibility for the abuse, effects on the family, and legal consequences.
4. Absolve the child victim of blame.
5. Affirm the victim for telling and talking about the abuse.
6. Absolve the family of blame.
7. Take full responsibility for the abuse.
8. Take full responsibility for family separation (if separated).
9. Take full responsibility for the impact on the family.
10. Take full responsibility for any legal consequences.
11. Apologize for all behaviors.
12. Tell the family about your own treatment and what you are learning.
13. Provide safety instructions to prevent reabuse.
14. Make commitment to nonviolent parenting and new family rules.

Box 14.2 | Sample Abuse Clarification Letters

Case Background: Two siblings, Harvey—age 12, and Hannah—age 14.

The parents divorced when the children were preschool age. The mother was the custodial parent. The mother was in a plane crash and sustained a head injury. The children went to live with the father while the mother was hospitalized, and during the initial stages of her recovery, the father was granted temporary custody. When it was evident that the mother would survive, her physician recommended that the children return to her to "take care of her and help her recover." The family court judge ordered custody returned. The children were removed from the mother when she beat Hannah with a blow dryer and covered her face with a pillow from the couch. The children were returned to the father's custody and entered treatment. The mother entered treatment to reestablish contact with the children through phone calls or supervised visitation.

First Draft of the Letter

Dear Harvey and Hannah:

I am writing to say I am sorry for all the times I have mistreated each of you. Especially you Hannah. I especially want to apologize for

Box 14.2   *continued*

the events that happened on August 13th. I am sorry for losing my cool the way I did. For example, I had to hit you with the belt, snatched the blow dryer out of your hands, and tried to keep you quiet by putting the pillow over your face. I have tried to remember other times I mistreated you, but can't remember any, so I really don't know what you're talking about. I know that when I was trying to recover from the crash that you both just about drove me crazy always wanting to be with your friends or on the phone and Hannah you were always working on your hair. I am trying to learn to deal with my temper with my doctor's help and I hope that you two will straighten up and help me also.

Harvey, I am sorry for the time I slapped you and yelled at you for no reason. And I lost my temper one time when you spilled a soda. You always were my clumsy child!

Hannah, I am sorry for thinking of you as a little adult instead of a child. I thought that you were the oldest and should set a good example for Harvey. But I was wrong. I should have set the example for both of you.

Please forgive me and I will forgive you too. I love you a lot.
Mom

Eighth Draft of the Letter

Dear Harvey and Hannah:

I am writing this letter to you both to apologize for the times I mistreated you, the times that I embarrassed you in front of your friends by hitting/yelling at you or by making negative comments about them.

Hannah, I especially want to apologize for the events that happened on August 13th. I carried my anger too far when I hit you with the belt, blow dryer, and tried to keep you quiet by putting the couch pillow over your face.

Harvey, I want to say I am sorry for the times I slapped you and yelled at you. I want to say that I am sorry for yelling at you when you did something that I thought was wrong or for standing up for your sister. I want to say I am so happy that you called your father when the situation got out of control. That really helped.

I know that there are other times that I mistreated both of you and I am very sorry for these times. I realize that after the crash I did not give you both the love, attention, guidance, and patience you needed. I am sorry that you both thought that I wanted to kill you and that you were afraid of me. I did not want to kill you, and I handled things really bad.

Harvey and Hannah, I love you both very much. I am working on getting myself back on the right track so that I can spend time with you both again. I am learning how to control my anger with the aid of Dr. Carnes. I am also learning to respect you both for who you are.

Box 14.2   *continued*

I am responsible, not the two of you, for us not being able to spend time together. I realize that when my anger and stress get too high I am more likely to lose control of my temper. I have learned to remove myself from a confrontation before it gets out of control and I lose my temper and take it out on you.

When we all are ready to begin seeing each other, Dr. Carnes will meet with us to help me learn to watch for my temper rising. If this happens, I will leave the room and go get myself calmed down. Controlling my temper is my job and not yours. Our visits will be supervised by Dr. Carnes and later by another adult who can help me watch my temper. I love you both and will try very hard to make sure you are safe.

Love,
Mom

PREPARING THE CHILD VICTIM

The child victim will have an opportunity to speak about his or her experiences and to ask questions at the family clarification meeting. Therefore, some preparation is necessary. Box 14.3 outlines some of the components of child preparation. If the child has a lot of anxiety when discussing the abuse, preparation should include the anxiety management procedures discussed in Chapter 9. The structure that may be helpful in preparing children includes simply processing what the child would like the parent and family to know about how the abuse made him or her feel and determining what questions the child would like the parent to answer. This can be accomplished by helping the child develop a list of feelings that children his or her age experience. From that list, the child can pick out any that describe how the abuse made him or her feel. Then, the child can add to that list additional feelings experienced. Next, the child may make a list of questions he or she has for the maltreating caregiver. These could be questions about the abuse (e.g., *"Why did you do it?"*) or statements explaining what the child would like the parent to know about his or her experience.

In the course of preparation, the child may introduce events that the parent has not made known. The therapist should gain permission from the child to discuss these events with the parent and have those events included in the apology. As the child determines what he or she would like to have said and asked in the family meeting, the child can decide how this should be done. The therapist may introduce options, such as that the child reads what is prepared, that the grandmother speaks for the child, that the therapist gives the child's prepared statements, or that the child gives statements through a puppet. The technique used to relay the child's feelings and questions should be comfortable for the child and developmentally appropriate.

Box 14.3 Components of Preparing the Child Victim for the Clarification Family Meeting

1. Develop a list of feelings that kids your age have.
2. Pick out what feelings you may have experienced from the abuse.
3. Add to that list other feelings you experienced.
4. Develop a list of questions for your parent.
5. Develop some statements you want to make sure are said to your parent in the meeting.
6. Set up a list of rules for the clarification meeting.
7. Decide who will help with the communication of what you want said.
8. Practice.

A second function of child victim preparation is structuring the family clarification meeting. The child will have an opportunity to be the original designer of the rules for the session. This helps the child feel some degree of control and comfort in an intense and potentially emotionally difficult session. Rules are set regarding where the child and maltreating parent will sit, who the child would like to sit by, the sequence of the session (i.e., whether the letter will be read first or whether the child or family will speak), boundaries around touching, and managing the maltreating parent's emotional reactions. Rules are reviewed with another primary adult who will attend the session. Box 14.4 gives an example of clarification family meeting rules.

Box 14.4 Example of Clarification Family Meeting Rules

1. Suzy sits between Grandma and Uncle David.
2. Mom is not allowed to give gifts to Suzy during the meeting.
3. Mom is not to expect or ask for hugs or lap sitting during the meeting.
4. If Mom feels like she is going to cry, she needs to leave the room, get herself together, and return when calm.
5. Mom will not ask the family to forgive her.

PREPARING OTHER FAMILY MEMBERS

Preparation of other family members for the clarification will depend on the structure of the family. If there is a second parent, then that parent's role will be to review the letter and give a final approval on what is read in the session. When the maltreating caregiver is a single parent, extended family may play that role. Other children in the family who will be present for the clarification family session should be briefed on what will take place in there. Some preparatory work may need to be done with them regarding what they might like to contribute to the session.

❏ The Clarification Family Meeting

The clarification family meeting will include all family members involved in the household where the abuse occurred, except for very young children. In addition, extended family or other key individuals in the family's social ecology may attend if the family so desires. The therapist directs the meeting. Unless the structure previously determined dictates otherwise, the session will start with the maltreating parent reading the clarification letter, acknowledging all abusive behaviors, and assuming responsibility for the occurrence of those behaviors and their impact on the child and family. Upon completion of the reading of the letter, the child victim or other family may comment or ask questions. If the therapist determines that additional information may be helpful to the family, the therapist may also ask questions or give comments. Information from the maltreating parent should lead the family to understand triggers that precede abuse (e.g., drinking alcohol, having a bad day at work, or experiencing certain interactions within the family) and how the parent plans to manage differently. Further discussion with the family can lead to discovery of external cues that might elicit fear in family members or suggest increased risk (e.g., seeing the parent's face turn red). These external cues can be incorporated into the family safety and reabuse prevention plan. The family should leave the clarification family meeting with the safety and reabuse prevention plan agreed upon and in writing (for a sample, see Box 14.5). The safety part of the plan includes changes that will take place in the family to support the safety of the child victim or other potential victims. The reabuse prevention part of the plan includes identification of triggers or situations that increase risk and specification of what the parent will do to lower risk and what other family members may do to help.

Box 14.5 | Sample Safety and Reabuse Prevention Plan

What Will Happen in Our Family to Make It a Safe Place to Be

Mom will remove the paddle from the house.

Each family member must knock on the door of someone's personal room before entering.

Everyone will practice using a low voice instead of screaming.

All guns will be removed from the house.

All alcohol will be removed from the house.

If guns or alcohol come back into the house, grandma will be notified and she will remove them.

Our Family Plan to Help Keep Mom From Hurting Anyone Again
Mom's Triggers:

Having a drink

Seeing that kids did not clean the house

Being upset about work

When the kids and television are loud

Mom's Inside Cues That Mean Danger

Face feels hot

Heart racing

Thinking, "I'm gonna hurt somebody"

Mom's Outside Cues That Mean Things Are Getting Worse

Scrunches up her face real mean

Starts shaking her fist

Starts getting loud

Plan

When mom recognizes her triggers are present or feels inside cues that signal things are getting worse, she will leave the room and change her thoughts and get her body to relax.

If the trigger is that the house isn't clean, when calm, she will come from her room and sit down with the kids and give the consequences we decided on for not cleaning.

If mom is upset about work, she will call her friend Tameka to discuss.

If the kids and television are loud, she will turn the television down and talk to the kids in a low voice. If they are still loud, she will send them to their rooms.

> ## Box 14.5 *continued*
>
> If mom slips and has a drink, she will call her friend James to help.
>
> If mom comes in, has been drinking, and doesn't call James, the kids will call grandma for help.
>
> If mom cannot get herself calmed down, and sees that things are getting worse and thinks she might hurt someone, she will go to her room and call grandma for help.
>
> If mom has a gun out and kids are worried that she will use it on the family, the kids will call grandma. Grandma will call 911. If the kids can't reach grandma, they will call 911.
>
> If the kids see mom scrunch up her face real mean, start shaking her fist, or start getting loud and are worried that she will hurt someone, they will call grandma right away, or if they can't call, will run to Miss Clara's next door.

❏ Summary

In this chapter, we have presented the abuse clarification process. This process occurs throughout treatment, but functions as a bridge in that it offers the therapist a forum for taking work completed in individual parent and child treatment and incorporating that into family treatment. As such, this procedure is consistent with the integration of multiple participants and treatment targets as found in the comprehensive individual and family cognitive-behavioral therapy approach. Specific treatments directed towards the family system are described in the next chapter.

References

Bradley, E. J., & Peters, R. D. (1991). Physically abusive and nonabusive mothers' perceptions of parenting and child behavior. *American Journal of Orthopsychiatry, 61*, 455–460.

Bugental, D. B., Mantyla, S. M., & Lewis, J. (1989). Parental attributions as moderators of affective communication to children at risk for physical abuse. In D. Cicchetti & V. Carlson (Eds.), *Current research and theoretical advances in child maltreatment* (pp. 254–279). New York: Cambridge University Press.

Conte, J. R., & Schuerman, J. R. (1987). The effects of sexual abuse on children: A multi-dimensional view. *Journal of Interpersonal Violence, 2*, 380–390.

Everson, M. D., Hunter, W. M., Runyon, D. K., Edelsohn, G. A., & Coulter, M. L. (1989). Maternal support following disclosure of incest. *American Journal of Orthopsychiatry, 59*, 197–207.

Feshbach, N. D. (1989). The construct of empathy and the phenomenon of physical maltreatment of children. In D. Cicchetti & V. Carlson (Eds.), *Current research and theoretical advances in child maltreatment* (pp. 349–373). New York: Cambridge University Press.

Frazier, P. A. (1991). Self-blame as a mediator of post-rape depressive symptoms. *Journal of Social and Clinical Psychology, 10,* 47–57.

Furniss, T. (1987). An integrated treatment approach to child sexual abuse in the family. *Children and Society, 2,* 123–135.

Lipovsky, J. A., Swenson, C. C., Ralston, M. E., & Saunders, B. E. (1998). The abuse clarification process in the treatment of intrafamilial child abuse. *Child Abuse & Neglect, 22,* 729–741.

Morrow, K. B. (1991). Attributions of female adolescent incest victims regarding their molestation. *Child Abuse & Neglect, 15,* 477–483.

Ralston, M. E. (1982). *Intrafamilial sexual abuse: A community system response to a family system problem.* Unpublished treatment and training manual.

Ralston, M. E. (1995). *Clarification: A process for assigning responsibility for protection and victimization in child sexual abuse cases.* Unpublished training manual.

Ralston, M. E. (1996). Child protection must be first priority in family preservation. *National Resource Center on Sexual Abuse News, 5,* 1–6.

Trepper, T. S. (1986). The apology session. *Journal of Psychotherapy and the Family, 2,* 93–101.

Trepper, T. S., & Barrett, M. J. (1989). *Systemic treatment of incest: A therapeutic handbook.* New York: Brunner/Mazel.

Wyatt, G. E., & Newcomb, M. (1990). Internal and external mediators of women's sexual abuse in childhood. *Journal of Consulting and Clinical Psychology, 48,* 758–767.

15

Family Treatment
Setting the Foundation

Earlier chapters have considered how to orient the child, parent, and family to the initiation of treatment and to establish expectations and conditions likely to maximize the benefits of treatment. In this chapter, we discuss some adaptations of family treatment procedures that have been tailored to address the needs and characteristics of physically abusive families. The objectives for the therapist as outlined in this chapter are to build rapport; conduct an assessment of parental child rearing, parent-child relationships, and family interactions and functioning; and promote family engagement, focusing on both children and parents. Certainly, considerable therapist discretion must be used in determining when to initiate family sessions and how much effort needs to be expended in addressing the family's structural and functional characteristics. We draw upon both structural elements (e.g., Alexander & Parsons, 1982; Minuchin, 1974; Minuchin & Fishman, 1981) and various behavioral or functional elements in this approach to family work (e.g., Alexander & Parsons, 1982; Morris, Alexander, & Waldron, 1988; Patterson, 1971, 1982; Patterson, Reid, & Dishion, 1992; Robin & Foster, 1989).

❏ Overview of Treatment

PHASES OF THERAPY

There are three primary phases to the family treatment approach we describe in this chapter. These phases parallel those used in earlier cognitive-behaviorally oriented, family-systems treatments described by Alexander and Parsons (1982) and Robin and Foster (1989) for use with general adolescent patient populations. Several aspects of these models have been incorporated into the present chapter, with several modifications designed to address the unique aspects of physically abusive families. As noted earlier, much of this material was included in the family treatment protocol evaluated in the Project IMPACT (Interventions to Maximize Parent and Child Togetherness) outcome study (see Kolko, 1996a, 1996b).

In our adaptation of these existing materials, the first phase of the present treatment program—setting the foundation—involves three primary tasks: (1) promoting a constructive view of family problems using reframing, (2) developing a no-force contract, and (3) assessing the family's pattern of interactions with a focus on abusive behavior. In general, this phase takes place during the first few sessions when efforts are made to engage the family in treatment.

Phases two and three will be presented in Chapter 16. The second phase—family skills training and applications—seeks to increase positive interactions within the family by teaching the family problem-solving and communication skills, addressing problems that interfere with the acquisition of these skills, and encouraging involvement with outside systems. The third phase—applications and extensions—is concerned with the maintenance and reinforcement of new family routines and skills. The clinical impetus here is to evaluate and promote the family's ability to examine how well they use their skills and to make modifications in its routines as new challenges arise.

❏ Setting the Foundation

The tasks to be completed in this phase generally occur after the child and parent have received exposure to some of the materials and treatment procedures described in prior chapters. In the context of family work, important tasks for the therapist include introducing the family to certain parameters of treatment (e.g., duration, type of work, and their responsibility), allowing the family to talk about feelings regarding treatment and each other, gaining an understanding of key aspects of family functioning in relation to the referral incident, helping the family view the problem in a systemic way, and developing a treatment contract. Because general introductions to the therapist and treatment have already been conducted, the following sections begin with treatment-specific content.

BEGIN TO REFRAME THE FAMILY'S BEHAVIOR AND INTENT

A major task of the therapist in this first phase of treatment is to enable the family to view what has happened in a constructive and therapeutic manner (see Morris et al., 1988). Reframing, or providing a more positive interpretation of a given event or situation, is done in the context of assessing the family's concerns and functioning. There are a number of goals of reframing, or *relabeling* as it is sometimes called.

To help join with the family and reduce any blaming for what has happened, the therapist can offer an open invitation to *"talk more about what you want from this service."* Even if the answer is *"Nothing"* or *"I think this is a waste of time,"* the therapist can respond with an affirmation of the process of that comment (e.g., *"It must be frustrating to feel like nothing can help"* or *"You sound as if you do not feel that anything will help"*). Although this still has a focus on something negative, it has the effect of putting the therapist and family on the same side.

The therapist is encouraged to maintain a nonblaming atmosphere, to look actively for ways to focus on positive family characteristics, and to reduce any apparent negativity or hostility. At the same time, it is important for the therapist to not be perceived by the family as sanctioning harsh punishment. Therapist Example 15.1 provides some examples of therapist relabels that focus on the parent's ultimate desire to help the children.

THERAPIST EXAMPLE **15.1**

Examples of Therapist Relabels to Promote Family Engagement

Therapist: Tell me about the kinds of things that happen in your family that you feel brought you here today.

Parent: My children are just out of control, and I get so mad at them.

Therapist: So, one reason you are here is because you want to help your children. One way you care is by getting angry or having high expectations. You wouldn't put that much energy into it if you didn't care about them.

Parent: I'm here because my caseworker told me I had to come.

Therapist: Sometimes, when you feel like you are being forced to do something, it becomes really hard to do. Some people would feel that if a caseworker told them to come, they really wouldn't want to come *because* a caseworker told them to do it. I really give you a lot of credit for coming tonight, because it must have been hard to do. It makes me think you must care a great deal about your children.

Parent: You have to do something with these kids—they are horrible.

Therapist: It sounds like you feel that you have tried to do different things to help your children and have found that things aren't working. I think it's great that you care enough about them that you are willing to come and see us for some help with that.

These brief examples demonstrate how the therapist should focus on positive intent and help the family to perceive the problem in a relational way. However, reframes such as those in Therapist Example 15.1 run the risk of alienating other members of the family. Thus, it is important, whenever possible, to give reframes that join the family members together. It is important to include some comment directed toward the child, such as *"It seems to me that one of the things that your intense anger is expressing is that you care greatly about John, but to you, John, the caring does not show through; you just feel the anger."* This type of discussion about how the *intent* of the person acting and the perception of the person being affected can be so disparate helps the family to see that different people in the family can have different perceptions of the same event.

One function of the reframe is to explain a pattern of interaction in a way that is different from how the family or participants currently understand it. For instance, a mother might be discussing how she feels when her child disobeys her. Reframes begin by stating underlying intent, as illustrated in Therapist Example 15.2

THERAPIST EXAMPLE 15.2
Sample Relabels Related to the Child's Behavior and Intent

Mother: When he misbehaves, I smack him so he won't do it again.

Therapist: You feel that you are trying to teach him something by smacking him. *[To the child]* What do you think when she smacks you?

Child: She is mad at me.

Therapist [to the mother]: So, he thought you were mad at him, but you think that you are mad about what he is doing. That is an important difference.

Mother: Well, I'd just never hit him for no reason, but he acts so bad I worry for him.

Therapist: So, again we get back to your caring about him. It sounds as if when this incident happened you were thinking, "I really care and worry about my son," but *[speaking to the child]* you were thinking, "Boy, my mom is really down on me."

Such information ideally will help the therapist to examine the family's typical interaction patterns and, where applicable, to understand how a given pattern may represent an ineffective but genuine attempt at solving the family's problems. For example, a parent who sends the child to his room for four hours may be attempting to administer a severe punishment for a behavior the parent wishes to stop. The parent probably is not aware that this discipline is unlikely to have the desired effect. The therapist reframes this as evidence of the intensity of the parent's concern for the child, rather than as evidence of the parent being bad or neglectful. The behavior of the parent is not sanctioned, but the underlying intent is stated.

RESPONSES TO FAMILY CHALLENGES

Obviously, parents are going to report challenging or hostile interchanges between family members during treatment. Much can be said about maintaining a low-key profile with the parent when some form of agitation or confrontation is demonstrated and showing an openness to communication rather than appearing disappointed in what has happened. For example, it is not uncommon to hear parents express outright displeasure with the therapy (e.g., *"I think this is stupid and I'm not coming back"*). Some therapists find themselves using a power- and control-based stance in responding to the parent (e.g., *"Well, didn't your caseworker say that if you didn't come back, you may lose your children through the courts?"*). An alternative approach is to use negotiation to address the parent's position (e.g., *"Okay, so let's talk about what you do not like about the process and we'll see if we can make this a more helpful experience for you"*).

At this point, it is useful to remind the family that they have at least some control over what happens to them in therapy. When a family is reluctant to participate, the therapist can try to find a middle ground that would reflect some willingness to maintain contact with treatment.

If you do not feel this is helpful after we have had a few sessions, I really want to know so that we can figure out how best to continue. How about if at the end of the next session—or the third session—we stop a little early so that we can discuss if we should go on or not?"

The therapist might then arrange the next visit, remind the family about the contract, and encourage the family to identify treatment goals.

There also may be times when it is necessary to reframe any challenges to the therapist as a reflection of the family's sincere interest in getting the best help for their family (see Alexander & Parsons, 1982). Here is one example from a recent case: *"It sounds as if you really want to make sure that you are going to be working with someone who can help you. I really respect someone who is a good advocate for his or her family."* Pay close attention to any such reframes to ensure that they do not sound patronizing or minimizing. Of course, offer answers to any specific questions about training or competence directly in advance.

EVALUATE AND SUBTLY CHALLENGE ATTRIBUTIONS

After the therapist recognizes the underlying intent of the family's statements, reframes should be used to evaluate (and subtly to challenge in the process) the parent's/caregiver's attributional stance, as well as the child's views. This is done by looking at how each participant perceived the event and at what each one assumed about the other's motivations during the exchange. For example, the therapist can ask a general question to ascertain the parent's attributions (e.g., *"What was the first thing you thought when he misbehaved?"*), which the parent can hopefully articulate (e.g., *"That he refuses to listen to me and has no respect for me"*). Then, the therapist can offer some form of validation of this response while seeking any additional interpretations or attributions that any of the family members may make (e.g., *"Okay, I could see that. Now, what else could it mean?"*).

During this routine, the therapist should allow the family to identify other behaviors conveyed by the term "misbehaving" with the hope that they identify at least some behaviors that are less negative (and more specific) than "giving no respect." At that point, it may be helpful to say something to the parent about the different interpretations of significant behaviors and events, such as the following:

> Often, what we think people mean when they say or do something is different from what they do mean. So, one thing we're going to do during our meetings is help me understand what each of you means when you say or do certain things.

PROMOTE A SYSTEMIC VIEW OF THE PROBLEM

One of the goals of a relational reframe is to develop a systemic view of the family's problem; that is, to move the family away from the perception that one person causes the problem or is the "bad" one in the family. For the family who has a child with a behavior problem, the therapist sometimes reframes the behavior as the child's attempt to achieve more autonomy, but this reinforces the view that the problem lies in the child (see Minuchin & Fishman, 1981). Instead, the therapist might make a connection between the family's need for connection and closeness and the child's behavior; here, the child is seen to behave a certain way in response to the family. The distinction is subtle. The focus, however, is on spreading the cause of behavior among the family system when there is at least some plausibility to this description.

ESTABLISH A NO-FORCE AGREEMENT OR CONTRACT

We try to encourage each family to consider adopting some type of preliminary treatment contract in this phase, even if it is only for the family to agree to attend the next session. One form of behavior contract we discuss is designed to address the family's (or parent's) use of physical force, if relevant. The therapist can attempt to provide the overt message that the *parent and child/children* must take responsibility for refraining from any such negative interactions. There is a choice point in each episode where alternative choices can be made. In addition, other members of the family should be provided with skills for making alternative choices in the same situation.

The focus of the contract is, at least, to suspend use of a strategy they already use in order to give the use of other strategies a chance. The contract specifies that the family should try not to use any negative remarks or behavior. However, the contract also indicates that various problematic or negative behaviors will be discussed in the session, with the goal of helping the family find alternative and more efficient methods of solving their interpersonal problems.

The involvement of the child or children within the context of this initial agreement is designed to encourage all of the family members to use a set of skills with each other that may encourage appropriate problem-solving choices, choices other than the use of physical force. For the parents, however, the focus is less on making a compromise choice upon which both the children and the parents can agree (although that is optimal) than it is on providing parents with something concrete to do when they feel frustrated and overwhelmed. The problem-solving search for this compromise will also serve as a timeout for parents when they feel enraged and may turn their anger towards their children. If a family is being followed by Child Protective Services, the therapist may choose to give a copy of the no-force contract to the social worker. Doing such gives public recognition to the family for agreeing to refrain from the use of force and may help to ensure a consistent overall safety plan. Therapist Example 15.3 provides an overview and explanation of the no-force agreement to be reviewed with the family.

THERAPIST EXAMPLE 15.3

Overview and Explanation of the Family No-Force Agreement

"One of the things that we will do is learn ways of interacting that are viewed as positive by your family during times when parents are disciplining their children or when kids are trying to get their parents to listen. We will also discuss alternative ways of solving problems and interacting with each other, other than spanking, beating, hitting, punching, or shoving. Because we will practice nonphysical ways of solving problems and because I want to give these new strategies as much of a chance as possible, we ask all families to agree to a very important treatment goal. We ask all family members to agree to try their best not to use any kind of physical force with members of their household while they are in therapy here. Can you all do that? . . . I'd like you to think about that." *[The therapist then elicits from the family which behaviors would be involved—hitting, slapping, grabbing, pushing, beating, shoving, pinching, washing someone's mouth out with soap, forcing food down someone's throat, or any other way of physically hurting or controlling others. Try to solicit every person's cooperation in this agreement.]*

"We know that this may not be easy to do. But, we ask all families to try to do this, not just yours. This doesn't mean that you will never do these behaviors again. Learning some new techniques of parenting or general family interaction takes time. It just means that we are asking you not to use these behaviors now so that we can give other problem-solving strategies a chance to become stronger." *[The therapist then gets their reactions to this, and why they might find it difficult.]*

"However, there may be times over the coming weeks when you may find yourself using some kind of hitting and slapping. You may feel overwhelmed, stressed out, or angry, so you reach out and shove or slap when you don't mean to. If this does happen, we want you to come in and talk about it so that we can discuss alternative ways of dealing with that problem. We will not get mad at you, view you as a 'bad' parent or person, or consider it a failure by any means. What we *will* do is talk about the behavior in some detail, then identify and practice an alternative way of coping with that problem. This will also help you in similar situations. Remember that it takes time to learn new skills, and we don't expect things to change fast. In fact, the good thing about a problem is that there is an opportunity for improvement. So, I hope very much that you *will* talk to us if something does happen, so that we can work on alternatives. During the weeks that you keep to the contract, we will also want to talk about what you are able to do differently." *[The therapist then takes any more questions and clarifies the content.]*

DEVELOP A PROBLEM LIST

One final step to be completed in this section involves helping the family to identify a few goals on which they can work during family treatment. We prefer to ask each family member to take responsibility for identifying his or her own goals separately, recognizing that they will in all likelihood differ in scope, relevance, and feasibility, among other characteristics. Each person is asked to write down his or her ideas on a piece of paper for review in the next session.

❏ Assessment of Family Functions and Interactions

DISCUSS THE REFERRAL INCIDENT

Although we discussed various assessment measures and recommendations in Chapter 4, this section describes some of the specific issues to be examined during a family-based assessment. If the family did not discuss the referral incident in a previous session, the therapist should elicit details as to the circumstances of what happened. At the same time, the therapist should remain sensitive to the possibility that the family has had repeatedly to "tell their story" about what happened. Therapist Example 15.4 provides a brief introduction to this topic.

THERAPIST EXAMPLE **15.4**

Therapist Reference to the Referral Incident

"I know that you've been asked a number of times about the situation with your child that brought you here. But I feel that it is important to discuss it at least briefly and for me to hear it directly from you so that I can understand better how you felt that day, how you think and feel about disciplining *[the child]*, and what would help in situations in which you are feeling very strongly about getting your point across to him *[or her]*. It will also help me understand what you want for your child, and how you can obtain those goals without hurting him *[or her]*."

[If the therapist encounters reluctance, she or he can add the following]

"I understand that it is uncomfortable even to have to talk about it—anyone would feel that way in your shoes—but could you tell me in your words and from your perspective what happened that day with *[the child]*? Different people in the family may remember it differently. Now, I'd like to ask everyone about it. Is it okay if I ask the kids too?"

In capturing a brief but useful description of the incident, it is useful to ask questions about the context in which it happened, to assess any apparent attributions of both parties about what happened, and, if possible, to fit these viewpoints into the reframes that have been discussed above. This is a time to show some empathy for the intent of the parent (as discussed above) and the stress she or he may have experienced (if this was the case), but care should taken to avoid giving any impression of sanctioning the abusive behavior. This discussion may help the therapist determine whether the parent's use of physical punishment is a product of enormous stress placed on the parent influencing the level of anger control, of the feeling of being out of control and unable to identify anything else to try with the child, or of the need to seize or maintain control due to the belief that this is the only legitimate or effective discipline strategy. The choice of problems to be selected for family work may be influenced by the underlying reason for the parent's use of this form of discipline.

GENOGRAM AND TIMELINE

Definition and Description

The genogram interview we use here is drawn from the work of McGoldrick and Gerson (1988) and McGoldrick, Gerson, and Shellenberger (1999), which includes information about parenting techniques used by the parents and grandparents, as well as suggestions on developing a basic genogram. For our purposes, it is useful to complete a genogram containing an assessment of family of origin issues. Such information can be incorporated into the diagram of system influences on the family's use of violent behavior. For instance, if the therapist learns during the course of constructing the genogram that the parent was subjected to force as a child, this potential early influence on the parent deserves notation. One could call it "how mom (or dad) was raised." If the parent's experience with force as a child is part of a parent's child rearing beliefs, then one might record it as "parenting beliefs."

As noted in Chapter 2, the literature on physically abusive caregivers usually describes the role of prior abuse and/or deprivation in the parents' families of origin for a modest minority of cases. Thus, it is important to try and gain a sense of what are those family issues at work in any case and how do they relate to the family's current circumstances. The goal here is to help the therapist show greater sensitivity for the historical and attitudinal stance of the family and/or parents by having some understanding of their history of exposure to and use of violence. The genogram may also include the entire social network support system. This will allow the therapist to determine the family's level of social isolation and the supports available to the family system. Ultimately, such information will be used in the later phases of our treatment model.

Comments and Caveats

Of course, the therapist may encounter some or substantial parental denial of any negative perceptions of their children or family. It is important that the therapist not assign blame or draw any specific conclusions prematurely about personal responsibility upon discussing this historical information. Therapists might frame the genogram as a way of helping them keep track of "who is who" within the family; this task may last for a few sessions. For each category below, descriptions, including questions and definitions of observable behavior, are provided that may be used in the assessment of family functioning. The therapist should be flexible and judicious by addressing only those topics in the following section that seem applicable and based on the family's particular problems.

Family of Origin Issues

The following list of questions may help caregivers to articulate details regarding their own family situations:

- *"How did you know, in your family, if you did something good?"*
- *"How did you know, in your family, if you did something bad?"*
- *"What kind of relationship do you have with your parent now?"*
- *"Is there anyone in your family with whom you are close now?"*

- *"As an adult, what do you wish your parents had done—done more of or less of—when you were a child?"*
- *"What did your parents do that caused you to say, 'When I have kids, I'll never do X,' or 'I'll always do Y'?"*

We have also found it helpful to ask the parent to respond to the following assignment, either in a session or as homework:

1. List an incident in which somebody did something that bothered, offended, or angered you.

2. Go back to the time it happened and remember why, at the time, you thought they did this to you.

3. As you think about it now, list three alternative reasons why they could have done this to you.

Power and Control

It is important to elicit information about who is in control in the family. The therapist must look closely at process as well as content. Other areas to observe include who answers most of the questions, whether there one person who answers when you ask someone else something, and if the children look to the parent or someone else for permission before they talk in the session.

Listed in Therapist Example 15.5 are examples of several questions that may be asked about the family and specific types of interactions that may be observed during the assessment.

THERAPIST EXAMPLE 15.5

Examples of Family Assessment Questions

"Tell me about how rules get made in the family." *[Ask about the most recent rule that was made, what led up to it, who was involved, has it been stuck to.]*

"How do decisions get made in the family?" *[Consider having them do the task of planning a family outing to get a sense of the patterns of control and power in the family.]*

"Who is the family news anchor—who tells everyone about the latest developments?"

"Tell me about something the family recently did together—for example, watch TV, eat dinner, go visiting, etc.). Who decided who would go, what they would do, and so forth?" *[If someone chose not to attend, ask how that was handled.]*

"What happens when someone wants to change a rule or not participate in a family activity?"

"Tell me about your family life—describe a typical day to me. *[Look for the levels of chaos, the problem solving, and the interactions. Does each member describe a very separate day, or do they sound like there is connection?]*

"What do you do when you are upset about something?" *[Ask this of each of them.]*

Family Dynamics: Structure, Hierarchy, and Alliances

Below is a list of some other family interactions or patterns to be assessed in abusive families and observations about family process that can be used during this procedure (see Alexander & Parsons, 1982; Minuchin & Fishman, 1981). Please be aware that one is looking for patterns of behavior, not individual incidents.

Enmeshment. We look for diffuse boundaries within the family. Here, the roles in the family may be ill defined. Areas to observe in understanding this domain include the following: (a) the therapist asks a question and someone other than the person to whom the question was addressed offers the answer; (b) the children seem to act like parents to each other; (c) the parent seems to act like a child; (d) there is a high level of chaos most of the time; and (e) no one in the family endorses having any time alone. The following is a suggested question to ask in assessing this domain: *"Do people in this family spend time alone?"*

Parentified Child. Look for a child in the family who is in the role of a parent to other children or to the parent as well. Areas to observe include the following: (a) one child who seems to function on the executive level (e.g., makes decisions, disciplines others, takes care of other children, etc.); (b) the child answers questions asked of the parent; (c) the child acts and sounds like an adult when conversing; (d) the child helps the therapist keep control of other children in the session; (e) the child may have anxiety about adult issues, food money, clothing, heating bills, and such; (f) the parent defers to the child as if he or she was an adult or partner; and (g) the child seems more organized and competent than the parent. One question to ask in evaluating this domain is, *"What responsibilities does the child have in the home, like chores or caring for other children?"*

Negativity. Negativity refers to a lack of positive interaction in the family. One should make observations in the following areas: (a) the child is unable to describe any pleasant family activities; (b) family members always qualify a positive statement with a negative one; (c) the parent believes that making positive statements about a child will spoil him or her or jeopardize the child; (d) the parent does not use praise; and (e) the parent holds negative attributes about the child because of his or her connection to a "bad" person within the family (e.g., *"This child is just like my Uncle Michael"*). A few questions to ask in evaluating this domain are listed here: *"Tell me something good about your family"*; *"How do you know, in this family, that you have done something good?"*; and, *"Tell me about the last time that your family did something fun together."*

Powerlessness. Does the parent or the entire family feel powerless to improve their quality of their life? Areas to observe include the following: (a) all problems are seen as related to outside forces that the family has no control or ability to change (e.g., the neighborhood, school, or the economy); (b) withdrawal, which may include the use of drugs or alcohol, is used as a problem-solving mechanism; and (c) there is anxiety about the future and a sense of hopelessness that things will improve. Questions to ask about this topic include the following: *"How do you let the children know if you are dissatisfied with their behavior?"*; *"How do you know if mom or dad is unhappy with something that you have done?"*; *"Describe how you feel when you pick up the phone and your child's teacher says she wants to discuss your child's behavior with you"*; and, *"Describe how you feel when you decide that you have to discipline one of your children for anything?"*

Significant Daily Stress. The concern with significant daily stress is that the parent spends so much time just working to survive that there is no energy left for parenting. Areas to observe are as follows: (a) the parent seems tired or burned out, or expresses the feeling of being overwhelmed; (b) the children seem to be in control; and (c) the parent may exhibit some depressive symptoms. Questions to ask in evaluating this domain include the following: *"How often does the school call about your kids?"*; *"Are there health problems in the family?"*; *"Are you unemployed and looking for work?"* (i.e., is the parent dealing with the stress of rejection?); *"Is there trouble paying the utilities and rent?"*; *"Has anything recently been shut off?"*; *"Are you getting any help?"*; and, *"Do you have anyone you can go to if things get really bad?"*

Other Child and Family Characteristics

Social Support. It is important to document whether the child or parent has friends or relatives whom they can call, to learn what they do in their spare time, and to understand how available they are to the family.

Child's School Functioning. Some attention should be paid to learning about the child's performance and behavior at school. Questions to ask include the following: *"How is the child doing in school?"*; *"What are his [or her] grades?"*; and, *"How does he [or she] get along with the teachers there?"*

Child's Peer Relationships. The nature and extent of the child's friendships and how well the child gets along with others can address social interaction concerns: *"How does the child get along with other children at school?"*; *"Does she [or he] play with kids outside of school?"*; *"Does she [or he] have a best friend?"*; and, *"What are the kids like with whom she [or he] is friendly?"*

❏ Summary

In this chapter, we have reviewed some specific procedures designed to enhance family engagement in treatment and to better understand both the parent's prior history and the family's interactional patterns. The length of this particular phase of treatment may vary considerably, given wide differences in the extent to which these personal and family histories reveal problems worthy of clinical attention. Furthermore, families vary in their level of candor and motivation, especially when discussing past or current family problems. This section has highlighted the need to appreciate the family's overall willingness to report these types of problems as one seeks to understand key family processes for incorporation in treatment. One important purpose of this section has been to promote initial family engagement and participation, in part through a somewhat systematic process of assessing family characteristics and interactional styles, rather than seeking to implement any specific changes in family activities or behavior. Of course, once such information is obtained, it may be appropriate to initiate the next phase of treatment designed to enhance family skills and interactions.

References

Alexander, J. F., & Parsons, B.V. (1982). *Functional family therapy.* Pacific Grove, CA: Brooks/Cole.

Kolko, D. J. (1996a). Clinical monitoring of treatment course in child physical abuse: Child and parent reports. *Child Abuse & Neglect, 20,* 23–43.

Kolko, D. J. (1996b). Individual cognitive behavioral treatment and family therapy for physically abused children and their offending parents: A comparison of clinical outcomes. *Child Maltreatment, 1,* 322–342.

McGoldrick, M., & Gerson, R. (1988). Genograms and the family life cycle. In B. Carter & M. McGoldrick (Eds.), *The changing family life cycle: A framework for family therapy* (pp. 164–169). New York: Gardner.

McGoldrick, M., Gerson, R., & Shellenberger, S. (1999). *Genograms: Assessment and intervention.* New York: Norton.

Minuchin, S. (1974). *Families and family therapy.* Cambridge, MA: Harvard University Press.

Minuchin, S., & Fishman, H. C. (1981). *Family therapy techniques.* Cambridge, MA: Harvard University Press.

Morris, S. B., Alexander, J. F., & Waldron, H. (1988). Functional family therapy. In I. R. Falloon (Ed.), *Handbook of behavioral family therapy* (pp. 107–127). New York: Guilford.

Patterson, G. R. (1971). *Families: Applications of social learning to family life.* Champaign, IL: Research Press.

Patterson, G. R. (1982). *Coercive family process: A social learning approach.* Eugene, OR: Castalia.

Patterson, G. R., Reid, J. B., & Dishion, T. J. (1992). *Antisocial boys.* Eugene, OR: Castalia.

Robin, A. L., & Foster, S. L. (1989). *Negotiating parent/adolescent conflict: A behavioral-family systems approach.* New York: Guilford.

16

Family Treatment
Skills Training and Applications

In extending the techniques described in the prior chapter on family engagement, this chapter describes the second and third phases of treatment for families involved in child physical abuse. The focus of this chapter is on implementing skills training procedures designed to enhance the family's prosocial interactions and extend clinical efforts with any important outside systems. Initially, however, it is important to determine how well the family has responded to their initial involvement in therapy.

❏ Review of Initial Progress

COLLECT AND REVIEW GOAL HOMEWORK

In a prior session, the family was assigned the task of setting goals. To begin the review of their initial progress, each person is asked to read his or her answers, if doing so feels comfortable. The family's concerns should then be assessed in an effort to formulate them into workable goals. Certainly, it is helpful if one of the goals for every family relates to the use of nonphysical methods of problem solving or discipline. The therapist should also offer suggestions for the details of a general treatment contract. Such a contract should include information on the following points: (a) who will attend, (b) the frequency of sessions, (c) how a session will be cancelled, and (d) the duration of treatment (for a very reluctant family, one may contract session by session). The contract provides both parties with clear expectations in advance about the scope and requirements of treatment. Once developed, the family is asked to sign the treatment contract or review sheet.

ASSESS ADHERENCE TO NO-FORCE AGREEMENT

At the beginning of each session, we encourage the therapist to ask each family member about the progress that has been achieved in keeping the no-force agreement (e.g., *"So how did everybody do with our no-force contract?"*). If anyone has questions about the reason for maintaining this contract, the therapist can explain that the use of force varies on a continuum ranging from mild physical discipline to hitting, to even more serious forms of disciplining that may hurt a child. If the therapist suggests that parents in some families use physical force as a way of showing strict discipline, it is also helpful to mention that such strict discipline is often shown by caring and committed parents who are attempting effectively to discipline their children. This is an important caveat, because certain families may mean well, even though their behavior may be punitive. However, it is still important to help challenge their rationalization for the use of such behavior.

Therapists should ask the family to describe any conflict situation in detail, using an enactment, if necessary, so that the therapist can understand and observe what actually happened. Therapists should track the corresponding interpersonal communication and level of closeness reflected in the situation, identifying and reframing intentions as applicable. After doing this, family members can be asked to identify additional options to aggressive or violent behavior in that situation. This step is a precursor to the structured problem solving to be discussed soon. In addition, the therapist may choose to clarify alternative attributions regarding the actor's behavior.

The therapist should use discretion in presenting any new material on the use of force and violence, but some introduction for this discussion might be as follows: *"Violence, physical force, and power may seem like strong words to use, and let's talk about that for a minute.*

When you watch TV, you often see violence. What is it that you see? [e.g., hitting, punching, shooting.] *All of these are forms of violence, although some are more extreme than others.*" It may be helpful to then talk about revenge and violence as main methods of getting problems solved on the television programs and movies that they may see on a regular basis.

Then, continuing with this theme, the therapist may add the following:

> *Let me explain why this is important. Let's talk about whether hitting solves problems in your family. First, we can talk about parents and children. Parents usually hit children because they are trying to help them or teach them something. Certainly, even caring parents may use hitting or some physical force. However, there might be problems with it sometimes. You may find that using physical means is sometimes effective in getting your child (or your brother or sister) to do what you want in the short term. However, it won't usually solve your problem in the long run, because it may not teach the person what you want them to do differently; it just shows them you are angry with them. It may not help them make a better choice themselves about what to do differently next time.*
>
> *Your goal for your children is to have them become better, more responsible decision makers without your help as they grow up, right? Hitting or other forceful responses tends to just make them afraid and angry at you, and sometimes feel badly about themselves.*

The therapist should distinguish fear of parents' disapproval, which is normal, from fear of being physically hurt. Try to make this as much of a discussion as possible. Again, reframe their intent positively, in light of this behavior being secondary to their being a caring committed parent.

❑ Family Skills Training

OVERVIEW

Whereas the therapist has focused upon engagement, relabeling, and family assessment in the prior phase, the therapist emphasizes the teaching of interactional skills in this phase. The caveat for the therapist is that being more directive does not mean that the therapist ceases to continue to reframe and reinforce behavior. It does mean that the therapist is very focused on encouraging the family to participate and that the therapist moves away from the role as the mediator into the role of the teacher.

The therapist should look for certain changes in the family that signify that the family is ready to move to this second phase. These include being engaged in the treatment process and shifting their attributions about each other. Concrete examples include (a) a family who has insisted on session-to-session contracts agrees to attend the next several sessions; (b) a family who has canceled some sessions begins to attend regularly; (c) the negativity within the family is decreased, as evidenced by fewer negative comments or an increase in hopeful comments; and (d) the family accepts or repeats reframes stated earlier by the therapist.

The problem-solving steps drawn upon in the next section have been used with children and adolescents. In general, the approach taken here encourages the family to solve problems together in the context of negotiation in each problem area, using clear and noncritical communication between the parent and the child. Here, the problem-solving approach will place greater emphasis on the parent when children, rather than adolescents, are involved. Either way, children are encouraged to use the same problem-solving steps; however, the parent should be empowered to make and enforce parenting decisions (even unpopular decisions), albeit without the use of physical force. There are several goals to this section: (a) teaching the problem-solving model, (b) teaching communication skills, (c) continuing reframing parental intent or behavior, (d) working on specific family problems as they arise, (e) assigning homework, and (f) intervening with outside systems.

TEACHING PROBLEM-SOLVING SKILLS

There are numerous problem-solving skills curricula, many of which include similar types of skills or steps. Some have been implemented primarily with children on an individual (Kazdin, Esveldt-Dawson, French, & Unis, 1987; Shure, 1992) or group basis (Guerra, Moore, & Slaby, 1995; Weissberg, Gesten, Liebenstein, Doherty-Schmid, & Hutton, 1980; Weissberg et al., 1981); others have been implemented with parents, either with or without their children or teenagers (see Fleischman, Horne, & Arthur, 1983; Robin & Foster, 1989). For purposes of illustration, examples of the problem-solving steps or skills contained in a few of these programs are shown in Box 16.1.

Regardless of the skills selected for training, it is helpful to place all of the steps on a diagram and to review each step with the family. What follows in this section is a more thorough description of six steps to solving problems derived from the manual by Weissberg,

---

Box 16.1   Examples of Problem-Solving Skills or Steps

Steps as described by Weissberg et al. (1980)

1. State the problem.
2. Decide on a goal.
3. Stop and think.
4. Think of as many solutions as possible and consequences of each one.
5. Try the best solution and, if it doesn't work, try another.

Steps as described by Fleischman et al. (1983)

1. What is my goal?
2. What am I doing now?
3. Is what I am doing helping me to achieve my goal?
4. If it is not helping, what do I need to do differently?

Steps as described by Kazdin et al. (1987)

1. Say what the problem is.
2. Decide on your goal.
3. Stop to think before you act.
4. Think of as many solutions as you can.
5. Think ahead to what might happen next.
6. When you have a really good solution, try it.

Steps as described by Robin and Foster (1989)

1. Define the problem.
2. Generate alternative solutions.
3. Evaluate the solutions and decide upon a mutually acceptable alternative.
4. Plan the details of solution implementation.
5. Verify the outcome of the solution implementation

SOURCES: Fleischman et al. (1983), Kazdin et al. (1987), Robin and Foster (1989), and Weissberg et al. (1980).

Gesten, & Doherty (1978), which was evaluated in a school-based outcome study with young children that was reported two decades ago (Weissberg et al., 1981). These skills appear fairly clear and complete, and were among the first to be disseminated in the context of a procedural manual. We have successfully applied these skills to training with aggressive children and adolescents (Kolko, 1995) and with physically abusive families in the Project IMPACT (Interventions to Maximize Parent and Child Togetherness) outcome study (Kolko, 1996). Each skill is described and illustrated below.

Step 1: Is There a Problem?

Some problems are obvious, some are ambiguous, and some nonproblems. One of the points to get across with this exercise is that the parent needs to prioritize the problem behaviors of their child. That is, there are certain behaviors they definitely will not tolerate, whereas others are less important. It should be explained to parents that children need *some* control over their lives, and if they are not allowed it from parents, then they will take it in ways that are bound to be unacceptable to the parents. In addition, these problem-solving skills will help the child grow into a more independent-thinking teenager—the therapist can tie this into the parent's goal of wanting a more responsible, self-motivated child, if they have indeed said this. The other main point is to make the parent more aware of criteria useful for defining a problem and of factors that may influence whether something is seen as a problem or not.

There are several factors to consider when deciding whether something is a problem, and these topics can be part of this discussion. These factors, summarized from the work of Weissberg et al. (1978), are listed in Box 16.2.

Box 16.2 | Factors to Consider in Determining When Something Is a Problem

1. Do you feel bad when you or others engage in this behavior?
2. Are your plans blocked or are you inconvenienced by this behavior?
3. Do you have to do something you can't do or don't feel comfortable doing?
4. Is it a high priority for you to have this behavior stop?
5. Is this behavior unsafe?
6. Does the behavior bother you more when you are tired, lonely, sad, or angry?
7. Can you understand the other person's behavior in such a way that it doesn't bother you? (e.g., understand it as a result of the person's age.)

It may be useful to go over examples and ask the parents whether they think these problems are obvious, ambiguous, or non-problems, and the reasons for their opinions. Sample problems might include the following:

- A small child runs out into the street and a car is coming.
- A boy wants to go out to play after school. His mother asks him to clean his room now, because relatives are coming over after dinner.
- A child is in her room alone doing her homework and she is tapping her feet. Her door is shut and no one can hear her tap.
- A child is in her room alone doing her homework and she is tapping her feet. Her door is open and her mother can hear her.
- A child is tired and complains about going to bed, but is walking toward his bedroom anyway.
- A father says "No" to his child, and then the child swears at father.

The therapist can also ask the parents to make a list of problems of one or more children, and then to ask them to prioritize them. At the top of the list should be the things to tackle, whereas those at the bottom might be ignored for awhile. This relates to the issue of children needing some control over their lives, and if there are areas in which parents can yield some control, then it will help minimize their conflicts.

Step 2: What Is the Problem?

At this stage, you can ask the family to generate some problems if they have not already done so. It is best to begin with minor or simple problems, with the goal of tackling one problem (or reworking a problem) per session. It may be that you find yourself getting stuck at the "What is the problem?" phase with some problems, and it is important to explain to the family that this is the hardest phase, because problem definition directly affects how one solves the problem. The family will sometimes define their problems differently from the way the therapist does. This is where the time spent using reframing earlier may prove useful, as the family should be more receptive to therapist reframes of the problem now.

If the family wants to move ahead and generate solutions, slow them down and suggest, without discouraging participation, that they focus just on the first two steps. As part of problem solving, communication training can be slowly introduced. Guidelines for problem definition appear below:

1. Make sure the parents address specific aspects of the problem situation, not just how they would feel in the situation. If they generate

more than one problem, focus them on what is the most pressing part of the problem.

2. Key attributes of problem definition are clarity, specificity, the use of nonaccusatory ("I") statements, and brevity. All family members should come up with ideas. Have individual members role-play what they would say to the other, even if the above examples were not a problem for their family. Coach them as to good problem definitions. The therapist can explain to the family that the only way to know if a problem-solving strategy is successful is to have a measurable problem. This allows us to see the before-after change.

3. If their ideas are inappropriate or off base, ask another family member what their perception of the problem is.

4. It is helpful if different parties can acknowledge some part of blame for the problem. Others can then acknowledge some part of blame in turn. This tends to help family members be less defensive.

5. Ask the family to develop a few simple ground rules for discussing problems. One could be avoiding name calling during problem definition. Another might be allowing others a chance to speak.

6. There is a balance between sticking to the topic and allowing enough discussion to really understand what the problem is. Often, the problem as defined by the family is different from how the therapist feels it ought to be defined, and enough discussion may have to take place to help the family see the problem in a new way. However, the therapist also has to exercise good judgment in responding to conversations in which the family wanders from the topic.

7. Encourage the family to use "When you do X, I feel Y" types of statements. Members should focus on the problem, rather than on personal qualities of the other parties.

8. Family members can be taught to reflect how other members see the problem. This is not a skill used commonly in everyday life, and will probably not be carried over, but practice of it can shake up old ways of seeing problems and help reduce defensiveness.

Here are two examples of exchanges that can occur regarding problem definition. In the first situation, Billy does not like the dinner his mother has cooked and wants her to make him something else. The mother says, "*I feel inconvenienced because you won't eat what I cook. That means I have to make two dinners instead of one. It takes me more time and I have other things to do.*" Billy replies, "*I don't want to eat food that I don't like the taste of.*"

In the second situation, cereal has been found spilled in the kitchen. The father says, "*I felt mad when you didn't clean up this mess that you made. That means I have to clean it up, and it's not my mess. I feel disrespected when you ignore the mess.*" Sally says, "*I wish you would ask me if I spilled it before you accuse me of spilling the cereal. Also, I don't want to be told to clean it immediately. I will clean it after I am finished eating my cereal."*

Often in negative parent-child interactions, one may find the following pattern (see Azar & Gehl, 1999): (a) the parent has unrealistic expectations of a child that age; (b) the child's behavior disconfirms this expectation; (c) the parent then makes an attribution that the child misbehaved for a reason that may not be accurate (e.g., the child acted out of spite); and (d) the parent overreacts to the situation. When parents are in the problem-definition phase, some education as to normal child development and appropriate expectations may be necessary. The four steps of the negative parent-child interaction are some of the topics that can be targeted.

Sometimes, it is difficult for participants to understand someone else's view of the problem. Therapist can have different members role-play each other or relevant people outside of the family (e.g., a teacher) in order to help them step into each other's shoes. In these roles, they can discuss their respective views of the problem.

Step 3: What Do We Want? What Is Our Goal?

Ask each family member what she or he would want in the problem situation under discussion. Try to get them to express their desire in positive, constructive terms that are specific to their own and to others' behaviors. The goal may vary depending upon whether you are talking about a one-time incident or a more persistent problem. Encourage the participants to state what they want, not what they do not want. Instead of *"I want you to stop loafing around,"* they could be coached to say, *"I want you to do your homework every night."*

Following are some examples of good goal definitions:

Mother: I would like to have one meal for the two of us.

Billy: I want to eat dinners that I like, and want to choose what I eat.

Father: I want you to clean up your mess now, because I am stepping on the cereal.

Sally: I want to eat my cereal first, and then clean up.

Step 4: What Can We Do? (Brainstorming for the Solution Generation)

There are several steps to follow and general suggestions to consider when trying to brainstorm a particular problem. Most families, especially abusive families, may not have these steps in mind when decisions are made. Box 16.3 lists several steps and guidelines for the therapist to review with the family.

Box 16.3 | Brainstorming Steps and Guidelines

1. Explain the difference between brainstorming and other methods of problem solving (i.e., thinking of one solution, deciding if it's good or not, then using it or thinking of another).

2. Explain that there are two problems with the latter method. First, it doesn't give you chance to consider all solutions you may not have thought of yet; and second, you often decide too quickly on a solution which may not be the best one.

3. If needed, you can help the family with the concept of brainstorming by asking them to generate uncommon (or alternate) uses for common objects (e.g., a pencil, a brick, a tire, grass, chocolate milk, a bracelet, etc.) on an impromptu basis.

4. Think of as many solutions as possible. Tell the family, *"Don't worry about whether it is a good solution or not; just say whatever comes to mind."* Help them along by suggesting some outlandish solutions. Solutions should come from everyone in family. You should reinforce effort, not the quality of the solutions.

5. Explain that brainstorming is good because it allows for more solutions from which to choose and it gets all the alternatives out in the open so the family can see which one is likely to work best to solve the problem.

6. Explain that this allows them to resist doing the first thing that comes to mind, which is not always the best thing. Tell them they can break old habits or ways of handling problems, but that old habits are sometimes hard to change without tips for doing it differently.

7. Prevent any evaluation while someone is listing solutions. Solutions should be spelled out clearly, specify positive change (not just stopping a behavior), and be future-oriented.

8. Encourage each family member to take some part in alleviating the problem. A spirit of compromise should be encouraged. Family members should acknowledge the positive aspects of solutions offered by others and build on them.

9. In the context of having alternatives to harsh or abusive discipline, encourage members to identify examples of problem-solving techniques in these examples that would involve using this type of discipline. You can suggest some if the family offers few alternatives.

10. Sometimes, family members can state their solutions as rules they would want to have in their family (e.g., *"He doesn't wear my clothes without asking"; "I get to stay out until 9 p.m. on weekdays and 10 p.m. on weekends"; "If I clean up on Wednesdays, I get extra play time"*).

Step 5: What Are the Consequences? (Evaluate All Possible Solutions)

It is possible that certain, more obviously inappropriate or ineffective solutions can be discounted. These are solutions that present a clear danger, are illegal, or are against the family's moral code. Once these are identified, the therapist and family can then identify the negative and positive consequences of each solution. This is a good chance for the therapist to discuss with the family pros and cons of different solutions, including the solution of physical force. The family should be encouraged to think through the pros and cons themselves. However, topics for discussion when evaluating physical force can include both advantages (i.e., the child will probably stop the behavior in the short term, the child learns who is in charge, and the parent takes action and feels effective) and disadvantages (i.e., the child's misbehavior is not stopped in the long term, thus the problem is usually not solved; the child learns to see violence as a problem-solving tool; some children become fearful and experience low self-esteem; and the child gets physically hurt).

Evaluations should include comments about how the solution would work, consider the impact of all solutions on others in the family, and involve further specification if needed. Evaluate the solutions using a (+) or (–) rating. Combine solutions where appropriate. After considering the remaining solutions, identify potential negative and positive consequences by placing a (+) or (–) next to the solutions from each person. Look for the best solutions, ones that have the most (+) signs and the least (–) signs. The therapist should acknowledge that the combination of pluses and minuses may be different for each person. Of course, ultimately, the parent has the last decision. If novel solutions come up during this step, simply add them to the list.

Step 6: What Should We Try? (Decide on One or More Solutions)

After eliminating solutions that have the most negatives next to them, family members can be asked to choose one or more solutions that they will try during the following week. Concurrently, discuss the possibility that the family's first choice solution might not work and the advantages of having considered alternatives. Obviously, have them try the solutions. The problem may need to be reworked if the solution does not work. The solution that is finally chosen should be the one with the most positives and the least negatives, but it should be explained to the family that there is no such thing as a problem-free solution. Obviously, the choice of a final solution is the parent's (as the parent may need to be encouraged to be in charge), although it is helpful to do so after considering the child's viewpoint.

In addition, it is important that implementation be well-planned because the failure rate for unplanned solutions is generally high. The family should be coached to discuss the implementation fully and include discussion of all the things that could go wrong. When they plan for these eventualities, they will be more likely to describe the experience as successful, even if there are numerous difficulties with the implementation.

After the implementation occurs, the family should be encouraged to evaluate whether or not it solved the problem as initially defined and stated. If one or another member is not totally happy with the solution, but it seems to be the best, ask them if they can come up with an alternative. If this is difficult, you can ask them to "try it for a week." If the parent expresses concern about giving the child too much power, reframe the effort as modeling flexible decision making, and that their "giving" a bit will make it more likely that the child will "give" a bit in the future. Steps to planning implementation are as follows: (a) operationalize the behaviors of the solution, (b) delegate tasks to family members, and (c) formulate record-keeping systems if appropriate. If they come in next time and the solution did not work, reframe lack of success as difficulty with new skills.

TEACHING COMMUNICATION SKILLS

As the family is learning and applying the problem-solving skills, it is likely that certain communications will cause distress or even more serious conflicts with at least one other family member. These communications have the potential of obstructing the problem-solving process and, ultimately, the family's active participation in treatment. Many of the specific communication obstacles commonly observed in parent-adolescent interactions have been articulated by Robin and Foster (1989). These obstacles include, for example, calling each other names, being critical or sarcastic, giving commands or lectures, denying or exaggerating a complaint, and moving off topic. Indeed, abusive families may exhibit numerous forms of communication blocks during sessions and, equally important, during routine interactions at home. Some of these negative forms of communication reflect their use of coercive or hostile statements, threatening gestures or comments, references to a sudden withdrawal of attention or assistance, and double messages wherein both positive and negative comments about the other person are made. Our observation suggests that it is important to determine the degree to which family members are even aware of their use of these types of communication problems; indeed, some individuals may not fully appreciate the nature and impact of their statements.

During sessions in which such obstacles occur, it is important to pay attention to the family's communication patterns and to offer some training suggestions to minimize any potential disruption to treatment. In encouraging the family to incorporate alternative patterns of communication, the therapist can follow these steps to accomplish this objective: (a) illustrate each communication problem and its effect(s), (b) instruct the family in alternative communication patterns or skills, (c) model the alternative, and then (d) have the family practice the alternative. If not already done in the course of this discussion, the therapist is advised to ask each family member to make a list of observed and/or reported communication problems or obstacles that might need to be addressed, and then to offer recommendations for their remediation. Therapists might also construct their own lists as a backup and to identify any other obvious problems that the family may have missed. This routine can be incorporated into problem-solving skills training. Communication problems may become most apparent during the problem-definition step, when family members begin to communicate their concerns about one another. This discussion may deteriorate into a fairly critical encounter that is likely to inhibit any further problem-definition activities.

Therapists should avoid entering into he-said-she-said discussions (i.e., where each person indicates the other is lying). Instead, the therapist should stop the family, point out the patterns of interacting that are occurring and interfering with their relationship, and refocus the family on stopping these patterns. For example, the therapist might say,

> You said she did this; she said she didn't. You have different opinions, but continuing to argue over who said what is a great example of what keeps you from communicating. Let's look at what each of you is feeling and how you might tell each other what you're feeling without being negative. Then we can discuss some possible solutions.

We suggest suspending specific work on problem solving when such obstacles occur. Furthermore, therapists ought to monitor carefully any attempts by family members, especially parents, to shame or embarrass the child, which may seriously threaten any efforts to enhance communication. It is useful to select one problem (and its opposite or alternative skill) at a time and to remind the family that the discussion may be interrupted to help them continue the conversation in a more productive manner; that is, in such a way as to promote the likelihood that they will get the result they want. To minimize any ensuing adverse reactions to the therapist's comments (e.g., being defensive), each problem should be related to the entire family or target a specific interactional pattern.

Once the problem is clearly identified, the therapist can describe and illustrate an alternative, positive communication skill. Certainly, the specific form of the skill to be promoted will depend upon the nature of the communication problem. What is important here is the focus these alternatives place on directly improving the communication process and showing how family members are motivated to help one another. By way of example, the parent who routinely uses threats could be encouraged to offer choices to the child, still highlighting the consequences of each choice. Or, the child who simultaneously exhibits both positive comments (e.g., *"I do like your cooking"*) and negative nonverbal cues (e.g., scowling and making a spitting movement with his mouth) could be encouraged to include two clear statements that relate to both of these mixed messages. Finally, parents who criticize their children by saying what the child does (e.g., *"You always . . ."*) could be encouraged to use "I" statements to indicate how the behavior affects or influences them (e.g., *"I get upset when . . ."*). In some instances, it may be more effective to review these skills before seeking to modify a family's idiosyncratic communication problems. A few general skills designed to enhance communication in all families, regardless of their specific problems, are outlined in Box 16.4 (see also Fleischman et al., 1983; Robin & Foster, 1989).

| **Box 16.4** | Skills to Facilitate Communication, Especially During Conflict |

Speak for yourself and acknowledge your own subjectivity.

Get to the point—be brief, clear, and direct.

Focus on behavior or actions, rather than invoking someone's personal characteristics.

Be willing to reciprocate and be ready for change.

Listen carefully.

Demonstrate and show support for open self-disclosure.

Show empathy for and validate other's feelings.

Ask questions, especially for information, when you don't understand something.

Check to make sure that you and others understand what is being communicated.

Pay attention to your (and others') nonverbal behaviors (e.g., eye contact, facial expressions, physical touching, or voice tone and loudness).

Avoid using obstacles to communication (e.g., yelling or using threats, sarcasm, or silence).

Once these skills have been explained and are understood, the family should be encouraged to use the skills when applicable, both during sessions and at home. The family can be asked to practice the skills in role plays or simply asked to use them as they are appropriate. It is our experience that this practice element often feels awkward to various family members, which is generally an indication that the skills are not comfortably integrated into their repertoire. One benefit of practice is that the therapist can offer and solicit feedback regarding the impact of the communication skill, and, thus, can make suggestions to enhance the family's use of each skill. With encouragement, family members will ideally do this on their own and in an appropriate manner.

HOME PRACTICE

At the end of each session, a home practice exercise can be assigned. These assignments may focus on having the family monitor their communication over conflict situations and/or test the skills they are learning in sessions, but are also designed to ensure that the family remain active between the sessions. For example, the therapist can give the family a handout on which they check if they have used a variety of negative or positive behaviors (e.g., name calling, minimizing, and using "I" statements to express feelings) to communicate during the week (Robin, Bedway, & Gilroy, 1994). In fact, the therapist may develop a form tailored to the specific negative behaviors shown in a given family. Family members can also track their use of the alternatives decided on in session (e.g., the decision that, instead of name calling, they would strive to use "I" statements and clearly express their feelings). Difficulties that arise with getting the assignments done will be dealt with by the therapist modeling the problem-solving skills during a discussion about the problems that kept the home exercise from being done.

The home exercise also should be designed so that the family can have a successful experience. We keep the assignments very simple and request that all tasks be completed by the family together. The responsibility for the completion of the home exercise is given to the appropriate person or persons in the family (i.e., the person who should be in charge). However, it is important that the family show mastery at each step. Thus, home assignments, which merit review at the beginning of each session, should be given that measure the family's skill level at each step. If home exercises are not completed, the therapist can model the problem-solving technique with the family while exploring the stated impediments to getting the homework completed. There must be a clear message given to the family that the therapist believes that this will help the family. The therapist also should give a great deal of encouragement and support to the family for all attempts at incorporating these skills into their everyday interactions.

❏ Family Skills-Training Applications

ESTABLISHING FAMILY PROBLEM-SOLVING ROUTINES

In this final phase of treatment, families are asked to work on problems specific to them, with family members doing more and more of the work. That is, the therapist moves to the final phase after the family has achieved some mastery of the skills and has shown the ability to use them outside of the sessions. The goals of this phase include (a) giving the family a clear message that therapy is not needed at this point in time, (b) offering to be available to the family for consultation, (c) discussing what the family's caseworker will be told about their work in the treatment, (d) identifying some options (possibly in a contract) for follow-up care, and (e) reinforcing all that the family has learned. (Caution: If a therapist says, "*I think that you are so much better,*" the family, who may be resistant to termination, can respond by trying to prove to the therapist that they are not really better. Therefore, the therapist should stay away from global comments and instead provide reinforcement about specific behaviors or events.)

At the conclusion of this phase, the family should receive a clear message about their progress and what they have learned. This should include a discussion about how it is difficult to use a new skill versus relying upon the skills they have always used. The therapist can reframe any incident in which the family does not use the new skills as an expected occurrence given the typical learning curve, rather than as a failure. Of course, problem-solving sessions should continue to address any specific behaviors and responses.

Within this time frame, the therapist should increase the time between the sessions. Instead of meeting once or twice a week, the therapist should schedule two or three weeks between sessions to give the family the chance to terminate from the therapy slowly. Going two or three weeks without sessions will give them the experience of being away from the therapist, but with the security of knowing that they will have a few more sessions before therapy ends.

It is imperative that the therapist be very positive, albeit realistic, at this time. She or he should conscientiously attempt to reinforce all efforts and to help the family focus on their successes. The therapist should remember that these families have not traditionally experienced many successes and should, therefore, concentrate a good deal of time and focus on reinforcing the family's attempts to change or modify their behaviors.

TRANSFER OF CONTROL TO THE FAMILY

The therapist should spend some time helping the family to set the structure for handling their own subsequent problems internally using the skills described in this chapter. We often include our phone number in the event they need to contact us in the future or to discuss a follow-up session. The therapist and the family should discuss any expectations for treatment termination conveyed by the caseworker and what information will be communicated to the caseworker about the course of treatment. Although the family does not have veto power, they should know before the final information exchange occurs exactly what the worker will be told.

Once termination of family work has begun, the therapist can anticipate with the family that problems will arise. The focus of these discussions is upon helping the family solve problems that arise out of a variety of concerns (e.g., child behavior) and to anticipate their responses in order to increase the likelihood that the family will be able to respond appropriately during the actual event. A secondary goal of this exercise is to help the family understand that if setbacks occur, they are typical and to be expected rather than indications of treatment failure.

Finally, the therapist should attempt to ensure that the family has a success experience outside of treatment before family work ends. A focus of this phase is on helping the family get a sense of themselves as competent individuals. The therapist should be reinforcing competence and accomplishment throughout this phase of treatment. Accordingly, the therapist should focus almost exclusively on giving the family positive reinforcement about their improved skills and/or the efforts they have made in treatment.

❏ Summary

We have reviewed several clinical recommendations and skills-based applications for helping the family involved in physically abusive behavior. Quite often, these families are involved in multiple forms of coercive or even violent behavior, which is the reason we focus on promoting their use of appropriate problem-solving and communication skills. Some families will find these skills fairly easy to incorporate into their everyday routines, whereas others will have significant problems being committed to such a systematic approach to interacting with each other. Obviously, the therapist may have to move more slowly in working with the latter family and may need to supplement this work with additional explanations about the relative advantages of and need for skills of this nature.

References

Azar, S. T., & Gehl, K. S. (1999). Physical abuse and neglect. In R. T. Ammerman & M. Hersen (Eds.), *Handbook of prescriptive treatments for children and adolescents* (pp. 329–345). Needham Heights, MA: Allyn & Bacon.

Fleischman, M. J., Horne, A., & Arthur, J. L. (1983). *Troubled families: A treatment program.* Champaign, IL: Research Press.

Guerra, N. G., Moore, A., & Slaby, R. G. (1995). *A guide to conflict resolution and decision making for adolescents.* Champaign, IL: Research Press.

Kazdin, A. E., Esveldt-Dawson, K., French, N. H., & Unis, A. S. (1987). Problem-solving skills and relationship therapy in the treatment of antisocial child behavior. *Journal of Consulting and Clinical Psychology, 55,* 76–85.

Kolko, D. J. (1995). Multimodal partial/day treatment of child antisocial behavior: Service description and multilevel program evaluation. *Continuum, 2,* 3–24.

Kolko, D. J. (2002). Child physical abuse. In: J. E. B. Myers, L. Berliner, J. Briere, C. T. Hendrix, C. Jenny, & T. Reid (Eds.), *The APSAC handbook of child maltreatment* (2nd ed., pp. 21–54). Thousand Oaks, CA: Sage Publications.

Robin, A. L., Bedway, M., & Gilroy, M. (1994). Problem solving communication training. In C. W. LeCroy (Ed.), *Handbook of child and adolescent treatment manuals* (pp. 92–125). New York: Lexington Books.

Robin, A. L., & Foster, S. L. (1989). *Negotiating parent-adolescent conflict: A behavioral-family systems approach.* New York: Guilford.

Shure, M. B. (1992). *I can problem solve: An interpersonal cognitive problem-solving program.* Champaign, IL: Research Press.

Weissberg, R. P. (1978). *The effects of social problem-solving training on the problem-solving skills and adjustment of third grade children.* Unpublished doctoral dissertation. University of Rochester, Rochester, NY.

Weissberg, R. P., Gesten, E. L., Liebenstein, N. L., Doherty-Schmid, K., & Hutton, H. (1980). *The Rochester Social Problem-Solving (SPS) Program: A training manual for teachers of 2nd–4th grade children.* Rochester, NY: University of Rochester Press.

Weissberg, R. P., Gesten, E. L., Rapkin, B. D., Cowen, E. L., Davidson, E., Flores de Apodaca, R., & McKim, B. J. (1981). Evaluation of a social-problem-solving training program for suburban and inner-city third-grade children. *Journal of Consulting and Clinical Psychology, 49,* 251–261.

17

Community and Social System Involvement

To paraphrase an old saying, "No therapist is an island." To provide therapeutic services for a child and family and not have significant interactions with existing professional systems may render the treatment incomplete. When physical abuse occurs, families are likely to be involved with Child Protective Services (CPS), family court, law enforcement, pediatricians or family practice physicians, and schools. Developing a working relationship with professionals from these systems can be a valuable service to the family and of paramount importance for treatment outcome. In this chapter, we discuss potential systems involved in child physical abuse cases and stress the importance of working with professionals from those systems.

❏ Service Settings and Systems

CHILD PROTECTIVE SERVICES

CPS is tasked with taking reports of suspected maltreatment, conducting an investigation, developing an initial safety plan, deciding whether or not to take the child into protective custody, providing court testimony about the case, linking the child and family with treatment, monitoring safety, and determining when to reunite the family, close the case, or recommend termination of parental rights. Often, CPS workers must make these monumental decisions rapidly and on top of a caseload bulging at the seams. These tasks are tremendous, and mistakes in decision making can have an impact on the remainder of a child's life.

Having the input of other professionals who know the family and their needs can be of great help to CPS. As soon as a therapist obtains a release or exchange of information signed by the legal guardian, an initial contact to CPS should occur. Through this contact, therapists can determine CPS's goals and form a collaborative relationship to advocate for the family. Ideally, the family and protective services should have shared goals. As noted by Azar and Wolfe (1998), this collaboration should balance the need to provide therapeutic intervention with the need to safeguard the child. As needed, the therapist can facilitate improvements in the relationship between the family and CPS to guide them toward shared goals. In some cases, collaboration with CPS may lead the family to view the therapist as adversarial. To avoid this view, the therapist should always let the parent know that CPS is being contacted, the reason for doing such, and the proposed content of the contact. Together, the therapist and parent can give direct input into the family's safety plan. Also, the therapist should listen to the family's complaints, but never engage in negative judgments about CPS; all discussion of the adversarial relationship should be focused a solution. Therapists can empathize with parents' feelings of unfairness or anger, but should help them see that getting along and working collaboratively can more quickly "get CPS out of their life," reduce the stress they feel from being involved with the system, get their child back, and help to get on with their life in a more positive way. Likewise, at no time should the therapist engage in "parent bashing" with the CPS worker. Therapists can help CPS workers remain focused. That is, conversations can focus on strengths the parent has, what the parent is currently doing right, and goals that continue to be the focus of treatment.

A collaborative relationship with CPS can accomplish multiple goals, including meeting concrete needs of the family and working out details regarding the court process in a nonadversarial way. With regard to concrete needs, oftentimes the therapist will find that a family needs help purchasing clothes for their child or paying a utility bill or rent. The Department of Social Services (DSS) worker can be an excellent resource for figuring out how to cover those costs. Some cities even have collaborative programs specifically designed to meet the concrete needs that families have. For example, in Charleston,

South Carolina, the HALOS Project (Helping and Lending Outreach Support) founded by Dr. Eve Spratt created a partnership between DSS and area churches (Spratt, 1997). The churches basically adopted a DSS worker and, through church membership, purchased goods to meet concrete services for families assigned to that particular worker. Furthermore, in some cases, DSS workers can be instrumental in helping families who have no transportation find ways to get to treatment.

Working out details involving the court process can take many forms. When a child is in out-of-home care, the therapist's role can involve making recommendations for telephone contact, visitation, and family reunification. When children remain in the home, therapists can keep the CPS worker informed of treatment progress and any concerns around child or family safety. Therapists can also render an opinion regarding completion of treatment, closing of the case, and discontinuance of CPS involvement.

FAMILY COURT

The therapist's involvement with the family court is essential to lending a clinical perspective to decision making. Involvement with the courts can occur in a more informal consulting capacity or formalized through serving as a fact or expert witness. In a consulting capacity and as an advocate for the child and family, therapists can be invaluable in helping to set up a family court treatment plan. Working closely with CPS legal council and the family's attorney, the therapist can offer recommendations for the treatment plan regarding who needs treatment, the nature of that treatment, the risk, and parent-child visitation. Such negotiations can save the court time and money. Rather than arguing each side in a hearing, both sides can go before the judge being "on the same page." Doing such reduces the adversarial nature of the process for parents.

Often, therapists will be needed to take the stand in family court and provide information. This experience can be intimidating, especially for new therapists. However, court testimony provides an opportunity for the therapist to teach the judge, family, and CPS about the needs of the family and what it will take to reduce the risk for reabuse.

When therapists testify on a case involving a child with whom they are working and their testimony is about what they did, saw, or heard, their role is that of fact witness. If the therapist is needed to give testimony, it is imperative to talk with the attorney regarding the purpose of the testimony and what will be asked. The therapist should become intimately familiar with the family's treatment chart to answer specific questions regarding dates or events in particular sessions. The therapist can then talk with the family about what will take place during the hearing. On the day of the hearing, there should be no surprises for either the therapist or the parents.

In some cases, judges may look to therapists for reports on treatment progress, as well as recommendations for visitation, family reunification, and other services that may be needed. When the purpose of testimony becomes drawing conclusions, offering an opinion, or interpretation of those facts, the role drifts into that of expert witness. Therapists often serve as expert witnesses to offer the court scientific information regarding child maltreatment issues and child and adult disorders. The reader is referred to two excellent books by Brodsky (1991) and Stern (1997) that prepare professionals to serve as expert witnesses. Prior to attending court, the therapist should know if the attorneys will try to have him or her qualified as an expert. This level of testimony takes even more preparation, in that the expert must have a strong working knowledge of the research literature. Experts also must demonstrate that through special knowledge and experiences they can provide information most people cannot. Before serving as an expert, it is essential to understand the role of an expert. In addition to the two books mentioned earlier, many workshops occur throughout the nation to teach individuals how to be an expert witness. The American Professional Society on the Abuse of Children (APSAC) conducts annual workshops that are specific to expert testimony with child maltreatment cases.

In some cases, the therapist will not be the only party to testify. The child, too, may be required to testify. In such cases, preparation of the child is important to his or her comfort on the stand. A solid court preparation protocol such as that described by Lipovsky and Stern (1997) should assist the therapist in covering all bases.

Secondary to testifying, in some family courts, the guardian ad litem provides an independent assessment of the family situation and can carry substantial weight regarding decisions made. Developing a working relationship with the guardian ad litem allows the therapist to understand the guardian's perspective on the family and to perhaps come to an agreement on recommendations.

LAW ENFORCEMENT

When a therapist begins a physical abuse case, chances are that law enforcement has already completed their investigation. Thus, the therapist may have little contact with law enforcement. Regardless, it is essential for therapists to be familiar with the juvenile officers in the jurisdictions from which their cases come. Therapists who work in the child abuse field and who do not know juvenile officers in the area should contact those officers and introduce themselves. In cases where an officer is still involved in the case, the therapist, with a release from the parent or guardian, should contact that officer and determine how best to work together. Especially when domestic violence is involved, the officer will be very important in assisting with family safety. An example is provided in the discussion of Case 1 in Chapter 18.

MEDICAL AND HEALTH PROFESSIONALS

Pediatricians or family practice physicians may uncover the abuse during an examination, or they may be providing needed treatment for medical difficulties. Early in the case, therapists should obtain a release of information so that they can discuss the case with the physician. The role of the therapist may just be to gather information to understand better both what happened and any medical implications for the child (e.g., treatment that will be needed for burns and prognosis). However, in many cases, a certain physician will have followed the family over a period of time and that individual will know the family and have insight into their situation. This information can be valuable to the therapist for understanding the strengths and needs of the family and their functioning over time. In some cases, physicians will be following children who are taking psychotropic medication for disorders such as attention deficit/hyperactivity disorder (ADHD). Therapists, physicians, and parents working together can ensure compliance with medication. Furthermore, information given to the physician can help ensure that the dosage is correct and that the child is benefiting from this intervention.

THE SCHOOL SYSTEM

Schools are a key system with which the therapist often works in partnership. Physically abused children's social and behavioral difficulties will likely be manifested at school through poor peer or teacher relations, disruptive classroom behavior, difficulty with attention or work completion, and low achievement. The aggressive behaviors increase the risk for suspension and expulsion, which in turn increases stress within the family and may increase the risk for reabuse. Chances are that the parent has received many phone calls from the school or has had to take time off from work in an effort to quell the behavioral problems. Multiple interactions around negative behavior may leave the parent with negative feelings toward the school and the school with frustrated feelings toward the parent.

One of the most important functions the therapist can serve in relation to the school is to help the parent and school personnel develop a positive, collaborative relationship. A positive linkage between the parent and school has been shown to affect a child's academic success (Fine & Carlson, 1992). The partnership between parents and schools is facilitated by parents ensuring that children attend school, complete homework, and study, and that the parent has contact with the teacher and supports the school's goals for the students. The school can facilitate the relationship by providing parents with ongoing feedback about their child's performance, keeping an open line of communication, and being available to parents in a way that is considerate of the parent's schedule. Although this exemplifies the ideal relationship, parents with problematic children are often a long way from achieving this. Toward developing positive relations between the parent and school, the therapist must not engage in "school or teacher bashing" with the parent or in "parent bashing" with the school. Empathizing with frustrations is appropriate and can lead to the view that "we are all on the same page," that everyone is frustrated because behavioral improvements have not occurred, and that everyone has the child's welfare in mind. The focus should clearly be on the strengths of each system (i.e., on the parent, family, and school) and goals that need to be addressed.

The second role of the therapist is, in collaboration with the parent and school personnel, to develop evidence-based interventions to address the child's school problems. Everyone involved should understand that interventions might need to be intense at first, until the behavior problems decrease. The behavior plan for managing the child's problem behavior should target specific behaviors determined by the parent and teacher, and should establish concrete criteria for whether the child has met the goal for the class period or day (e.g., the child completed the class assignment or did not engage in physical fights). Each person involved in the plan must clearly understand his or her role and be able verbally to specify that role.

Given recent media reports of increased school violence, therapists must be clear that schools will need a lot of support to manage aggressive children in the classroom. Strongly advocating keeping the child in school will be an important third function of the therapist. Children who have a medical or psychiatric diagnosis and do not qualify for special education services may qualify for a federally-mandated school accomodation plan (504 services). This service basically calls for the child and all his or her teachers and parents to come together to staff the case and determine classroom modifications necessary to manage the problem. Being 504 eligible gives a small measure of protection against expulsion and is an example of a good standard practice for any child with behavioral difficulties. Some children whose emotional and behavioral difficulties impair their learning may qualify for special education services. The therapist and parent will need to request a psychological assessment by the school district. If the waiting list for assessments is long, the parent may have the assessment completed by a psychologist outside the school system. However, before doing so, the parent will need to make sure that an assessment by an outside source will be accepted by the school district.

GENERALIZATION WITH CASE MANAGEMENT

In discussing work with each of the systems involved in physical abuse cases, it is apparent that the therapist has a heavy case management role. As case management is conducted, generalization should always be kept in mind. That is, therapists should not only allow but expect parents and professionals to take on their own specific role, and should not do those jobs for them. From the start, therapists should approach interventions, advocacy, and all case management functions with an eye towards how the family will do this when the therapist is out of the picture. The faster the family takes on the responsibility, the sooner they can function on their own and not need treatment.

❏ Summary

In summary, many systems will be involved when physical abuse occurs. Although the therapeutic work is done directly with the child, parent, and family, these interventions occur within a context of other system interventions. That is, professionals from other systems will be making recommendations or decisions about a child or family that could potentially change the course of treatment or the outcome originally sought. Also, other professionals may have information crucial to helping the family that the therapist may not attain without contacting those professionals. Indeed, each system may provide useful observations and impressions about aspects of the adjustment of the child and family that may enhance the therapist's own clinical formulation. One may learn other useful information from these sources (e.g., failed behavior change efforts or obstacles to clinical improvement) likely to influence the content of treatment. Thus, it is not surprising that these sources may be helpful in designing and implementing interventions and in ensuring that there is cooperation when such efforts are coordinated across settings.

Typically, other systems with which the family may be involved include child protection, family court, law enforcement, physicians, and the schools. Mere contact with professionals from these systems may not be sufficient. Joining with these professionals to create a partnership in which the family is included will increase the likelihood of attaining the outcomes sought. In addition, involving all key people as part of the treatment team will help reduce the potential for strained interactions. If families can feel empowered by professionals rather than be in an adversarial relationship with them, then together all may achieve positive outcomes. The following chapter illustrates the integration of the content of this chapter and the remaining treatments mentioned in this book in three clinical case descriptions.

References

Azar, S. T., & Wolfe, D. A. (1998). Child physical abuse and neglect. In E.J. Mash, & R.A. Barkley (Eds.), *Treatment of childhood disorders* (2nd ed., pp. 501–544). New York: Guilford.

Brodsky, S. L. (1991). *Testifying in court: Guidelines and maxims for the expert witness.* Washington, DC: American Psychological Association.

Fine, M. J., & Carlson, C. (Eds.). (1992). *The handbook of family-school intervention: A systems perspective.* Boston: Allyn & Bacon.

Lipovsky, J. A., & Stern, P. (1997). Preparing children for court: An interdisciplinary view. *Child Maltreatment, 2,* 150–163.

Spratt, E. G. (1997, April). *Joining hearts, hands, heads, and halos: Strengthening a community outreach child protection team through adoption of a Department of Social Services worker.* Collaborative community meeting, Mt. Pleasant, SC.

Stern, P. (1997). *Preparing and presenting expert testimony in child abuse litigation.* Thousand Oaks, CA: Sage.

18

Case Examples and Applications

This chapter presents three cases. Within each case, we present background information, discuss the course of treatment, and set forth outcomes and information regarding extended treatment needs. As the reader reviews each case, it should be noted that each case provides treatment for several people and addresses multiple problems. The comprehensive individual and family cognitive-behavioral therapy (CIF-CBT) model is shown throughout each case.

❏ Case One: James

BACKGROUND AND RELEVANT CLINICAL INFORMATION

James, age 12, was referred for treatment by the Department of Social Services (DSS) following an investigation of physical abuse by his biological father. The abuse had been ongoing for 3 years, and consisted of beatings with a belt, belt buckle, extension cord, fist, and board. James was kicked, shoved, thrown against the wall, and made to kneel on rice for hours at a time. In addition, the father was verbally abusive—hurling insults and cursing. The father was physically violent toward the mother—and had a lengthy criminal history of violence toward persons and property. DSS founded physical abuse and threat of harm from physical abuse, and placed the children in protective custody and foster care. The mother was physically isolated from the children by the father's command, and they had no contact with her for 6 months. The father was subsequently arrested for a strong-armed robbery, and sent to prison for this crime and violation of parole. The children were returned to the mother.

James was the oldest of five children, and his siblings were ages 10, 8, 6, and 3. He attended a local middle school. Prior to removal from the home, he was failing in school and had numerous referrals for fighting, cursing at teachers, and excessive absences. After the beatings, the father would make James stay home until the marks were gone. When moved to foster care, James's grades improved dramatically, but he continued to have difficulties with the aggressive behavior. Upon return home, his school performance plummeted and he was described as "extremely angry all the time, disrespectful, and violent." He was also aggressive at home and would frequently put holes in the wall or break up furniture when angry. His mother was clinically depressed and frightened. She struggled with posttraumatic stress disorder (PTSD) from her own history of childhood abuse and the domestic violence. She received weekly threatening phone calls from the father in prison who threatened to kill her, the children, the DSS worker, the former foster parents, and the therapist. She was able to provide meals for the children, but unable to provide any discipline. She felt stressed over child-rearing tasks and stated she had given up, but continued to maintain the dream of raising her children under her care to be productive, nonviolent adults. There were no nonabusive extended family members, but the foster parents maintained contact with the children. The children were angry about the return home from foster care because of feelings about the family violence and because they had to give up nicer homes and toys that they had never been able to have in the past.

COURSE OF TREATMENT

James and his mother participated in treatment. Information gained from the initial assessment set the course for the focus of treatment.

Treatment Techniques for the Mother

First, although the family was safe from physical harm by the father, his calling the home from prison and threatening the mother and children created a situation of psychological harm. James's father demanded specifics from the mother regarding the comings and goings of the family, the name of the therapist, and the content of treatment sessions. When the mother disclosed that the phone calls were happening, two interventions were set up to assure family safety: first, the mother and the therapist called the prison, spoke to officials about the phone calls, and requested assistance in stopping the father's behavior; and second, the mother changed her phone number and made sure that it was not published. James's mother and the therapist made a plan regarding who among family and friends could have the phone number.

Second, James's mother was having significant difficulties with depression and poor sleep. PTSD symptoms from childhood abuse were resurfacing when the father called and the children acted out. The therapist immediately began working with the mother on anxiety reduction techniques, such as relaxation and exposure work related to her own history of abuse and domestic violence. The mother made an appointment with her family physician for a complete physical exam and medication assessment.

Third, James's mother had stopped disciplining the children out of fear of them becoming violent, exhaustion over life tasks, fear that they would not love her, and limited parenting skills. The mother and the therapist worked together to set up rules for the children and consequences that could be implemented. Furthermore, the mother and the therapist talked with the foster parents, who agreed to help with respite and to make sure the children knew that the mother was in charge and that they would have to abide by the same rules made by the mother when they were in the foster home.

In addition to changing parenting techniques around discipline, a functional analysis was conducted with the mother to set up self-management techniques to reduce arguing between her and James. This analysis revealed that the mother's anger and yelling were triggered by an angry look that James gave when asked to help around the house. This look was very similar to a look given by her husband before he became violent with her. The yelling was an attempt, in her thinking, to emotionally separate her son from her and protect herself. In reality, she could see that the yelling escalated James and increased the likelihood of aggressive behavior against property. He had never become violent with his mother. To address this problematic interaction, the therapist, the mother, and James role-played, catching the triggers and de-escalating the situation. They handled this by self-instruction to calm down or by leaving the room, getting calm, and then returning to problem solve during family therapy (FT).

Treatment Techniques for James

Simultaneous with the above interventions, the therapist began to work with James on individual techniques for anger management, social skills, and anxiety reduction related to thoughts and worries about the abuse. His mother was included in the sessions so that she could help follow up with the homework assigned. Conjoint treatment was efficient, because the mother and James were learning some of the same skills they needed to manage anxiety and depression.

Treatment Techniques for School Problems

The therapist and the mother made a visit to the teacher and principal at James's school. The mother had been reluctant to go to the school. She felt the school personnel were judging her because of the family violence and because a teacher had spoken harshly to her three years earlier, and she felt put down. The mother was candid with the teacher and principal about what the family had gone through, and was relieved that the school personnel were understanding and supportive. The principal suggested that they involve James in the school wrestling program to help him create a positive connection with his school. The school agreed to provide in-school consequences for his argumentative behavior in lieu of sending him home, which he liked. The principal invited the mother to volunteer in the office until she had secured employment outside the home. James's mother agreed to do so. This helped in two ways: first, the mother got out of the house, and second, the mother's presence in school alleviated James's need to go home. He had been working to get sent home because he was worried about his mother and wanted to be with her.

OUTCOMES AND EXTENDED TREATMENT NEEDS

CBT techniques the family used helped them reduce James's aggression at school and home, decrease the mother's depression and anxiety, and improve family interactions. After the family settled and was functioning well, the father escaped from prison. The fears around his behavior resulted in upheaval in the family and a return to depression and aggression. The mother initiated a call to the police to ask them to drive through the neighborhood periodically. She also took pictures of the father to the children's schools and made sure that all personnel knew of the situation. The mother called her Child

Protective Services (CPS) worker and enlisted her help in finding other housing so that she could move. Several family meetings were held to allow the children a time to express what they were feeling and develop a safety plan should they see their father. The mother's proactive behavior and her standing strong with discipline even though the children were acting out, coupled with additional help for respite from the former foster parents and a regular forum to discuss their fears and be reassured that the adults were working on it, helped the children quickly return to positive functioning. After three weeks, the father was recaptured and placed in a higher security prison. The family maintained their new levels of functioning and the mother successfully obtained employment.

❏ Case Two: Tanisha

BACKGROUND AND RELEVANT CLINICAL INFORMATION

Tanisha is an African American girl, age 13, who was referred for treatment by Child Protective Services (CPS) following an investigation of physical abuse by her mother. The mother acknowledged that she had beaten Tanisha with an extension cord because she skipped school and did not return home until later that evening. Tanisha told her mother that she was late because she was abducted by three men who held her captive for several hours, but later recanted her story, saying that she made it up out of fear of getting into trouble. The girl sustained welts on her wrists and buttocks from this beating, but received no medical attention for these injuries. The mother reported no other stressors or use of alcohol or drugs at the time of the incident. The only consequence following this event was the referral to CYS and the family's referral for treatment. The mother did acknowledge increasing use of mild physical punishment.

Residing with Tanisha is her mother, her 7-year-old half-sister, and her maternal grandparents. Tanisha had a history of behavior problems, notably, lying and stealing for the past four years. These problems were evident at home and at school. The mother admitted to being inconsistent with her discipline and limit setting, and with her expectations of her daughter's behavior. She reported using grounding and withdrawing privileges. The mother was employed as an account specialist in a local bank. She saw her daughter as sensitive, caring, bright, and able to get along with many people. The girl saw her relationship with her mother as positive; she also got along well her mother's fiancé and her half-sister. She had a good relationship with her father, but there has been little contact between them since the mother's divorce several years earlier. The father was reported to be an alcoholic; the mother has a history of diabetes related to obesity, and had made a suicide attempt by ingesting pills five years earlier. She received counseling at that time for this incident.

On clinical/diagnostic interview, Tanisha was found to meet no criteria for a DSM-IIIR Axis I or II disorder. She and her mother denied any problems with mood or anxiety, or any psychotic symptoms. She did present for treatment three years earlier following an incident in which she was fondled by a 17-year-old cousin, at which time she was diagnosed with adjustment disorder with disturbance of conduct.

COURSE OF TREATMENT

Tanisha and her mother participated in parallel individual CBT treatment. They received 17 sessions, 10 of which were conducted in the clinic with seven sessions conducted in the home. They either cancelled or failed to show for a total of four sessions.

Treatment Techniques for the Mother

The mother's individual treatment was coordinated with Tanisha's treatment, so it emphasized some similar concepts and training materials. In general, she was very talkative and difficult to keep on task. She reported having exhibited similar behavior problems to her daughter when she was a teenager. After seeing and discussing the movie *Ordinary People*, about an abusive parent, the mother maintained that her discipline did not seem harsh in her view, but recognized how it might have some of the consequences for children that was reviewed in the protocol. She was especially receptive to the material on emotional abuse and took seriously the message about avoiding the use of words that hurt others. Material regarding the mother's expectations of her daughter was discussed, and agreements were made as to which ones made the most sense for them. The mother also cooperated with a discussion of negative distorted thinking, and was able to identify specific exaggerations she has made about her daughter's behavior. These types of negative perceptions were acknowledged and then reviewed on three occasions during treatment. The mother learned anger-control skills, which allowed her to recognize the importance of maintaining self-control. A home contingency plan was developed, and then implemented, in which specific reinforcers were to be delivered for positive behaviors shown at home and school. Privilege restrictions were selected for use in a response-cost procedure, and time-out was also trained to provide the mother with another nonphysical punishment strategy. However, time-out did not need to be implemented more than once. Just prior to termination, the mother reported having to remove a privilege for a rule violation (i.e., the unsanctioned use of the phone) and that the child had responded well to the procedure.

Treatment Techniques for Tanisha

In terms of Tanisha's treatment, she generally was very cooperative and seemed to understand the material reviewed across sessions. Specific attention first was paid to teaching her to identify feelings in herself and others (e.g., anger at her sister); discussing the abusive incident and other mild physical punishment she received (e.g., occasional slaps on the arm), including relevant contextual variables; and teaching her about how to understand stressors in her life. She seemed to have a realistic understanding of the impact of violence on children, but tended to minimize her involvement in and responsibility for some of the behavior problems in which she engaged (e.g., saying, "It's really my friends"). She reported having automatic and negative thoughts on various occasions, which were discussed in the context of her anger control program. At one point, she reported having a problem with a peer at school that she felt she had handled appropriately. Part of this work included training in relaxation exercises. A safety plan then was developed in which she identified a support person. Training emphasized relevant assertion and social skills.

OUTCOMES AND EXTENDED TREATMENT NEEDS

During this time, Tanisha reported improvements in her relationship to her sister and her ability to talk to her mother about various personal issues. She also noted a decline in any school behavior problems or oppositional behavior at home. She concluded in the final session that she had "opened up a lot more." Her mother reported that she had made gains in handling her daughter's behavior problems in a more positive way and had refrained from using physical discipline. She also claimed that she could see how their relationship was improving and becoming more open and honest. The mother's fiancé, who sat in on a session dealing with expectations, reported that mother had become much more explicit about her expectations of her daughter and that there had been a big improvement in their interactions. In fact, the mother reported that even Tanisha's grandmother had become more calm since her granddaughter's behavior problems had declined and her respect for others had increased (the grandmother is reported as saying, "*We don't scream and holler like we used to*"). Furthermore, the mother reported that her blood sugar had become normal and that her medication dosage had been reduced since starting treatment. Reports during a school open house revealed an improvement in Tanisha's academic progress and behavior. On the Weekly Report of Abuse Indicators (WRAI; Kolko, 2002), reports from the two informants revealed no use of any physical discipline or force, and anger ratings never reflected a level higher than "a little anger." The discharge was planned after resolution of all treatment goals and completion of all treatment materials.

❏ Case Three: Marvin

Background and Relevant Clinical Information

Marvin, an 8-year-old male, was in his father's custody and had visitation with his mother. Several years earlier when the parents' relationship ended, the mother had been battling drugs and had decided that "a boy would do better with his father." So, Marvin was living with his father at the time of referral. Marvin's mother referred him for treatment. He reported to a school counselor that his father had hit him with a board. During the CPS investigation, physical abuse was founded and he was placed in his mother's custody. Marvin had been struck with a small board that had been used as a ruler. He was left with welts and bruises. Behaviorally, Marvin was failing in school and was destructive at home. At school, he harmed himself by applying an eraser to his arm until the skin was removed from a medium sized area and by pinching at his skin until it bled. Strengths of the family included the mother's recovery from cocaine addiction, a supportive extended family, and the father's desire to get treatment and have nonabusive contact with his son.

Marvin was the second oldest of four children. His older sister, age 12, a 4-year-old sister, and 2-year-old brother lived with the mother. All of Marvin's siblings were in the mother's care. Marvin was a first grader at a local elementary school. He had been retained two years. In addition, he had been hospitalized psychiatrically twice previously due to suicidal statements. Aside from the hospitalization, he had not participated in treatment.

COURSE OF TREATMENT

Marvin, his father, and his mother were involved in the treatment process. The mother was involved in treatment to help her manage Marvin's home and school behavior problems. The father was involved in treatment to manage his own physically abusive behavior, help with Marvin's recovery, and restore the relationship between father and son.

Treatment Techniques for the Father

To help Marvin's father learn to manage his son's behavior appropriately, behavioral parenting techniques were taught and practiced. In addition, from the functional analysis we determined that the father had few skills for actually managing anger. Anger management training was begun with the father. As the therapist began to talk with the father about the physical abuse and getting the father started on writing the clarification letter, the father disclosed that he had molested Marvin. He also disclosed that he had molested another boy a year earlier. The therapist informed the father that a report would be made to CPS and that he would be required to undergo specific treatment related to the sexual abuse. The father was applauded for being honest, and his disclosure was framed as a way to help protect his son and other children. Subsequently, the father began attending a sex-offender group. We also determined that substance abuse was part of the father's abusive behavior, and he began treatment for the substance abuse problem. Because of the heavy demands from these treatment programs, Marvin's father met with the CBT therapist once a week. In session, he worked on his clarification letter and addressed errors in thinking related to the abuse. The therapist worked closely in conjunction with the sex-offender group therapist so that the individual sessions could augment the group treatment process.

Treatment Techniques for the Mother

To help the mother manage Marvin's behavior, behavior management techniques were employed. At home, the mother set up rules to create a routine for Marvin. She established meal times, homework times, bed times, and rules for behavior. Compliance with home rules resulted in increased free time and privileges. In addition to a focus on Marvin's behavior, the mother held a lot of anger toward the father for the physical abuse. Her anger increased exponentially following the disclosure of sexual abuse. Time was spent with the mother to help her process her feelings of anger about the abuse and of guilt that her son experienced this when he could have been living with her, and to assure her that the abuse would be addressed with the father before he resumed contact with Marvin. As soon as the mother learned of the sexual abuse, she had Marvin assessed by a pediatrician trained to complete child abuse examinations to assure that he had not experienced physical damage and to establish current health status. When the father was near completion on the clarification letter, the mother began to read and comment on the drafts.

Treatment Techniques for School Problems

To address the school problems, especially the self-harm, the mother, teacher, therapist, and Marvin established a home/school behavior plan. Marvin earned rewards at home for meeting the behavioral goals at school of completing work, staying out of fights, and not hurting himself. The school agreed to provide remedial academic instruction and assess Marvin for possible participation in their resource program.

Treatment Techniques for Marvin

Marvin was diagnosed with PTSD. He was highly anxious about reminders of the abuse. His self-harm behavior in school related to re-experiencing the abuse. The therapist taught Marvin anxiety management skills and conducted graduated exposure with him. After the father disclosed sexual abuse, additional exposure sessions were conducted about those abusive incidents. Marvin not only was anxious but also had significant problems managing anger. He was taught CBT anger management skills. Finally, Marvin and his mother really wanted an apology and acceptance of responsibility from the father. So, Marvin participated in preparation for the clarification session. Marvin wanted to resume contact with his father, but wanted reassurance that his father was learning what he needed to do to not hurt Marvin again.

OUTCOMES AND EXTENDED TREATMENT NEEDS

The mother established her home as a safe place and began behavior management. Despite the increased structure, Marvin's aggression initially increased as the exposure sessions began, and he had difficulty sleeping. He argued with his mother to help him by not bringing him to the sessions. She brought him anyway, and he worked through the avoidance. The aggression started to decrease and finally stopped at home. The teacher monitored his anxiety and reminded him of the CBT techniques. His aggression at school decreased at a slower rate than at home, but finally extinguished. He was very pleased at the rewards he was earning at home. The father's struggle with alcohol and cocaine abuse was difficult, and he was admitted to a detoxification unit due to heavy alcohol use after he disclosed the sexual abuse. As he began to progress in his group and on the clarification letter, the alcohol and cocaine use decreased. Samples of the first and ninth draft of his clarification letter are shown in Box 18.1. The mother approved the ninth draft of the letter and she, Marvin, the father, and the paternal and maternal grandparents attended the clarification meeting. The meeting went well: The father was appropriate, and the grandparents also apologized to Marvin for not protecting him. After the successful clarification meeting, Marvin and his father began supervised visits and parent-child dyadic sessions. Their interactions improved, but no plan was made for the father to have Marvin at his home at all or to be anywhere alone with him.

Box 18.1 | Sample Clarification Letters

First Draft of the Letter

Dear Marvin:

I just wanted to tell you how sorry I am for hurting you. And about the time I thumped you on your wee-wee. That morning I tickled you in between your legs. But you know when you and me get to wrestling, you are getting to be so strong that dad tickled you so you would get off of me. So we can't do that no more, o.k.? And the time you and me was over at Randy's house and you keep telling me you wanted to go back to the swing set. Dad got mad at you and came running after you like I was going to spank you. I am sorry for that. Don't worry dad was drinking at the time and he learned a big lesson. When I drink I'm not the same dad and you know that I feel a whole a lot better now that I don't drink. I just want you to know I love you too much to hurt you. Marvin, I hope you accept my apology.

Love you very, very much,
Daddy

[NOTE: The father was still drinking at the time of this letter.]

Ninth Draft of the Letter

Dear Marvin:

I just wanted to tell you how sorry I am for hurting you. There are 3 ways I behaved wrong. I yelled at you, I touched you sexual and physical hurt you wrong. You were very brave and did the right thing when you told the school counselor that you were afraid of me and that I had hurt you. The time we cooked out at great granny's house, I got mad at you and hit with the broom. I should have talked to you instead. I want you to know I am sorry.

Box 18.1   *continued*

And the time I hit you with the ruler wrapped with duct tape one time and hit you two more times with my hand, that was wrong too. The time I got you out of bed and touched you on your privates that was very wrong too. The time we were at Randy's house and I called you a bad name and grabbed you around the neck. That was wrong too. And I came running at you yelling at you that it was time for you to get a beating, that was wrong too. I want to say I am sorry and I will try not to ever hurt you again. I am sorry for the past and every time I hurt you and touched you in the wrong way.

Marvin, I have learned different ways to raise you. I have been working on my drinking and stopping the cocaine and feel better than I ever have. I am learning a lot in my counseling. There are going to be new rules when I see you. I just wanted you to know we are not allowed to see each other because of my ways and not because of you. I just want you to know that I love you and appreciate you telling about what you did. This has helped me very much.

At first I told great granny and granddaddy that you lied and I did not hurt you. They believed me because I was bigger than you. I will make sure everybody will know that I was wrong and you were right. I have learned that if I talk to you instead of telling you that you are going to get a beating for everything, I will probably do better. When we get to see each other, our visits will be supervised. If ever you feel unsafe, you can let the supervisor know.

Love,
Dad

❏ Summary

Each of the three cases presented in this chapter illustrate that multiple factors are involved in abuse risk. Furthermore, each case shows how individual CBT and FT techniques are integrated to address the multiple abuse risk factors. The reader will note that interventions used in each case differed according to the problems identified in the assessment, but in no case was only one system involved in the treatment.

The first case, James, presented a special situation involving family violence. CBT techniques were used to address the mother's depression and PTSD, and to teach her behavior management techniques. To target child behavior problems, CBT techniques were used to reduce aggression shown at school. FT techniques were used to reduce conflict by addressing patterns that escalated the mother's and James's arguing. Noteworthy in this case was the role of other providers and the schools in helping keep the children and mother safe.

The second case, Tanisha, illustrates the importance of involvement of extended family and how a parent can shift from the view that the abuse was not that bad to understanding the impact on the child. For the mother, CBT techniques were used to target negative attributions about the child, teach behavior management, and address anger management. For Tanisha, CBT techniques were used to address her beliefs about the abuse, teach anger management, and develop a safety and support plan. FT techniques were used to address cohesion between mother and daughter and issues that the grandmother faced. The role of other health professionals was key in that the mother had problems regulating her diabetes and this complicated the family picture.

Case three, Marvin, highlights the course of treatment when multiple forms of abuse have occurred. In this case, CBT techniques were used to address the father's problems with anger and distortions about the abuse. Furthermore, through CBT techniques, the therapist taught the mother behavior management and processed her anger about the abuse. For Marvin, CBT techniques were used to reduce school aggression and self-harm behaviors. Using FT techniques, the entire family and extended family addressed the abuse. This case shows how the clarification process can occur and promote healing even when the parent is not going to be living with the child.

The major thrust of this chapter is that treatment must be tailored to fit the strengths and needs of families, and that treatment must address more than individual factors within the child or parent. Furthermore, one can see how efforts to treat the child and parent need to be integrated with any family-level interventions. Although working with a comprehensive model can be labor-intensive, to do less is to provide incomplete and/or inadequate treatment. The additional effort is likely to pay off in both improved outcomes and clinician satisfaction. We conclude this book with some final comments in the next chapter.

Reference

Kolko, D. J. (2002). Child physical abuse. In: J. E. B. Myers, L. Berliner, J. Briere, C. T. Hendrix, C. Jenny, & T. Reid (Eds.), *The APSAC handbook of child maltreatment* (2nd ed., pp. 21–54). Thousand Oaks, CA: Sage Publications.

19

Conclusions

❑ **Summary of Chapter Contents**

We have introduced and explained in this book a multimodal approach to treating children and families when child physical abuse (CPA) has occurred. The Comprehensive Individual and Family Cognitive-Behavioral Therapy (CIF-CBT) model on which we draw considers both the strengths and clinical needs of the child, parent, and family. In accord with this model, treatment is designed to target multiple factors that may help child victims to adjust from a recent abuse experience, parents to manage social-emotional difficulties to help prevent reabuse, and families to implement changes in their interactional styles that can support a safe environment. The clinical techniques proposed within the model, primarily cognitive-behavioral in nature, have empirical support from the research literature and emerging clinical utility from the practice arena.

We presented empirical evidence in Chapter 2 that child victims of physical abuse are at risk of experiencing a variety of mental health consequences related to their experiences. These experiences broadly include maladaptive cognitions about aggression and violence; poor management of affective problems, such as anger, anxiety, and depression; and poor interpersonal competence. In addition, physically abused children are at risk of carrying these mental health problems into adulthood in such forms as involvement in substance abuse and violent crime. Furthermore, evidence was provided that multiple parent factors relate to physical abuse. These factors broadly include maladaptive cognitions about the abuse and violence in general; unrealistic expectations of child development; poor management of stress, anger, anxiety, and depression; and low knowledge of child behavior management. In addition, multiple family factors relate to abuse risk, including family violence, limited psychosocial resources, general stress within the family, and unsafe community activities. Finally, parental substance abuse may affect parenting and family functioning, exponentially increasing abuse risk.

One salient implication of having multiple risk factors for abuse and multiple consequences from abuse is the need for an assessment and treatment model that addresses both risk factors and consequences. Unfortunately, as shown in Chapter 3, there are few treatment models being used with physically abusive families that address multiple factors. Instead, most current treatments are provided to the child or the parent, but none explicitly integrates child, parent, and family procedures.

The CIF-CBT model targets certain gaps found in current research literature and practice. In Chapter 4, we described a comprehensive assessment model that provides the reader with an understanding of some of the state-of-the-art assessment tools for use with children, adults, and families. Assessment is vital for two reasons. First, assessment provides information regarding strengths and problem areas that need to be targeted. Second, assessment is a tool for providing objective information as to whether individuals participating in treatment are truly getting better. It seems essential to measure progress on an individual basis using, for example, the specific problem areas being treated. With a broad-based model such as CIF-CBT, assessment will be conducted with children, adults, and the family. Of course, this can be a challenge given diversity in the content, format, and psychometric underpinnings of such a wide array of measures. Suffice it to say that various domains related to the evaluation of an intervention are worthy of being assessed (see Kolko, 1998a, 1998b).

Before beginning comprehensive treatment with children, parents, and families, several background factors and clinical prerequisites must be considered. In Chapter 6, we discussed key elements for facilitating treatment when abuse has occurred. These include engagement of families, gaining a cultural understanding and safety, confidentiality, and abuse reporting. Given that the initial contacts made with the family help to facilitate the development of a therapeutic connection, suggestions for providing clients with a proper orientation to treatment also were made in this chapter.

The treatment section of this book is in accord with our emphasis on the multiple risk factors and consequences of abuse and the implementation of a comprehensive assessment of each system. Four chapters (Chapters 7–10) constituting the child treatment section provide fairly in-depth strategies for addressing child issues, such as maladaptive cognitions about violence and the abuse; poor management of such affective problems as anger and aggression, anxiety, and depression; and poor interpersonal competence. Three chapters (Chapters 11–13) constitute the adult treatment section and provide strategies for addressing maltreating adult issues, such as maladaptive cognitions about the abuse and violence in general; unrealistic expectations of child development; poor management of stress, anger, anxiety, and depression; and low knowledge of child behavior management. By offering diverse content, the therapist will be better able to match certain treatment strategies to the family's needs.

Chapter 14 is the bridging chapter because it integrates clinical work conducted with both the child and parent. Although the clarification process runs throughout treatment, an in-depth description of this process is covered just prior to the family treatment section because the culmination of ongoing clarification work signals the start of family therapy strategies. The clarification process is an effort to assure that the responsibility for the violence that occurred in the family is assumed by the person who committed the violence: the maltreating parent. The maltreating parent is empowered to take responsibility for the abuse and that acceptance of responsibility is conveyed to all of the family in detail. Then, all family members may contribute to the development of a safety and reabuse prevention plan.

Chapters 15 and 16 provide recommendations on family therapy techniques adapted from the work of Robin and Foster (1989), Minuchin and Fishman (1981), and Alexander and Parsons (1982). Work with the entire family initially focuses on reframing behavior and intent, challenging attributions that may not have been challenged in the clarification, and reinforcing a no-force contract within the reabuse prevention plan. Further work to identify family interactional patterns that sustain maladaptive behavior is conducted and families are taught to change those patterns. Primarily, the cognitive-behavioral skills training component in this section emphasizes problem solving and positive communication.

When child maltreatment occurs, multiple systems outside the family, such as the greater community, become involved. Chapter 17 offers tips for engaging other professionals and systems that are key to the success of the family. These include Child Protective Services

(CPS), family court, law enforcement, physicians, and the school system. Truly, partnering with professionals from these systems in a way that advocates for the family can affect a decision-making process in which the therapist would otherwise have no input.

Three cases that employ strategies from the CIF-CBT model are presented in Chapter 18. These cases illustrate the importance of tailoring treatment to the strengths and needs of a family and the integration of CBT and family therapy (FT). The reader will note that the treatment strategies differed for each family. The cases also identified some special concerns that may happen in some cases, such as a resumption in family violence.

In conclusion, the CIF-CBT model seeks to address the need for individualized, but family-centered treatment models that incorporate empirically validated components. Likewise, the CIF-CBT model addresses a gap in clinical practice in that it offers practical, hands-on, empirically supported strategies. As such, the practitioner has the opportunity to provide evidence-based practice in a comprehensive way.

The treatment procedures and content of therapy presented in this book were selected on the basis of both empirical support and clinical experience. Although our studies and those of our colleagues provide supportive research findings for these techniques, it is important to point out that no single study has evaluated all of the many comprehensive treatment strategies described herein. An actual test of the impact of integrating these individual child, individual parent, and family treatment procedures must await empirical investigation. We cannot underscore enough the need for practitioners to use evidence-based strategies and to evaluate objectively the course of treatment with each and every abusive family. In this way, the practitioner may be in the best position to understand whether the needs of the child and family indeed have been addressed.

❏ Final Comments

Several issues relating to the treatment enterprise bear some mention in order to place much of this content in its proper context. Even with the application of various techniques designed to introduce the therapist, minimize mistrust and hostility, enhance cognitive-behavioral skills, and promote positive family interactions, abusive parents and their children may show limited motivation and may, in fact, seem disinterested in treatment. Finding the right message that will enhance the family's level of participation in and commitment to treatment may require considerable ongoing effort. Indeed, there are times when the use of coercion and legal leveraging may have an influence and other times when they seem counterproductive. Also, therapists must be careful to not interpret fear or mistrust as resistance or lack of interest in change. With serious multi-need families, it will not suffice to set an appointment and assume that nonattendance means lack of desire to change. Engagement strategies, as described in Chapter 6, are vital to helping parents and families participate as team players and maximize benefit from treatment. Of course, no single treatment approach is likely to work with all clients and there will frequently be a need to incorporate other treatment strategies or methods to achieve a better outcome.

Other principles of providing effective treatment also bear reiteration. The first principle involves truly recognizing a family's strengths and using those as part of the change process. Often, lip service is given to assessing family strengths as a politically correct thing to do, but nothing is done with that information. Providers should actually determine strengths that the child, parent, family, extended family, and key systems involved bring to the table. These strengths should be noted on the treatment plan and interwoven within the interventions.

Second, services should be provided in an ecologically relevant setting that permits an understanding of the contextual influences on the family's problems. Not all therapists have the luxury of working in a situation that allows them to provide home- and community-based treatment. Working within the family's environment permits overcoming several practical barriers to treatment participation, such as transportation. Also, providers have an opportunity to see how the home is structured, understand the community norms, and observe how the child behaves in his or her usual environment. If the structure of a therapist's work prohibits home-based treatment, at least making several home visits can help with engagement and an understanding of the greater context within which the family functions.

A third principle reflects the benefit of drawing upon multiple informants within the ecology. It is highly unlikely that a family presenting for treatment has no extended family, no close friends, or no neighbors; the family will be influenced by those people. That influence can work for or against treatment goals. Bringing key people within the family's ecology on board as part of the treatment team can help with meeting goals and generalizing behaviors. Furthermore, other people in the ecology can help the therapist understand how well the interventions have worked. These sources provide a perspective that is different from the parent and that may guide the techniques used.

Finally, therapists are encouraged to maintain a balance between addressing the abusive incidents and experiences that elicited referral and the many other presenting problems acknowledged or being experienced by the family. A careful assessment will help determine the major factors that are driving the problem, and these will have to be triaged in terms of which factors have the strongest influence. Thus, attention should be paid to promoting disclosure and discussion of abusive experiences, and targeting various domains likely to enhance the child's, parent's, and family's overall adaptive skills and competencies. Certainly, many intervention programs integrate experiential and skills-training targets. Furthermore, the materials described in this book are designed both to reduce the impact of any sequelae for the child following an abusive experience (e.g., to reduce symptoms and teach skills) and to minimize or eliminate parental and family environmental risk factors for another incident of abuse. It is hoped that the comprehensive interventions targeting these two domains as described in this book offer direct, concrete strategies that can enhance the child's welfare while reducing the likelihood of being reabused.

In closing, we would like to acknowledge that this book presents a labor-intensive comprehensive model. We certainly do not propose that the work with abusive, multi-need families is easy. On the other hand, our intent is not to overwhelm providers with the notion that the needs are so great as to preclude conducting treatment. We have seen through our own work that successfully carrying out this model is possible. One caveat is that, to provide this level of intensive treatment, which is certainly implicated in the research, a strong level of community and agency support is required. That support comes in the form of an adequate case load, competent supervision, ongoing quality assurance strategies, a referral process that maximize use of resources, collaboration in goal development, agreement on the range of strategies that will and will not be employed, and funding policies that allow adequate treatment for families. Providing treatment in accord with a comprehensive, empirically supported model that addresses child, parent, family, and community factors related to the processes supporting abusive behavior will, we hope, provide the greatest opportunity to reduce the impact of CPA both in the families referred for treatment and the larger society that must serve them in the long run.

References

Alexander, J. F., & Parsons, B. V. (1982). *Functional family therapy*. Pacific Grove, CA: Brooks/Cole.

Kolko, D. J. (1998a). CPS operations and risk assessment in child abuse cases receiving services: Initial findings from the Pittsburgh Service Delivery Study. *Child Maltreatment, 3*, 262–276.

Kolko, D. J. (1998b). Integration of research and treatment. In J. R. Lutzker (Eds.), *Handbook of child abuse research and treatment: Issues in clinical child psychology* (pp. 159–181). New York: Plenum.

Minuchin, S., & Fishman, H. C. (1981). *Family therapy techniques.* Cambridge, MA: Harvard University Press.

Robin, A. L., & Foster, S. L. (1989). *Negotiating parent/adolescent conflict: A behavioral-family systems approach.* New York: Guilford.

Index

About the Authors

David J. Kolko, PhD, is Professor of Psychiatry, Psychology, and Pediatrics, at the University of Pittsburgh School of Medicine. At Western Psychiatric Institute and Clinic, he directs the Special Services Unit, a treatment research program for sexually offending youth referred by the Juvenile Court. Dr. Kolko is a consulting psychologist for the Pittsburgh Child Advocacy Center at Children's Hospital of Pittsburgh, a multidisciplinary child abuse program. He has just concluded a second term on the Board of Directors of the American Professional Society on the Abuse of Children (APSAC) and was chair of its research committee.

Dr. Kolko's federal and state grant funding has been directed towards the study and treatment of disruptive disorders, juvenile sexual offending, child physical abuse, and adolescent depression. Much of the work described in this book is based on a treatment outcome study with physically abused children and their parents or families (NCCAN 90-CA-1459) and was informed by other work directed towards understanding the service delivery system in child abuse (NCCAN 90-CA-1547). His other research has involved the development and evaluation of integrated mental health treatments and probationary services for juvenile sexual abusers (*Pennsylvania Commission on Crime and Delinquency*), the evaluation of a multimodal community-based treatment protocol for young children with disruptive, called REACH (Resources to Enhance the Adjustment of CHildren; NIMH

Grant 57727), and behavioral health services for children with behavior problems in primary care, called SKiP (Services for Kids in Primary Care; NIMH Grant 63272).

Dr. Kolko received his BA in Psychology from the University of Cincinnati, his MA in general psychology from the New School for Social Research, and his PhD in clinical psychology, with a specialization in behavior therapy, from Georgia State University.

Cynthia Cupit Swenson, PhD, is Associate Professor of Psychiatry and Behavioral Sciences at the Medical University of South Carolina. Her work primarily consists of research on community-based treatment for youth violence, child physical abuse, family violence, and community violence. Currently, via a grant funded by the National Institute of Mental Health, she is involved in examining treatment for adolescents and their families when physical abuse occurs.

Dr. Swenson is a frequently invited speaker around the United States, and has written numerous publications in the field. At the national level, she is a member of the Board of Directors of the American Professional Society on the Abuse of Children (APSAC) where she serves on the Executive Council. Dr. Swenson also participates on a number of state boards related to child maltreatment and youth drug court. In addition, she is on the board of a youth West African dance and drumming company, as well as other community-based service and development organizations.

Dr. Swenson received her MS in psychology from Northeast Louisiana University and her PhD in clinical psychology from The Florida State University.